Francis Wolle

**Desmids of the United States**

And List of American Pediastrums with Eleven Hundred Illustrations

Francis Wolle

**Desmids of the United States**
*And List of American Pediastrums with Eleven Hundred Illustrations*

ISBN/EAN: 9783337187774

Printed in Europe, USA, Canada, Australia, Japan

Cover: Foto ©ninafisch / pixelio.de

More available books at **www.hansebooks.com**

Francis Wolle
Born Dec. 17 1817.

**NEW AND ENLARGED EDITION.**

# DESMIDS

OF THE

## UNITED STATES

AND

## LIST OF AMERICAN PEDIASTRUMS

WITH NEARLY

FOURTEEN HUNDRED ILLUSTRATIONS

ON

SIXTY-FOUR COLORED PLATES.

BY THE REV. FRANCIS WOLLE,
*Member of the American Society of Microscopists.*

BETHLEHEM, PA.:
MORAVIAN PUBLICATION OFFICE.
1892.

TO

Dr. Otto Nordstedt,

OF THE UNIVERSITY OF LUND, SWEDEN,

THIS LITTLE WORK IS

Dedicated,

IN RECOGNITION OF HIS GREAT AND VALUABLE CONTRIBUTIONS

TO THE HISTORY OF CRYPTOGAMIC PLANTS,

BY HIS GRATEFUL FRIEND,

THE AUTHOR.

# PREFACE.

In the "American Journal of Science and Art," A. D. 1847, Prof. J. W. Bailey, of West Point, said:—"With the exception of six or eight, I am not aware of any published account of Marine *Algæ*. Of our fluviatile (fresh-water) *Algæ*, I find no published notice, although they appear to have been studied with some care by the indefatigable Schweinitz," and at a little later date he adds:—"It appears that to Schweinitz is due the credit of being the *first* to collect and to study any of our fresh-water *Algæ*." I refer with all the more pleasure to these remarks concerning the late Rev. L. D. von Schweinitz, of Bethlehem, Pa., that he was a friend of my youth, and the first to draw my attention to the study of cryptogamous plants. It is only proper that ample credit should be given to this the first collector of our fresh-water *Algæ* in this the first monograph published in the United States, on that class of *Algæ* known as DESMIDS.

Nearly forty years ago Prof. J. W. Bailey contributed to the "American Journal of Science and Art," two papers, one describing a few new species of Desmids from the Catskill mountains, and the other, "Notes on the *Algæ* of the United States;" following these we have "Microscopical Observations made in South Carolina, Georgia, and Florida—Smithsonian Institute, A. D. 1850, 50 pp." These observations cover *Infusoria* and *Algæ*, the latter comprising a list of one hundred and twenty-five species, among which appear a few newly discovered Desmids which are illustrated and described.

Horatio C. Wood, Jr., M. D., published in 1872, through the Smithsonian Institute, "A Contribution to the History of the Fresh-Water *Algæ* of North America." In this publication Dr. Wood brought together all the recorded observations that had been made up to that time, in this country and in Europe, upon the *Algæ* of the United States. His list of *Algæ* includes about one hundred and sixty species of Desmids.

In a collection made by Stephen J. Olney, near Providence, R. I., during the years 1846-48, there were about fifty species of Desmids.

My first contribution to the literature of the fresh-water *Algæ* appeared in the "Torrey Botanical Bulletin of New York," in 1877, wherein are described thirty Desmids not heretofore found in the

United States. Every succeeding year up to 1883, I have recorded in the same journal the results of my observations upon this interesting class of American flora; what my success has been, may be inferred from the fact that I have in my herbarium nearly five hundred well authenticated species and varieties of American Desmids.

Only the great pleasure I derived from collecting, and studying the life-history of this heretofore neglected class of plants, enabled me to make light of, and to overcome, the serious obstacles I met with at the outset of my labors. There were no home correspondents with whom to co-operate and no accessible good works to guide me in my researches over this almost wholly unexplored field. My first encouragement came from abroad. The late Dr. L. Rabenhorst, of Meissen, Prussia, and the late Alexander Braun, of Berlin, sent me many valuable communications, and to the former particularly, I furnished many sets of mounted specimens of our *Algæ* for his serial of decades of *Algæ Exsiccatæ*. I am particularly indebted, however, to Dr. Otto Nordstedt, of the University of Lund, Sweden, for his kindness in determining the identity of certain American species discovered by me with those already known in Europe; and also in confirming my impressions concerning the restriction of others solely to the United States.

My grateful acknowledgments are also due for valuable notes and papers, to Dr. V. B. Wittrock, of the Scientific Academy of Stockholm; N. Wille, of Christiana, Norway; F. Hauck, Trieste; Dr. J. Rostafinski, Cracow; G. Lagerheim, Stockholm, and others.

Meanwhile, the subject had awakened interest in various parts of the United States, and specimens began to come in from places it would have been impossible for me to have visited. Among those to whom I am particularly indebted for favors of this kind, are:—Mr. H. W. Ravenel, Aiken, S. C., who during the past eight or more years, has sent me many interesting specimens, from his own State, Georgia and Florida; Capt. J. Donnell Smith, Baltimore, Md., who, in 1878 and 1879, sent me over seven hundred specimens of freshwater *Algæ* gathered in Florida; in his collections the Desmids were not numerous, but they included specimens not found elsewhere; Mr. F. H. Horsford, assisted by Mr. C. G. Pringle, Charlotte, Vt., whose collections were copious in northern Vermont; and Miss Eloise Butler, Minneapolis, Minn., who was a most successful collector of Desmids; I am indebted to her for all the species in the list which are assigned to Minneapolis. My acknowledgments would not be complete did I omit to mention the practical interest taken in my labors by the Rev. H. D. Kitchel, and his son, Mr. H. S. Kitchel.

In the descriptive parts, I have abbreviated the name of the discoverer of each plant, the reader being referred, for additional information, to the appended list of names alphabetically arranged with their abbreviations, and with the title of the books consulted in the compilation of this work.

## PREFACE.

Although this work is believed to be exhaustive of all now known concerning the Desmids of the United States, yet the author regards it only as the pioneer to others much larger and **therefore** more valuable, wherein will **be** recorded the achievements of those who will perhaps be indebted **to** this work for their first introduction to so fascinating a study as that of the fresh-water *Algæ* of our country.

F. W.

BETHLEHEM, PENNSYLVANIA,
FEBRUARY, 1884.

---

## PREFACE TO SECOND EDITION, 1892.

September, 1891, found us unable to supply the occasional demands for a copy of DESMIDS OF THE UNITED STATES. Some of the plates were reproduced by means of the camera; these, in connection with other plates and some copies of letterpress remaining from the original publication made a very limited number of complete copies, which, however, soon proved insufficient. The demand for more encouraged the idea of another edition of the work.

Since the original publication in 1884 quite a number of discoveries were made. Some of these were published on eight plates, and issued in connection with the FRESH-WATER ALGÆ OF THE UNITED STATES. Still later discoveries fill two more plates. Putting these together we get a volume with one-fifth more plates than the original.

To make a new edition the fact is evident that the demand for a book of the kind, naturally limited, has been pretty well supplied, and hence the risk of sale greatly increased. The author's consideration must be to curtail expenses. This he hoped to do in a satisfactory way by furnishing a book with many additional plates, figures all hand-colored, without an increase in price. The plan was to omit the descriptive part of the book as far as it relates to species, believing the distinct forms of the Desmids sufficient for identification, but upon maturer consideration and advice have concluded to make a COMPLETE REPRINT, adding all known later discoveries. This will add greatly to the size of the volume and proportionately to the expense, but in every other regard will make the most satisfactory work for reference.

The discoveries of species new to the United States the past few years, have not been as numerous as might have been expected in so great a territory as belongs to us. A few have worked with success. W. L. Poteat, of North Carolina, published a preliminary list of Desmids from his State. W. N. Hastings, Rochester, New Hampshire, has been doing a good work as is evidenced by the plants acknowledged to his name. G. Lagerheim, of Sweden, received material from Massachusetts containing a number of new forms. W. Joshua;

W. West and W. B. Turner, of England, in like manner, made researches in American waters. F. W. Harvey, Orono, Maine, has been active in researches among the *Algæ*. Many others might be named who have made a beginning. Personally have done very little collecting. The explorations so delightful in the past have become impossible by the advance of years, failing health and consequent loss of vigor of body.

In foreign countries much interest prevailed, judging by the numerous papers which made their appearance the past few years. Dr. Otto Nordstedt, of Lund, Sweden, a veteran in the field, has added to his previous achievements his contribution to the *Algæ* of Brazil; his discoveries in the Arctic regions, in Greenland and Spitzbergen and in Bornholm; he worked up also the collections made by Dr. S. Berggren in New Zealand and Australia. Dr. Wille, of Stockholm, made three contributions to the Desmids of Norway, of South America and of Nova Zembla. Dr. Schaarschmidt has taken care of the Desmids of Hungary. W. M. Maskell presented three valuable papers on the *Algæ* (Desmids) of New Zealand. Dr. Lagerheim tells of Bengal plants; Roy & Bisset of Japan gatherings; W. Joshua, of Burmah; Eug. Warming of Central Brazil; A. W. Bennett of North Cornwall and English Lake Districts; Maria Lewin of collections in Spain; W. West, gatherings in Yorkshire; J. P. Bisset in Lake Windermere; John Roy in Scotland, and probably many others not represented in my library.

# NAMES OF AUTHORS

Which are abbreviated in the text, together with the titles of the works consulted in the preparation of this monograph.

---

A. Br.—Alexander Braun. Algarum Unicellarium genera nova et minus cognita. Leipzig, 1855.

Arch.—W. Archer. Desmideæ in Pritchard's History of Infusoria. London, 1861.
    Notes, in the Proceedings of the Natural History Society, Dublin, 1862–1863. Notes in the Journal of the Microscopical Society, London.

Ag.—C. A. Agardh. Species Algarum, Lundæ 1820 and Systema Algarum. Lund, 1824.

Bail.—J. W. Bailey. Microscopical Observations made in South Carolina, Georgia and Florida. Washington, 1851.
    Notes on Algæ of the United States; American Journal of Sciences and Arts. 1846 and 1853.

Breb.—A. de Brebisson. Liste des Desmidiées observées en Basse-Normandie. Cherbourg, 1856.

Bulnh.—O. Bulnheim. Einige Desmidieen; Beitraege zur Flora der Desmidieen Sachsens. Dresden, 1863.

Cleve.—P. T. Cleve. Bidrag till Kännedomen om Sveriges Soetvattensalger af familjen Desmidieæ. Stockholm, 1864.

Cohn.—Ferdinand Cohn. Desmidiaceæ Bongoenses. Halle, 1879.

Corda.—A. J. Corda. Observations sur les Euastrées et les Cosmariées. Carlsbad, 1835–1840.

D. By.—A. de Bary. Untersuchungen ueber die Familie der Conjugaten. Leipzig, 1858.

De Not.—G. de Notaris. Elementi per lo Studie delle Desmidiaceæ Italiche. Genova, 1867.

Delp.—J. B. Delponte. Specimen Desmidiearum subalpinarum. Augustæ Taurinorum, 1873.

Ehrb.—C. G. Ehrenberg. Verbreitung und Einfluss des mikroskopischen Lebens in Süd und Nord-Amerika. Berlin, 1843.

Gay.—Fr. Gay. Essai d'une monographie locale des Conjugacées. Montpelier, 1884.

Klebs.—G. Klebs. Ueber die formen einigen Gattungen der Desmidieeen Oestpreusen. Königsburg, 1879.

Grun.—A. Grunow. Ueber die in Rabenhorst's Decaden ausgegebenen Suesswasser Diatomeen und Desmidiaceen von der Insel Banka. Leipzig, 1865.

HASS. - A. H. Hassall. A History of the British Fresh-water Algae. London, 1845.
HOFM. - W. J. B. Hofmeister. Ueber die Fortpflanzung der Desmidieen und Diatomen. Leipzig Berichte 9, 1857.
KIRCH.—O. Kirchner. Kryptogamen flora von Schlesien. Breslau, 1878.
KG.—F. T. Kuetzing. Deutschlands Algen in buendigen Beschreibungen. Nordhausen, 1845. Species Algarum. Leipzig, 1849.
LUND.—P M. Lundell. De Desmidiaceis quae in Suecia inventae sunt, observationes criticae. Upsal, 1871.
MENEGH. - J. Meneghini. Synopsis Desmidearum hucusque cognitarum. Halle, 1840.
MEYEN.—F. J. F. Meyen. Beobachtungen ueber einige niedere Algenformen. Bonn, 1829.
NAEG.—C. Naegeli. Gattungen einzelliger Algen. Zurich, 1849.
NORD.—O. Nordstedt. Desmidieae Arctoae. Stockholm, 1875.
18 Fam. Desmidieae Brasiliae. Stockholm, 1869.
Desmidieae ex insulus Spetsbergensibus et Beeren Eiland. Stockholm, 1872.
Bidrag til Kaennedomen om Sydligare Norges Desmideer. Lund, 1873.
Desmidieae in Italea et Tyrolia. Stockholm, 1876.
De Algis Aquaedulcis ex insulis Sandvicencibus. Lund, 1878.
De Algis nonnullis, praecipue Desmidicis inter Utricularius Musei Lugduno-Batavi. Lund, 1880.
RAB.—L. Rabenhorst. Flora Europaea Algarum Aquae dulcis et Submarinae. Leipzig, 1868.
RALFS.—J. Ralfs. On the British Desmidieae. London, 1848.
REINSCH.—P. Reinsch. Die Algenflora des mitleren Theiles von Franken. Nürnberg, 1867.
De Speciebus Generibusque nonnullis novis ex Algarum et Fungorum classe. Frankford, 1867.
WALL.—G. C. Wallich. Descriptions of Desmidiaceae from lower Bengal. London, 1860.
WILLE.—N Wille. Ferskvandsalger fra Novaja Semlja samlede af Dr. F. Kjellman paa Nordenskioelds Expedition, 1875. Stockholm, 1879.
Bedrag til Kundskaben om Norges Ferskvandsalger. Christiania, 1880.
WITTR.—V. B. Wittrock. Anteckningar om Skandinaviens Desmidiaceer. Upsal, 1869.
Algae aquae dulcis exsiccatae praecipue scandinavicae, quas adjectis algis marinis chlorophyllaceis et phycochromaceis distribuerint V. R. Wittrock et O. Nordstedt. Fasc. I.-XII. Upsalie, 1873-1883.
WOOD.—H. C. Wood. A Contribution to the History of the Fresh-water Algae of North America. Washington, D. C., 1874.

# INTRODUCTION.

The following preliminary remarks may prove interesting to those who have not heretofore paid much attention to the subject which has inspired the preparation of this volume.

The term *Algæ* signifies *Sea-weeds*, and is used to designate certain marine and fresh-water plants, which because they bear no flowers, stamens nor pistils, and in fructification produce spores instead of seeds, are styled cryptogamous plants. The *Algæ* comprise not only sea-weeds properly so-called, but likewise the gelatinous, or scum-like substances found floating on or near the surface of ponds, ditch water and placid streams; only a very small proportion of the entire class of fresh-water *Algæ* is confined to trunks of trees, shady recesses, or to rocks dripping with moisture.

Owing to the life-like peculiarities exhibited in some stages of their development and growth many of the *Algæ* were believed by Ehrenberg and other microscopists of his time, to belong to the animal kingdom, but the wholly vegetable character of the *Algæ* is now too well established to admit of further controversy.

Howsoever great in other respects their individual differences may be, the *Algæ* possess certain characteristics which are common to them all. They are cellular, flowerless and devoid of roots; their home is in the water; the very few which affect other localities, die when deprived of moisture. Their nutriment is absorbed through their entire surface from the medium in which they live. They are totally devoid of vascular tissue, in fact, are merely congeries of simple cells on the arrangement of which depends their structural differences.

Few classes of plants present greater diversities of form than do the *Algæ*. Some are minute enough to tax the powers of our best microscopes, while others are a constant source of astonishment because of their enormous size, stretching as some of them do, nearly two hundred feet across their marine beds, and with stems sufficiently thick wherefrom to manufacture handles for small tools and cutlery.

Those which consist of only a few cells, contrast very forcibly with others which in appearance, but in appearance only, present the branches, stems, twigs and foliage of highly developed plants; nor are they less opposite in what may be termed their sociality, from the fresh-water hermits scattered more or less sparsely in secluded places, up to those immense aggregations in mid-ocean which resemble sub-aqueous forests, or form floating islands miles in diameter, where multitudes of marine creatures find permanent homes.

Equally diversified is their range of habitat; no geonomic condition suffices to exclude the *Algæ*; they greet the traveler on the confines of vegetation, near the highest mountain tops, amid snow and ice[1], and are brought up by marine explorers from great depths below the surface of the sea.

To overlook their color would be to neglect a very striking characteristic. The predominant tint of the entire class, including both marine and fresh water varieties, is green; then pink grading off into all the shades of purple, and finally olive, from golden green and bright tawny to black; indeed there are few if any colors, from the most gorgeous to the dullest, but are to be found among the *Algæ*. They are also interesting for the many useful purposes to which they have been and are applied. We are under no small obligation to them for aiding to keep the atmosphere in a wholesome condition, since they absorb carbonic acid largely and exhale immense quantities of oxygen. The extinction of certain kinds would prove an annoying loss to our *materia medica*. They nourish a large variety of fish and molusca, and in some localities, constitute a nutritious fodder for cattle and pigs; moreover, of some kinds there are made sauces, soups and blanc-mange which are highly appreciated by epicures, while others as fertilizers, are largely used by sea-coast farmers.

Of what further benefit they may be to mankind it would be rash to predict, but it is within the bounds of probability, that the microscopic study of the fresh-water varieties, if pursued hereafter as ardently as during the past few years, will result in

---

[1] In a recent publication by V. B. Wittrock, of the Scientific Academy of Stockholm, he describes the Snow and Ice flora of the Arctic Zone. The Snow flora comprises about 40 species and varieties of fresh-water *Algæ*, and the Ice flora about 10 species. They belong to 25 genera. Ten species and varieties are new.

a considerable modification of our ideas concerning the generation and growth of certain life-germs.

For the behoof of the uninitiated, a few words may here not be out of place, on

## HOW TO FIND, HOW TO COLLECT, AND HOW TO PRESERVE

Fresh-water *Algæ*. As a large majority of them, especially the DESMIDS, are free-floating plants, it would be a waste of time to seek them in rapid waters; they affect pools, sluggish streams and ponds; the latter afford the most satisfactory results to the explorer, when the pond is a mile or more in length and is fed by one or two creeks; the indentations on the margins of such a pond and its tributaries, usually abound in water grasses and mosses which shelter and support the floating *Algæ*.

The outfit need not consist of more than a nest of four or five tin cans (tomato or fruit) one within the other for convenience of carriage; ten or a dozen wide-mouthed vials, and a small ring-net of fine muslin at the end of a rod about four feet in length. Should a boat be needed it can usually be hired on the spot. After selecting what seems to be a good locality, drag the net a few feet among the grasses and mosses, above indicated, allow the bulk of the water to drain through the muslin, and then empty the residue into one of the cans; repeat this process as often as may be desirable. Ten or fifteen minutes after the cans have been filled, most of the surface water may be poured off, and the remainder transferred to a glass vial, where the solid contents will gradually sink, and the superfluous water can be again poured off, and the vessel filled up with deposits from other vials. In shallow places, what is known as swamp-moss (*Sphagnum*), bladderwort (*Utricularia*), water-milfoil (*Myriophyllum*) or other finely cut-leaf water plants are likely to abound; these should be lifted in the hand and the water drained, or squeezed from them into a tin can to be subsequently treated as already stated. A few drops of carbolic acid in each vial, just enough to make its presence perceptible, will preserve the contents for months and even years from deterioration; the green coloring matter (*Chlorophyl*) may fade, but this in the case of the DESMIDS, is of little importance; nevertheless, when practicable, always examine the material when fresh. When dried on paper for the herbarium, the specimens can still, after being moistened with water, be microscopically examined, but not with the best results, since the drying is apt to collapse, or otherwise distort the cells.

The collector will not know the value of his find, until it has been brought drop by drop under the lens of his microscope, and out of the entire mass he may discover nothing to reward his labors; this however should not discourage him, as one or two failures are to be expected prior to meeting with an adequate reward. His interest in the study will be greatly enhanced if he keeps a record of it in sketches of what the microscope reveals to him. These sketches should, of course, be very exact, and in order that they may be so, it is necessary that the microscope should be provided with an eye-piece micrometer with which to measure the length and breadth of the figure to be sketched; a half inch per $\frac{1}{1000}$ (.001″) or 25 $\mu$ is the most convenient, though $\frac{1}{4}$ or $\frac{1}{2}$ of an inch may be a preferable scale for the larger forms. It is so difficult to separate specimens from their accompanying foreign matter, that it is seldom amateurs can mount them satisfactorily on slides, and therefore this method of preserving specimens is not open to recommendation.

Although in the microscopic study of the fresh-water *Algæ* much has been done within the past few years, much more remains to be accomplished. The field, instead of growing smaller, seems to widen out with every fresh discovery; localities thought to have been exhausted of additional possibilities, have in subsequent seasons, yielded ample returns to the patient explorer; and if the old territory is not sufficiently attractive, there are vast regions into which no student has yet penetrated, where, doubtless, the harvest awaiting the reaper dwarfs all that has been heretofore garnered.

# DESMIDS.

*Order,* ZYGOSPOREÆ; *Family,* CONJUGATÆ.

The DESMIDS form a large group, nearly equal in number of species, to that of all the other orders of fresh-water *Algæ*. They are microscopic plants, and are to be found floating free in pools, ponds and sluggish streams in all parts of the world; at least representatives of them are to be met with in every clime, from the frigid arctic latitudes to the torrid equatorial zone; but unlike the higher order of plants this wide difference in temperature is not in these *Algæ* always accompanied by corresponding structural difference; for in New Jersey, varieties have been discovered, which previously were thought to belong exclusively to the hottest parts of South America, and in the same State are also found species peculiar to the region of Nova Zembla, and Spitzbergen; we may assume these latter to have been a northern legacy to New Jersey upon the breaking up of what is known as the Glacial period, but we have no plausible reason to give for the presence in the same localities of species which are indigenous to Brazil and the East Indies. In every country, however, there are varieties of Desmids that have not been found elsewhere; a remark which applies peculiarly to the United States, where nearly one hundred species wholly distinct from any heretofore known, have been discovered, and are now for the first time collectively described in this work.

The Desmids are all more or less gelatinous; certain genera as *Hyalotheca, Desmidium, Sphaerozosma,* and some species of *Cosmarium,* and of *Staurastrium,* have a distinct, wide, colorless envelope; but the majority are provided with nothing more than an extremely thin mucous covering, which, though hardly perceptible under the microscope, becomes sufficiently evident in the firmness with which the Desmids adhere to the paper on which they are dried.

The cell, that is to say, the plant, is multiform, varying from the simple cylindrical and fusiform, to the denticulate, crenulate, lobed and otherwise much indented margins of the equal parts into which the cell is with few exceptions, beautifully and symmetrically divided. The division of the cell into two equal parts is effected by a transverse constriction, usually so deep as to leave about a third of the diameter of the constricted cell for a connecting link between the two parts; sometimes, however, the constriction is so slight as to produce merely an obtuse angled sinus on each side of the cell; a few have no constriction.

The wall (*cytioderm*) of the cells is not constituted alike for all the genera; in some cases it appears to be of a silicious character, judging by the appearance of the empty case, and by the firmness with which it retains the contour of the cell, even years after the Desmid had been collected; but usually the wall is more fragile and easily liable to collapse or rupture, unless the specimen is kept in a preservative fluid.

One of the characteristics of Desmids which confirmed many of the earlier microscopists in the belief of their animal character, was their seemingly voluntary movements. These movements are most apparent in the larger forms of *Closterium* and *Cosmarium*, but are more or less evident in all of them; they consist of slow, steady oscillations, and sometimes they go forward and backward, similar to the movement of diatoms, but slower, therefore less observable. By means of this locomotive power, they work themselves to the surface when gathered into a vessel with dirt and other foreign matter, and collect in such positions as are most exposed to the light. Many theories have been advanced to account for this phenomenon, but hitherto all have failed to establish a satisfactory explanation.

Another movement belonging to the Desmids is that of the granules within the cells. This is always present in good living specimens, and consists in a circulation of granules in the watery fluid next to the cell walls; they appear to be constantly passing to and fro between the center and the ends of the cells.

A third motion belongs to the so-called *vacuoles* of *Closteriums, Docidiums* and *Peniums*. In the end of many of these cells is a well-defined globular, transparent space (*vacuole*) filled with a number of small granules, significantly called, by the Germans, *tanzenden körnchen*, or dancing granules, because of their sprightly activity. A similar behavior of the granules in the bodies of smaller Desmids, and in the cells of filamentous *Algæ*, is often observable, particularly in unhealthy plants. No satisfactory explanation of these movements has yet been given. To some they appear a mystery, but, are they more mysterious than the circulation of blood in our arteries and veins, or than that of the so-called *cyclosis* in the higher plants? Nearly, if not quite all vegetable germinal matter, displays some spontaneous activity, and it is more than probable that the like characteristic seen in the Desmids, must be ascribed to the same causes whatever they may be.

### MULTIPLICATION.

Multiplication among the Desmids takes place by two processes. The one is simply a division and growth, the other is through what may be termed sexual intervention.

The first process is merely a modification of ordinary vegetative growth, that is to say, a peculiar cell multiplication by division. Plate XV, figs. 5, 6, are two semi-cells of a *Docidium*, which have separated by the development of short processes (fig. 7); these, primarily very small, commence their growth from out of the center of the base of each semi-cell. The figure represents them somewhat advanced; they develop rapidly, and soon become exact counterparts of the original mother-cells, then they separate. Thus two cells are developed from one; the same process is repeated, the two produce four, the four eight, and so on.

Plate XVII, figs. 12, 13, represent a *Cosmarium*, the one the perfect plant, the other in process of division; the ends are the halves of the mother-cell; the parts between, the partially developed forms of the new semi-cells. Plate XIX, fig. 27, represents a similar growth of a denticulate form; the teeth are not apparent until the young parts have attained nearly their full size.

Plate XLIV, fig. 8, is a series of four *Micrasterias truncata*, which represent the stages of growth by division; a cell producing two, and the two, four, under the rather unusual circumstance of adherence after division; only a fragment of the series is shown in the figure. Fig. 11 is a similar fragmentary series of adhering cells which must originally have numbered no less than sixty-four. I counted thirty-eight which could not have occurred in a regular course of division.

There are some peculiarities attending the process of multiplication. The new semi-cells are not always exact counterparts of the mother semi-cell. Plate XVIII, fig. 18, *Cosmarium moniliforme*; here there is an enlargement of the new, central semi-cells, probably developed under more favorable circumstances than the original cell. An impoverished condition is more frequently the result. Plate XXXIV is a striking illustration of such an instance in *Micrasterias Torreyi*. Fig. 1 is nearest the typical form described by Bailey, the other seven are varieties which occurred by division. I found them variously attached one to the other; one half distinct from the other half, and some so different from the typical form that had they not been mingled with many others they could easily have been mistaken for other species. Did these departures from the normal type continue indefinitely, the original form would soon be lost, but the true type as described nearly forty years ago by Prof. Bailey is preserved to this day. The changes are probably due to an impoverished condition of the plant. This suggests the cause of the second mode of multiplication, viz.:—that by

## REGENERATION.

This process is figured to some extent on many of the plates of our illustrations. Plate I, figs. 7-12, show how the separated, floating joints of a *Hyalotheca* are drawn together, and unite by means of a gelatinous tube (fig. 9) into which the contents of the cells gradually empty; the tube enlarges as represented in the figures of the progressive stages (figs. 10, 11) to the perfected *zygospore* (fig. 12). The three circular forms united, are the divided cells or semi-cells.

Plate III, fig. 3, are two cells separated from the filament (fig. 1) drawn together and united by a gelatinous tube mutually protruded; through this the green cellular contents (*Chlorophyl*) of the one passes out into the other, thus producing the regenerated spore (fig. 4).

Plate II, fig. 8, is a simpler process; the contents normally separated in each joint, flow together (fig. 9), and condense; then enlarge (fig. 10) and finally break loose (fig. 11) to produce the new plant. Plate III, figs. 5-9, illustrate another method of reproduction; two cells are drawn together, when they unite (fig. 6) and bind themselves closely until they fuse into one body, (figs. 8, 9).

Plate IX, fig. 2, is another instance, varying only in form, the two cells in the first stage of conjugation; fig. 3, the developed *zygospore* with the empty semi-cells or husks still attached. Figs. 4, 9, 10, 11, 16, are zygospores of various species of *Closterium*. This condition of copulation and developed spores, *zygospores*, or *sporangiums* as often termed, is frequent; the next step or GERmination is, if not of rare occurrence, very rarely detected. Dr. de Bary, of Germany, enjoyed a favorable opportunity; he describes the whole process substantially thus: Two cells are drawn together by a conjugal influence which we have no means of detecting; the semi-cells separate (Plate XXVII, fig. 27), and pour out their contents; those of the one cell unite with those of the other, at first without a distinct investment, but soon the mass acquires a membranous envelope (figs. 28, 29), forms a matrix, or sporangium in which are reproduced new plants possessed of invigorated vitality. The envelope of the matrix or *zygospore* is primarily thin and smooth, but by degrees it acquires increased thickness, and in the *Cosmariums*, usually a granular, tuberculated (fig. 28), or more frequently a spinous surface (fig. 29); the spines being sometimes simple but commonly forked at their extremities. The next step so difficult to be traced is the opening of the wall of the zygospore (fig. 29), setting free small spheres of sarcode; as they issue they enlarge and acquire a gelatinous, or thin membranous wall. The wall thickens and the sphere enlarges (fig. 30), the contents constrict (fig. 31), first in one direction and then transversely to the plane of the first incision (fig. 32); these parts develop and set free two or four new plants in size and form like the mother-cell, except in the cytioderm or membrane; this is not granular, but smooth, and so remains until after the multiplication by division takes place. After the first division the new semi-cells assume the characteristic granular surface; the result of this first division is two plants each composed of one granulated and one smooth semi-cell. The second division will make two perfect cells and two which retain the one smooth semi-cell; the third division produces eight cells, all of which except the original two semi-cells will be of typical form.

Hofmeister's views are somewhat at variance with those of De Bary in regard to numbers; he affirms that the contents of the sporangiums of *Cosmariums* are transformed by repeated binary subdivisions into eight or sixteen cells, which assume the orginal form, but not full size of the parent, before they are set free by the rupture or diffluence of the wall of the sporangium.

The sporangiums of *Closterium*, *Staurastrum* and of other genera are supposed to germinate in the same manner as *Cosmarium*. Plate XXVII, fig. 33, is a cluster of *Closteriums* surrounded by a membrane, found by Ralfs; he however questions whether this is a germinating sporangium.

Encysted clusters of Desmids are not necessarily evidence of germination. I have found many such cysts enclosing sometimes only one large specimen, as *Euastrum verrucosum*, but more frequently six, or eight smaller Desmids in one cyst; these were at first a source of perplexity. Upon consultation with men and books I found Huxley to say: "Encystment is very common among all the *Ciliata*; and a species of *Amphileptus* has been seen to swallow, or rather envelope a stalked bell-animalcule, and then become encysted upon the stalk of its prey."

Prof. Smith writes with reference to a case of encysted diatomes: "the group of *Navicula* seen, are simply a group that were devoured and their protoplasm digested by an *Amoeba*. They constantly are ejected in this way from the body of the *Amoeba* after the nutriment has been abstracted, and look like an encysted mass with an envelope complete."

This subject of multiplication by regeneration is full of interest for the microscopist, and opens a large and unexplored field.

The frequent variations in outline of form in certain species is calculated to mislead, and perhaps suggest notions of variation of species, but close observation will soon dispel such notions, and prove that they are merely temporay results of exhausted vitality in the process of multiplication by division; they occur most frequently in the latter part of the summer season. After regeneration through copulation, the zygospores become winter resting spores and lie dormant until the following spring, then germinate and reproduce the true counterpart of the original form of the species.

# DESMIDS OF THE UNITED STATES.

### Order, ZYGOSPOREÆ.

Green or brown *Algæ*, unicellular, either free cells or united into filamentous *fascia*. Sexual propagation takes place by an act of copulation followed by conjugation or *zygose*. Two cells of like appearance are attracted to each other, and unite; the contents of the two cells flow together, commingle, and form a primordial cell called a *zygospore;* this develops a double or triple episporium, or membranous envelope.

In rare cases twin *zygospores* are developed.

### Family, CONJUGATÆ.

Cells free, or united into simple series or filaments; no branches and no terminal growth. Contents of cells *(cytioplasm)* chlorophylous green, arranged in parietal bands, axillary lamina, or stellate nuclei.

### Sub-Family or Group, DESMIDIEÆ.

Composed of symmetrical cells, usually constricted in the middle, often of beautiful, ornamental forms, single or conjoined into filiform series, and sometimes involved in a maternal jelly. Asexual multiplication takes place by transverse division, or separation of the semi-cells (Plate XVII, fig. 13; Plate XIX, fig. 27); and development of new parts similar to the mother semi-cells.

Copulation takes place between two floating or free cells (Plate XXVII, fig. 27), and produces a *zygospore* with a firm middle membrane, and usually a more delicate inner and outer coating. The *zygospore*, after a longer or shorter period of rest, develops one or more regenerated daughter cells.

### Genus, GONATOZYGON, D. By.

Cells long, cylindrical, or truncate spindle form, without constriction, united into fragile, filiform straight series; at maturity they separate and become geniculate, copulate and produce spherical zygospores; these separate quickly from the empty cells.

Two species only have been recognized in this country.

**G. ASPERUM, (Ralfs) Rab.** Probably identical with G. RALFSII, De By. Plate I, fig. 1.

Cells long, cylindrical, ten to twenty times as long as wide, very slightly, or not at all reduced in thickness at the ends. Cytioderm fine-granularly roughened.

Diameter 11–12 $\mu$.

Occurs frequently in ponds of New Jersey.

**G. PILOSUM, Wolle. Plate I, fig. 2.**

Cells twelve to twenty times as long as wide, loosely connected; cytioderm more or less densely clothed with small, straight hairlike spines; cells cylindrical, terminal one of a filament slightly attenuated, end rounded.

**Diameter** 15 $\mu$.; with spines 25 $\mu$.

Habitat the same as the preceding.

### Genus, HYALOTHECA, Ehrb.

#### Plate I, figs. 3–14.

Cells short, cylindrical, usually with a slight obtuse constriction in the middle; disciform in end view, closely united into long filaments, which are inclosed, each in an ample, colorless mucous sheath. Chlorophyl mass in each cell, end view, six to ten radiate.

**H. DISSILIENS, (Smith) Breb.** Plate I, figs. 3, 4, 5.

Filaments elongated, cells slightly contracted in the middle, usually about half as long as broad. Variable in size.

**Diameter** 20–36 $\mu$.

**Var. HIANS, Wolle. Plate XII, figs. 14–16.**

Differs from the typical form in having the lateral margins of the cells arched with an acute notch in the middle.

Diameter 25–50 $\mu$.

Budd's Lake, N. J., and Florida.

Frequent in ponds and sluggish, shallow waters. The frequency of this plant soon familiarizes it; usually it is found intermingled with other forms, but sometimes it has entire control of small pools, trenches and outlets of springs. In its younger state it is attached to the muddy bottom, or sticks or stones; but more commonly it is found in floating masses. The filaments are generally fragile, but sometimes they occur elongated and strong. When gathered in proper season, **and kept in water for a few days, the cells separate at the articulations, and float in free joints, which being nearly square, readily turn over and present the circular end view,** with the stellate arrangement of the *chlorophyl*. **I have had a quantity in** good condition for observing the successive stages of conjugation. The cells separated the same day **the collection was made**; and soon thereafter copulation of **cells commenced.** Plate I, figs. 7, 8, are two floating cells, one in front and **the** other in transverse view, they are drawn to each other by some hidden conjugal influence, put forth a mucous tube and unite as fig. 9, then each cell breaks into two; thus four parts are united; sometimes all present themselves to view, but more commonly only three are visible, as figs. 10 and 11. **The** *chlorophyl* concentrates to the space between the cells; fig. 10, shows an early stage; fig. 11, a more advanced condition; and fig. 12, the developed *zygospore*. Single matured *zygospores* are frequently noticed in gatherings from waters where the plant prevails.

H. MUCOSA, (Mert) Ralfs. Plate I, fig. 13.

Filaments scarcely fragile; joints not constricted, but having at one of the ends a minute bidentate projection, **the adjoining end of the next joint being similar. These projections are** visible only in older plants.

Diameter 19–21 $\mu$.

This plant is not so frequent as the preceding, but it appears to be widely distributed, not in masses, but frequently mingled with other filamentous forms. Had it from ponds of Pennsylvania, New Jersey, Vermont, Rhode Island, South Carolina and Florida.

It is easily distinguished from the preceding by its wider mucous sheath, by the straight margin of the cells, by the longer joints and by the central gathering of the *chlorophyl*. The mucous sheath, being entirely colorless, is not easily discerned, except when surrounded by turbid water.

H. UNDULATA, Nord. Plate LXIV

**Cells about twice** as long as wide, sides concave and angles **rounded, closely** connected; filaments are involved in a **wide, colorless,** gelatinous sheath. The constriction of the **cells, and the** rounded angles make an undulate margin.

Diameter 9–12 $\mu$. without sheath.

Frequent in ponds of New Jersey, Pennsylvania, etc. There are two forms very nearly allied, this *H. undulata*, and *Sphaerozosma exearatum* (Ralfs), both about the same thickness and same length of cell, and both in a colorless gelatinous envelope; the only point of separation is in the attachment of the cells; in the *Hyalotheca* the cells adhere by the whole plane of the end, and in the *Spaerozosma*, they are connected by two sessile glands on the margin. To my mind this distinction is scarcely tenable.

### H. DUBIA, Kg. Plate I, fig. 14.

Cells about as long as wide, not constricted, closely united into short fragile filaments, without gelatinous sheath.

Diameter 13–21 $\mu$.

This form occurs now and then in waters of ponds in New Jersey. As the name implies, it holds a somewhat dubious position. It is without the mucous envelope characteristic of the other species and is usually smaller. Fruiting specimens have not been observed.

Reasoning from observations on the life history of an allied genus, *Bambusina*, I venture to suggest that the forms referred to this species are merely undeveloped conditions of other species.

## *Genus*, BAMBUSINA, Kg.
### Plate I, figs. 15–24.

Cells or joints barrel-shaped, surrounded by one or two narrow median bands, closely united into articulate, nodose filaments. Chlorophyl bodies and zygospores as in *Hyalotheca*.

### B. BREBISSONII, Kg. (*B. Borreri, Cleve; Didymoprium Borreri, Ralfs*). Plate I, figs. 15–21.

Cells somewhat longer than broad, hub or barrel-shaped, surrounded in the middle with two narrow bands, and another often visible between these and the ends of the cells.

Diameter 18–25 $\mu$.

Frequent in quiet waters from Maine to Florida and far west. A pond at Pleasant Mills, New Jersey, furnished me with good conditions of development. The lowest traceable stage is represented by fig. 17. A gelatinous sheath enclosing a series of green cells; fig. 18, four cells around which the envelope is diffusing; these unite, end to end, then widen and produce a form as fig. 19; fig. 20 is somewhat more advanced, showing small notches in the sides; fig. 21, the beginning of the central inflation and the bands; these continue to develop until the perfect plant is produced.

Var. GRACILESCENS, Nord.

Wittrock and Nordstedt have, in their series of *Algæ exsiccatæ*, No. 367, a small variety under this name. It is very small, but the features are those of the typical plant. It was collected in Brazil. The same small form occurs here; have memorandum of it from Longwood Pond, and Wood Lake of northern New Jersey.

B. GRACILESCENS, Nord.  Plate XLVII, figs. 13, 14.

This form is described as a variety of *B. Brebissonii*. Whether viewed as such or as a distinct species, it was an interesting discovery to find it fruiting freely in a pond near Winter Park, Florida.

Diameter of cells 14 $\mu$; length 23 $\mu$; zygospores 15 $\mu$.

> The plant conjugates not like one of the *Desmidieæ*, but more like a *Zygnemaceæ*, in longer or shorter series; often when the zygospores are nearly matured, the cells of one side separate and cause the other side to bend backward.
>
> Judging by these specimens the correctness of the generic position of *Bambusina* may be questioned.

B. DELICATISSIMA, Wolle.  Plate I, figs. 22, 23, 24.

Cells sub-cylindrical, surrounded in the middle by two narrow, thick bands, twice the diameter of the cylindrical body, cells four times as long as wide.

Diameter of body, 6-8 $\mu$.; of bands, 13-17 $\mu$.

> Pond, Pleasant Mills, New Jersey.
>
> The characteristic features of this plant are the small size, the cylindrical form of the body, the elevation of the bands which surround it, and the elongated proportion of the body.

### *Genus*, DESMIDIUM, Ag.

#### Plate II, figs. 1-14; Plate III, figs. 1-4.

Filaments fragile, elongated, triangular or quadrangular, regularly twisted, two chlorophyl masses in each cell barely touching in the middle. Margin of cells incised or entire.

D. CYLINDRICUM, Grev.  (*Didymoprium Grevillii*, Kg.)  Plate III, figs. 1-4.

Cells about half as long as broad, with a thickened border at their junction, medianly more or less deeply incised; transverse view elliptic, with the angles somewhat drawn out. Filaments surrounded with a mucous sheath.

Zygospore spherical, formed by the conjugation **of two cells, the clorophyl passing through a gelatinous connecting tube from one cell to the other (figs. 3, 4)**

Specimens occur frequently in pools and ponds all over the **country, rarely** unmingled with other forms. It is readily **distinguished by its large size, deep incisions of the** border, **and twisted outline.**

D. QUADRATUM, Nord. **Plate LX, fig. 5.**

Differs from the **preceding in the cells being** nearly as **long as broad, and viewed from the side,** quadrate. The breadth **of the cells is** only about one-fifth more than the length ; **the thickness, the same as the length. Chlorophyl mass in each cell in** end **view, more or less radiate.**

Diameter 45 $\mu$. ; length, 33-38 $\mu$. ; thickness, 33-38 $\mu$.

**Found this form** repeatedly during the past four **years, but rarely, except in** ponds, Brown's Mills, New Jersey. It varies **in size** from the Norway typical plant, **in** being considerably **larger ;** othewise it appears to be identical.

D. LONGATUM. Wolle. **Plate LX, fig. 6.**

**Filaments thin ; cells in front view nearly twice as long as wide ; in side view nearly 2½ times longer than broad ;** closely **united without a thickened border at their junction ; end view broadly elliptic.**

**Diameter, widest part, 25-28** $\mu$.**; thickness, 16-18** $\mu$.**; length of cell, 35-40** $\mu$.

This interesting new species from **Brown's Mills and Egg Harbor,** New Jersey, was found late in the season (September **22, 1883) ;** no gelatinous sheath was observable ; the filaments **were hyaline** except two *chlorophyl nuclei* in **each cell.**

D. SWARTZII, Ag. **Plate II, figs. 1-6.**

Filament triangular, with a **single longitudinal, waved, dark line,** formed by the third angle, (compare figs. **6, 8, 13); joints in** front view somewhat quadrangular, broader **than long, with two** slightly angular crenatures on each lateral margin, united at the whole of their end margins by a thick-**ened border ; end** view triangular with the chlorophyl **three-rayed. Zygospores** oval.

**Diameter 36** $\mu$.**, more or less.**

Frequent in shallow pools, **trenches** and the like.

The spores are formed by the flowing together of the two masses of chlorophyl in each cell ; the united body **assumes a** spherical form; this enlarges, and as it increases in size, forces the sides of the cell apart to more than twice the original diameter (fig. 3); when mature the sides separate and the spores are set free.

D. QUADRANGULATUM, Kg.   Plate II, figs. 13, 14.

Filament quadrangular, varying in breadth from its twisting, having two longitudinal waved lines; joints in front view broader than long, with two somewhat rounded crenatures on each lateral margin.   End view quadrangular.

Diameter 50–60 $\mu$.

> This is a form which prevails in England and on the Continent, but has not yet been found in this country. I insert it from Dr. Wood's contribution in anticipation of yet finding it.

D. APTOGONIUM, Breb.   Plate II, figs. 6, 7.   Plate LX, fig. 7.

Joints in front view, quadrangular, broader than long, with two rounded crenatures on each lateral margin, united at the outer portion only of each end margin by mutual projections, thus producing intervening central oval or oblong foramina.

Diameter 25–38 $\mu$.

> Not so frequent as *D. Swartzii*, but it appears to be widely scattered from Pennsylvania and New Jersey as far south as Florida, and probably also northward and westward.

D. BAILEYI (*Aptogonium Baileyi*, Ralfs).   Plate II, figs. 8–12.

Filaments triangular, twisted as the preceding, joints united by each end of the lateral margins only, excavated between the angles as the preceding form; the lateral margins are straight, not bicrenate, a characteristic which separates it from the other species.

Diameter 25 $\mu$., more or less.

> Found frequently in sluggish waters, without being confined to any particular State or States.
>
> The process of fruiting is not unlike that of D. Swartzii, the separated portions of chlorophyl (fig. 8) unite and concentrate (fig. 9), then enlarge (fig. 10), press out the sides to more than twice the diameter of a sterile filament, then break apart and set the spores free.

### Genus, PHYMATODOCIS, Nord.

Cells closely united in sheathless filaments, not at all **or only** slightly twisted; cells deeply constricted in the middle, the two semi-cells somewhat twisted, giving the margins an irregular outline; filaments quadrangular with sides longitudinally ex**cavated.**

**P.** NORDSTEDTIANUM, Wolle. Plate LX, figs. 1-4.

Cells rectangular, about as long as wide, deeply constricted in the middle, the sinuses somewhat enlarged inwardly and **rounded at the base**; the sinuses between the cells similar, slightly deeper; end view quadriradiate with wide and deep sinuses between **the** rays, apices rounded, emarginate; **the** two semi-cells somewhat twisted, **so** that the end of **one ray** projects more than that of the other and **produces an irregular** outline; membrane smooth.

Diameter 37-40 $\mu$.

This new species in ponds at Brown's Mills and Egg Harbor, New Jersey, and at Kissimme, Florida, differs from the form collected in Brazil, in being one-fourth smaller; **in** having the lobes or rays in end view straight, not curved to one side, and in having the sinuses of the cells not narrow linear, but **somewhat enlarged** inwardly and rounded at **base.**

### Genus, SPHAEROZOSMA, Corda.

### Plate IV, figs. 1-16.

Cells **closely** united side **to side** by a narrow isthmus or by means of glandular processes, deeply incised on each side, thus forming bilobed cells, **and** often giving a pinnatifid appearance to the fragile filaments.

Filaments often surrounded **by a colorless gelatinous envelope.**

Brebisson separated the forms which have the cells united without glandular processes with **a new** genus SPONDYLOSUM. The distinction is **hardly tenable.** The modes **of** union, like the gelatinous sheaths, are inconstant, hence should not be made generic or specific characteristics.

This genus differs **from** the preceding in the *compressed, flat,* **not** round, triangular nor square filaments, but deeply incised **cells, and** especially in the frequent presence of the minute gland-**like** connecting processes.

S. PULCHRUM, Bailey.   Plate IV, figs. 1, 2.

Cells twice as broad as long, deeply incised on each side, ends rounded, junction margin straight, filaments twisted, frequently enclosed in a gelatinous envelope.

Diameter 60–82 $\mu$.

Var. PLANUM, Wolle.   Plate IV, figs. 3, 4.

Similar to typical form, except in size and in the absence of the twist in the filaments.

Diameter 30–38 $\mu$.

Var. INFLATUM, Wolle.   Plate LX, fig. 8.

Differs from the preceding in the central inflation, producing a short isthmus between the cells.

Diameter 38 $\mu$.

> The typical form appears to be widely scattered throughout many States: Rhode Island, Massachusetts, Pennsylvania, New Jersey, South Carolina and Florida. The variety *planum* I found in a trench aside the railroad near Metuchen, N. J. The water was green with the abundance of it. The variety *inflatum* occurs sparsely in ponds of New Jersey.

S. FILIFORME, Rab.   Plate IV, figs. 5, 6.

Cells about as long as wide, constricted in the middle with a deep, acute incision; ends of lobes rounded, connected by two sessile glands.

Diameter 12–18 $\mu$.

> Pond waters of Pennsylvania and New Jersey.
> General appearance very near *S. pulchrum* variety, but smaller, and length of cell equal to the diameter. Did not observe a gelatinous sheath mentioned by Rabenhorst; Kirchner admits no sheath.   Fig. 6 is very near Corda's *S. lamelliferum*.

S. PULCHELLUM (Arch.) Rab.   Plate XII, figs. 8, 9.

Cells in outline oblong with the middle much inflated, sharply incised and angles rounded; ends narrower because not at all or very slightly inflated; apices square; varying in length from one to nearly two diameters.

Diameter 9–10 $\mu$.

> Pond waters, not rare.   *Syn. Spondylosium bambusioides*, Witt.  *S. pulchellum*, Arch.

S. MONILIFORME, Lund.  **Plate XLVII**, fig. 11.

Series of cells often long, firm, somewhat twisted ; usually included in a mucous envelope. Cells average **one-half longer than broad, deeply constricted, sinus obtuse outwardly enlarged, back more or less produced** ; seen from **the vertex triangular, sides somewhat retuse** ; angles rounded, **isthmus sub-elongate, membrane smooth.**

Diameter about 20 $\mu$.

Not infrequent in quiet waters, Florida ; **less frequent in** New Jersey, Minnesota and Pennsylvania.

S. EXCAVATUM, Ralfs.  **Plate IV**, figs. 8, 9, 10–12.

Cells twice as long as broad, with a deep, wide sinus on each side, **connected by two small sessile glands.**

Diameter 9–12 $\mu$.

Not infrequent in ponds ; sometimes it **occurs with, and** sometimes without, the gelatinous sheath.

S. VERTEBRATUM (Breb.), Ralfs.  Plate **IV**, fig. 13.

Cells about half as long as broad, **with a deep narrow constriction, connected in** the center by a simple, rather **thick gland ; more or less remote.** Semi-cells narrow, elliptic, smooth. **Filaments twisted,** usually surrounded by a mucous sheath.

Diameter 12–14 $\mu$.

Rather rare ; the best specimens found were from Splitrock Pond, Sussex Co., New Jersey.

S. SERRATUM, Bailey.  **Plate IV, fig. 7.  Plate XLIII,** figs. 7, 8.

**Cells** broader than long, **deeply notched,** or divided into two transverse portions with acute, spinelike projecting ends which give **a** serrated outline to the **chain.** Cells closely united by **two short** glandular processes. **Usually surrounded by a wide gelatinous sheath.**

Diameter 22–33 $\mu$., including the projections.

**Prof.** Bailey collected this species in South Carolina, Georgia, and Florida, 1848 ; it is found frequently in New Jersey, Pennsylvania and other Northern States.

According **to** Wallich this species should be classed with *Onychonema*, a new genus made by him to take in the forms **which** have the glandular processes **long.**

The glandular processes connecting the cells are sometimes long, nearly equal to the length of a semi-cell ; in this condition it approaches very near to *Onychonema laeve*, Nord., a Brazil **form. The specimens** vary considerably, but they do not seem to admit of separation. The cells are often only slightly inflated, sides nearly straight; the spines, in young condition nearly obsolete, or very small and straight, and the glandular processes sometimes short, barely discernible, and again so long that they lap over the cells.

S. (Onychonema) NORDSTEDTIANA, Turner. Plate XLIII, figs. 9, 10.

Cells forming filaments of fifty to sixty cells or more connected by subcapitate claspers peculiar to the genus. Length of cells 14 $\mu$.; breadth 18 $\mu$.; breadth of sheath 30–40 $\mu$.

The rather unusual size, and that it has not been found where other forms prevail, Mr. Turner considers evidence of a distinct species rather than a merely young form.

S. WALLACHII? Jacobsen. Plate IV. fig. 15.

A peculiar form of which I found only two short specimens in pond, Brown's Mills, N. J. They are not identical with the form described by Jacobsen. I record the figures of them provisionally until other specimens may be found to verify a good species.

Diameter 10–12 $\mu$.

S. SPINULOSUM? Delph. Plate IV, fig. 14.

Another variety of which I found only a single specimen, in a pond known as Chain Dam, Northampton Co., Pennsylvania. In a Florida collection are numerous well developed specimens, which agree with Delpont's diagnosis in being really spinous. They have the form of cell, the measure, and the arrangement of the spines, except perhaps that there are more frequently only two, than three spines, on the margin of each semi-cell. A fine and distinct species. If the granules of the figure (Plate IV, fig. 14) were drawn out into short spines, the typical plant would be well represented. It is not the same, but near Delpont's described form.

Diameter 10 $\mu$.

S. RECTANGULARE, Wolle. Plate LX, fig. 9.

Filament wide; cells twice as wide as long, deeply constricted in the middle; semi-cells somewhat tapering near the ends, producing acute-angled sinuses between the cells, and between the semi-cells; ends truncate concave, and angles often cuspidate. Membrane smooth.

Diameter 50–55 $\mu$.; thickness 18–20 $\mu$.

This form was recorded with hesitation; it was one of **the latest finds in the fall of 1883; but since it occurred frequently in ponds at Brown's Mills, Manchester and other waters, New Jersey.

*Genus.* **MESOTAENIUM,** Naeg.

*Palmogloea,* **Kg.** Plate III, figs. 5-15.

Cells straight, short cylindrical, or **oval, ends** rounded, not constricted in the middle. *Chlorophyl lamina* axillary, sometimes divided in the middle.

Copulation takes place by two cells uniting side **by side, the** contents flowing together.

Kirchner remarks that copulation in this genus is **a** simple union of two cells, leaving no husks or remains of empty cells; (compare figs. 5-9). This process accords with my observations, **but** Wood illustrates another mode transferred **in figs. 13-15, in** which the contents of the cells flow **together and are surrounded** by a new membrane; **in this case the** remains **of the old cells** are present.

These plants occur frequently in small pools, on dripping rocks, damp walls, **wet** ground and the like; sometimes singly, but more frequently associated in families in **a** gelatinous **mucus.**

**M. Braunii,** D. By. (*Palmogloea macrococca,* **Kg.**) Plate III, figs. **5-9.**

Cells cylindrical, 2-2½ times **longer** than wide, ends flatly rounded. Zygospore square, angles rounded, sides usually somewhat concave.

Diameter 16-19 $\mu$.

**Found** floating, in families, in gelatinous scum, mountain **pools.**

**M.** micrococcum, Kg. Plate III, fig. 10.

Cells oval or elliptical, about twice as long as wide, ends sometimes slightly narrowed and rounded.

Diameter 6-11 $\mu$.

Usually in gelatinous **masses on** old wet wood, timbers of sluices, etc.

**M.** Endlicherianum, Naeg. Plate III, fig. 11.

Cells cylindrical, 3-4 times as long as wide, ends bluntly **rounded.**

**Diameter 9-11 $\mu$.**

Occasionally intermingled with filamentous forms, in gelatinous gatherings.

M. CLEPSYDRA, Wood.  Plate III, figs. 12–15.

Living on rocks and mosses, swimming in a transparent, sometimes light-green jelly; **cells obtusely** truncated, **rounded at the ends,** 2–3 times longer than broad; *chlorophyl lamina* **axillary,** mostly indistinct, often wanting; *endochrome* **light green;** nucleus generally distinct; *zygospores subfuscous*, **either** globose or of an irregular form, somewhat resembling **that** of an hour-glass; **external coat irregularly excavated and sulcate.**

Diameter given by **the author** is $\frac{1}{1000}''$, this would be .00173 = 43 μ.  Evidently an error, the plant cannot be so large.

> The author adds, "This species was found near Chelten Hills, growing amid mosses on the rocky juttings over which the water was dripping. It occurs as a rather firm, transparent jelly, mostly of a light greenish tint, in which the cells are often placed quite thickly."

## *Genus,* SPIROTAENIA, Breb.

### Plate III, figs. 16–22.

Cells **straight** fusiform, single **or aggregated in a gelatinous mucus; not constricted** in the middle, ends round.  *Chlorophyl* **arranged in one or** more spiral *laminæ* **on the inner surface of the wall.**

S. CONDENSATA, Breb.  Plate III, figs. 21, 22.

Fusiform, or cigar-shaped, ends **rounded, eight to ten times as long as broad,** with a single, broad, closely wound chlorophyl **spiral band,** its revolutions numerous.

Diameter 18–25 μ.

> Found in meadow pools, ponds, etc.  Has been collected in many States of the Union, from New York and New Jersey, south to Florida, and westward to Minnesota.

S. OBSCURA, Ralfs.  Plate III, figs. 16–19.

Fusiform, deep green, five to eight **times longer than broad, ends attenuated, apices rounded.  Chlorophyl arranged in a number of narrow spiral, parietal bands.**

Diameter 8–15 μ.

> The locality in which this species occurred most frequently to me, was in small pools aside streamlets on the open slope of our mountain sides, but found it also in New Jersey. European specimens are quoted as large as 30 μ. in diameter. I have found none so large.

S. BRYOPHILA, (Breb.), Rab. (*S. muscicola*, D. By.) Plate III. fig. 20.

Cells cylindrical, two to four times as long as broad, ends obtusely rounded, chlorophyl a single, broad, smoothly defined, widely wound spiral band; its revolutions one or two.

Diameter 8 $\mu$.

> Dr. Wood reports this species, measure and form, from near Philadelphia, **growing among some mosses** which were kept **constantly wet** by overhanging dripping rocks. It formed little transparent masses of almost colorless jelly, looking like little drops of **dew**.

## *Genus*, PENIUM. Breb.

(Netrium, Naeg. Cylindrocystis Menegh.)

Plate V, figs. 1-22.

Cells straight cylindrical or fusiform, not incised nor constricted in the middle; ends more or less obtusely rounded. *Chlorophyl lamina* axillary; when seen transversely, radiately divergent, arms often forked, and containing starch granules.

Individuals swim free, scattered, or associated in gelatinous masses; cell membranes smooth or finely granulate, transparent or fuscous, or reddish, often longitudinally striate.

Multiplication takes place by division, and by zygospores developed by the copulation of two cells. Comp. Introduction.

P. DIGITUS, (Ehrb.), Breb. Plate V, figs. 1, 2. Plate LXIV, fig. 1.

Cells ovately cylindrical, or broadly elliptical, 3-5 times longer than broad, each end subtruncately rounded, (Plate LXIV, fig. 1). *Chlorophyl lamina* lobate in the periphery, interrupted in the middle. Plate V, fig. 1, is a variety, more elliptic than the typical form. Fig. 2 is a transverse section.

Diameter 60-80 $\mu$.

> This species appears to be widely distributed from Maine to Florida and westward. Very variable in size and outline.

P. LAMELLOSUM, Breb. Plate V. fig. 4.

Cells oblong or fusiform cylindrical, often with a slight depression in the middle, more or less attenuated towards the obtusely rounded ends. Arrangement of chlorophyl usually somewhat like the last, but not separated in the middle.

Diameter 55–80 $\mu$.

Not so common as the preceding.

P. OBLONGUM, D. By.   Plate V, fig. 17.

Cells oblong cylindrical, 3–4 times as long as wide, not constricted in the middle, slightly tapering towards the ends; apices flatly rounded. Zygospore spherical, not unlike Plate V, fig. 7.

> I find this form mostly in fresh spring water, in gelatinous gatherings.

P. MARGARITACEUM, Breb.   Plate V, figs. 5, 6, 11.

Cylindrical, usually 8–9 times longer than broad, rarely, only twice as long; not at all, or scarcely constricted in the middle; ends rounded, ornate with pearly granules arranged in longitudinal series which often give a denticulate appearance to the margin.

Diameter 24–28 $\mu$.; length ordinarily about 225 $\mu$. I have had specimens measuring 375 $\mu$.

> Prevails over a wide range. I have it from Vermont, Connecticut, and almost every State southward to Florida, also from the west to Minnesota.
>
> It varies somewhat in size, but is easily recognized by the arrangement of the granules.

P. SPIROSTRIOLATUM, Barker.   Plate X, fig. 17.

Large, elongated; single cells somewhat swollen in the center and tapering slightly towards the rotundo-truncate ends; the cell walls possessing a number of superficial, conspicuous, rather coarse striae, running in a spiral direction; these somewhat interrupted at a number of annular rib-like projections varying in number; these projections most numerous towards the ends.

Mr. Turner, of England, who reports this form from Minnesota remarks, "As I do not know of the publication of any measurements or authentic figure of this species, I may possibly be in error in referring these American forms to it: the figures therefore must speak for themselves."

Diameter of cells 23–31 $\mu$.; length of double cell as figured 227–260 $\mu$.

Another form, Plate X, fig. 19, which may for the present be referred to this species, I found frequent in the Tocoi marshes, **Florida.** It is unlike the preceding in the absence of the transverse sutures or rib-like projections; **in the variableness of diameter and** proportionate lengths. Diameter of smaller forms 15-18 $\mu$ and of larger form 37 $\mu$. The smaller are 10-14 and the larger 7 times longer than broad. Chlorophyl usually thrice interrupted.

P. INTERRUPTUM, Breb. Plate V, figs. 14, 15.

Broad cylindrical, not **constricted, 5-6** times as long as wide, suddenly tapering, **cuneate near the ends,** apices rounded. Chlorophyl deep green, in matured plants interrupted by three transverse pale bands; **cytioderm** smooth.

Diameter 38-50 $\mu$., rarely only 16-20 $\mu$.

> Habitat the **same as the preceding, rather more frequent;** readily distinguished by its **transverse** bands and **cuneate** ends.

P. CLOSTERIOIDES, Ralfs. Plate V, fig. 18.

Cells narrowly lanceolate, **5-6 times** longer than the greatest diameter; sensibly attenuated from the middle to the rounded apices. Chlorophyl contents interrupted in the center.

Diameter 30-44 $\mu$. Ten times **longer.**

> Ponds, New Jersey, Pennsylvania **and Minnesota.**
>
> In its general appearance and in **the arrangement of the** chlorophyl, this plant **has a strong resemblance to a** *Closterium,* but varies in **being always straight** and having the opposite margins symmetrical.

P. TRUNCATUM, Ralfs. Plate V, figs. 9, 10, 21, 22.

Cylindrical, not **constricted, 3-4 times longer than wide,** ends truncate, **square. Zygospores smooth, spherical.**

Diameter 11-12 $\mu$.

> **Ponds, northern** counties of New Jersey. The chlorophyl **is usually more or** less interrupted **in** the middle, producing **a pale transverse band;** membrane smooth or finely punctate.

P. MINUTUM, Cleve. Plate V, figs. 19, 20.

Slender, cells 4-6 times longer than **broad, sides straight,** ends rounded, without inflation, **and without punctures.**

Diameter 11-15 $\mu$.

> **This small** form, **perhaps** more properly a *Calocylindrus,* (Plate XV, fig. 12), has **not** come under my notice. It **is** reported by Bailey and Olney, from Florida and from **Rhode Island.** The measures are taken from Rabenh. Fl. Alg. **The** figure **in** Ralfs, Br. Desmids, and referred to as belonging to this species is certainly distinct and is a *Docidium.*

**P. polymorphum**, Perty. Plate V, fig. 12.

Sub-cylindrical, smooth, various sizes usually intermingled in larger families; 3–4 times longer than broad, ends more or less attenuated, apices rounded; **cytioderm somewhat longitudinally striated.**

Diameter 11–15 $\mu$.

Pools, or wet earth, Charlotte, Vermont. Collected by F. Hosford.

**P. Brebissonii**, (Menegh.), Ralfs. Plate V, figs. 7, 8.

Cells smooth, cylindrical with rounded **ends, transverse central band inconspicuous;** conjugating **cells persistent.**

Diameter 16–17 $\mu$.

Usually congregated **in a mucous stratum in** small **pools and on wet** grounds, Princeton, New Jersey (Bailey) and other localities in the State. The plant mentioned by Wood **appears** to be nearer *Closterium obtusum*, Breb.

**P. Navicula**, Breb. Plate V, fig. 16.

Small, broadly fusiform, **4-5 times** longer than broad, tapering from the center to the rounded **apices.** Chlorophyl lamina entire; cytioderm smooth.

Diameter 12–17 $\mu$.

Zygospores are said to **be nearly** square, somewhat drawn **out** between the attached remains of the copulating cells. **The** plant occurs frequently in trenches and small ponds of Pennsylvania and New Jersey; **the fruiting cells, or zygospores** have **not come under my personal observation.**

**P. Jenneri**, Ralfs. Plate XXXVII, figs. 1, 2.

Smooth, cylindrical with rounded ends, zygospores orbicular, situated between the conjugating cells which are deciduous.

Diameter 14–15 $\mu$.

I have not **recognized** this **form.** Bailey **reports it from** Florida. Rabenhorst describes it as scarcely distinguishable from *P. Brebissonii*; 2½–5 times longer than broad; zygospores mostly globose, membrane somewhat fuscous, sub-granulate.

**P. crassa**, D. By. Plate V, fig. 3.

Cells short, ovate-cylindrical, 1½–2 **times as long as wide,** chlorophyl not separated, but concentrated **into two or more nuclei** in each cell.

Diameter 25–29 $\mu$.

Collected **by** E. S. Cheeseman, Knowlesville, **New York,** in gelatinous mucus in an aquarium.

**P. RUPESTRE.** Kg. Plate V, fig. 13.

Cells ovate elliptical, length about two diameters; **apices rounded.**

Diameter 20–25 $\mu$.

> Rabenhorst unites the preceding with **this form.** They are very near in size, but not the same in shape; the one is more cylindrical and the other inclines more to an ellipse in form. Collected in a mucous gathering on dripping rocks.

**P. CLEVEI,** Lund. Plate LXI, fig. 27.

See *Calocylindrus*.

**P. CRUCIFERUM,** (D. By.), Wittr. Plate X, figs. 9–11.

Cells cylindrical, nearly twice as long **as wide,** scarcely constricted, ends roundly truncate; **seen from vertex orbicular;** chlorophyl laminae arranged in form of a cross **as seen** in transverse section; cytioderm smooth.

Syn. *Cosmarium cruciferum*, **D.** By.

Marsh pools, Florida.

**P. (Cylindrocystis) TUMIDUM,** F. Gay. Plate XLV, figs. 7, 8.

Cells twice **as** long as broad; each semi-cell **a broadly truncated cone. Cytioderm smooth.**

Diameter 28 $\mu$.

Frequent in Tocoi marshes, **Florida.**

## Genus, CLOSTERIUM, Nitsch.

Cells simple, elongated, lunately **curved or crescent-shaped,** entire, in the center not constricted but **frequently marked with** from 1–5 transverse striae; **the cytioderm or wall, thin, moderately firm, smooth or more or less distinctly striate.**

The chlorophyllous cytioplasm is mostly arranged in **longitudinal parietal laminæ, broken in the middle by a pale transverse band;** at each end there is usually a **clear, circular, colorless or** straw-colored vesicle, or *vacuole*, which contains **minute** granules **in constant** motion. As the specimen dries **the** "dancing **granules"** disappear, and **the vesicle vanishes.** Compare Introduction, page 16. Compare also **Addenda.**

A distinct circulation of **granules may be noticed in good** living specimens.

The *Closterium* in normal condition is always green, but may be found of various tints of reddish brown; these changes of color take **place as** life becomes extinct. The striated forms have a firm cytioderm and retain their outline when dry or empty; others, not striated are more flexible and collapse when dried. The chlorophyl escapes by a slight separation of the semi-cells, and leaves the case colorless.

Faded specimens of the striated forms are best adapted for examination; the striae, barely discernible in green condition, become distinct; the cases flatten somewhat in drying, the breadth in center increases and the ends appear more attenuated, hence some allowance should be made in describing them.

Conjugation takes place by a process which appears the same as in other *conjugatæ*. Two cells drawn into close proximity, put forth small tubular prominences by which they unite, the chlorophyllous cytioplasm of the two cells concentrates at their junction, in the connecting tube; this enlarges more and more until the whole of the contents of the two cells are commingled, and condense into a seed-like mass. This becomes smooth, spherical, sometimes quadrangular, and is known as the zygospore. Compare Plate IX. The coupling usually takes place from the concave sides, but not universally; have found them united from the convex sides also.

SECTION 1.—Cells more or less cylindrical, slightly bent, ends scarcely, or not at all tapering; zygospores orbicular or square

C. OBTUSUM. Breb. Plate VII, fig. 1.

Cylindrical, lightly curved, 5-10 times longer than broad, ends not tapering, broadly rounded, cytioderm colorless and smooth.

Diameter 5–11 $\mu$.

Often in gelatinous masses on planks, on the sides of flumes, Pennsylvania.

C. JUNCIDUM, Ralfs. Plate VII, figs. 2, 3.

Cells long cylindrical, somewhat curved and tapering towards the ends; 20-30 times longer than broad, apices obtusely rounded; vacuole small and indistinct.

Diameter 11–12 $\mu$.

Variable in thickness and length; occurs frequently in ponds from Maine to Florida.

C. JUNCIDUM, forma GRACILLIMA-LAEVISSIMA, Breb. Plate VI, fig. 21.

Very much smaller than the type-form and destitute of striae.

Frequent in ponds near Maitland, Florida.

C. MACILENTUM, Breb.  Plate VII, fig. 6.

Very long cylindrical, slightly curved and reduced in thickness near the ends, apices rounded; 20–40 times longer than the diameter.  Cytioderm smooth, colorless, or yellowish, usually with 1–4 transverse striae.  Zygospore spherical, smooth.

Diameter 12–13 $\mu$.

Ponds, Pennsylvania, New Jersey.  Not rare.

C. ENSIS, Delp.  Plate VI, figs. 13, 14.

Cell elongate, about twenty times longer than broad, sublinear, or slightly attenuated from the middle to the apices; ends not curved; cytioderm smooth.

Diameter 36 $\mu$.

Not rare in ponds, Minnesota, Pennsylvania and New Jersey.

C. GRACILE, Breb.  Plate VII, figs. 4, 5.

Long cylindrical, 20–30 times as long as broad, nearly straight, ends somewhat curved and slightly reduced in thickness; cytioderm smooth and colorless.  Zygospores according to Brebisson quadrangular, with rounded angles, each of which bears a short spine.

Diameter 5–6 $\mu$.; zygospores 28–30 $\mu$. long; 22 $\mu$. broad.

Not infrequently intermingled with other desmids from ponds, New Jersey, Pennsylvania, etc.

C. LANCEOLATUM, Kg. (*C. tenue*, Bailey).  Plate IX, fig. 14.

Cells semi-lanceolate, 6–10 times longer than broad, gradually tapering, ends subacute, chlorophyl fillets several; larger granules in a single series.  Empty frond colorless and destitute of striae.

Diameter 40–50 $\mu$.

Pools, Florida; New York, (Bailey).  Hundreds of specimens in a gathering made by Prof. Cragin, Kansas.  Stouter and proportionately shorter than *C. acerosum*.

C. DIDYMOTOCUM, Corda.  Plate IX, figs. 12, 13.

Broad cylindrical, slightly curved, 6–12 times longer than broad, slightly tapering towards the ends which are broadly truncate, square; vacuole distinct containing many "dancing granules;" cytioderm yellowish, finely longitudinally striate.

Diameter 30–32 $\mu$.

Not abundant, but turns up now and then with other forms, in smaller ponds of Pennsylvania, New Jersey and Minnesota.

Plate V, fig. 10, represents a large form and distinct variety corresponding to description by Delponte. Cytioderm not longitudinally striate, but smooth and apices obtusely rounded.

Diameter 50–60 $\mu$.

Minnesota and New Jersey.

C. DECUSSATUM, Kg. Plate VII, figs. 9, 10.

Cylindrical, curvature scarcely appreciable; 7–12 times longer than broad; very slightly tapering near the obtusely rounded ends, cytioderm distinctly decussately striate.

Diameter 20–25–30 $\mu$.

Frequent in ponds, Mt. Everett, Massachusetts, August, 1882, and ponds northern part of New Jersey. Kützing of Germany appears to have been the only individual who observed this species. He sent a drawing to Ralfs, but he questioned the correctness of his friend's vision; he remarks, "Prof. Kützing represents the striae as regularly crossing each other, so as to form diamond-shaped reticulations. As this appearance is not unusual in dried specimens, when the flattened cell permits the striae of both surfaces to be visible together; I will venture to suggest the possibility that Prof. Kützing's drawing may have been taken from a cell in that condition."

The correctness of Kützing's observations is readily established by an examination of the plants as found in Gilder and other ponds on Mt. Everett. They are cylindrical and may be rolled over to display the decussated striae on every side alike.

C. ANGUSTATUM, Kg. Plate VII, figs. 21, 22, 23.

Cells sublinear, 16–18 times longer than wide, very slightly attenuated; ends obtusely rounded. Cells present 4–5 somewhat prominent longitudinal striae; 2 or 3 transverse bands or striae are also frequently distinct; vacuole subremote from the apex, small. Dried specimens brownish yellow.

A variety is frequent with the striae loosely crossing each other, decussately.

Diameter 15–25 $\mu$.

Ponds, Berkshire Mountains, Mass.

Section II.—Cells slightly bent, the back (dorsum) more or less convex, the opposite (ventral) side almost straight, distinctly attenuated from the middle to the ends. Zygospore globular, smooth.

### C. Lunula, Ehrb. Plate LXI, fig. 26.

Cells large, semilunar, 5–6 times longer than broad, smooth, or very finely striate, indistinct, back high convex, lower side straightish, ends attenuated, rounded. Chlorophyl globules numerous; vacuole usually distinct and contains many actively moving granules.

Diameter 80–110 $\mu$.

Frequent in small ponds.
The figure is not a good typical form. It should not be curved so much at the end.

### Var. striatum, Wolle.

Differing from the ordinary form by having the cytioderm finely, but distinctly striate.

### C. Cucumis, Ehrb. Plate VII. figs. 17, 18.

Cells smooth, stout, semilunate; ends broadly rounded.

Ehrenberg's figure represents this species about five times longer than broad; in form somewhat resembling *C. Lunula*, not so large, and lower side more concave. Ehrenberg collected it in the State of New York. The figures are from plants found in New Jersey and Pennsylvania. They are evidently closely allied to *C. Lunula*.

### C. subtile, Breb. Plate VIII, fig. 2.

Cells very slender, acicular, slightly curved, narrow lanceolate, apices acute, cuspidate.

Diameter 3–4 $\mu$.

Ponds, New Jersey. Rather rare.

### C. acerosum, (Schrank), Ehrb. Plate VII, figs. 7, 11.

Linear fusiform or slightly curved, 15–24 times longer than wide, lightly tapering towards the ends; apices narrowly truncate, or obtusely rounded, transparent or yellowish; cytioderm rather indistinctly, or not at all striate. Chlorophyl globules 11–14 arranged in a simple axillary series in each semi-cell; vacuole small with numerous corpuscles. Zygospore globose, or broadly elliptic.

Diameter variable, 35–62 $\mu$.

Plate X, figs. 1, 2. A specimen finely in fruit; presenting the peculiarity of two forms of zygospores, single and twin, oval, the longer axis at right angles with the axis of the cells. Cell walls finely but distinctly striate.

One of our most common species, often forming gelatinous floating masses on small ponds and pools. I have it from many States, and probably it exists in every one.

The entire chlorophyl of this species often retracts itself from the cell-wall and breaks up into a number of oval or globular forms, every one of which acquires a firm envelope. Plate IX, fig. 17, represents one of these forms.

C. PRELONGUM, ‹Breb.›, Delph.  Plate VI, figs. 15, 16.

Cells somewhat linear, cylindrical, elongate, about thirty times longer than broad, slightly curved, apices obtusely rounded, sometimes slightly recurved; cytioderm striated.

Diameter 20–21 $\mu$.

Ponds, Pennsylvania and Minnesota.

C. SUBCOSTATUM. Nord.  Plate VII. fig. 11.

Cells usually four to five times longer than broad; back rather high arched, below nearly straight, may be either slightly concave or convex; apices obtusely rounded. Membrane usually yellowish brown with 9–12 longitudinal costae.

Diameter 50–60 $\mu$.

C. NASUTUM, Nord.  Plate VII, fig. 12.

Large, fusiform, only slightly curved, about five times as long as wide, gradually tapering from the middle to near the ends, then suddenly contracting, making the sides parallel, to the truncate or rounded apex. Cytioderm smooth. Specimens of this species from Cypress Swamp, Florida, appear perfectly straight and somewhat thicker and longer than the forms hitherto noted, apical vacuole distinct. Chlorophyl arranged in five or six fillets; centrally separated, length seven times more than the breadth. Coll. A. C. Stokes.

Diameter 75 $\mu$. more or less.

Ponds, Berkshire Mountains, Massachusetts.
The only counterpart to this form, hitherto found, is from Brazil, and is represented in Witt. and Nord's *Algæ Exsiccatæ* No. 366.

C. TURGIDUM, Ehrb.  Plate VII, fig. 15; Plate VI, figs. 3, 4.

Dorsum convex, lower margin somewhat concave, inclining upward at the rounded ends; upper margin with a depression near each extremity; empty cells reddish brown, striae numerous, fine but distinct.

Diameter 64–75 $\mu$.

Wet, marshy places, Pennyslvania.

C. ATTENUATUM, Ehrb.   **Plate IX, fig. 5.**

Somewhat curved, attenuated, suddenly contracted at the end into a narrow conical point; empty frond reddish, faintly striated.

Diameter 34–42 $\mu$.

> I quote this diagnosis from Ralfs' Br. Desmids; think we ought **to find, but am** not satisfied that I had a genuine species.

C. STRIGOSUM, Ehrb.   **Plate VII, figs. 13, 14; and Plate LXIV, figs. 9, 10.**

Long fusiform, at the ends somewhat bent, 19–24 **times as long** as broad, slightly tapering from the middle to **the thin,** finely rounded apices. Vacuole small and indistinct. **Cytioderm colorless, smooth.**

Diameter 10–16 $\mu$.

> **Pond** waters, Pennsylvania and New Jersey. Plate LXIV, figs. 9, 10, represent a fruiting form, collected in abundance, near Ocean Beach, July, '83. In form near *C. parvulum*, but **proportionately so** much longer than the species, I take it for a variety of *C. strigosum*. Diameter **of cells** 10 $\mu$.; length 200 $\mu$.; twenty times longer than wide.

SECTION III.—Cells more or less falcate; dorsum and ventral margins both convex, arched in the same direction, ends tapering. § A. form slightly **curved.** § B. forms strongly curved, sometimes almost semi-circular.

C. STRIOLATUM, Ehrb.   **Plate VII, figs. 8, 20.**

Cells slightly bent, 8–16 times longer than broad, ends reduced **to one-fourth the** largest diameter, apex obtusely rounded. Vacuole full size, containing many active gran**ules.** Cytioderm **of older** forms, reddish brown, distinct striate. Zygospore orbicular, smooth.

Diameter, 30–48 $\mu$.

**Plate VI, figs. 5–8. Distinct from forms on Plate VI. Fig. 8 may be considered of doubtful value.**

> Frequent in shallow pools.
> 
> I find three varieties, the one 6–8 times longer than broad (Plate VI, fig. 8); another 10–15 (Plate VI, fig. 20); and the third only 4–5 times longer than broad. They may be recognized as varieties, *intermedium*, Ralfs; *elongatum*, Rab.; and *tumidum*, Rab. The latter is very near Nord's. *subcostatum*. **The** variety *elongatum* is more slender and more delicately striate than the others.

C. COSTATUM, Corda. Plate VII, fig. 19.

Fusiform, more or less curved, 6–8 diameters in length, ends rounded; tapering from the middle to about one-third the largest diameter; vacuole large, containing many dancing granules. Membrane in front view has 5, or rarely 6–8 longitudinal striae or costae. Zygospores spherical or ovate. Diameter 63–70 $\mu$.

Frequent in marsh pools and the like localities.

C. DELPONTII. Klebs. (*C. Crassum*, Delp.) Plate VI, fig. 9.

Cells cylindrical, somewhat inflated in the middle, gradually tapering to an obtusely rounded apex; distinctly striate with one, two or three sutures about the middle; cell twenty times (more or less) longer than broad.

Diameter 35–45 $\mu$.

Delponte's name of *Crassum* having been previously applied to another species by Rabenhorst, Klebs changed it.

C. LINEATUM, Ehrb. Plate VII, fig. 16.

Long, straight and cylindrical in the center, ends greatly attenuated and slightly incurved, apices obtusely rounded, distinctly striate; chlorophyl globules, about twenty in each semi-cell, placed in a single axillary series; vacuoles small, remote from the apices.

Diameter 24–36 $\mu$.

Pennsylvania, New Jersey, and probably every State.

Var. COSTATUM. Plate 10, fig. 3.

This variety differs from the usual form in having the striae very thick and few in number. The figure represents one of many fruiting specimens found by W. N. Hastings, Rochester, N. H.

C. BRAUNII, Reinsch. Plate LIV, fig. 19.

Frond large, nearly straight, linear in front view, tapering rather suddenly near the obtusely rounded apices, a central suture; 5 to 10 distinct longitudinal costae. Cells usually brownish yellow about 12 times as long as wide.

Pictou, Nova Scotia.

C. DECORUM, Breb. Plate VIII, fig. 1.

Moderately arched, 12–16 diameters in length, gradually tapering from the center to one-fourth or one-fifth of largest diameter; ends rounded; vacuole small. Cytioderm finely striate. Zygospores angular in European specimens.

Diameter 34–41 $\mu$.

Occurs occasionally in sluggish waters, Pennsylvania and New Jersey. This form is separated from *C. striolatum*, mainly by the larger number of striae; the one has 12-15 and the other 20-30.

C. AREOLATUM, Wood. Plate VIII, figs. 3, 4.

Fusiform, straightish, or very slightly curved, the ventral side often a little concave in the middle; 9-10 times longer than broad, moderately attenuated at each end; the apices truncately rounded; cell-membrane reddish brown, thick and firm, distantly profoundly striate, and very minutely but distinctly granulate or areolate; median sutures very distinct, 4-10 in number.

Diameter 60 $\mu$.

Dr. Wood remarks: "I found this species growing in a quiet pool of pure water, in a wild, deeply wooded ravine, near Danville, Central Pennsylvania. It was in great abundance, forming a translucent greenish jelly, one or two gills of which might have been readily gathered." "This species is very closely allied to *C. turgidum*, Ehrb., agreeing pretty well with it in general outline and size. I think, however, the peculiar markings upon the membrane are sufficient to separate it." "The turning up of the ends, generally so marked in *C. turgidum* is mostly entirely absent in this species, rarely there is some tendency to it."

C. SUBDIRECTUM, West. Plate LIV, fig. 20.

Frond about fifteen times longer than broad, gently tapering, the middle portion nearly straight, slightly curved near the ends, which are truncate with rounded corners, cytioderm finely striate, with three distinct transverse sutures.

Diameter 26-27 $\mu$.; length 390-400 $\mu$.

Ponds, Massachusetts. J. R. M. S., Nov., 1888.

C. AMBLYONEMA, Ehrb.

A form bearing this name was accredited to the United States by Dr. Ehrenberg. Prof. Bailey, about thirty years since, examined the character of the plant, and pronounced it the same as *C. lineatum*.

C. ACUTUM, Breb. Plate VIII, figs. 11, 12.

Small, slightly bent, 6-12 times longer than broad, gently tapering from the middle to the rounded ends; cytioderm colorless and smooth. Zygospores angular.

Diameter 9-11 $\mu$.

Not rare in marsh pools, Pennsylvania and New Jersey.

C. DIANÆ, Ehrb.   Plate VIII, figs. 8, 9.   Plate IX, fig. 4.
Plate VI, figs. 1, 2.

Crescent shape, sometimes a full semi-circle as variety *arcuatum*, Breb., attenuated from the middle to the rather sharp ends, vacuole not definitely defined; transverse striae sometimes evident. Ends are separated by about 10 diameters. Specimens Plate LV differing somewhat in size. Not rare. Zygospores spherical, smooth.

Diameter 16-20 $\mu$.

Quiet waters, Rhode Island to Florida.

C. ACUMINATUM, Kg.   Plate VIII, figs. 18, 19.

Similar to *Dianæ*, somewhat larger and less curved, ends sharper, vacuoles more distinct; membrane very finely striate, or smooth.

Diameter 25-28 $\mu$.

Not rare in marsh pools; conjugated cells frequent. Pennsylvania.

C. JENNERI, Ralfs.   Plate VIII, fig. 5.

Crescent shaped, small, slightly tapering, six to eight times longer than broad, ends obtusely rounded; vacuole large, containing many active granules; cytioderm colorless, smooth.

Diameter about 14 $\mu$.

Rhode Island (Bailey); Pennsylvania, New Jersey.

C. VENUS, Kg.   Plate VIII, fig. 6.

Small, more or less slender, nearly semi-circular, eight to twelve times longer than the diameter; gradually tapering from the middle to the sharp ends; vacuole distinct; cytioderm colorless and smooth; chlorophyl homogeneous.

Diameter 8-10 $\mu$.

South Carolina, (Ravenel); Pennsylvania, New Jersey, frequent.

C. PARVULUM, Naeg.   Plate VIII, fig. 7; and Plate IX, fig. 16.

Six to eight times as long as wide; differs from *C. Venus* in being rather less arched and stouter, vacuoles not so well defined, and chlorophyl lamina more evident.

Diameter 12 $\mu$.

SECTION IV.—Cells falcate as the preceding; upper margin very convex, **lower side** concave with a more or less conspicuous central inflation, **ends tapering**. Zygospores spherical, smooth.

**C. EHRENBERGII**, Menegh.   Plate VIII, fig. 16.

Large, stout, five to six times as long as the central diameter; upper margin very convex, lower side ventricosely much inflated; ends rounded; cytioplasm with large granules, numerous, scattered; no striae, and no central suture evident. Of the zygospore, Archer says, "it is smooth, placed betweeen the slightly connected empty conjugating fronds, the endochrome during the process of conjugation emerging from the opened apex of a short conical extension from the under side of each younger segment (or shorter one) of each pair of recently divided fronds; the conjugating fronds being produced immediately previously by the self-division of a pair of old fronds—two sporangia (zygospores) being thus the ultimate produce of the two original fronds."

Diameter 75-110 $\mu$.   Delp. 57-79 $\mu$.

Ponds, Pennsylvania and New Jersey; common.

**Var. IMMANE**, Wolle.   Plate VIII, fig. 17, similar to the typical form except in size.

Diameter 208 $\mu$.

Not infrequent in Budd's Lake, and larger ponds of New Jersey.

**C. ROBUSTUM**, Hast.   Am. Mic. J., July, 1892.

Cells large, semi-lunar, a little more than four times as long as wide; cytioderm smooth; dorsum high convex; ventrum somewhat concave, ventricose; chlorophyl globules large, numerous scattered; vacuoles large, terminal distinct, with many moving granules.

Diameter 100-120 $\mu$.

Rochester, N. H., Dec., 1890. Had very much the appearance of *C. Ehrenbergii*, with the ends less attenuated.

**C. MONILIFERUM**, Ehrb.   Plate VIII, fig. 16.

Very near *C. Ehrenbergii*, but somewhat smaller, six to nine times longer than broad, ends subacute; cytioderm light straw-colored, smooth or finely striate; large chlorophyllous granules in a single longitudinal series in the center of the cell.

Diameter 46-55 $\mu$.

There appear to be two varieties of this species; **one with rather broad truncately rounded ends**; the **other, smaller with more pointed ends.**

Georgia; Rhode Island; (Bailey). Pennsylvania and New Jersey; occurs frequently.

C. LEIBLEINII, Kg. Plate **VIII**, figs. 13 **and 20.**

In outline bears a strong resemblance to the two preceding, but is shorter, stouter, **upper** margin more convex and ends more acute; **lower margin concave** with a central inflation.

Diameter 40–60 $\mu$.

Found in ponds with the two preceding.

Var. CURTUM, West. **Plate XLIII**, fig. 22.

Differs from the **typical form** by its shortened ends. Has the appearance **of a miniature** C. Ehrenbergii.

J. R. M. S., Nov., 1888.

C. RALFSII, Breb. Plate **VIII, fig. 10.**

Stout, finely and densely striated, curved, rapidly **attenuated** into somewhat linear beaks which are shorter than the **ventricose body**; 6–8 times longer than **broad.**

Diameter 42–47 $\mu$.

Pond near Perth Amboy, New **Jersey.**

Color of this species changes from green **to a** yellow brown; the upper margin is convex, the lower concave but ventricose at the center; chlorophyl vesicles rather irregularly disposed **in a single row : a transverse suture** is usually evident in **the middle.**

SECTION V.—Cells more or less curved, ventral margin also somewhat inflated, but the end drawn out into beak or seta-like extensions. Zygospores angular.

C. ROSTRATUM, Ehrb. Plate **IX**, figs. 1, 2, 3. Plate XLIII, fig. 21.

Lanceolate-fusiform, **ends thin**, drawn out to nearly half the length of **the body**; **cytioderm** light yellowish, densely but finely striate; chlorophyllous vesicles and vacuoles usually indistinct; the latter when seen has 12–15 actively **moving corpuscles.**

Diameter 23–40 $\mu$.

Var. BREVIROSTRATUM, West.

Differs from the usual form in its short and less attenuated beak.

Ponds, Massachusetts. J. R. M. S., Nov., 1888.
Frequent in ponds, Pennsylvania, New Jersey, Vermont, Connecticut, Florida.
In this vicinity, Bethlehem, Pa., copulating specimens are of common occurrence.

C. PRONUM, Breb. Plate VI, fig. 22.
Cells very small, sublanceolate, each end **drawn** out into a setaceous beak about half as long as the body; cytioderm finely **striate**.

Diameter 7–12 $\mu$.

Ponds, Florida.

C. KUETZINGII, **Breb.** Plate IX, fig. 8.
Straight in the middle, smaller than the **last**, narrow lanceolate, each extremity tapering into a long slender setaceous **beak**, which is curved at the obtuse ends, and less than the length of the **body**.

Diameter in middle **17** $\mu$.

Rather rare in ponds, Pennsylvania and New Jersey.

C. SETACEUM, Ehrb. Plate IX, figs. 6, **7**, 9, 10, **11**.
Very slender. Smaller than the preceding; 20–25 times longer than broad, upper and lower margins equally convex; ends tapering into long seta-like beaks, colorless, somewhat enlarged at extremities, longer than the length of the body; striae close, faint, central suture solitary. Zygospore **cruciform**.

Diameter 10–11 $\mu$.

Frequent in Pennsylvania, New Jersey, Massachusetts, etc. Solitary **and** conjugating. Bailey reports it **from** Rhode Island, Georgia and Florida.

## *Genus*, DOCIDIUM, Breb.

Cells straight, cylindrical or **fusiform, elongated, apices** rounded, truncated or divided; transverse view **circular**; constricted at the middle, with or without a suture **between the** semi-cells which are usually inflated at the base.

*Docidium*, like *Closterium*, has **in most** instances terminal vacuoles which contain numerous "dancing granules." The presence or absence of these vacuoles, **and** the arrangement of the chlorophyllous cytioplasm, whether parietal or axillary, have been made points for generic separation between otherwise **similar forms.** These distinctions seeming **too uncertain and** variable in different stages of growth, I put them all together, and retain DOCIDIUM in preference to *Pleurotaenium*, as the older name.

D. ARCHERII, Delp.   Plate XII, fig. 2.

Cells smooth, cylindrical, about twenty times longer than broad; scarcely attenuated from the middle to the ends; apices broadly rounded or truncate; base of semi-cells with one or two undulations. Chlorophyl usually arranged in numerous small parallel bands.

Diameter 50-60 $\mu$.

Numerous in pond, Luzerne Co., Pa.

D. CRENULATUM, (Ehrb.), Rab.  (*Pleurotaenium nodulosum*.  D. By. *Docidium nodulosum*, Ralfs.)   Plate XI, fig. 1.

Cell very stout, the thickened sutures forming a projecting rim; 8-16 times longer than broad, scarcely attenuated; regularly inflated at intervals so as to form an undulated margin; the basal inflation the most prominent; ends suddenly contracted and truncated, furnished with three or four teeth in view, below the margin; cytioderm coarsely punctate.

Diameter 40-60 $\mu$.

Frequent in ponds from Vermont to Florida; Minnesota.

D. CLAVATUM, (Kg.), D. By.   Plate XI, fig. 8.

More slender than the last, suture not prominent, 16-24 times longer than broad, sensibly enlarged at the ends, more or less clavate; apices broadly rounded or truncate; cytioderm firm, colorless, densely and irregularly punctate.

Diameter, smaller forms 23-25 $\mu$., larger forms 36-42 $\mu$. Figure 8 has not the proportionate length.

Pennsylvania, New Jersey, South Carolina and Georgia.

D. TRABECULA, (Ehrb.), Naeg.   (*Docidium Ehrenbergii*, Ralfs.) Plate XI, figs. 2, 3, 4; and Plate XV, figs. 1-7.

Long cylindrical, eight to twenty times longer than broad; tapering moderately from the center to the ends; apices truncately rounded, not dentate; suture forming a sharply defined rim, the inflation adjoining often having a smaller one above it. Sometimes there is a contraction near the apex (fig. 2). Cytioderm smooth. Zygospore globose, smooth, surrounded by a colorless gelatinous envelope.

Diameter 25-35 $\mu$.   Length 180-450 $\mu$.

Occurs frequently, and will probably be found in every State in the Union.

D. TRUNCATUM, Breb.  Plate XI. figs. 6, 7.

Cells stout, six to eight **times longer than broad, with a** single inflation at the base of the semi-cell, **tapering to the** truncate, **or** broadly rounded, entire, **ends; suture forms a** thick rim, which projects on each side.

Diameter 50–75 $\mu$.

Florida, Minnesota, Pennsylvania.

Peculiarities of this species are the large diameter and shortness of cells in comparison with the breadth; the **attenuated ends, truncate, or** broadly rounded apices, solitary **inflation at** the base of the semi-cells and consequent even **sides.** Florida furnished the best developed forms.

D. RECTUM, Delp.  **Plate X,** figs. **20, 21.**

Cells cylindrical, straight, **twelve or** more times longer than broad; slightly narrower **at** the truncate apex than at the base; moderately swollen **at the** base of the semi-cells.

Diameter 25–28 $\mu$.

The distinction which **Delponte makes between this form and** *D. Baculum,* to which it is **very closely related,** is, that **it is** perfectly straight, while **the former is** "straightish," **somewhat** bent, although not so represented, Plate XI. figs. **3, 4, Des. U. S.** The central inflations are usually larger in *D. Baculum* **than** in *D. rectum.*

D. FLOTOWII? Rab.  A variety.  Plate XI. fig. 5.

Large, about eight times longer than the **larger diameter;** suture distinct; solitary inflation at base of semi-cells; sides straight, tapering slightly in straight lines **from the center to the broad truncate apex, each angle furnished with a** prominent tooth; cytioderm firm, coarsely verrucose.

Diameter at base of semi-cell 68 $\mu$.; at apex 50 $\mu$.

From pond **on** Mt. Everett, Massachusetts. A large, firm and distinct form; not identical with the described plant, but it is tolerably near it.

D. BACULUM (Breb.), D. By.  **Plate XIV,** figs. 3, 4.

Rather long, cylindrical, straightish margins slightly tapering towards the ends, or nearly parallel; apices truncate, rounded. Cytioderm smooth and colorless.

Diameter 14–22 $\mu$.

In general **form** very near *D. Trabecula,* but smaller and devoid of the terminal vacuoles.

Ponds, Pennsylvania, New Jersey **and** Florida. Bailey **found it also** in Georgia.

DOCIDIUM.   53

D. BACULUM, var. FLORIDENSE, Wolle.   Plate XII, fig. 5.
    Differing from the typical form, having the margins wavy from base of semi-cell to apex.
        Diameter 15-17 $\mu$.; length of cell often thirty times greater.
            Frequent in pond near Maitland, Florida, March, 1885.
            Probably the same as the next following.

D. EHRENBERGII, Ralfs.   Var. FLORIDENSE, Wolle.
    Differs from *D. Trabecula*, Naeg., described, page 2, and from the typical form of *D. Ehrenbergii*, of Ralfs, Delponte, and others in its **more slender cell**, and in the larger number of umbonations.  Cell twenty or more times longer than broad; medianly distinctly constricted, without an evident suture or projecting rim.  Semi-cells tapering slightly, in direct lines from the center to the end, with not only one or two inflations (umbonations) at the base, but four, five or more, often extending in slight undulations to near the end; apex squarely truncate, bordered by three to five minute tubercles.
        Diameter 16-20 $\mu$.; length 300-400 $\mu$.
            Cypress Swamp, Florida.

D. CORONATUM, Rab.   Plate XIV, figs. 9, 10.
    Cells stout, cylindrical, slightly tapering from middle to ends; suture projecting on each side; semi-cells inflated at the base and bordered by one or two rows of tubercles at the apex, which produce a crenulate appearance.
    A smaller form has the suture imperfectly developed. Vacuoles, with active granules, are usually large and distinct.
        Diameter 22-56 $\mu$.
            Ponds, Pennsylvania, New Jersey, Massachusetts.

D. CORONULATUM, Grun.   Plate LXIV, fig. 16.
    Smooth or finely punctate, subcylindrical, slightly attenuated near the ends; apices truncate, ornate with a crown of pearly teeth.  Twelve times as long as broad.
        Diameter in middle 38 $\mu$.   Near the ends 33 $\mu$.
            The original form of this species was found in the East Indies; the plant was somewhat thicker, but of about the same proportionate length, and so near otherwise, I adopt the name.  Collected it in northern New Jersey; found the finest specimens in Green Pond, commonly several united; had as many as ten cells in a series.  They are without a suture, and apparently without vacuoles.  Found the same in Florida.

D. CONSTRICTUM, Bail.  Plate XIV, fig. 2.

Cells with moderately deep constrictions, which separate **four** equal, gently curving prominences on each semi-cell; end view entire. **Apex** furnished with a **few** conspicuous **teeth** of which four **are** ordinarily in view. Plant 10-12 **times longer than broad.**

Diameter 40-50 $\mu$.

> **This species bears** some similarity to *D. nodosum* in its wavy margins, but the undulations are less prominent, and the transverse sections are quite distinct; in the one they are circular, in the other undulate; compare **Plate XI, fig. 11,** sections of *D. nodosum*.

D. (PLEUROTAENIUM) BREVE, Wood.

Robust, 4-8 times longer than broad, distinctly constricted, but not undulate in the middle; slightly attenuated towards **the ends;** apex truncate and somewhat rounded; cytioderm very thick, densely minutely granulate; margins **either** straight **or** shortly **undulate.**

Diameter 20-24 $\mu$.

> **Dr. Wood** remarks, "**This** species **was** sent **to me** by Dr. Billings, who obtained **it** near Washington, D. C. The margins are sometimes straightish, but in other fronds there are three or more distinct, short undulations or rounded **projections in each half margin.**"
> 
> The shape of the semi-cell is very near Plate X, fig. 12, **but only** about half the size, not so undulate and not spinous.

D. NODOSUM, Bail.  Plate XIV, **figs. 11, 12, and Plate XV, fig. 20.**

Semi-cells with **four** prominent nodes separated by constrictions; **end view** six crenate, formed by whorls of tubercles; **8-10 times longer** than broad.

Diameter **45-55 $\mu$.** in center; **ends about half** as thick.

> Frequent in ponds, Pennsylvania, New Jersey, Massachusetts.

D. REPANDUM, Wolle.  Plate XIV, fig. 1.

**Smooth** or punctate, about twenty times longer than broad, margins repand or undulate from the base of the semi-cell to near the end; only slight variation in **diameter from** base **to** end; **apices** truncately rounded, and sometimes slightly dilated. **No suture.**

Diameter 25 $\mu$.

> **Sparsely found in Pennsylvania and New Jersey.**

D. WOODII, Delp.  Plate XII. fig. 4.

Cells cylindrical, six to ten times longer than broad; apices rounded; basal inflation of semi-cell large, wide and high; cytioderm smooth.

Diameter at ends 50 $\mu$.; inflation 65 $\mu$.

Pond, Ocean County, New Jersey.

D. GEORGICUM, Lagh.  Plate X, fig. 16.

Cells large, twelve times longer than broad; moderately constricted in the middle; suture none; semi-cells much swollen about the middle; basal part with four larger and smaller undulations, alternating large and small; ends somewhat attenuated; apices roundly truncate; membrane hyaline, punctate, thickest at the ends—no aculei nor teeth.

Diameter of cells, basal parts 54 $\mu$.; middle 75 $\mu$.; apices 39 $\mu$.

Pond waters, Georgia.

D. DILATATUM, (Cleve), Lund.  Plate LXI, fig. 32.

Cells slender, cylindrical, 15–20 times longer than broad, undulate-nodose; base moderately inflated and longitudinally plicate; no suture evident; semi-cells usually with eight inflations and corresponding constrictions; apices roundly truncate and more or less dilated.

Diameter 13–16 $\mu$.

Brown's Mills, and other ponds, New Jersey.

D. SINUOSUM, Wolle.  Plate XIV, figs. 6, 8; variety fig. 7.

Slender, undulate, smooth, cylindrical; 20–24 times longer than broad; semi-cell with eight constrictions; ends truncate, straight or slightly concave, each angle furnished with a short, stout tooth; basal inflation not plicate.

Diameter 12–14 $\mu$.

Var. BREVE, Wolle.  (Fig. 7) only half the length, and only four constrictions to a semi-cell.

Diameter 12–14 $\mu$.

Very near the preceding, but armed with teeth at the apex, not plicate, and sometimes only half the length. Pond, Pleasant Mills, New Jersey.

D. UNDULATUM, Bail.  Plate XIV, fig. 5.

Cells small, cylindrical with undulating margins, 18–20 times longer than the diameter; moderately constricted in the middle; inflation at base of semi-cells very slightly larger than the undulations, apices rounded.

Diameter 10–12 $\mu$.

Bailey found this species in fresh waters of Florida; I have it from the same State, and from ponds at Hammonton and Dennisville, New Jersey.

**D. HIRSUTUM,** Bail. Plate XIII, fig. 13.

"Semi-cells many times longer than broad, slightly inflated at base, surface hirsute, a small species resembling *D. Trabecula* in form, but strongly hirsute on its outer surface." These, the words of Prof. Bailey; his figure has the appearance of a *Gonatozygon*, but guided by his comparison with *D. Trabecula*, I judge my figure represents the same **plant.** The cytioderm is densely hirsute throughout.

Diameter 24–30 $\mu$.

Sluggish waters, eastern Pennsylvania.

**D. SPINOSUM,** Wolle. Plate XIII, fig. 12.

Cells large, subcylindrical, 8–10 times longer than the larger diameter; margins undulate with three or four more or less prominent inflations; central constriction deep, and suture conspicuous; apex truncate, about two-thirds as wide as the base of the semi-cell, cytioderm firm, clothed with densely set spines; two or three rows around the apex firmer and longer than the others.

Diameter 40–48 $\mu$.

Pond, Dennisville, New Jersey.

*D. crenulatum,* **Ehrb.,** *D. nodosum,* Bail.. *D. hirsutum,* Bail., have features in common with this form. I have separated it in view of the armor of spines with which it is clothed; these are not hairs, nor gelatinous contractions, but decided **and firm spines.**

**D. VERRUCOSUM.** (Bailey), Ralfs. Plate XIII, figs. 4, **5.**

Cells cylindrical, tapering very slightly from the center **to** the apex; margins made crenate by numerous whorls **of** quadrangular prominences. Length about twelve times the breadth.

Diameter 25–33 $\mu$.

Occurs frequently in ponds, Mt. Everett, Mass., and sparsely in quiet waters, northern New Jersey. Bailey found it originally in Rhode Island and New York.

D. MINUTUM, Ralfs. Plate LXI, figs. 29–31. Plate XIII, fig. 9.

Slender, elongated, smooth, cylindrical, linear or slightly tapering, ends round; 10–30 times longer than broad; a single inflation, more or less prominent at the base of the semi-cell.

Diameter 7–9 $\mu$., or more rarely 10–12 $\mu$.

Ponds, Florida, Massachusetts and New Jersey

This minute plant is near a form described by Delponte as *P. rectum*, but it has twice the diameter. Ralfs describes his *D. minutum*, which has the same diameter as ours, only five or six times longer than wide. Our forms vary greatly in proportionate length and breadth; the shortest, however, is ten times as long as broad. They vary also much in thickness and in the central inflation; sometimes the constriction is barely perceptible, and again marked by a strongly inflated border. The various forms frequently occur in groups, and evidence specific relationship.

D. TRIDENTULUM, Wolle. Plate XIII, fig. 10.

Near the preceding in form and structure but average somewhat larger, and often granulate; apices crowned with a few prominent teeth, usually three in view.

Diameter 12–13 $\mu$.

Pleasant Mills, Brown's Mills, etc., New Jersey.
The inflation at the base of the semi-cells is more prominent than is usual in *D. minutum*.

D. COSTATUM, Wolle. Plate XIII, fig. 2.

Fusiform, 7–8 times longer than broad; slightly constricted in middle; inflated gradually from the base of the semi-cell to about one-third the length, then gradually tapering to the truncated, slightly dilated and dentate apex; margins with regular crenae, produced by twenty or more distinct transverse costae or rib-like lines.

Diameter, widest part 25 $\mu$., constriction 20 $\mu$., ends 15–17 $\mu$.

Found by H. D. Kitchel in pond, Berkshire Mountains, Massachusetts, 1882.

The specimens which came under my observation were not vegetative—too old; this species needs verification.

D. VERTICILLATUM. (*Triploceras verticillatum*), Bail. Plate XIII, figs. 1, 11.

Cells large subcylindrical, with numerous whorls of small, oblong, often tooth-like prominences; 7–16 times longer than broad; ends with three bidentate diverging processes.

Diameter ordinarily 38–45 $\mu$.

Var. TURGIDUM, (fig. 11), Wolle. Shorter and stouter, often 60 $\mu$.

Of frequent occurrence in pond waters, Maine to Florida. The number of whorls varies from 12-16 in a semi-cell. In living condition the cells are green, but more commonly they are found of brownish red color.

Plate X, fig. 18. This illustration **given as** another of many forms in which this species often occurs. The third diverging **process of the** apical termination not always evident.

W. N. Hastings, Rochester, New Hampshire, reports this form frequent in the Cocheco River.

D. GRACILE, (*Triploceras gracile*), Bail. **Plate XIII**, figs. 3, 6, **7, 8.** Differs from the last in usual smaller size of cell, smaller and more acute tooth-like prominences of **the** whorls.

### Diameter 20-28 $\mu$., exceptions, up to 40 $\mu$.

Habitat the same as the former.

The whorls appear to be composed of a double series of teeth, but frequently the second row is barely evident. Fig. 3 is of unusual size. Fig. 7 represents a condition of dissolution; the contents have escaped, and the parts constituting the cell have separated, contracted and assumed a partially inverted position.

## *Genus*, CALOCYLINDRUS, D. By.

Cells straight, cylindrical, **ends** rounded **or** truncate; semi-cells without basal inflation, **or** longitudinal plication; **chloro-phyl** parietal or axillary.

C. RALFSII, (Kg.), **Kirch.** (*Cosmarium cylindricum*, **Ralfs**). Plate XV, fig. 17.

Cells cylindrical, about twice as long as wide. Semi-cells subquadrate in front view, broadest at the extremity; **cytio-derm** more or less granulated.

### Diameter about 24 $\mu$.

Pools fresh water, Pennsylvania and **New** Jersey.

C. DE BARYI, Arch. Plate **XLV**, fig. 12.

A specimen from Minnesota, the typical form, unlike the **one fig. 5**, Plate XV, which is more like a form of *C. Cucumis;* the constriction is not deep, linear, but merely a shallow notch, hence De Bary classified it with ***Pleurotaenium.***

C. MINUTUS. (Ralfs), Kirch. (*Penium minutum*, Cleve). Plate XV, fig. 12. Plate V, figs. 19, 20.

Cylindrical, 4-6 times as long as broad, slightly constricted in the middle, ends rounded, membrane smooth.

Diameter 11-16 $\mu$.

> Florida, South Carolina, (Bailey), Rhode Island, (Olney). This minute and apparently variable plant has not come to my notice. It is classed by different authors both as a *Penium* and a *Docidium*.

C. CUCURBITA, (Breb.), Kirch. (*Cosmarium Cucurbita*, Breb.) Plate XV, fig. 14.

Cells punctate, cylindrical, about twice as long as broad, slightly constricted at the middle, rounded at the ends.

Diameter 22-25 $\mu$.

> Pennsylvania and New Jersey.

C. CURTUS, (Breb.), Kirch. (*Cosmarium curtum*, Breb.). Plate XV, figs. 15, 16.

Cells somewhat fusiform cylindrical, about twice as long as wide, slightly constricted at the middle, the ends subconically rounded, cytioderm smooth.

Diameter 20-32 $\mu$.

> Pennsylvania, New Jersey, and other States.
> Fig. 16 represents a small form collected several succeeding Summers, in gelatinous masses on the muddy bottom of a small pool; thousands were present; the other (fig. 15) is the larger, typical form.

C. CORDANUM, Breb. Plate XLIX, fig. 28.

Diameter about half the length; gentle and slightly constricted in the middle; ends round or somewhat truncate; cytioderm lightly granular or punctate. End view circular.

Diameter 26-27 $\mu$.; length 47-50 $\mu$.; isthmus 17-19 $\mu$.

> This form is reported by W. B. Turner, as found in Nova Scotia.

C. CONNATUS, (Breb.), Kirch. (*Cosmarium connatum*, Breb.) Plate XV, figs. 8, 9.

Cells short and thick, subcylindrical, about one and one-half to two times longer than broad, ends broadly rounded; constriction forms a wide, shallow sinus; cytioderm distinctly punctate.

Diameter 45-75 $\mu$.

> Pennsylvania, New Jersey, Florida, New York, Vermont, Minnesota, etc.; probably distributed everywhere.

**This is** one of the largest species of the genus and most **common**. The end view is nearly a perfect circle; front view of a semi-cell constitutes about two-thirds of a circle; a distinct border is always present, and often appears striated.

### Var. MINOR, Nord.   Plate XV, fig. 10.   Plate LX, fig. 18.

**This form is in** all essential points like the last, **except in** dimensions.

> I have found almost every possible variety of size, measuring in diameter from 20 to 40 $\mu$. This fact furnishes a presumptive evidence that the smaller forms are merely undeveloped conditions; young plants evolved from sporangiums, in accordance with Hofmeister's theory. See INTRODUCTION, p. 19.

### C. PSEUDOCONNATUS, Nord.   Plate **XV, fig. 11.**   Plate LX, figs. 10, 11.

Similar to the two preceding in form and structure, but in size usually smaller than the typical plant. The distinctive feature is in the arrangement of the chlorophyl; this is not homogeneous, but divided in each semi-cell, in front view, **into** two parts, and in end view, into four parts.

> Marsh pools, Pennsylvania.
> The value of the arrangement of the chlorophyl as a specific character, needs, I think, further corroborative evidence.

### C. CLEVEI, (Lund.), Wolle.  (*Penium Clevei*, Lund.)  Plate LXI, fig. 27.

Cell subcylindrical, 2½–3 times longer than broad, somewhat constricted in the middle; semi-cells cylindric-sub-conical, ends distinctly attenuated and rounded at apices; vertical view a perfect circle. Nuclei large, elliptic single or rarely twinned. Membrane finely punctate, at apices subgranulate punctate.

> Diameter **40–50** $\mu$.   Length 115–118 $\mu$.
>> Brown's **Mills**, New Jersey.
>> The plant is slightly larger than Lundell's form, but so **good** a counterpart in form and structure, I take it to be the **same species**; by measurement the constriction is somewhat deeper. The decided constriction makes the natural position of this form, I think, a member of the present genus, notwithstanding the observations made by Lundell in the arrangement of the chlorophyl.

### C. THWAITESII, Ralfs.   Plate XV, fig. 19.   Plate LXI, fig. 28.

Cells **two** or three times longer than broad, fusiform in **front** view; circular in end view; constriction **a shallow** sinus; ends high-rounded, cytioderm not at all, or very indistinctly punctate; chlorophyl scattered.

Diameter about 30 $\mu$.

Florida, (Bailey); frequent in pond, Spring Lake, Monmouth County, New Jersey.

C. DIPLOSPORA, Lund. Plate XV, fig. 18.

Cell large, twice as long as broad, subcylindrical, moderately constricted in the middle, very slightly but distinctly enlarged from the center towards the ends; apices broadly rounded; end view circular; cytioderm colorless and smooth. Cytioplasm has usually a tint of reddish brown.

Diameter 25–30 $\mu$.; length 53–58 $\mu$.

Frequent in ponds, Berkshire Mountains, Massachusetts.

C. COSTATUS, Wolle. Plate XV, fig. 13.

Cell ovaliform, nearly twice as long as wide; moderately constricted in the middle. Front view a constricted oval, end view circular; cytioderm longitudinally costate; costae 5–7, distinct, converging at the apices. Color of older plants reddish brown.

Diameter 50 $\mu$.; length 90 $\mu$.

Pond, Mount Everett, Massachusetts, 1882.

According to some authors this plant might be classed with *Docidium*, but having no inflation at the base of the semi-cells, and no plication in the cell walls, I give it a place here.

*Genus*, COSMARIUM. Corda.

Cells oblong, cylindrical, elliptical or orbicular with margins smooth, dentate or crenate; always more or less deeply constricted in the middle; ends rounded or truncate and entire, not emarginate, lobed or sinuate; end view oblong or oval, sometimes with a swelling in the middle of the longer sides; chlorophyllous cytioplasm parietal, or more or less concentrated in the center of the semi-cells, or divided into two masses; cytioderm (cell-walls), smooth, punctate, warty, or very rarely, spinous. Zygospore spherical, tuberculated or spinous, seldom smooth or angular.

The plants of this genus are recognized by their short form and entire end. They are usually about 1½ times as long as wide; sometimes shorter and sometimes longer, rarely over two diameters in length. Ends always entire, not emarginate or incised.

They may be conveniently divided as follows :
1. Chlorophyl parietal—distributed on the inside of the walls of the cells.
2. Chlorophyl more or less concentrated into **one or two** masses, (nuclei,) in each semi-cell
   § End view **round, oval** or elliptic without central inflation.
   1. Cytioderm (cell-wall) smooth, **or** punctate.
   2. Cytioderm verrucose.
   3. Cytioderm spinous.
   § End view round, **oval or** elliptic, with a central inflation on **each side.**
   4. **Cytioderm smooth or punctate.**
   5. **Cytioderm verrucose or spinous.**

C. OVALE, Ralfs.   Plate XVI, figs. 8, 9.

Large, oval or elliptical, nearly twice as long as **broad, ends rounded**; **central** constriction deep linear; isthmus about one-third **of** the diameter of the cell; semi-cells with straight base, angles rounded and sides convex, gradually converging. Cytioderm granularly rough, with one or two rows of larger pearly granules near the margin, producing **a** dentate appearance.

Diameter about 100 $\mu$. (range **from 62 to 112 $\mu$.**).

Ponds, Pennsylvania, **New** Jersey, New York, South Carolina, Rhode Island, Minnesota, etc.

C. DE BARYI, Archer.  (*Pleurotaenium cosmarioides*, De By.)
Plate XVIII, fig. 5.   Probably the same as *Calocylindrus De Baryi*.   Plate XLV, fig. 12.

Cells oblong, twice as long as broad, with **flatly** rounded ends; **constriction narrow,** straight, linear.   **Cytioderm** smooth **or** finely **punctate;** chlorophyl parietal.

Diameter 50-54 $\mu$.;  length 104-110 $\mu$.

Ponds, Berkshire Mountains, Massachusetts.

C. CUCUMIS, Corda.   Plate XVIII, figs. 6, 7, 8, 9.

Cells oval, one and one-half to one and three-fourths times longer than broad, ends broadly rounded; constriction linear; cytioderm smooth; chlorophyl covering the inside **of** the **walls** of the cells.

Diameter 46-56 $\mu$.   **Thickness** 36-40 $\mu$.   Isthmus about one-third **of the diameter of** the cell.

Frequent from Maine to Florida.

Besides the measures given, forms are found of much smaller dimensions. Figs. 7, 8, 9 represent such; every possible size, from the largest to the smallest, and down to **a**

COSMARIUM. 63

diameter of 15 μ. are not rare. These I consider undeveloped, or young conditions of the plant evolved from zygospores. Compare Introduction, p. 19.

C. CONSTRICTUM, Delp. Plate LXI, figs. 1-4.

Cells smooth, about one-half longer than broad; deeply constricted; sinus acute-angled; semi-cells near a three-fourth circle, with inferior angles rounded; end view oval; lateral view of cell an oblong with ends rounded and middle constricted. Somewhat in character with *C. Cucumis*, but proportionately shorter.

Diameter 30-38 μ.

Frequent in small ponds, New Jersey, Pennsylvania, etc.

C. SCENEDESMUS, Delp. Plate LXI, figs. 7, 8, 9.

Cells smooth, not as long as broad, depressed, constriction deep, sinus narrow linear; semi-cells subsemicircular, base nearly straight, ends a depressed arch, angles rounded; end view elliptic; side view circular.

Diameter 32-38 μ.

Reminds strongly of *D. Phascolus*, but has no reniform base, and no central inflation. Sinus of fig. 7 too much am-plinted.

Occurs frequently.

C. QUADRATUM, Ralfs. Plate XXI, figs. 8, 9, 10.

Smooth, deeply constricted at the middle; semi-cells in front view quadrate, with a slight protuberance on each side above the base, giving the sides a retuse appearance, angles rounded; chlorophyl in larger forms usually divided into two masses.

Diameter, smaller form 20-23 μ.; larger form 40 μ.

Ponds, Pennsylvania, rather rare. Minnesota.

The apices of the two forms differ; the smaller ones are more or less retuse, and the larger ones convex. The length of each is twice the diameter.

C. ANCEPS, Lund. Plate XXI, fig. 11.

Small, full twice as long as broad, hexagonal-oblong; sinus narrow linear; side view oblong with sides slightly emarginate; apices rounded; semi-cells quadrate, rather longer than broad, tapering moderately from base to end; end view sub-circular. Membrane smooth; isthmus half the diameter of the cell.

Diameter 17-18 μ.; length 45-50 μ.

The only plant I have found to harmonize with **this description**, was collected by J. D. Smith in Florida. **It agrees very well except** in length, being nearly equal to **three diameters.**

**C. PARVULUM, Breb.**   Plate XXI, figs. 12, 13.

Cells small, ovate elliptical, slightly constricted, apices truncate, two to nearly three times as long as wide; margins entire, or **sometimes** lightly crenulate; semi-cells short conical, broadly truncate or sometimes with apex retuse; cytioderm **smooth or finely punctate.**

Diameter 18–22 $\mu$.

**Florida,** collected by J. D. Smith.

**C. AMERICANUM, Lagh.**   Plate XLIX, figs. 15, 16.

Cells small, **sinus** rather obtuse and widening outwardly; **semi-cells** sub-circular, the center with seven larger granules (six peripheral and one central) and twelve, more or **less** distinct, around these; vertical view elliptic; lateral **view sub-circular.** Membrane smooth **excepting** the central **granules.**

Diameter of cell 22 $\mu$.; length 40 $\mu$.; **thickness** 18 $\mu$.; diameter isthmus 6 $\mu$.

**Pond near Tewksbury,** Massachusetts.

**C. GRANATUM, Breb.   Plate LXI, fig. 13.**   Plate **XVIII, figs.** 14, 15.

Cells one and one-half times as long as broad; constriction narrow linear; semi-cells trapezoidal, with straight bases, rounded angles, sides gradually converging; apex truncate; variable in size.

Diameter 20–32 $\mu$.; isthmus about **one**-third the diameter.

Frequent in quiet waters. Pennsylvania, New Jersey, Massachusetts, Florida and Minnesota.

Plate LXI, fig. 13, is the typical form; the others, Plate XVIII, figs. 14, 15, are varieties, near Wille's variety *elongatum*.

**C. WOLLEANUM,** Lagh., var. GRANULIFERUM, Lagh.   **Plate** XLIX, figs. 1, 2.   **Syn.** *C. pseudogranatum*, Wolle.   Des. U. S., p. 158.

**Cell rather** large, one-fourth longer than **wide; sinus somewhat** ampliated inwardly and outwardly; semi-cells sub-semi-circular, **base** subreniform, dorsum narrowly rounded, angles rounded, margins finely crenulate-dentate;

in vertical view oval; in lateral view broadly oval. Membrane distinctly punctate.

Diameter 54 $\mu$.; length 66 $\mu$.

Tewksbury, Massachusetts.

The author of the present name for a *Cosmarium*, G. von Lagerheim, of Stockholm, Sweden, finds that we have duplicated the name *pseudogranatum*, previously used by *Nordstedt*, hence re-names the form as above. The new variety *granuliferum* reminds one of *C. cymatopleurum*, Nord., *C. de Notarisii*, (Witt.), Nord., and *C. capense*, Nord., but it is distinct.

C. MONILIFORME, Ralfs. Plate XVIII, figs. 16, 17, 18, 19.

Cells twice as long as wide; semi-cells spherical, united by a narrow isthmus; four semi-cells often in series; cell membrane smooth.

Diameter 16-24 $\mu$.

> Frequent in ponds, Pennsylvania, New Jersey, Massachusetts, Florida, etc. Fig. 18 represents a peculiarity noticed now and then, that in multiplying by division, (Introduction p. 17), the new daughter semi-cells are larger than those of the mother cell; if this is not always the case such are frequently found.

C. GLOBOSUM, Bulnh. Plate LX, figs. 14-17.

Cells small, light green, bicocciform, scarcely compressed, nearly one-third longer than wide, very slightly constricted, sinus acute; semi-cells circular, exclusive of the confluent bases, entire, cytioderm smooth or finely punctate.

Diameter 20-24 $\mu$.; length 25-33 $\mu$.

> Not infrequent in ponds intermingled with other forms.
> Plate XV, fig. 20, represents a variety which stands between this species and *moniliforme*.
> Diameter about 20 $\mu$.
> Pennsylvania, New Jersey, Massachusetts.

C. PERFORATUM, Lund. Plate XLVIII, fig. 32.

Somewhat circular, slightly longer than broad, moderately constricted in the middle, sinus acute angled, enlarged outwardly, rarely linear; semi-cells sub-semi-circular, back high convex, with the middle slightly flattened or rarely slightly retuse; end view broadly elliptical; lateral view circular with base broadly truncate. Membrane distinctly but sparsely punctate, often with larger granules arranged in triangular form on basal part. Isthmus fully half of the diameter of the cell.

Diameter 57–63 $\mu$.; length 60–68 $\mu$.

Ponds, Minnesota.

C. BIOCULATUM, Breb. Plate XVIII, figs. 21, 22.

Cells small, somewhat longer than broad; constriction deep, producing a gaping notch on each side. Semi-cell compressed, oval, with convex base, short convex sides and rather flat apex. Cytioderm smooth or finely punctate. Zygospore globose, without spines.

Diameter 15–16 $\mu$.; length about 17 $\mu$.

Rhode Island, Massachusetts, Pennsylvania, New Jersey, etc.

C. RHOMBUSOIDES, Wolle. Plate XLIX, figs. 6, 7.

Cells nearly as long as wide; semi-cells in form of a rhombus, sides all equal, straight or slightly convex; nearly half as long as broad; sinus between, deep and wide; isthmus one-fourth of diameter; end view rhombus-like; membrane finely punctate.

Diameter 55–65 $\mu$.; length 50 $\mu$.

From collections made by Mrs. Hanson and Miss Haggin in pools near Lake Tahoe, California, August, 1886.

C. LOBATULUM, Wolle. Plate XLVIII, figs. 33, 34.

Small, one-third longer than broad, end of semi-cell broadly truncate; sides convex with a slight contraction near the apex; side view circular with end truncate. Membrane finely and closely punctate, or granular.

Diameter 25 $\mu$.; length 33 $\mu$.

Ponds, Minnesota.

C. QUIMBYII, Wood.

Cells small, subelliptical, profoundly constricted in the middle, joined by translucent bands into families; semi-cells seen from the front elliptical, and nearly twice as long as broad; from the vertex elliptical, from the side roundish. Chlorophyl masses single in each cell. Cytioderm thin, smooth.

Diameter 18 $\mu$.; length 25 $\mu$.

"This plant was found in a spring near Camden, N. J., upon whose bottom it formed a gelatinous translucent, greenish mass. The cells are joined by bands into families, in which the little parent cell is generally very distinct, it, or rather the two cells into which it first divides, remaining in the center of the group." Wood, p. 35.

I would suggest this to be very near, or identical with *C. tinctum*, Ralfs.

C. TINCTUM, Ralfs. (*Sphaerozosma tinctum*, Rab.) Plate XIX, fig. 31.

Cells small, somewhat longer than broad; **isthmus broad, constriction outwardly enlarged; semi-cells** oval; chlorophyl **a single mass; cytioderm smooth, often tinted with** yellow, brown or red.

Diameter 10–15 $\mu$.

> Of the sporangium, Ralfs writes, "It is large in proportion to the cells, and quadrate with an empty segment of the fronds permanently attached at each corner. Sometimes the fronds couple in a crossed position, when the sporangium appears variously twisted or distorted."
>
> I find single specimens of this plant occasionally, but have not had a satisfactory group of them, or fruiting specimens.

C. TUMIDUM, Lund. Plate XVIII, fig. 23; Plate XXI, fig. 20.

Cells somewhat longer than broad, constriction narrow linear. Semi-cells suboval, rather flat base, apex broad convex, with one chlorophyllous mass. Cytioderm punctate and more or less granularly rough in the central part, margin smooth. Plate XXI, fig. 20, appears to be a variety of this form, coarsely granular.

Diameter 20–33 $\mu$.

> Pennsylvania, New Jersey, etc.
>
> In front view this species bears some resemblance to *C. Phascolus*, Breb., but differs in being proportionately longer, and in not having the base of the semi-cells reniform, and in not having an entirely smooth membrane. Some specimens are very distinctly punctate, others not so evidently except away from the margins. Kirchner makes two varieties; *a. genuinum*, cytioderm distinctly granular in the middle; *b. subtile*, cytioderm finely punctate over the whole cell.

C. INFLATUM, Wolle. Plate XLVIII, figs. 18, 19.

Cells one-half longer than broad; semi-cells gradually enlarged from a narrow base to a broadly dilated end; end view broadly elliptic; lateral view circular, with somewhat flattened sides; membrane finely punctate or smooth.

Diameter 25–28 $\mu$.; length about 40 $\mu$.

> Ponds, Minnesota.

C. SEJUNCTUM, **Wolle.** Plate LXI, figs. 18-20.

Membrane smooth, slightly **longer** than broad; **semi-cells semicircular** with angles **rounded,** separated by a **wide, nearly linear sinus;** isthmus connecting **the semi-cells is narrow, less than** one-fourth the breadth of cells.

Dameter 20-25 $\mu$.; length 25-30 $\mu$.

Pond, near Malaga, New Jersey, and Minneapolis, Minnesota.

Usually two forms **of this plant** are recognized, the one longer than the other; the longer slightly retuse, which is the typical form; **the other** not retuse, and not so long.

Sometimes **found in** considerable numbers in **gelatinous gatherings on** dripping rocks and in small pools. **The variety** SEPTENTRIONALE, found **near** Amherst, **Mass.,** not so frequent.

C. VARIOLATUM, Lund. Plate XIX, figs. **3, 4.**

**Small** elliptical, **twice** as long as wide, constriction deep, **narrow,** linear; semi-cells, base straight, sides rising at right **angles, then** curving **gradually** and producing an **almost circular apex,** sometimes slightly retuse; **end view broadly elliptical; side view obovate.** Cytioderm more or **less punctate;** isthmus one-third of the **whole** diameter. **Chlorophyl** nucleus single.

Diameter 15-17 $\mu$.

Ponds, southern New Jersey, Hammonton, etc.

C. CIRCULARE, **Reinsch.** Plate XLVIII, fig. 37.

Cells nearly circular; present form slightly shorter than broad; sinuses narrow linear; lateral view ovoid, end view elliptic; isthmus **one-third of diameter of cell;** membrane finely punctate.

Diameter 75-85 $\mu$.; length 70-75 $\mu$.

Frequent in marsh pools, Tocoi, Florida. **This form is considerably** larger than the one described by **Reinsch, and not** quite equal in length and breadth, **but otherwise very** near it, **and** certainly nearer **than the** plant **described** by Lundell **under** the same name.

C. CONTRACTUM, Kirch. Plate **XIX, fig. 1.** Plate LXI, **fig. 24.**

Cells one and one-half times as long as wide; sinus produced by the constriction, deep and narrow, widening **outwardly from the base.** Semi-cells oval, with **convex base** and convex apex, containing each one chlorophyl nucleus; cytioderm distinctly punctate.

Diameter 24 $\mu$.

Denmark, and other ponds, New Jersey.

C. SEXANGULARE, Lund.  Plate XIX, figs. 8, 9.  Plate LX, fig. 13.

One-fifth part longer than wide; constriction deep; sinus linear within and widening outwardly. Semi-cells more or less hexagonal-elliptic; ends truncate, sides obtusely rounded; end view elliptical; side view circular. Cytioderm finely punctate.

Diameter 25–42 $\mu$.

Occurs frequently in ponds, Pennsylvania, New Jersey. The hexagonal feature of the semi-cells is not always as distinct as described; in the figures 8 and 9 it was inadvertently omitted altogether, nevertheless, they represent a common form of the species.

C. DEPRESSUM, (Naeg.), Lund., not Bailey.  Plate LXI, figs. 10, 11, 12.

Cells usually slightly shorter than wide; constriction deep; sinus widening outwardly; semi-cells compressed oval; the long sides flattened, the others rounded; one chlorophyl mass in each. Membrane finely punctate.

Diameter 20–25 $\mu$.

Frequent in pond, Spring Lake, N. J. They are smaller in size than the European form; otherwise identical.

Bailey in his contribution, describes another plant under the same name. Naegeli's description has claim of priority, hence must stand. In order to avoid further confusion, I change the name of the former, and in honor of the author call it *C. Baileyi*.

C. BAILEYI, Wolle.  (*C. depressum*, *Bailey*.)  Plate XIX, figs. 17, 18.

"Elliptical, binate, division in the plane of the longest axis. Segments entire, nearly twice as long as broad, rounded above, very much flattened at base;" cytioderm punctate.

Diameter 36–48 $\mu$.

Florida, (Bailey); and ponds, Mount Everett, Mass.

"This species resembles *C. bioculatum*, Breb., but the segments are much closer together, and are angular, not rounded at the basal extremities." Compare Note under *C. depressum*.

**C. obsoletum.** Reinsch. Plate LX, fig. 12.

Cells elliptic, about one-fourth more in breadth than length. Deeply **constricted**; sinus rounded at the base, then gradually narrowed towards the lateral angles of the semi-cells, which come close together; semi-cells in end **view** elliptical; side view circular. Isthmus about **one-third the** diameter of the cell. Membrane punctate or smooth; chlorophyl concentrations **or nuclei,** two.

**Diameter 110 $\mu$.; length 80 $\mu$.**

I adopt Reinsch's name for this plant. In general form it is the same; **the two distinct** nuclei also correspond, but in **size it** is much larger and the angles of the semi-cells are not at all or but slightly contracted. I collected it in a sluggish streamlet, Ocean Grove, N. J. It is near *C. Baileyi*, but **differs in the form** of the sinus, and in having two nuclei in **each semi-cell; it** is also twice the size.

**C. Regnesi,** Reinsch. **Plate XLIII,** fig. 4.

Rare and of doubtful value. **Has** the appearance of a cell of *Sphaerozosma*.

**C. sinuosum,** Lund. **Plate XIX,** fig. 2.

Twice as long **as** wide, rectangular, constriction **not deep,** sinuses narrow linear, not widened outwardly; semi-cells quadrangular, equilateral, sides and apices somewhat retuse; end view subcircular; **lateral** view elliptic-oblong; **membrane** smooth; isthmus one-third of the diameter **of cell; nucleus single.**

Diameter **16–18 $\mu$.**

Pond, Berkshire Mountains, Mass.

**C. Meneghinii,** Breb. Plate XIX, **fig. 7.**

Cells 1–1½ **times** as long as **wide;** constriction forms a narrow linear sinus; semi-cells subquadrate, base straight, apex flat, truncate or slightly concave; sides straight or concave, corners rounded, diagonally **truncate or** slightly retuse; single chlorophyl mass **in each semi-cell.** Very variable. Kirchner makes three **varieties**:

*a. genuinum,* with **sides and ends and upper angles retuse.**

Diameter **20–22 $\mu$.**

*b. angulosum,* Rab., **sides and** ends straight, **upper and** lower angles diagonally truncate.

Diameter 18 $\mu$.

*c. concinnum*, Rab., more elongated, semi-cells nearly quadrilateral, all angles truncate, or rounded.

**Diameter 9–26 $\mu$.**

Found frequently; probably has a wide range north, south, and west.

*d. simplicissimum*, Wille. Plate XLIII. figs. **11–13.**
A variety of *forma octangularis*, Wille.

Pond near Amherst, Massachusetts.

C. OCTOGONUM, Delp. Var. CONSTRICTUM, Lagh. Plate XLIX, figs. **34, 35.**

Cells in front view oblong-tetragonal deeply constricted; semi-cells trapezoidal; in vertical view elliptic with middle somewhat inflated; isthmus one-third of diameter of cell. Membrane smooth. Var. *constrictum* is more deeply constricted, sinus wider and semi-cell in vertical view not inflated.

Tewksbury, Massachusetts. From these specimens the significance of the name is not evident. Instead of three crenulations or angles on each side of the semi-cell, Delponte describes "sometimes four," or *eight* to the semi-cell. Has some resemblance to *C. Braunii*, Reinsch, but is not so regular.

C. POLYGONUM, Naeg. Plate XIX, fig. **30.**

Small, polygonal, about as long as wide, entire, sinus very narrow; semi-cells hexagonal-oblong, angles subacute or obtuse; apices straight or rounded; cytioderm smooth or punctate.

**Diameter 15–20 $\mu$.**

Ponds, New Jersey and Massachusetts. Not frequent.

C. LUNATUM, Wolle. Plate XIX, fig. **16.**

Cells nearly as long as wide, circular, constriction deep and forms a wide rounded or oval sinus; semi-cells lunately curved, back circularly arched, base concave; angles of the two semi-cells, more or less acute, approximate closely. Cytioderm punctate; isthmus usually less than one-third of the diameter. End view elliptical; side view circular.

**Diameter 25–28 $\mu$.**

Brown's Mills, N. J.

C. ACULEATUM, Wolle. Plate XIX, fig. **15.**

Medium size, suborbicular, length slightly less than the diameter; constriction deep, forming, by the incurving of the angles of the semi-cells, two elliptical sinuses; cytioderm primarily more or less densely aculeated; later the aculei drop off and leave short granule-like stumps; **end view elliptical.**

Diameter 33 μ.; length 30 μ.; breadth of constriction 10 μ.

Pond, Minneapolis, Minn. Collected by Miss E. Butler, 1882 and 1883.

C. SMOLANDICUM, Lund. Plate XIX, figs. 35, 36.

**Cells somewhat** longer than wide; isthmus narrow, constriction deep, **sinus narrow** linear; **semi-cells semicircular with** straight base **and** arched back sometimes subtruncate, **angles** (inferior) obtuse, mounted with a papilla; **end view elliptical; lateral** view circular. Membrane distinctly **punctate. Chlorophyl masses** two in each **semi-cell.**

Diameter, 34–48 μ.

Various localities, Pennsylvania and New Jersey.

Usually the cells are about one-eighth longer than broad; they vary considerably in size. At Pleasant Mills, New Jersey, there is a variety which **is somewhat** depressed, measuring one-eighth less in length than **breadth. The distinguishing feature of this species is the papilla at each angle.**

C. EXIGUUM, Archer. Plate XIX, figs. 13, 14.

**Cells very small, smooth, oblong, 1½–2 times as** long as **broad; medial constriction slight; semi-cells** subquadrate, **containing one chlorophyl nucleus; ends** obtusely rounded.

Diameter 12–15 μ.

Florida, collected by **J. D. Smith, 1878.**

C. NOTABILE, Breb. Plate XIX, fig. 11.

Cells small, **about twice as long as broad,** margins entire or moderately **undulate-crenate; ends truncate;** semi-cell **more or less pyramidal,** base somewhat reniform, end broadly **truncate; angles** rounded, cytioderm smooth or finely **granulate.**

Diameter 22–28 μ.

**Ponds of eastern Pennsylvania.**

C. UNDULATUM, Corda. Plate XIX, fig. 20.

Cells 1½ times **as** long as **wide, ends broadly rounded,** margins undulate; deeply **constricted, sinus gradually enlarged** outwardly; **semi-cells semi-orbicular;** sides and back broadly rounded, margins undulate crenate, **usually with** nine crenae to a semi-cell; cytioderm smooth. **Zygospores** spherical, armed with long spines bi- or tri-fid at apices.

Diameter 40–44 μ.

C. Braunii, forma major, Reinsch. Plate XLVIII, figs. 28, 29.

Cells small, one and one-half times longer than broad, sinus narrow linear; sides with two emarginations; ends truncate, membrane smooth; lateral view oval; vertical view elliptic.

Diameter 25–28 $\mu$.; length 36–40 $\mu$.

Ponds, Stillwater, Minnesota.

C. (*Euastrum*,) Sendtnerianum, Reinsch. Plate XLVIII, figs. 30, 31.

Cells nearly twice as long as wide; sinus narrow linear; semi-cells nearly as long as wide, ends rounded, lateral margins each with four or five crenulations; lateral view of whole cell elliptic with more or less of a constriction in the middle; end view oval.

Diameter 25 $\mu$.; length 44 $\mu$.

C. nitidulum, De Not. Plate XXI, figs. 16, 17, 18; and Plate LXIII, figs. 9, 10.

Cells small, smooth, of nearly equal length and breadth; constriction deep, sinuses narrow linear; basal angles of semi-cells obtusely rounded, sides rounded, ends roundly truncate; viewed from the vertex elliptic; from the side, subovate.

Diameter 22–30 $\mu$.; length 25–35 $\mu$.

Not infrequent in pond waters. The figs. 16, 17, should have the ends moderately flattened.

C. pseudonitidulum, Nord. Plate XXI, fig. 19.

Varies from the preceding in its somewhat larger size and more quadrangular form. The basal angles of the semi-cells besides being rounded, protrude slightly.

Diameter 38 $\mu$.

Found this form only in Northampton County, Pennsylvania.

C. laeve, Rab. Plate XVIII, fig. 10. Var. Septentrionale, Wille. Plate XLIII, fig. 14.

Cells one and one-third to one and two-thirds longer than broad, constriction deep; sinus narrow linear; semi-cells with high-rounded ends, usually somewhat retuse. Cytioderm finely granular.

Diameter 14–16 $\mu$.

Var. CRENULATUM, Wolle. Plate XIX, figs. 10, 19, is usually smaller in size and numbering ten to fourteen crenae to a semi-cell. This variety is near *C. crenatum*, but is separated by the rounded ends. The typical form is from South Carolina and Rhode Island, (Bailey); the variety from ponds, eastern Pennsylvania and New Jersey.

C. CRENATUM, Ralfs. Plate LX, figs. 31, 32.

Cells oblong, usually nearly twice as long as wide, deeply constricted in the middle; semi-cells crenulate at the margins, flattened at the ends; generally have twelve or fourteen crenae; cytioderm punctate. Zygospore globose, studded with protuberances which terminate with a divided apex.

Diameter 30–38 $\mu$.

> Rhode Island, New Jersey, Pennsylvania, and other States. Not frequent, but occurs every now and then.

C. NAEGELIANUM, Breb. (*C. crenatum*, *Naeg.*) Plate LXI, fig. 21.

Small, somewhat longer than broad, sinus narrow linear; semi-cells, with sides sinuate-crenate, converging from the broad flat base to the broadly truncate, entire or imperfectly quadricrenate ends; cytioderm finely granulate or smooth.

Diameter 20 $\mu$., or a little more or less.

> Not rare. Bears some resemblance to *C. crenatum* in front view, but is smaller and proportionably much shorter; the crenae of the sides are usually less in number, and those of the ends imperfectly developed.

C. VENUSTUM, Rab. Plate XIX, fig. 37.

Length of cell equal to about 1½ diameters; constriction deep; sinus narrow linear; semi-cells have a flat base, rounded lower angles, sides somewhat convergent; each with two notches of equal size; ends truncate, and slightly retuse. One chlorophyl mass in each semi-cell; membrane smooth.

Diameter 24–30 $\mu$.

> Occasional in ponds, Pennsylvania and New Jersey.

C. REINSCHII, Arch. (Dublin Microscopical Club.) Plate XIX, fig. 12.

Somewhat longer than broad, deeply constricted, sinus narrow linear; ends truncate; sides convex, erose, dentate or notched. Membrane smooth; end view elliptic, without a central inflation.

Diameter 30–35 $\mu$.

> Not frequent, but is found in Lake Hopatcong, N. J., and in ponds, eastern Pennsylvania.

C. HOLMIENSE, Lund.  Plate XIX, fig. 23.

Cells twice as long as wide, elliptic-rectangular, moderately constricted, sinus narrow linear;, semi-cell subquadrate, sides straight or subconvex, slightly converging until **near the** somewhat dilated apices; ends obsoletely crenulate; dorsum truncate-undulate, angles rounded.  Viewed from **the vertex** elliptic with the poles obtuse-angled; side view rectangular-elliptic; membrane smooth.  Chlorophyl homogeneous or in a single mass.

**Diameter 33 $\mu$.; length 63 $\mu$.**

Collected by F. H. Hosford, Mt. Mansfield, Vt., **1881**. Differs slightly from Lundell's figure in the crenulations, **and in being** less restricted near the ends.

Var. INTEGRUM, Lund.  Plate XIX, figs. 24, 25.

Differs from the typical form **in** having no crenulations nor plications near the apices, and **no undulations on the** ends.

**Diameter 32–36 $\mu$.**

Mountain spring, Rockdale, **Pa.**

C. ANSATUM, **Kg.**  Plate XIX, fig. 22.

Cells twice as long as broad; constriction wide but not deep; semi-cells have a flat base, rounded lower angles, sides converging, concave; **ends truncately** rounded; membrane punctate; **end** view oval.

**Diameter 28–31 $\mu$.**

Ponds, Pennsylvania, **rather rare.**

Scarcely separable from a variety (fig. 28) of *C. Holmiense*, except by the punctate membrane and the usually wider sinus; the latter is not correctly represented in fig. 22, should be two or three times wider and not quite so deep.

C. PYRAMIDATUM, Breb.  Plate XVII, figs. 16, 17.

Cells scarcely twice as long as broad, **suboval**; constriction deep, linear; semi-cells pyramidal, **rounded** at basal **angles**, sides convex, gradually converging **to** the somewhat truncate ends; punctate; **end view** broadly elliptic.

Diameter 50–85 $\mu$.

A common **species found probably in every State of the Union.**

Var. STENONOTUM, Nord.  Plate XVII, figs. 18, 19.

This subspecies is separated from the typical **form by the shape** of the sides of the semi-cells, which are **somewhat** retuse near the apices; for perfect identity the ends ought not to be retuse; my specimens are slightly concave.

Size about the same as the typical plant.

> Found this variety in collections made by Miss E. Butler, Minneapolis, Minnesota, and by A. D. Balen, Plainfield, New Jersey.

C. PSEUDOPYRAMIDATUM, Lund. Plate XVIII, figs. 11, 12.

In habitat, in form and proportions like the true plant, but only about half the size. It corresponds with *C. pyramidatum*, variety *minus*, Reinsch; Rab. Alg. Exsic. No. 1902.

Besides these, Ralfs has a *Forma major*, which I have included in my general grouping (fig. 17).

C. RALFSII, Breb. Plate XVIII, fig. 1.

Orbicular or suborbicular, deeply constricted, sinus narrow linear; semi-cells nearly semicircular; inferior angles obtuse, dorsum high convex; cytioderm smooth or finely punctate.

Diameter 60–100 $\mu$.; length 70–120 $\mu$.

> Pennsylvania, New Jersey, not frequent, but turns up every now and then, sometimes in considerable numbers.
>
> In size, form, and arrangement of chlorophyl, this species is often a good representative of *C. Candianum*, Delp.

C. PACHYDERMUM, Lund. Plate XVIII, figs. 2, 3.

Cells 1½–1½ times longer than broad; sinus narrow linear; semi-cells with straight base, rounded angles; sides rise nearly at right angles and then converge, forming a high arch; they contain two chlorophyl masses; viewed from the vertex, oval; isthmus wide, cytioderm firm, distinctly punctate.

Diameter 75–100 $\mu$.

> Had specimens from Budd's Lake, New Jersey; from Nebraska Notch, Vermont, collected by C. G. Pringle; and from Mt. Everett, Massachusetts.
>
> This species is separated from *C. Ralfsii*, by its usually greater proportionate length, firmer cytioderm, and wider isthmus.

C. GALERITUM, Nord. Plate XIX, figs. 46, 47, 48.

Cells slightly longer than wide, with narrow isthmus, deep constriction and narrow, slightly gaping sinus; semi-cells triangular with straight, or somewhat reniform base, rounded lower angles, convergent, straight, or slightly convex sides; ends more or less truncate; membrane smooth; end view oval; side view circular.

Diameter 40–55 μ.

> Springs and ponds, Pennsylvania and New Jersey.
>
> Fig. 47 represents a small form found in a pond on Mt. Everett, Mass., measures only 29 μ. diameter. The smaller size, straight sides, and more broadly truncate ends may prove it to be a different species. I note it provisionally a variety of the typical plant.

C. SPHALEROSTICHUM, Nord. Plate XLVIII, figs. 26, 27.

Cells small, somewhat longer than broad, sinus narrow linear; semi-cells subreniform-trapezoid, base straight; inferior angles nearly right; ends in middle truncate and nude, granulate, granules often in two or three vertical series, often scattered, inconstant as name implies. In vertical view elliptic, margins granulate; in lateral view circular, granulate. Zygospore globose or subglobose, smooth.

Diameter 13–14 μ.; length 16–20 μ.

> New Jersey and Pennsylvania. Resembles *C. orthosticum*, Lund., but is somewhat smaller, ends truncate and granules not so regularly arranged.

C. POLYMAZUM, Nord. Plate XIX, figs. 38–40.

Cells about as long as wide, deeply constricted; sinus narrow linear, widening somewhat outwardly; semi-cells subelliptic, margins with about sixteen crenae, and within the margins a concentric series of granules to correspond; area smooth with six papillae arranged in the form of a triangle, three in the first row nearest the margin, then two, then one; seen from the vertex, elliptical, truncate at ends, with a papilla at each angle and from these two longitudinal series of granules; three papillae on each side (omitted in the figure); lateral view circular, with end truncate, and two rows of granules extending from the angles of the truncate end of one semi-cell to those of the other; the margins of the sides ornate with three papillae.

> Nordstedt made this form, found by him in Norway, a variety of Lundell's *C. monomazum*, which has not occurred here; the other *C. polymazum*, is frequent in Denmark Pond, N. J.

C. OCULIFERUM, Lagh. Plate X, figs. 7, 8.

Cells small, deeply constricted, sinus inwardly and outwardly more or less dilated; semi-cells semicircular-triangular, ends retuse, sides slightly convex or straight, inferior angles obtuse; above the middle a single large granule and below it a series of six small granules arranged in a semicircle, ends tending towards the retuse apex; viewed from apex oval, from sides subcircular. Membrane smooth.

Diameter of cell 24 $\mu$.; length 32 $\mu$.

Pond, Tewksbury, Mass.

C. DONNELLII, Wolle. Plate XIX, figs. 41, 42.

Cells nearly as long as wide, suborbicular; sinus narrow, gaping; semi-cells somewhat flattened, semicircular with angles rounded; margin formed of about eighteen large pearl-like granules; area smooth with a series of three larger granules, or papillae in the center. End view oval, three papillae on each side.

Diameter 37–45 $\mu$.

Found in collections made by J. Donnell Smith in Florida, 1879.

C. TAXICHONDRUM, Lund. Plate XIX, figs. 32–34.

Cells suborbicular, slightly longer than broad; sinus deep, narrow, linear, barely widened at the mouth; semi-cells semicircular, margin of base nearly straight, membrane thickened at the angles; face ornate with a single large granule at the isthmus, and two somewhat arched rows near the dorsal margin, one with three and the other with five or six granules; seen from the vertex, elliptic with five or six granules on each side; cytioderm punctate; isthmus one-fourth of the diameter of the cell. Chlorophyl nuclei two.

Diameter 40–50 $\mu$.

Occurs frequently in ponds, northern New Jersey, Pennsylvania and Massachusetts.

Var. BIDENTULUM, Lagh. Plate XLIX, figs. 17, 18. Distinguishing feature; in vertical view elliptic, somewhat contracted at ends, the angles bidentate.

C. PSEUDOTAXICHONDRUM, Nord. Plate XLIX, figs. 22, 23.

Scarcely as long as broad, deeply constricted, sinus considerably widened outwardly; semi-cells semicircular with the middle more or less truncate or depressed; the angles somewhat thickened and often terminating in a tooth-like point; above the basal line is an arched transverse series of four granules; end view elliptical with four granules on each side; lateral view circular, with two inconspicuous granules on opposite sides; membrane punctate. Isthmus about one-third of the diameter.

Diameter 30 μ.

> Brown's Mills, New Jersey, is the only locality which has hitherto furnished this form. The original, found in Brazil, differs somewhat in the "*sinu lineari, extrorsum vix ampliato.*" **Our form has the sinus** decidedly enlarged towards the mouth.

**G. von** Lagerheim **appears to** give **too much prominence** to simple differentiations—mere vagaries of the same species. They **may** be briefly noted.
1. *C. taxichondrum*, var. *bidentulum*, as above.
2. *C. pseudotaxichondrum*, **cells** more depressed.
3. *C. pseudotaxichondrum*, var. *trichondrum*, semi-cells ornate with a single **row of** three granules.
4. *C. pseudotaxichondrum*, var. *quadridentulum*; in front view, **the** inferior angles bidenticulate.
5. *C. pileigerum*. Merely a depauperated form of the above.

Pond, Tewksbury, Massachusetts.

C. ANISOCHONDRUM, **Nord.** Plate XIX, figs. 43–45.

Cells subquadrate, length and breadth nearly equal; sinus, narrow linear; semi-cells subsemicircular, dorsum broadly truncate; in center two horizontal rows of large granules of three each, and two intermediate granules below and above; smaller granules, more scattered on each side; viewed from the vertex, elliptic, with three larger granules on each side **and** a number of smaller ones within the margin; the middle **bare**; lateral view obovate, **circular. Isthmus one-third the diameter of cell.**

Diameter 30–38 μ.

> Denmark Pond and other ponds of northern New Jersey. The original of this species was collected on **the** Sandwich Islands and described by Dr. Nordstedt.

C. QUINARIUM, Lund. **Plate XLIX, figs.** 10, 11.

Cells subhexagonal, **about one-fourth** longer **than broad**; constriction deep linear; **semi-cells subtrapezoid, narrowed toward** the subtruncate apex, **sides somewhat convex, inferior** angles obtuse, margins obsolete granulate-dentate; within the margin a series of prominent granules, in center five obtuse granules arranged **in** two transverse **series**;

membrane punctate; in vertical view elliptic granulate around the margin; in lateral view circular.

Diameter 33–35 $\mu$.; length 39–42 $\mu$.

Tewksbury, Massachusetts.

C. KITCHELII, Wolle.  Plate XXI, figs. 1–3.

Cells suborbicular, about one-fourth longer than broad, deeply constricted; sinus narrow linear; semi-cells semicircular, margins crenulate, with about 18 crenae; within, two concentric rows of granules corresponding with the crenae; area smooth excepting two, rarely three, transverse rows of three larger granules each, in the middle; viewed from the vertex, ovate-elliptic with three larger granules on each side, and four series of smaller granules extending from end to end; lateral view circular with two granules on each side, and four central series.

Diameter 40 $\mu$.

> Collected by Rev. H. D. Kitchell in a pond near Hammonton, New Jersey. This species is readily recognized by the large marginal granules, end and side view, and by the four parallel central series of smaller granules. It bears some resemblance to *C. polymazum*, but differs in the central granules and in the double row of marginal smaller granules.

C. TRACHYPLEURUM, Lund.  Plate XIX, figs. 26–29.

Cells about one-fourth longer than the diameter; isthmus narrow; sinus narrow, enlarged outwardly; semi-cells subreniform; ends truncate, nude in center; the margins of the sides armed with **five** or six conical spines; the area close to the margin, is set with numerous conical spines arranged in short concentric series; **the middle is** ornate with **seven** granules, six **in a circle and one in** the center; between these granules punctate; viewed from the vertex, elliptic with three prominent granules on each **side**; within the margin, and near it, is a series of conical granules; lateral view circular.  Chlorophyllous **nuclei, two.**

Diameter 33–40 $\mu$.

> Frequent in ponds, eastern Pennsylvania and **New Jersey.**

C. TRIPLICATUM, Wolle.  Plate XXII, figs. 3–6.

Cells about one-fourth longer than **broad, subrectangular**; angles obtuse; sinus between the semi-cells linear; margins **irregularly granulate crenate**; membrane rough with larger and smaller granules: the larger ones arranged in series of three; **three on the** margin of each of the three superior rounded angles, three within the margins, and three near margin between the angles (sometimes the granules appear to border the whole semi-cell); on the margin of the sides near the inferior angles two larger granules, and within the margins a few scattered smaller ones; end view quadrangular-oval, with two series, usually of six larger granules, on each of the longer sides, one of the series on the margin, and the other within. Zygospores spherical, with long spines, fig. 6.

Diameter of cell 40 $\mu$.; length about 50 $\mu$.

Ponds, Pennsylvania and New Jersey.

The nearest approach to this species is *C. Ungerianum*, Naeg. It is separated by its smaller size, the details of outline and the arrangement of the larger granules.

C. NORDSTEDTII, Delp.  Plate XLVIII, figs. 23-25.

Cells somewhat longer than broad, constriction deep; semi-cell rectangular oblong about twice as wide as long, granulate around the margins, center usually nude.

I adopt this name for a form widely distributed, but variable; sometimes it resembles *C. triplicatum* in size and shape, but differs in the number and arrangement of the granules, which are not in series of threes, but in continuous eccentric rows. Sometimes they cover the upper half of the semi-cell, then again only one or two rows occur within, but close to the margin; the center and basal half are usually nude. The sides are not so straight as figured by Delponte, but the front and end views are always more or less rectangular-oblong.

Reinsch has named a very different form *C. Nordstedtii*; it is nearly, if not entirely, identical with *C. cyclicum*, Lund.

C. SEELYANUM, Wolle.  Plate XXI, figs. 33-35.

Cells small, quadrangular, deeply constricted; sinus narrow linear; semi-cells twice as wide as long, with a small rounded notch in the middle of the sides, the superior angles somewhat produced laterally; dorsum slightly produced in the middle and crenated; membrane at the superior, and at the inferior angles and near the margin of the ends, each with three or four granules; in the center a circular cluster of larger granules.

Diameter 25-30 $\mu$.

Frequent in pond at Elmira, N. Y., 1882.

? Membrane granular without a central inflation.

C. MICROSPHINCTUM, Nord. var. PARVULA, Wille. Plate XLIX, figs. 20, 21.

Cells small, elliptic, one-half longer than wide, moderately constricted, sinus narrow linear; semi-cell subelliptic, apex in vertical view broadly elliptic, granulate within the margin, center nude; in lateral view suborbicular, end truncate.

Diameter of cell 25 $\mu$.; length 33 $\mu$.

Tewksbury, Massachusetts.

C. MARGARITIFERUM, Menegh. Plate XVI, figs. 1-3.

Cells about one and one-half times longer than broad, sinus narrow, usually more or less enlarged outwardly; semi-cells semiorbicular, somewhat reniform or oval, with rounded interior angles, convex sides and broadly rounded, not truncate end. Cytioderm rough with pearly granules; end view elliptic; zygospores orbicular.

Diameter 25-50 $\mu$.

This species varies in size and form. The rough membrane distinguishes it from *C. crenatum* and *C. undulatum*; its rounded ends from *C. Botrytis*, its smaller size and less positive kidney form from *C. reniforme*. It appears to be as widely distributed as the most common of this genus.

C. PUNCTULATUM, Breb. Plate XVI, fig. 4.

This form is very similar to *C. margaritiferum*, but it is smaller, the pearly granules less conspicuous, and the ends more flattened. The membrane is sometimes not granular, but punctate. It is found in the same localities, and appears very nearly related.

Diameter of cells 20-30 $\mu$.

C. POLYMORPHUM, Nord. Plate XLIX, figs. 31-33.

Suborbicular, deeply constricted, sinus narrow linear; semi-cells semicircular, base straight, ends truncate; two granules above the base, three about the middle of the area; punctate between the two series; granulate near the margin; in vertical view broadly elliptic, granulate within the margin, center nude; in lateral view suborbicular, end truncate.

Diameter of cell 25 $\mu$.; length 33 $\mu$.

C. BOTRYTIS, Menegh. Plate XVI, figs. 5-7.

Cells one, and nearly two times as long as broad; sinus narrow linear; semi-cells with nearly straight base, sometimes inclining to reniform; sides converging from the inferior rounded angles to the flat, truncate end; cytioderm evenly covered with large pearly granules. Zygospores orbicular, spinous with long, thin spines, the ends much divided.

Diameter 35–62 $\mu$.

A very common plant, and very variable in the size, and in the proportions of length and breadth.

Var. TUMIDUM, Wolle. Plate XX, figs. 3–5.

In outline, front view, very near *C. Botrytis*, yet entirely unlike it in side and end views, which show a central inflation. Found it in only one locality in a meadow pool, near Bethlehem, Pa. Further observation may prove it a distinct species.

C. BREBISSONII, Menegh. Plate XVI, figs. 10, 11.

Cells somewhat longer than broad; semi-cells semiorbicular, rough with conic spines or granules; end view elliptic or oval.

Diameter 45–65 $\mu$.

Cells generally larger than *C. margaritiferum*; semi-cells more oval, but separable only by the armor of conical granules. Not so frequent as the preceding, but appears to be widely distributed.

C. CONSPERSUM, Ralfs. Plate XVII, figs. 1, 2.

Cells somewhat longer than broad, quadrilateral, angles obtusely rounded; constriction deep, produces a linear notch on each side; granules pearly, large, depressed, giving a crenulate appearance to the margin.

Diameter 50–73 $\mu$.

A beautiful and conspicuous species, frequently found in large numbers; it is easily distinguished by its large size and quadrangular form.

C. CONSPERSUM, var. RETUSUM, Wolle. Plate XLVI, fig. 5. (Comp. Des. U. S., p. 75.)

Unlike the true form in the depressed or retuse ends; sides also incline inwardly from the base of the semi-cell to the end.

Diameter averages the same as the type-forms.

Ponds, Minnesota.

C. TETROPHTHALMUM, (Kg.), Breb. Plate XVI, fig. 13.

Cells one-third to one-half longer than broad; semi-cells semiorbicular somewhat elevated, rough with pearly granules which give a crenate appearance to the margin; chlorophyl masses two, often very conspicuous.

Diameter 60–78 $\mu$.

> Rather common. The semi-cells are usually near in form to two-thirds of a circle. The transverse view is broadly elliptic. The four chlorophyl nuclei, which are frequently very prominent, two in each semi-cell, probably suggested the name, *four-eyed*.

C. PARDALIS, Cohn.   Plate XLIX, figs. 3–5.

Cells suborbicular or subquadrate, equal or slightly longer than broad, constriction narrow linear or often somewhat dilated inwardly, and more or less ampliated outwardly; semi-cells transversely oblong, subreniform; base and vertex truncate or concave, angles inferior and superior rounded; lateral view suborbicular; vertical view oblong, sides straight; membrane verrucose, verrucae (papillae) obtuse, regularly arranged in diagonal rows.

Diameter 54–57 $\mu$.; length 75–80 $\mu$.; thickness 39 $\mu$.; isthmus 18–20 $\mu$.

> Lagerheim reports this *African* plant from Tewksbury, Mass. It has not come under my notice. Looks like a close relation to some form of *C. conspersum*. The figures represent a front, a lateral and a transverse view, copied from Cohn's figures.

C. INTERMEDIUM, Delp.   Plate XVI, fig. 12.

Cells very near the preceding (*C. tetrophthalmum*), somewhat smaller, semi-cells more absolutely semiorbicular, not so elevated.

Diameter 45–50 $\mu$.

> Habitat same as the preceding.

C. DENTATUM, Wolle.   Plate XVI, fig. 15.

Cells about one-half longer than wide; constriction deep, forms gaping sinuses; cytioderm rather closely set with small pearly granules; the margins of the rounded sides of the semi-cells dentate with large and distant conical projections, or teeth; ten to twelve on each side. The ends broadly rounded are devoid of projecting teeth. End view of cell oval; lateral view elliptic with a constriction in the middle.

Diameter 90–100 $\mu$.; length 145–160 $\mu$.

> This plant has hitherto been found only in Pennsylvania, New Jersey, Florida and Massachusetts.
>
> It is separated from *C. ovale*, its nearest kin, by the shape of the semi-cells, which are not triangular, or conical, but broadly oval, and by the nudity of the apices.

C. LATUM, Breb.   Plate XVI, fig. 14.

Large, slightly longer than broad; constriction deep, sinuses narrow, somewhat enlarged within; semi-cells broad reniform, sides rounded, and back (dorsum) broad, rather flatly rounded, margins dentate-crenulate; cytioderm covered with pearly granules which are disposed in curved, concentric series.

Diameter about 60 $\mu$.

> Bears a resemblance to *C. margaritiferum*, but it is somewhat larger; and according to Brebisson, more flatly rounded in the middle, and base more reniform. Find it rather rarely intermingled with other forms, and sometimes question the characters for a good species.

C. RENIFORME, (Ralfs), Arch.   Plate XVII, figs. 10, 11.

A diagnosis of this species would not differ from the last, *C. latum*, except in the size of pearly granules, which are nearly twice as large, (well shown in the empty cell fig. 11) and in the more decided reniform figure of the semi-cells.

> The only habitat hitherto found for this form is a pond in Florida; collected by J. Donnell Smith, of Baltimore, Md., 1879.

C. OCHTHODES, Nord.   Plate XVII, figs. 3, 4.

Cells one and one-half times longer than broad, somewhat elliptic-oblong, deeply constricted, sinuses narrow linear; semi-cells semicircular or subtriangular, sides convex; apices truncately rounded, or frequently slightly retuse in center; margins densely crenated; viewed from the vertex, elliptic, from the side, obovate. Membrane densely verrucose, verrucae large, depressed, arranged in subregular or concentric series.

Diameter 52-70 $\mu$.

> Hitherto have found this variety only in eastern Pennsylvania. The original of the species was found in northern Sweden, and described by O. Nordstedt; it bears the resemblance to *C. Botrytis*, and *C. tetrophthalmum*, but differs in the form of the verrucae which are short cylindrical truncate; in *tetrophthalmum* the verrucae are triangular hemispherical obtuse, and in *C. Botrytis* triangular with subacute apices.

C. PORTIANUM, Archer.   Plate XVII, figs. 12-14.

Cells about one-third longer than broad, deeply constricted; semi-cells oval, remote, separated by a wide sinus; isthmus about one-fourth the diameter of the cell, membrane granular.

Diameter 25-33 $\mu$.

Frequent in ponds, Pennsylvania, New Jersey, Massachusetts, Minnesota and Connecticut.

C. ORBICULATUM, Ralfs. Plate XVII, figs. 20, 21.

Twice as long as wide ; semi-cells spherical, connected by a narrow isthmus ; cytioderm covered with large granules. Zygospore, according to Ralfs, orbicular, studded with large verrucae.

Diameter 20–33 $\mu$.

Met with it frequently in ponds of New Jersey and Pennsylvania.

C. EXCAVATUM, Nord. Var. *duplo major*, Lund. Plate LXIV, figs. 14, 15.

Cells nearly twice as long as wide, constriction wide and deep; end view orbicular; semi-cells subspherical with truncate base; verrucae of membrane, producing a crenulate margin.

Diameter 21–25 $\mu$.

Not rare in ponds, Pennsylvania, New Jersey, etc.

Wille, of Norway, describes a form *"elliptica,"* most nearly allied to ours in front view, but elliptical in end view. Nord.'s and Lund.'s described forms are orbicular in end view.

Var. TRIGONUM, Lagh. Plate XLIX, figs. 24, 25.

Cells in vertical view triangular, sides straight, or somewhat convex, angles rounded.

Diameter of cells 18 $\mu$.; length 20 $\mu$.; thickness 18 $\mu$.

Tewksbury, Massachusetts.

C. SUBORBICULARE, Wood. Plate XXVII, fig. 24.

Cells small, a very little longer than broad, with the margin irregularly crenate, or crenate-undulate; semi-cells from the side orbicular, from the vertex elliptical; sinus very narrow, but within somewhat excavated; cytioderm thick, sparsely coarsely granulated; granules subdistant, in each cell arranged in one or two curved marginal series and in a central group of two or three short rows.

Diameter 30 $\mu$.; length 33 $\mu$.

Saco Lake, New Hampshire, (Lewis).

C. AMOENUM, Breb. Plate XVII, figs. 5, 6, 7.

Cells twice as long as broad, sides parallel, ends rounded ; constriction deep, linear ; semi-cells rough with large, obtuse, papilla-like pearly granules; side view much compressed, about thrice as long as broad; semi-cells contain two chlorophyl nuclei.

Var. TUMIDUM, Wolle, has the sides, front view, not parallel, but swollen or rounded.
>Diameter 20–25 μ.
>>Rhode Island (Olney), Florida (Bailey).
>>Frequent in Pennsylvania, New Jersey, Massachusetts.

C. ORTHOSTICUM, Lund. Plate XXI. figs. 4, 5.
>Cells slightly **more** in length than the diameter, deeply constricted, sinus narrow linear; semi-cells subelliptic, sides rounded, base and dorsum nearly straight, coarsely verrucose; verrucae in 6–8 vertical series; from the vertex elliptic; **verrucose on or** near the margins, area punctate; from the side, circular. Chlorophyl nucleus single.
>**Diameter 20–30 μ.**
>>Ponds, northern New Jersey and **Mount Everett, Mass.**

C. ELEGANTISSIMUM, **Lund.** Plate XVII, figs. 8, 9.
>Cells **two to** two and one-half times longer **than** broad, perfectly cylindrical, **ends** arched; slightly constricted; viewed from the vertex, circular; margins verrucose-crenate; membrane with emarginate verrucae disposed in twenty-two **longitudinal** series, **of** which about nine are visible in front **view; these are** arranged transversely also, **in eight or nine** series on each semi-cell; **the same contains two chlorophyllous nuclei.**
>Diameter 29–33 μ.
>>I found **this plant in** collections made in Florida; **it** differs somewhat in size from Lundell's Swedish form, being more variable in length, varying from two to three diameters; the number of longitudinal series, if actual series, is greater than specified; the transverse series agree.

C. NOTABILE, Breb. **Plate XIX, fig. 11.**
>Length **of cell** nearly equal to two diameters, margins somewhat undulate-crenate, ends broadly truncate; semi-cells, base somewhat reniform, sides converging from the base to the broadly truncate end; **angles rounded;** cytioderm **smooth or** finely granulate.
>Diameter 25–30 μ.
>>Met **with** rather **rarely in shallow** pools and on dripping rocks.

C. HAMMERI, **Reinsch.** Plate XXI, figs. 27, 36–38.
>Small, smooth; semi-cells in form of a truncate cone, the end either straight or slightly retuse, the sides rounded below and slightly concave **above; the** truncate ends about

one-half the diameter of the cell; end view usually a regular ellipse; lateral view of cell oblong with central constriction.
Diameter 20–24 $\mu$.

> Frequent in ponds. Reinsch describes several forms; a larger and a smaller size, one with straight ends, another emarginate; end view usually elliptic. Among our varieties I find one with inflated cepter; of eleven drawings made in my sketch book nine are without central inflations, and two with them, the latter even more inflated than the variety *retusiforme*, found in Norway, and described by Wille.

C. NYMANNIANUM, Grun.

Cells somewhat hexagonal, finely punctate; semi-cells slightly broader than long; base rather flat, sides converging from the base to the broadly truncate end, lower part prominently rounded, sinuate near the end; apex often retuse.
Diameter 36–38 $\mu$.; length 50 $\mu$., more or less.

> In front view, this is a common form, barely separable from the following—*C. sublobatum*; in lateral, and in end view however, they ought to be distinct by the absence or the presence of a central inflation. All the specimens examined personally evidenced more or less of an inflation, or at least a tendency to it; have not been convinced of having a genuine *C. Nymannianum*. I set them down to *C. sublobatum*.
>
> Semi-cells with central inflation; cytioderm smooth or punctate.

C. TURPINII, Breb.  Plate XX, figs. 24, 25.

Cells of equal length and breadth; constriction deep, forms a narrow linear or acute-angled sinus, outwardly ampliated; semi-cells triangular, lower angles rounded, apex truncately rounded; sides somewhat concave; central inflation granulate, and sometimes emarginate; cytioderm finely granulate or punctate.
Diameter 55–70 $\mu$.

> Not rare; frequently in large numbers in ponds, New Jersey, Pennsylvania and other States.

C. SUBLOBATUM, Archer.  Plate XXI, figs. 21, 22.

Cells somewhat oblong, about one-half longer than broad, sinus linear; semi-cells swollen at the base, gradually narrowed toward the truncate ends; inferior and superior angles rounded; apex broadly truncate, sides sinuate; with central inflation.
Diameter 38–44 $\mu$.

> Ponds, Pennsylvania, New Jersey; not abundant, but probably widely distributed.

**C. RETUSUM**, Perty.   Plate XXI, figs. 25, 26.

Small, of nearly equal length and breadth, entire; sinus deep, linear; semi-cells with subreniform base, sides sinuate and converging to a truncate end; angles **rounded; end view** centrally protruding.

Diameter 22–30 $\mu$.

Pennsylvania and New Jersey.

**C. MARGARITUM, Wolle.**   Plate XXII, figs. 25, 26, 27.

**Suborbicular, from** one to one and one-third times as long **as wide; sinus** narrow **linear;** semi-cells somewhat semi-circular, margins undulate crenate, or emarginate; **two** or three surface swellings near the base which cause prismatic reflections from **the** smooth pearl-like membrane.

Diameter 22–25 $\mu$.

Found the first of this form in Splitrock pond, New Jersey, but **occasionally since in** other localities of the same State, **and in Pennsylvania.**

**C. TITHOPHORUM**, Nord.   Plate XXII, figs. **28, 29, 30.**

**Cells** about as long as wide, circular, deeply constricted; **sinus an** acute angle considerably ampliated (angle about **20°);** semi-cells from the base cuneate-semicircular; end view elliptical with a prominent central elevation; laterally **seen, obovate-circular with** a mamilliform prominence on **each** side.

Diameter **28** $\mu$.; length 30 $\mu$.

Collected this form from ponds on Mount Everett, Mass. It corresponds so nearly with a plant found on the island of Java, described **by** Dr. Nordstedt, I adopt the name as his choice.

**C. HOMALODERMUM**, Nord.   Plate XX, figs. 19, 20.

Slightly longer than broad, deeply constricted; sinus narrow linear with the mouth considerably ampliated; semi-cells trapezoid with a subreniform base; sides retuse; ends truncate, and often retuse; superior angles obtuse, inferior broadly rounded; seen from the vertex, elliptic-oblong with **the** middle somewhat inflated; lateral view ovate. Ends about half as wide as the breadth of the cell. Cytioderm finely, often indistinctly, punctate.

Diameter 40 $\mu$.

**Ponds, Mount** Everett, Mass.

**The** typical plant was found in the Arctic region, on the **island** of Spitzbergen. It is described by Dr. Nordstedt as measuring 48–51 $\mu$. in diameter, about one-fifth larger than our plant; hitherto found only in one locality, 1881 and 1882.

C. CRUCIATUM, Breb. Plate XXI, figs. 23, 24.

Length and breadth nearly the same, ends broadly **truncate**; deeply constricted; sinus narrow, enlarged outwardly; semi-cells trapezoid-reniform, inferior angles obtuse; **sides incline towards the truncate end**; margins somewhat crenate. Two nuclei in each semi-cell; membrane finely granulate or punctate.

Diameter 22–24 $\mu$.

Swamp and marsh pools; rather rare.

C. PHASEOLUS, Breb. **Plate XXI, figs. 28–32.**

Cells about as long as wide, smooth; constriction deep, forming a linear, excavated, notch on each side; semi-cells reniform; **end view elliptic** with a slight **projection in the middle of each side**.

A common species to be found, probably in every State of the Union.

C. BIREME, Nord. Plate XXII, figs. 23, 24.

Small, about **as long as wide, deeply constricted, sinus wide at the mouth**; **semi-cells elliptic, base and back somewhat truncate**; in the **center a large verruca**; viewed from the end, elliptic, with **a prominent cylindrical verruca in the center of each** side; lateral view, **obovate** furnished with a **similar verruca**. Membrane smooth.

Breadth 13 $\mu$.; length 14 $\mu$.

Denmark Pond and Budd's Lake, N. J.

C. SCHLIEPHACKEANUM, Grun. Plate XXI, figs. 14, 15.

Very small, subquadrate, as broad as long, smooth, entire, **deeply constricted**; semi-cells depressed, ends broadly **truncate, or plane-convex**; sides convex, often projecting at an obtuse angle; **center more or** less inflated.

Breadth 12 $\mu$.; if not equal, slightly less in length.

Occurs occasionally in large numbers, but more frequently it is found singly in ponds of Pennsylvania, New Jersey, **Massachusetts**, Minnesota.

§ Cells with a central inflation, membrane granular.

C. ORNATUM, **Ralfs.** Plate XXI, figs. 39–45; Plate LX, figs. 22–24.

**Cells** of nearly equal length **and breadth**, constriction deep, narrow; semi-cells with a somewhat reniform base, angles broadly rounded, end truncate; sides inflated below, and contracted and **concave near the end, thus** producing a truncate projection which in end view forms a rounded **lobe**; membrane rough **with** pearly granules **which give a dentate** appearance to the margin.

Diameter 33-45 $\mu$.

> Not uncommon; probably no form is more generally **distributed throughout the earth. It is variable in size, in the arrangement of the central granules and in the projection.**

Var. PROTRACTUM. Plate LX, fig. 22; Plate XX, fig. 29.

The figure (Plate LX) represents a form collected July, 1883, by my friend, Dr. Kitchel, in Lake Minnetonka, Minn. He found it freely intermingled with the typical form (fig. 23). It is in all its parts, except the more protracted ends, so like the true form, I consider it merely a variety of *C. ornatum*. Plate XX, fig. 29, is a good representation of *C. protractum*, Naeg., but the specimens, found in large numbers, clearly show their connection with *C. ornatum*. Compare note under *C. protractum*.

C. LAOENSE, Nord. Plate XLIX, figs. 26, 27.

Semi-cell in vertical view, in the middle much swollen and the ends inflated, granules large; center smooth. It is an exaggerated development of *C. ornatum* and hence a variety of it.

> Tewksbury, Massachusetts, and not infrequently in New Jersey ponds.

C. SPORTELLA, Breb. Plate LX, figs. 28-30.

Very nearly as long as broad, deeply constricted; semicells subreniform, sides somewhat dilated and rounded, end broadly truncate, margins erose-spinous or denticulate; cytioderm granular.

Diameter 33-36 $\mu$.

> Harvey Lake, Luzerne County, Pa. Bears some resemblance to *C. ornatum*, but ends do not protrude; granules are more spinous than rounded, producing the erose appearance of the margins. Found many specimens in this one **locality, but** did not recognize the form elsewhere.

C. PROTRACTUM, (Naeg.), Archer. Plate XX, figs. 27-28.

But slightly longer than wide, constriction deep, sinuses narrow linear, often ampliated from the acute angles; semicells with tumid base, twice as broad as long, angles rounded, sides deeply sinuate below the truncate end. Viewed from the vertex, elliptic with a central inflation; membrane granular.

Diameter 70-80 $\mu$.

The plants recognized by different authors as of the present species, by their protracted ends of the cells, are very variable in size and detail of form. Plate XX, figs. 27, 28 represents the true form; from pools in marshy grounds, Pennsylvania. Fig. 29 is another form, less than half the size, found in numbers in a pond near Branchville, Sussex County, N. J. Plate LX, fig. 22, is a third variety from Minnetonka Lake, Minn., intermediate in size, but so closely related to *C. ornatum* in size, form, and arrangement of granules, I call it a *variety* of that species. The other (fig. 29) is evidently of the same connection, hence I transfer it from the position given it by Naegeli to companionship with the latter.

C. COMMISURALE, Breb. Plate XXI, figs. 49-51.

Semi-cells short reniform, three times broader than long, rough with pearly granules; end view with a constriction between the central inflation and the extremities.

Diameter 34-38 $\mu$.; length 25-30 $\mu$.

Sparsely found in ponds in Pennsylvania, New Jersey, New Hampshire, and probably most of the States.

C. SUBCRENATUM, Hantzsch. Plate XXI, figs. 6, 7; Plate XXII, fig. 20.

Cells with apices or ends more or less distinctly quadricrenate, sides with (4-) 6 crenae; within the margins three or four series of granules; the swelling near the basal line has usually five short series of granules; viewed from the vertex, elliptic, apices truncate-retuse, sometimes rounded; on the swollen middle are often seen five prominent granules; lateral view, ovate, with basal swellings and truncate ends.

Diameter 20-26 $\mu$.; length 23-36 $\mu$.

Ponds, and sluggish streamlets, Pennsylvania, New Jersey, Massachusetts, Minnesota.

C. PROTUBERANS, Lund. Var. GRANULATUM, Wolle. Plate LXII, figs. 13, 14, 15.

Cells about one-fifth longer that broad; constriction deep, narrow linear; semi-cells nearly twice as wide as long, base straight, sides somewhat diverging from the basal line; superior angles nearly right, inferior angles obtuse; near the middle of the cell is a small granulated tumor; seen from the vertex elliptic with a central swelling on each side; lateral view nearly spherical; membrane granular.

Diameter 25-28 $\mu$.

From a small pond near Minneapolis, Minn. This desmid is evidently not the same as found in Sweden and described by Lundell, but it possesses the principal feature, the "protuberans" derived from the excess of the diameter of the end of the semi-cell over the measure of the base. It differs in the less prominent central inflation, and in having the membrane granular, not punctate. Kirchner describes a new species, *C. pseudoprotuberans*, **which** has no central inflation, **no granules nor puncta.**

C. QUASILLUS, Lund. **Plate XX, figs. 13, 14. 15.**

**Somewhat** longer **than broad, constriction** deep, **sinus linear.** Semi-cells trapezoid, **narrowed from the** broad, straight base to the truncate end; sides, below, granulate dentate, above undulate; end slightly undulate; angles, inferior and superior, obtusely rounded; cytioderm coarsely granulate, the verrucae in subconcentric lines; end **view** shows a basal, granulated protuberance.

**Diameter 60–70 $\mu$.**; length 66–75 $\mu$.

I found this form first in the vicinity of Bethlehem, Pa., **in** the year 1877, and then described **it in the "Bulletin** Torrey Bot. Club," of New York, **Vol.** VI, p. 186, **as a new species,** *C. irregulare*, in reference to the irregular **size** of the crenae of the sides. Later researches revealed Lundell's earlier description.

Since 1877, have found **the same** plant in various localities in Pennsylvania, Massachusetts and New Jersey.

C. EVERETTENSE, **Wolle. Plate XX, figs. 10, 11, 12.**

Cells as long as wide; constriction deep; sinus linear, often much ampliated; semi-cells with ends broadly **rounded**, or truncate, sides convex; membrane rough with large verrucae arranged **in** concentric series; apex usually nude, surrounded by short, **acute,** conical teeth; **end, and transverse view show a decided** central **inflation.**

**Length and** breadth, 50–52 $\mu$.

Ponds, Mt. Everett, **Mass.**

C. ELOISEANUM, Wolle. **Plate XXII, figs. 1, 2.**

Cells large, **one-third longer** than broad; constriction forming a deep, linear, **outwardly** widening sinus **on each** side; semi-cells semicircular, margins set with long **pointed** teeth or aculei; center inflated and granularly rough, **intermediate area smooth or** punctate; end view oval with a granular tumor on each side, and two somewhat converging series of teeth or aculei extending from end to end.

Diameter 75 $\mu$.; **length 100 $\mu$.**

A species originally found in Minnesota, by Miss Eloise Butler, now turns up also in New Jersey, Splitrock Pond, and more recently Mr. W. N. Hastings has been collecting fine specimens near Rochester, New Hampshire. The specimen represented, Plate XXII, is an old form and caused too many teeth to be illustrated. A single series on the periphery of a semi-cell does not exceed 23-25.

C. BROOMEI, Thwaites. Plate XX, fig. 6-9.

Usually as long as broad, sometimes slightly longer, obtuse-quadrangular; sinus narrow linear; semi-cell oblong-quadrangular, twice as broad as long, angles, inferior and superior, obtusely rounded, base plane, end broadly truncate and often slightly retuse, or moderately convex; end and side views evidence a distinct central inflation; cytioderm rough with pearly granules arranged in suberect lines.

Diameter 30-45 $\mu$.

Appears to be entitled to the term "common."

C. PSEUDOBROOMEI, Wolle. Plate LXII, fig. 36, 37.

This new species is in all its details of structure like the preceding, but entirely devoid of a central inflation.

Diameter 30-45 $\mu$.

Wood Lake, northern New Jersey, furnished scores of specimens of this species the past summer, 1883.

C. BIRETUM, Breb. Plate XX, figs. 1, 2.

Subquadrangular or polygonal; a deep constriction forms a narrow linear sinus; semi-cells obtuse-quadrangular, with subreniform base, and end broad, subplane-convex, dilated; cytioderm rough with pearl-like granules arranged in concentric series; end view shows a prominent central swelling.

Diameter 55-60 $\mu$.

Rather rare, singly among other *Algæ*, but occasionally in quantities. Had a cluster of *Oedogonium* from a sluggish stream near Closter, N. J., literally covered with specimens of this species.

Var. FLORIDENSE, Wolle. Plate XLVI, fig. 6.

Differs from the typical form in its somewhat larger size, but principally in the retuse ends.

Diameter 70 $\mu$.

Frequent along the shores of lake at Kissimme, Florida.

C. CAELATUM, Ralfs. Plate XXI, figs. 46, 47, 48.

Suborbicular, deeply constricted, sinus narrow linear; semi-cells subsemicircular, diameter equal to twice the length; margins scolloped or broadly crenate, with four crenatures at the **end**, one on each side at the base, and **one** intermediate between it and the end; the lateral, basal ones are the largest; membrane sulcated between the crenatures; rough with pearly granules; end view oval, **somewhat inflated at the middle.**

Diameter 40 $\mu$., more or less.

A distinct species which turns **up** frequently **in smaller** numbers.

C. QUADRIFARIUM, Lund. Plate XX, figs. 16, 17, **18.**

**About** one-fourth longer than broad, deeply constricted, sinus narrow linear; semi-cells, semicircular; inferior angles nearly right; margin composed of 17 emarginate-truncate verrucae; within the margin a similar series; basal tumor **orbicular, furnished** with 12–17 **larger** granules; viewed **from the** vertex, elliptic, with a granulated **tumor on the** middle of each **side, and** four series of **granules extending from end to end**; lateral view has a granulated swelling on **each side and four** granules on the end terminating four **series. Two** chlorophyllous nuclei in each semi-cell.

Diameter 33–36 $\mu$.; length 40–44 $\mu$.

Frequent in ponds, Mt. Everett, Mass.

C. KJELLMANII, Wille. Plate LX, figs. 19, 20, 21.

Nearly equal in length and breadth, deeply constricted in the middle, sinus linear with mouth considerably **ampliated;** semi-cells cordiform, sides **nearly** straight, or low **convex;** apex truncate with four or six light crenulations; the sides each with six indentations; granules arranged in radiating lines, none in the center, but a basal tumor has five vertical series **of granules;** observed from the vertex the semi-cells are narrow **elliptic,** with a tumor on each side.

Diameter 20–25 $\mu$.

Wood Lake, **Sussex County, New Jersey.**

C. SUBCRUCIFORME, Lagh. Plate XLIX, figs. 12–14.

Small, somewhat circular, the constriction introrsely and extrorsely ampliated; semi-cells reniform, the end rounded, not crenulate; angles rounded verrucose with margins denticulate; a central inflation granulate; in vertical view subcruciform, angles granulate; in lateral view ovate-circular. Membrane punctate.

**Diameter** of cell 32 $\mu$.; **length 36 $\mu$.; thickness 25 $\mu$.**

Reminds one of *C. ornatum*, Focke, and also of *C. subreniforme*, Nord.

Tewksbury, Massachusetts.

C. BLYTTII, Wille.   Plate XXII. figs. 31, 32, 33.

Small, somewhat longer than broad; semi-cells subreniform, apex truncate with four crenulations; sides erose-crenate (crenae three); semi-cells within the margin, granulate, granules arranged in two series of about fourteen and nine; in center a small prominence. Lateral view circular with a papilla on each side; end view elliptic, with a prominence or papilla on each side.

Diameter 14–15 $\mu$.; length 17–18 $\mu$.

Waters of Sussex County, N. J.; Longwood Pond; Wood Lake.

C. SPECIOSUM, Lund.   Plate XXII, figs. 7, 8, 9; 14, 15.

Cells about one and one-half times longer than wide; elliptic-oblong, constriction forms a narrow linear sinus; semi-cells with sides slightly convex, but moderately converging to the subtruncate end; inferior angles nearly square, base plane; margins crenate, crenae eighteen; within the margins granulate; granules arranged in regularly radiating, and concentric series; at the base seven to eight vertical series of smaller granules; viewed from the vertex elliptic with a central inflation, ends crenulate; lateral view subovate; thickness of cells about one-half of the diameter of the cell; isthmus equal to about one-third of the measure of the breadth.

Diameter 33–50 $\mu$.; length 50–75 $\mu$.

The plants recognized as the *C. speciosum* of Lundell, are usually larger than the Swedish forms, but they have the same outline, truncate end, swollen centers, arrangement of granules and crenulate margins.

C. SUPRASPECIOSUM, Wolle.   Plate LXI, figs. 5, 6.

Large, broadly oval, about one-third longer than broad, ends truncate; deeply constricted; isthmus rather less than a third part of the breadth of the cell; sinus narrow linear; margins crenulate with thirty or more crenae to each semicell; usually about sixteen on each side and five or six on the truncate end; ornate with large undivided granules arranged in concentric and at the same time, radiating series, extending from the margin nearly half way to the center; central area nude except five or six vertical series of smaller granules; end view shows a prominent central **inflation**; lateral view **broadly** ovate, sinuate towards the **ends**.

Diameter 65-70 $\mu$.; length 90-95 $\mu$.

> Occurs frequently in **ponds, northern New Jersey** and in Pennsylvania.

C. PECTINOIDES, Wolle.   **Plate XXII**, figs. 12, 13.

Suborbicular, **somewhat longer** than broad, constriction deep, sinus narrow linear within and widening outwardly; semi-cells semiorbicular with the angles rounded, undulate on the margins **with** twenty or more crenulations; rough with geminate **rows** of pearly granules symmetrically arranged **in** radiating **and concentric** lines. On green cells the united twinned granules appear oblong and the crenulations dentate; at the base of the semi-cells the inflation is marked with **six, more or less distinct, vertical series of** smaller granules; **end and side view evidence a distinct basal** protuberance.

**Diameter 45 $\mu$.; length 60 $\mu$.; somewhat variable in size.**

> A resemblance to forms of many seaside shells suggested the name. Not abundant, but is found frequently in smaller ponds of Pennsylvania and New Jersey.
>
> This form is near *C. pulcherrimum*, Nord., but differs in **the** gaping sinus, the rounded inferior angles of the semi-cells, the number of crenulations, and larger size.

C. PSEUDOPECTINOIDES, Wolle.   Plate XXII, figs. 16, **17**, **18**.

Differs from the typical plant in its smaller size, **less number of crenulations, and absence of the series of granules on the basal inflation;** instead the granules are scattered.

Diameter 30-35 $\mu$.

> Have this form from Florida, from the White Mountains, N. H., and the Lehigh Valley, Pa.

C. NASUTUM, Nord.   Plate XXII, fig. 19.

Nearly one-fourth longer than broad, constriction forms a narrow linear sinus; semi-cells semicircular, margins incised-crenate, crenae eight, smooth or granulate; cytioderm rough with eight radiating series of granules; end view oval with an inflation on each side.

Diameter 30-36 $\mu$.

> Rare, differs from the typical, Arctic form in being smoother, not so strongly marked with coarse granules.

C. PYCNOCHONDRUM, Nord.   Plate XXII, figs. 10, 11.

About one-fifth longer than the diameter; subhexagonal, constriction deep, sinus narrow linear; ends truncate quadricrenate; angles inferior and superior obtusely rounded; sides moderately convex with about six crenae each; at base nine to twelve vertical, or somewhat diverging series of granules; membranes ornate with additional granules arranged in lines, at the same time radiating and concentric; the former courses are double, and often triple near the margin; central area within the concentric rows, is nude. Seen from the vertex, or from the side, a basal inflation is evident; thickness of the cells, equal to about half the length; isthmus measures about half as much as the breadth.

Diameter 50 $\mu$.; length 79 $\mu$.

The only locality from which I had this form is Nebraska Notch, Vt., from collections made by C. G. Pringle. It differs from the typical, Arctic (Spitzbergen) form in its greater proportionate length.

C. PULCHERRIMUM, Nord.   Plate LX, figs. 25-27.

Cells oblong, ends rounded, about one-third part longer than broad, margins crenulate, constriction deep, sinus narrow linear, not ampliated towards the mouth; semi-cells subsemicircular, inferior angles square, basal center inflated and furnished with about five vertical series of granules; lateral view broadly ovate, end rounded, and base of each side more or less inflated; membrane granulate near the margins, granules arranged in about four to five concentric series; area nude between these and the vertical series.

Diameter 33 $\mu$.; length 40 $\mu$.

This desmid is proportionately shorter than the typical forms described by Dr. Nordstedt. The one from Brazil and the other from the island of Spitzbergen, which measures one and one-third to nearly twice as long as wide. My specimens are from Minnesota, and from several localities of eastern Pennsylvania.

C. RADIOSUM, Wolle.   Plate XXII, figs. 21, 22.

Cells orbiculate, about one-eighth longer than broad; semi-cells semicircular, separated by a deep narrow linear sinus; ends round or slightly depressed, clothed with semiorbicular granules arranged in about thirty-five radiating lines; basal inflation has about eight vertical, or somewhat diverging series of granules; lateral view subrectangular oblong; end view elliptic with central inflation.

Diameter 50 $\mu$.; length 56–58 $\mu$.

Sluggish waters, Northampton Co., Pa.

### Genus, TETMEMORUS, Ralfs.

Cells cylindrical or fusiform, slightly constricted in the middle, narrowly incised at each end, but otherwise entire. Cytioderm mostly punctate or granulate.

The cells are elongated as in *Penium*, from which, however, this genus may be distinguished by the incised ends and by the central constriction.

T. BREBISSONII, (Menegh.), Ralfs. Plate XXIII, figs. 1–2; Plate LXI, fig. 36.

Cells in front view cylindrical, not attenuated at the truncately rounded ends; in lateral view fusiform, attenuated from the middle to the rounded ends; cytioderm striately punctate. Cells four to six times longer than broad.

Diameter 18–20 $\mu$.

Frequent in ponds everywhere.

Var. TURGIDUS, Ralfs. Plate XXIII, figs. 4, 5.

This variety is larger, the constriction greater, and the semi-cells somewhat inflated. It approaches in form *T. granulatus*, but is more constricted at the middle, its punctae are arranged in longitudinal lines, and front and side views are unlike.

Diameter 40–48 $\mu$.

T. GRANULATUS, Ralfs. Plate LXI, figs. 33, 34.

Cells five to six times longer than broad, both in front and lateral views, fusiform, and ending in colorless projecting lip-like process; slightly constricted in the middle. Chlorophyl usually with a longitudinal series of large granules. Membrane irregularly punctate.

Diameter 38–50 $\mu$.

Frequent in ponds, and readily recognized by its figure, both in front and lateral views, fusiform.

T. LAEVIS, (Kg.), Ralfs. Plate LXI, fig. 35; Plate XXIII, fig. 3.

In front view somewhat tapering with truncate ends; lateral view fusiform; punctae none, or very indistinct; four to six times longer than broad.

Diameter 20–22 $\mu$.

Not so frequent as the preceding, but not confined to any particular localities.

T. MINUTUS, D. By.  Plate XXIII. figs. 7, 8, 9.

Smaller than the preceding, only three times longer than broad, membrane smooth.

Diameter 18-20 $\mu$.

Had this species from Florida, New Jersey and Pennsylvania.

T. GIGANTEUS, Wood.  Plate XXIII, fig. 6; Plate XII, fig. 1.

Very large, oblong, three times longer than broad, with the ends not usually attenuate but broadly rounded; suture profound, linear; cytioderm irregularly granulately punctate; somewhat plicate at the base of the semi-cells; cells often contracted near the end.

Diameter 75 $\mu$. more or less.

Ponds, Pennsylvania and New Jersey.

*Genus*, XANTHIDIUM. Ehrb.

Cells single or geminately concatenate, inflated, profoundly constricted; semi-cells compressed, entire, spinous, protruding in the center as a rounded, truncate, or denticulate tubercle. Cytioderm firm, the spines with which it is armed, simple or bi-tri-furcately divided at the ends. Zygospores globose, smooth or spinous.

X. ARMATUM, (Breb.), Ralfs.  Plate XXIV, figs. 1-4.

Semi-cells largest at the base, about as long as broad, armed with numerous, short, stout spines terminated by two, three or more diverging points.

Diameter 62-140 $\mu$.

Very variable in size. Fig. 1 is a finely developed form from Mt. Everett, Mass. The other two are more usual varieties found in all the States with which I had any communication.

This is the only species with spines divided at the apex. Wood has two more, as *X. arctiscon* and *X. coronatum*, but these must be separated from this genus, and placed with *Staurastrum*.

The following have subulate spines:

X. ACULEATUM, (Ehrb.), Breb.  Plate XXVI, figs. 10, 11, 12.

Spines subulate, more or less scattered; central projection truncate, obscurely dentate.

Diameter 62-70 $\mu$.

Prof. Bailey reports this species from South Carolina, Georgia and Florida.

X. COLUMBIANUM. **Wolle.** Plate XLV, figs. 10, 11.

Cells about one-third longer than wide; divided by a deep constriction forming much ampliated, acute-angled sinuses; semi-cells oblong hexagonal, superior and lateral angles each produced into a firm **aculeus**; within the margins, four, often indistinct, aculei; end view more or less regular hexagonal, each angle somewhat produced and surmounted by a firm aculeus; within the margin are four aculei, the ends of which often extend over the margin; cytioderm smooth.

Diameter 60 $\mu$.; length 80 $\mu$., **without aculei**.

Pond, Ocean County, New Jersey.

X. BISENARIUM, Ehrb. Plate XXVI, figs. 7, 8, 9.

Cells in front view broader than long; constriction **deep**, sinus acute angled; spinous; spines subulate, **marginal**, geminate; central projection somewhat truncated and margined with pearly **granules**.

Diameter 65-73 $\mu$.

West Point, N. Y. (Bailey.)

Ralfs suggests that this is the same as his *X. Brebissonii*. The number of spines appears to be variable. Bailey and Ehrenberg's figures have six pairs of spines, Brebisson's, eight; whilst some British specimens have ten to each semi-cell.

X. CRISTATUM, (Breb.), Ralfs. **Plate XXIV, figs. 5-8.**

Semi-cells with a solitary spine on each side at the base, the other spines geminate, in four pairs. Central protuberance, short **conical**.

Diameter 40-55 $\mu$.

Pennsylvania, New Jersey, South Carolina, Georgia, **etc.**

X. ASTEPTUM, Nord. Plate XXIV, figs. 9, 10, 11.

About one-fourth longer than wide; semi-cells octangular-oval, or truncate-triangular, with **two** diverging, somewhat curved, subulate spines on each side, and two geminate spines at each of the two superior angles. **Cytioderm** smooth or **punctate**.

Diameter 40-48 $\mu$, without the spines.

**Rather rare**; quiet waters, Pennsylvania and New Jersey.

X. FASCICULATUM, (Ehrb.), Ralfs.  Plate XXV, figs. 4, 5.

Semi-cells with four, rarely six pairs of long, subulate, marginal, spreading spines; central projection, minute conical, not beaded.

Diameter 55–65 $\mu$. without the spines.

Var. HEXAGONUM, Wolle.  Plate XXVI, fig. 5.

Large angular, with four pairs of short subulate spines.

Var. MINUS, Wolle.  Smaller in size, and spines short.

Plate XXV, figs. 6, 7, front and lateral view of a semi-cell which appears to develop a sporangium without copulation. I found but one specimen of the kind, and record it as a peculiar abnormal act.

Var. SUBALPINUM, Wolle.  Plate XLV, fig. 9.

Prof. Delponte, in his DESMIDIACEARUM SUBALPINARUM, p. 168, describes this species differently from that described above, the variation being mainly in the wider separation of the lateral spines. To distinguish the two I make the above variety.

Not rare in ponds, New Jersey and Minnesota.

X. ANTILOPÆUM, (Breb.), Kg.  Plate XXVI, figs. 1, 2.

Differs from the preceding in smaller size than the typical *X. fasciculatum*, and in the reverse curvature of the lateral spines.

Diameter 45–50 $\mu$.

Var. POLYMAZUM, Nord.  Plate XXVI, figs. 3, 4.

Unlike the true form in the series of bead-like granules over the central protuberance.

Var. TRIQUETRUM, Lund.  Plate XXV, figs. 1, 2, 3.

Instead of an oval, end view, this is triangular, similar to a form discovered by the author (Lund.) in Sweden, and to another from Brazil, described by Dr. Nordstedt.

The only locality for this variety, hitherto found, is a trench near Quakertown, Bucks County, Pa. The other forms may be called common.

Var. MINNEAPOLIENSE, Wolle.  Plate LXIII, fig. 16.

A new form from Minneapolis, Minn., possessing the peculiarity of a fifth pair of aculei immediately over the central protuberance and bead-like series of granules.

Var. TRUNCATUM, Hast.  Plate XLII, figs. 3–5.

Front, lateral and end views. Same as *X. Tylerianum*,

West. The former was published a year earlier than West's name, hence stands by right of precedence.

This variety differs in having the spines **at the superior angles** deflected horizontally and continuous with the margin of the truncate or slightly convex ends of cell.

> Ponds and streams, Rochester, New Hampshire, and Amherst, Mass.

**Var.** CANADENSE, Joshua. Plate XLIII, figs. 2, 3.

Front and end views. Cytioderm minutely punctate, possessing no protuberance or granulation, resembling the var. *Minneapoliense* in the possession of a fifth pair of spines, the extra pair in the center of each semi-cell.

> **Pictou,** Nova Scotia.
> Diameter of cells (S. acul.) 45–50 $\mu$. of all the varieties.

X. RECTOCORNUTUM, Wolle. Plate XXV, figs. 10, 11.

Cells as long as wide; constriction linear, sinus sometimes slightly excavated, and sometimes gaping; semi-cells semi-circular, finely punctate or smooth; two rows of beads above **the** central protuberance, the one with 6–10, and the other under it with half the number; another series of beads on **the** base forming a ring around the isthmus; ends broadly rounded, nude; basal angles with two pairs of aculei, or subulate spines; the one horizontal, the other vertical; transverse view somewhat in the form of an hourglass, truncate, crenate at the ends with **two** vertical aculei in the center.

Diameter without spines, **55–60** $\mu$.

> Frequent in ponds, Mount Everett, Mass.
>
> This species differs from *X. antilopaeum* in having the ends of the cells bare, the upper pairs of spines not incurved nor divergent, but erect, straight, attached to the sides, and springing from the basal angle. It is also quite unlike that species in **the** three series of beads, and in its transverse view.

X. TETRACENTROTUM, Wolle. Plate XXV, figs. 8, 9.

About as long as broad, smooth, constriction deep, sinus enlarged outwardly; semi-cells subreniform or subhexagonal, base somewhat convex, ends broadly rounded; basal angles on each side armed with **a pair** of subulate spines; central protuberance low, over it sometimes a series of bead-like granules.

**Diameter 33–37** $\mu$., without spines; 60 $\mu$. with spines.

> Pond, Sussex Co., N. J.
>
> The form and character of this species is very near *C. antilopaeum*, but it is smaller and bears only two pairs of aculei, not four or six.

## Genus, ARTHRODESMUS, Ehrb.

Cells simple, compressed, deeply constricted in the middle; semi-cells broader than long, with a single spine or mucro on each side, but otherwise smooth and entire.

A. CONVERGENS, (Ehrb.), Ralfs.   Plate **XXVI**, figs. 19, 20, 21.

Semi-cells elliptic, each having its spines curved towards those of the other semi-cell.

Diameter 38–40 $\mu$.

> Several varieties are acknowledged to this species, one with shorter and almost straight spines, another with broadly fusiform cells. Plate XXVI, figs. 22, 23, I place with the varieties.

This species is common.

A. FRAGILIS, Wolle.   **Plate XXVI, figs. 16, 17, 18.**

Semi-cells broad, **oblong-oval**; aculei straight and parallel, *i. e.*, the aculeus of one semi-cell is parallel with that of the other; deciduous. Chlorophyllous nuclei, two.

Diameter 33–38 $\mu$.; length somewhat less.

> Central New Jersey, pond at Hammonton, and other waters.

A. RAUII, **Wolle.**   Plate XXVI, figs. 13, 14, 15.

**Cells slightly** longer than broad, aculeated or verrucose; **aculei short and** stout, deciduous, leaving, after falling off, **large verrucae;** usually six on the margin of each end, and **two** curved series of about **six** each on the membrane within **margin;** semi-cell broadly elliptic, with a single outwardly curved aculeus at each end.

Diameter of cell without **aculei** 38 $\mu$.; **with** aculei 63 $\mu$.

> This species **was collected** with **swamp** moss (*Sphagnum*), by E. A. Rau, in a pond near Newfield, **N. J.** It bears some resemblance to *A. divergens*, Rab., but it is not *subtilissime verrucolosus;* also to *A. quadridens*, Wood, but it is twice the **size of** that plant, and not *quadridens*.

A. OVALIS, Wolle.   Plate XXVII, figs. 13, 14.

Cells small, smooth, often about one-fourth longer than wide; semi-cells oval, armed at each end with a straight or **diverging** aculeus.

Diameter 20 $\mu$., without aculei.

> Ponds, Mt. Everett, Mass.
> The smaller size, the straight, **erect** or slightly diverging spines, I **consider sufficient to separate** this form from *A. convergens*.

A. SUBULATUS, Kg. Plate XXVII, figs. 11, 12.

Semi-cells elliptic, larger than the preceding, with long, subulate, erect or somewhat diverging spines.

Diameter 30–35 $\mu$.

Ponds, New Jersey; rather rare. I have somewhat modified the original diagnosis, by putting *diverging* for *converging*, and thus claim for this plant a distinct position.

A. ORBICULARIS, Wolle. Plate XXVII, figs. 15, 16.

Very small, smooth, orbicular; semi-cells united by a narrow isthmus; aculei of the two semi-cells nearly parallel.

Diameter, without aculei, 12 $\mu$.

Ponds, Mt. Everett, Mass.

A. QUADRIDENS, Wood. Plate XXVII, figs. 17, 18.

Broadly oval or suborbicular, a little longer than broad, with the margin crenately undulate; semi-cells somewhat reniform, at each end armed with a subulate, moderately robust, acute, recurved, large spine; cytioderm with a few smallish tubercles arranged in three or four rows; semi-cells from the vertex acutely elliptical, with the margin crenate and the surface sparsely warty.

Diameter 19 $\mu$.; length 30 $\mu$.

Saco Lake, N. H., (Lewis) Wood.

A. INCUS, (Ehrb.), Hass. Plate XXVII, figs. 1-10.

Cells minute, smooth, as long as, or longer than broad, constriction a deep notch or sinus; semi-cells with inner or lateral margins turgid; outer, truncate; spines diverging, subulate, acute; sporangium orbicular, spinous; spines subulate.

Diameter very variable 10–36 $\mu$.

Turned up frequently in every State in which explorations have been made.

A. OCTOCORNIS, Ehrb. Plate XXVII, figs. 19-23.

Smooth, about as long as wide; the sinus produced by a deep constriction, a wide notch. Semi-cells much compressed, trapezoid, each angle terminating by one or two subulate, acute spines; the intervals between the spines concave. Some specimens without reference to size, have two spines at each angle.

Diameter 16–25 $\mu$.

Not abundant, but scattered from Maine to Florida.

A. INCRASSATUS, Lagh.  Plate X, fig. 6.

A large form, deeply constricted, sinus largely ampliated outwardly; semi-cells subellipsoid, sides convex, ends highly arched, superior angles surmounted each with a nearly straight aculeus; in middle two series of granules arched, nearly parallel with the ends; in vertical view rhomboid-elliptic; in lateral view somewhat circular; membrane in middle thickened and yellowish.

Diameter of cells 40 $\mu$.; length 50 $\mu$., without aculei.

Tewksbury, Massachusetts.

Var. CYCLADATUS, Lagh.

Somewhat smaller, eight granules in the middle of semi-cell, one central and the others in circle around it.

This variety is near my *Xanthidium tetracentrotum*.

Tewksbury, Massachusetts.

A. NOTOCHONDRUS, Lagh.  Plate X, figs. 4, 5.

In size and constriction like *A. incrassatus;* semi-cells sub-semicircular; sides convex, ends straight, with margins moderately granulate; angles armed with a long divergent spine; semi-cells in vertical view elliptic, with three longitudinal series of granules; in lateral view subcircular.  Membrane smooth, in middle somewhat thickened and yellowish.

Diameter of cells, without spines, 30 $\mu$.; length 32 $\mu$.

Tewksbury, Massachusetts.

A. TRIANGULARIS, Lagh.  Plate X, figs. 14, 15.

Sinus between the semi-cells wide, obtuse; semi-cells triangular, connected by a cylindrical isthmus, ends somewhat retuse in middle; angles subacute bearing a long straight spine, either parallel or slightly converging; semi-cells in vertical view lanceolate-oval; in lateral view subcircular. Membrane hyaline, in middle not thickened.

Diameter, without spines, 25 $\mu$.; length 30 $\mu$.

Georgia.

A. PACHYCEROS, Lagh.  Plate X, figs. 12, 13.

Cells small, constriction an acute-angled sinus; semi-cells suboval, sides convex, end arched, angles obtuse, each bearing a firm spine, straight or slightly bent, diverging; semi-cells in vertical view oval; in lateral view subcircular. Membrane smooth.

Diameter, without spines, 18 $\mu$.

Properly a Cuban plant.  Not sure that it was found within our borders.

### Genus, EUASTRUM, Ehrb.

Cells oblong or elliptic, deeply constricted into two semi-cells which are emarginate and usually incised at their **ends**; sides symmetrically sinuate or lobed; provided with **circular** inflated protuberances (rarely absent); viewed from the vertex, elliptic. Zygospores spherical, tuberculose or spinous.

E. CRASSUM, (Breb.), **Kg.** **Plate** XXVIII, figs. 1, 2, **3.**

Cells about twice as long as broad, smooth; semi-cells three-lobed; **basal lobes** very broad, with a wide shallow marginal **sinus; terminal lobe** cuneate, partly included in **a** notch formed by the lateral lobes; incision in terminal **lobe** linear or acute angled.

Diameter 68–82 $\mu$.

A **large, and** not rare plant in shallow **spring, and** pond **waters.**

Var. SCROBICULATUM, Lund. **Plate XXIX, figs. 4, 5.**

In outline very nearly the same **as the** type form, but differs in having in the middle of the semi-cell four scrobiculae. **Lundell represents only two;** our form has four; besides these excavations the plant has four papilla-like prominences towards the ends of the semi-cells, **which** I do not find alluded to; they may give claim for a distinct species.

**Pond, Malaga, New Jersey.**

E. ORNATUM, Wood. **Plate** XXVIII, fig. 4.

A species which **is very** close to *E. crassum*; perhaps **not** separable from it. **The** author, Wood, says "it differs **in** the proportionate length, being only twice instead of three times as long as broad; **in** the size being only three-fourths as large; and especially **in** the peculiar lateral splitting, as **it were,** of the **basal** lobes."

**In** our observations, very few specimens of *E. crassum* ever **exceed** two diameters in length; they vary greatly in size, and the "lateral splitting," a delusive appearance, is common to all of them when the cells are **empty.**

Saco Lake, New Hampshire (Wood).

E. OBLONGUM, (**Grev.**), Ralfs. Plate XXVIII, figs. **5, 6, 7.**

Cells smooth, oblong, semi-cells somewhat five lobed; lobes nearly equal, cuneate; lateral lobes, or the basal only, with a broad, shallow, marginal concavity; all their angles rounded; terminal lobe partly included between the lateral lobes, usually with a linear notch; sometimes this is obsolete or very indistinct.

Diameter 68–75 $\mu$.

This species is very variable, and if the end lobe, fig. 5, were constant with the apex so broadly sinuately excised, it should be separated; it is often incised with an acute-angled notch. The two forms, fig. 5, and fig. 6, are two distinct varieties.

Rhode Island, New Jersey, Pennsylvania, Minnesota, and other States.

E. MULTILOBATUM, Wood. Plate LXIV, fig. 11.

About twice as long as wide, profoundly constricted; sinus moderately large; from the lateral view somewhat enlarged and doubly biumbonate in the middle; semi-cells from the front trilobate, the lobes separated by very wide sinuses; the basal lobe broadly emarginate, the central lobe obtuse, the end lobe broadly and shallowly sinuately emarginate; semi-cells from the vertex five lobed; cytioderm smooth.

Diameter 62 $\mu$.; length 120 $\mu$.

Saco Lake, New Hampshire.
This form, described by Wood, has not yet come across my path.

E. PINNATUM, Ralfs. Plate XXXII, figs. 14, 15, 16.

Semi-cells five lobed; end lobe exserted, dilated, upper margin of all the lobes nearly horizontal. The basal lobes emarginate, and the intermediate ones smaller and entire. Membrane punctate; terminal lobe with a linear notch.

Diameter 60–70 $\mu$.

Meadow and mountain pools, Pennsylvania.

E. HUMEROSUM, Ralfs. Plate XXXII, figs. 12, 13.

Semi-cells with terminal lobe dilated, emarginate, neck sometimes partly included between the elongated lobes which resemble processes; basal lobes large, rounded, emarginate. Cells smooth, two or three times longer than wide; notch of the end lobe indistinct, or short linear.

Diameter about 75 $\mu$.

Sluggish waters, Pennsylvania.
If this form is not identical with Ralfs' figure, it is very near it. The plant bears some evidence of relationship also with *E. crassum* and with *E. oblongum*, and may possibly be merely a variety of these.

E. CUNEATUM, Jenner.   Plate XXIX, figs. 12, 13.
>Semi-cells cuneate, not lobed; terminal notch linear.
>Diameter of cell 24–28 $\mu$.; length about 75 $\mu$.
>>Not rare; seems of rather doubtful value as a species.

E. MAGNIFICUM, Wolle.   Plate XXIX, figs. 6–8.
>The largest of our *Euastra*; about twice as long as broad; semi-cell five lobed, the terminal lobe exserted; dilated, end somewhat convex, connected by a short neck; basal and intermediate lobes entire, with a deep obtuse notch between; upper margin of the basal lobes nearly horizontal and parallel with the base of the semi-cell; no prominent tumors, but one large central undulate inflation shown in lateral view (fig. 7). End view (fig. 8) shows the terminal and intermediate lobes notched at each side.
>Diameter 100 $\mu$.; length about 190 $\mu$.
>>Ponds, near Malaga and Manchester, New Jersey.

Var. CRASSIOIDES, Hastings.
>A form which may be described as intermediate between *E. magnificum* and *E. crassum*. In end view and size it is nearly like the first, but the intermediate lobe is, in this view, rounded, not "notched." In lateral view this lobe is notched and the central inflation is seen to be most prominent near the base of the semi-cell. In front view it has the outlines of *E. crassum*.
>>Collected near Rochester, N. H.

E. WOLLEI, Lagh.   Plate XXXIII, figs. 1–5.
>G. von Lagerheim, of Stockholm, Sweden, has seen fit to change the name of our *E. intermedium*, Cleve, for the reason that he finds that it does not correspond with the Swedish plant so named by Cleve. It has much of the form, but is much larger, having more than twice the diameter and twice the length. Cleve states the diameter of the plant described by him at 44 $\mu$.; and length 77–80 $\mu$. Diameter of our form is 112–120 $\mu$.; length 160–170 $\mu$.; moreover the end of the semi-cell of the Swedish plant is *two*-lobed, ours is *four*-lobed.
>>An apology for the error in choosing the name is unnecessary. Will only remark, a full description of Cleve's plant was not convenient at the proper time.

Var. QUADRIGIBBERUM, Lagh.   Plate XLIX, fig. 29.
>Semi-cells with four horizontal inflations; in vertical view elliptic, apices acuminate, sides quadriundulate.
>>Tewksbury, Massachusetts.

Var. CUSPIDATUM. Wolle. Plate XXXIII, figs. 3, 4, 5.

This variety differs in being more depressed, squatty, in having the lateral lobes cuspidate, end lobe not so wide, and greater thickness to the body of the cell. End view (fig. 5) shows a more angular figure with end lobe cruciform; cytioderm punctate.

> The typical form I found in various places in New Jersey; the variety only in a *Sphagnum* bed in a pond near Newfield, New Jersey.
>
> The original plant was found in Sweden; our true form agrees well in size and figure with it.

E. ANSATUM, (Ehrb.), Ralfs. (*E. Ralfsii*, Rab.) Plate XXVIII, figs. 8, 9, 10; and Plate XXXIII, figs. 11, 12.

Semi-cells inflated at the base, and tapering upwards to the notched but not dilated extremity; end view cruciform. Cytioderm punctate. There appear to be two distinct varieties of this species, perhaps distinct plants; the one twice the size of the other.

Diameter normally 25–36 $\mu$. Var. *major*, diameter 62–74 $\mu$.

> Frequent in ponds and quiet waters, widely distributed. The various sizes may represent different stages of development.

E. DIDELTA. (Turp.), Ralfs. Plate XXXIII, figs. 9, 10.

Cells rather more than twice as long as broad; semi-cells pyramidal, inflated at the base and again at the middle; end scarcely dilated, more or less rounded, notch linear; transverse view shows four shallow lobes on each side and one on each end. Cytioderm punctate.

Diameter 50–62 $\mu$.; length 100–125 $\mu$.

> There is a smaller form which measures about one-fourth less. Specimens often very close to the following, *E. ampullaceum*. Transverse view nearly the same.
>
> Frequent everywhere, north, south and west.

E. PECTINATUM, Breb. Plate XII, figs. 10–12.

Semi-cells three lobed, terminal lobe dilated, usually entire; lateral lobes broad, making the basal portion of the semi-cell somewhat quadrilateral, horizontal, at each side emarginate; lateral view cuneate, with two swellings near the base and one at the apex; transverse view oval with three lobules on each side and one or imperfectly two at each end.

Diameter 40–50 $\mu$.; length about 75 $\mu$.

Minnesota. A number of varieties of this species have been described by specialists in different countries. The present is not Ralfs' type-form, but a variety. It is common in England, but hitherto not found here.

E. VENTRICOSUM, Lund. Plate XXXI, figs. 1-3.

Large, twice as long as wide, outline subelliptic, deeply constricted, sinus narrow linear; semi-cell trilobed, base much dilated, polar lobe short somewhat dilated, incision narrow linear, sides sinuate, two-lobed, superior lobe obtuse tending upward, entire, not bifid in lateral view; basal tumors three, intermediate two, and two in end lobe; in vertical view elliptic, four undulations on each side; in lateral view narrowed towards the ends, sides undulate, apex subtruncate and dilated; shows the superior lateral lobule entire.

Diameter 60–69 $\mu$.; length 105 $\mu$.

Found this plant frequent in pond, Orange County, near Maitland, Florida. Zygospores not infrequent as fig. 1.

E. AMPULLACEUM, Ralfs. Plate XXXII, figs. 8-11.

Semi-cells less in length than breadth, base inflated, not emarginate, but having on each side, near the middle, a small tubercle, or prominence; end lobe exserted and dilated, its notch linear, or somewhat gaping. Membrane minutely punctate. Transverse view, four inflations on each side and one at each end.

Diameter 62–75 $\mu$.

Not as common as the preceding, but not rare.

E. PURUM, Wolle. Plate XXIX, figs. 9-11.

Small, short; semi-cells three-lobed, broader than long; basal lobe much inflated, terminal lobe short, dilated and notched; in lateral view the base and end are more or less inflated.

Diameter 35–45 $\mu$.; length 55–70 $\mu$.

The smaller form from Florida, the larger from New Jersey.

E. AFFINE, Ralfs. Plate XXVIII. figs. 11, 12.

About twice as long as wide; semi-cells three lobed; basal lobes somewhat emarginate; intermediate between them and the end lobe on each side is a prominence, the upper margin of which is nearly horizontal; end lobe exserted, dilated, its notch linear. Cytioderm minutely punctate; transverse view very near the two preceding.

Diameter 45–50 $\mu$.

Pennsylvania and New Jersey, to Georgia.

E. URNAFORME, Wolle.  Plate LXIII, figs. 11, 12.

Cells about one-third longer than broad; semi-cells urn-shaped, three lobed; terminal lobe dilated, centrally sinuate; lateral lobes horizontal with sides converging, sinuate, basal portion protruding, emarginate, upper part broadly rounded, a rounded sinus between them and the end lobe; protuberances, one at each angle of the terminal lobe; one at each of the basal angles, two intermediate, and one between the end and the lateral lobes.

Diameter 50 $\mu$.; length 55–60 $\mu$.

Wood Lake, Passaic County, N. J.

This form is nearest *L. pectinatum*, Breb., but differs in most essential points.

E. VERRUCOSUM, (Ehrb.), Ralfs.  Plate XXX, figs. 1, 5.

Cells somewhat longer than broad; rough with conical granules; terminal lobe cuneate, no incision, but a broad, shallow sinus; lateral lobes cuneate with ends more or less concave; semi-cells with one large central inflation, and a smaller one on each side; two on the end lobe.

Diameter about 75 $\mu$., for larger typical form.

Var. SIMPLEX, Joshua.  Jour. Bot., Feb., 1885.  Plate XLII, figs. 12, 13.

Of stout habit, terminal lobe very short and with shallow incision; central inflation either none or very small; no other. It is nearest to the *Cosmarium* in Reinsch's contribution. Plate XVI, fig. 9, the verrucae are perhaps somewhat larger than in the typical plant.

Diameter 65 $\mu$.; length 85 $\mu$.

Canada.

The following varieties deserve a separate note:

Var. CRUX AFRICANUM, Wolle.  Plate XXX, fig. 2.

The more angular, and more distended lobes, give this form a stronger resemblance to an African *Micrasterias*, described by Cohn, and suggests the name.

Pond, eastern Pennsylvania.

Var. ALATUM, Wolle.  Plate XXX, fig. 4.  Very near Corda's *Cosmarium alatum*.

Marsh pools near Minneapolis, Minn., and Bucks Co., Pa.

Var. REDUCTUM, Nord.  Plate XXX, fig. 3.

This specimen does not agree as well as many others found in the same locality and group. I therefore add a translation of the author's diagnosis from his *De Algis—Musci Lugduno-Batavi*:

"Sinus between the semi-cells linear; sides and angles close; end lobe scarcely dilated, apex retuse, middle lobe small; end view rectangular; tumor in the middle of the semi-cell obovate elliptic, others very small."

E. CIRCULARE, (Hass.), Ralfs.  Plate XXXII, figs. 1, 2.

Semi-cells three-lobed, mostly with three basal tubercles; end notched, scarcely dilated.

Ralfs makes three varieties: *a.* semi-cells inflated at the base and attenuated upwards; *b.* semi-cells emarginate at the sides, the basal portion with five tubercles; *c.* emarginate at the sides; tubercles smaller, more numerous and scattered.

Diameter 36 $\mu$., more or less.

Rhode Island, Pennsylvania, New Jersey; common.

E. GEMMATUM, Breb.  Plate XXXII, figs. 3, 4.

About one-half longer than broad; semi-cells three lobed, lateral lobes horizontal, deeply emarginate; the protuberances minutely granulate; terminal lobe dilated, broadly emarginate; transverse view broadly elliptic, with three granulate inflations on each side (not four, as incorrectly drawn) and one at each end; end view shows the terminal lobe, cruciform.

Diameter 38 $\mu$.

Found from Rhode Island to Minnesota, and southward.

E. EVERETTENSE, Wolle.  Plate XXXII, figs. 5, 6, 7.

Cells about twice as long as broad; semi-cells three lobed, basal lobes wide, emarginate; end lobe dilated, notch linear; two larger inflations near the middle, and several smaller ones on each side, and on end lobe. Transverse views broadly elliptic, with two protuberances on each side; side view shows one inflation on each side.

Diameter 50–55 $\mu$.

Collected in ponds, Mount Everett, Mass.

This form bears some resemblance to *E. affine*, but it is clearly separable by the broad basal lobe, by the absence of the intermediate prominences, and by the arrangement of the protuberances which produce distinct forms in transverse and lateral views.

E. INSIGNE, Hass.   Plate XXXI, figs. 39–43.

Semi-cells longer than broad, inflated at the base, sides entire, and tapering into a long slender neck; end lobe dilated with linear notch; end view quadrangular, with angles slightly protruding, and a swelling on each of the shorter sides; end lobe cruciform as shown on the middle of fig. **43**.

Diameter 30–35 $\mu$.

Rhode Island, Massachusetts, Pennsylvania, New Jersey and Florida.

E. MAMMILLOSUM, Wolle.   Plate XXX, figs. 14, 15.

**Cells in** length twice the diameter; semi-cells three lobed; basal lobes wide and nearly half as high as the semi-cell, drawn out in the center **into** a narrow column one-third **to** one-fourth the diameter **of** the body; dilated at the end, sinuate, four-parted; **base** with six mammiform protuber**ances**; membrane punctate; end view oval with three diverging mammiform prominences at each end.

Diameter of center of cell 68 $\mu$.; length 118 $\mu$.

Ponds, Mount Everett, Mass., and Sussex County, N. J.

E. HASTINGSII, Wolle.   Plate XLII, figs. **16,** 17.

Cells small, a little **more than one and** one-half **times as long as** broad; semi-cells three lobed, **lateral lobe horizontal, deeply** emarginate; terminal lobe a stout **column rather more than** one-third diameter **of the body and about the** same height, dilated **at the** end, apex **ornamented by a row** of tubercles, giving it a crenulate appearance; **lateral view similar** except that the **basal** lobes are one-third **or one-fourth narrower**; transverse **view** broadly elliptic, with **three inflations on** each side and **one** on each end; end view **shows terminal lobe a crenulate circle of about** a dozen **tubercles.**

Diameter 35–40 $\mu$.

Coll., W. N. Hastings, Cocheco River, New Hampshire.

E. ATTENUATUM, Wolle.   **Plate** XXX, fig. 17.

**Small,** twice as long as wide; semi-cells three lobed, basal lobes broad, emarginate; terminal lobe a column with nearly parallel sides, apex truncate.

Diameter 35 $\mu$.

Rather rare, but I found a considerable number in swamp **pools,** Bucks County, Pa., and near Ocean Beach, N. J.

E. Donnellii, Wolle.  Plate XXX, fig. 6.

Broadly ovate, somewhat longer than broad, profoundly constricted in the middle, sinus linear; semi-cells trilobed; basal lobes orbicularly tumid; terminal lobes semiorbicular; margin of each side armed with seven or eight short, stout, conical teeth. Semi-cells with one larger central and four smaller inflations; three of them in a series on basal part, and two on the end lobe. Cytioderm punctate.

Diameter 38 $\mu$.; length 54 $\mu$.

Florida. Coll., J. Donnell Smith.

E. formosum, Wolle.  Plate XXX, fig. 16.

Nearly twice as long as broad, oval in outline; semi-cell with six marginal lobes, apices trifid, or tridentate; central tooth erect and the other two divergent; the sections of the two basal lobules more rudimentary than the others. Cytioderm smooth.

Diameter 40 $\mu$.; length 62 $\mu$.

This plant bears some likeness to *E. Nordstedtianum*, but is separated from it by the less prominent teeth, and especially by the vertical position of the end lobules and the wide sinus between them.

E. divaricatum, Lund.  Plate XXX, figs. 18, 19.

Cells one-fourth longer than broad, constriction deep, sinus linear; semi-cells subtriangular, gradually narrowing from a broad base to a truncate apex; sides undulate; polar lobe short, not dilated, linearly notched; angles of the terminal lobe, and of the basal lobe, armed each with a short aculeus; vertical view elliptic, middle of each side granulate dentate, ends also dentate.

Diameter 32–36 $\mu$.; length 40–45 $\mu$.

Occasional in ponds, Pennsylvania and New Jersey.

E. Pokornyanum, Grun.  Plate XXXI, figs. 33, 34, 35.

Semi-cells trilobed; basal lobes, margins crenate or emarginate; terminal lobe erect, subcuneate, truncate, incised; membrane smooth.

Diameter 17–20 $\mu$.; length equal to two diameters.

Rather common, often intermingled with the following two forms which are so nearly allied, that it is almost impossible to separate them.

E. EROSUM, Lund.

Very near the preceding; in front view barely separable. End lobe usually rather wider, and not so deeply incised; notch obtuse-angled. End and lateral views somewhat quadrangular with ends imperfectly tricrenate.

E. INSULARE, Witt.

This form the author gives as a variety of *E. binale*. I prefer it separated because the basal lobes are emarginate, corresponding with the preceding two. It is distinguished by a greater breadth of the terminal lobe and the absence of an incision or notch; sometimes slightly sinuate. Size rather less.

E. INERME, Lund. Plate XXXIII, figs. 6-8; Plate XXXI, figs. 30, 36.

Subelliptic; semi-cells subtriangular, apex somewhat protracted, truncate, deeply incised, not dilated or dentate; sides biundulate, the basal crenae most prominent, obtuse, and angle obliquely truncate; tumors three, inconspicuous and sometimes wanting; end view subelliptic, sides bigibbous; side view ovate. Membrane finely punctate.

Diameter 32-38 $\mu$.

Rather common.

E. CRASSICOLLE, Lund. Plate XXXI, figs. 37, 38.

About twice as long as wide; sinus narrow linear; semi-cells slightly attenuated, three lobed; lateral lobes, lightly sinuate-bilobulate; polar lobe broad, barely dilated, apex emarginate; end view hexagonal, poles truncate, middle inflated.

Diameter 14 $\mu$.; length 28 $\mu$.

New Jersey — not frequent.

E. CUSPIDATUM, Wolle. Plate XXXI, fig. 32.

Diameter slightly less than length; semi-cells distinctly three lobed, basal lobes extending laterally their own width; end lobe subrectangular, twice the width of the other lobes, obtusely sinuate in the center; ends of the rounded basal lobes and of the two sections of the end lobe, surmounted each with three firm, diverging aculei.

Diameter without aculei 25 $\mu$.; with them 33 $\mu$.

Pond, Absecom, N. J. Coll., H. D. Kitchel, 1882.

E. PINGUE, Elf.  Plate XXXI, figs. 1, 2, 3.

Somewhat longer than broad; semi-cells three lobed, **each** lobe globularly rounded; the polar lobe with a small notch; side view oval with ends slightly truncate-crenate; end and side views show a slight central inflation of semi-cells. Isthmus about one-fourth the diameter of the cell.

Diameter 35–45 $\mu$.

Ponds, Atlantic **and** Passaic Counties, N. **J.** Our plants are often without the terminal notch, but otherwise so near the form described by Elfving, I adopt the name he has given.

E. NORDSTEDTIANUM, Wolle.  **Plate XXX, figs.** 7-13; and Plate LXIII, figs. 13–15.

Cells quadrangular-oblong, **not quite** twice as long as broad; semi-cells obscurely three lobed; basal lobes broad, each divided in the middle by a rounded notch into two lobules with tridentate or spinous ends; end lobe short, more or less emarginate, the two sides of the apex usually somewhat reflexed, with a subacute **or rounded** notch between; lateral margins furnished with two or three horizontal spines. End, transverse and side views (Plate LXIII, figs. 13, 14, 15) rectangular, with broad, square, and more or less sinuate **sides and ends; angles dentate.**

Diameter 45–50 $\mu$.; length 70–75 $\mu$.

Frequent in pond near **Minneapolis, Minn.; rarer in** New Jersey and Pennsylvania.

E. ELEGANS, Kg.  **Plate** XXXI, figs. **10-16; 25, 26.**

Oblong, one and one-half to two times as long as wide; central constriction **narrow** linear; semi-cells with sides somewhat converging, with a constriction near the truncate, angular end, and another, often very slight, between this and the base; ends divided by a linear or acute angled notch; side view oblong elliptic, apices acute-conic; end view oval **with** central inflation.

Diameter 18–36 $\mu$.  **Common.**

E. ROSTRATUM, Ralfs.  Plate **XXXI, figs. 8, 9.**

Varies from the preceding in the protuberant, emarginate, **or angular ends** having a prominent, horizontal spine on **each angle.**

E. SPINOSUM, Ralfs.  Plate XXXI, figs. 4–7, 17.

Nearly allied to the two preceding, but separated by the more decided lateral notch **in the** basal lobes forming two distinct lobules, each furnished with, usually, two horizontal or diverging spines. **Somewhat larger.**

Diameter 35-40 $\mu$.

E. INTEGRUM, **Wolle.** Plate XXXI, figs. 18-22.

Another form nearly allied to the above three species or varieties; separated by the absence of the **lower** constriction of the semi-cell. Size variable, diameter 16-36 $\mu$.

. **The preceding four forms** are closely related, and may be accounted mere varieties. They are frequent. Having for comparison, scores of sketches made of plants from as many localities in different States from Vermont to Florida and westward to Minnesota, this division suggested itself as the most feasible and **natural.** I retain the old names, but with somewhat modified diagnosis.

**The same** is described as *E. simplex*, Des. U. S., p. 106. **Since** the publication of the diagnosis, F. Gay, of Montpellier, France, is found to have anticipated the adoption of the same name for **another** *Euastrum* form. Hence we substitute *E. integrum* for *E. simplex*.

E. BINALE, (Turpin), **Ralfs.** Plate XXXI, figs. 23, 24.

Cells minute, **about one-half longer** than broad, oblong-oval; semi-cells with their basal portions entire; slightly **contracted beneath the ends; apex** dilated, its central notch **acute, broad,** gaping. Transverse view with **two** lateral inflations; ends truncate, angles rounded.

Diameter 15-25 $\mu$.

**Plants** of this species have features in common with *E. integrum*, but may be readily recognized by the proportionately shorter form and the pouting separation of the end.

E. COMPACTUM, **Wolle.** Plate XXXI, figs. 28, 29.

Very small, suborbicular, little longer than broad; semi-cell broad, **transversely oval;** apex a slight protuberance with a linear incision; two small prominences, one on each **side of the** apical projection.

Diameter 20-22 $\mu$.; length 28 $\mu$.

Pond, Pennsylvania.

E. OBTUSUM, **Wolle.** Plate XXXI, fig. 31.

Minute, **twice** as long as wide; semi-cells obovate, base **flattened,** sides somewhat diverging, end broadly rounded with linear incision in the center.

Diameter 14 $\mu$.; length 25 $\mu$.

Ponds, Pennsylvania.

E. ABRUPTUM, Nord.  Plate LXIII, figs. 21, 22.

Cells one and one-half times as long as broad; constriction deep, narrow linear; semi-cells trilobed, lateral lobes somewhat protruding above the base, near the middle; ends truncately rounded and usually dentate or granulate; end lobe incised bifid, with exterior angles furnished with short spines; transverse view rectangular with large central inflation, end margin more or less undulate granulate, or sometimes retuse.

Diameter 28–30 $\mu$.; length 40 $\mu$.

Passaic County (Wood Lake), N. J.

This species does not strictly conform to the description of the author, but it has so much in common that with his consent, I adopt the name he chose for his Brazilian plant.

## Genus, MICRASTERIAS, Ag.

Cells simple, lenticular, deeply constricted in the center; viewed from the front, orbicular, or broadly elliptical; from the vertex fusiform with acute ends. Semi-cells three to five lobed; lateral lobes entire or incisely-lobulate; end or polar lobe entire or sinuate or emarginate, and sometimes with angles produced and bifid.

In but few species have the zygospores been detected; they are large, globular and furnished with stout spines, which are at first simple, then become branched at the ends.

SECTION I.—Cell circular; segments five-lobed; lobes approximate, the end lobe narrower.

M. TORREYI, (Bailey), Ralfs.  Plate XXXIV, figs. 1–8.

Circular; lateral lobes deeply incised, making two or three subdivisions to each; all more or less tapering, and acute or bidentate at the extremities. End lobe narrow, not exserted, dilated at apex, concave, angles taper into acute points or spines.

Diameter 250–300 $\mu$.

Frequent in ponds of New Jersey, Mt. Everett, Mass., and few localities in Pennsylvania.

Often variable in the number and form of the subdivisions. Plate XXXIV represents eight varieties, the result of multiplication by dividing. Compare Introduction, page 18.

M. PSEUDOTORREYI, Wolle.  Plate XXXVI, fig. 1.

Large, circular, five-lobed; basal and intermediate lobes bisected, sections more or less conical, ends deeply furcate;

polar lobe broadly cuneate, end truncate-sinuate, angles cuspidate.

Diameter of cell 180 $\mu$.

Mt. Everett, Mass.

Separated from *M. Torreyi*, by its smaller size, the less number of lobules and their greater similarity of form.

M. RADIOSA, (Ag.), Ralfs.   Plate XXXV, figs. 1, 2, 3 ; Plate XLIII, fig. 1.

Cells orbicular, smooth; semi-cells rather indistinctly five lobed; lobes dichotomously divided; ultimate subdivisions, inflated, attenuated, furcate at the ends. End lobe narrow cuneate, emarginate, and its angles dentate.

Diameter 150–200 $\mu$.

A beautiful species and not rare, easily recognized by its many and deep incisions; it is variable in size and number of subdivisions; the latter range from twenty to forty in a semi-cell.

Var. PUNCTATA, West., J. R. M. S., Nov., 1888.   Plate XLIII, fig. 1.

This differs from the usual forms of *M. radiosa* in having a distinctly punctate cytioderm with the division of the lobes more like those of *M. papillifera*, especially the ultimate ones.

Pond, Massachusetts.

M. SWAINEI, Hast.   Plate XLII, fig. 1.

A form very near *M. radiosa*, differing mainly in the usually more or less elongated lower lobe of the basal division of the semi-cell, which is a constant feature; frequent in large gatherings made by Wm. N. Hastings near Rochester, New Hampshire.

Diameter variable, 190–250 $\mu$.

M. SPECIOSA, Wolle.   Plate XLV, figs. 1, 2.

Small, somewhat longer than broad, five lobed; lateral lobes unequal, the basal pair usually with only half as many divisions as the intermediate ones; each basal lobe consisting of one, and the intermediate of two lobulets, the angles of each section drawn out into two spine-like points; terminal lobe rather narrow, linear, the end exserted and much dilated, usually with three prominent mucros at each angle; center an obtuse angled notch, standing free with a rather wide gap between it and the adjoining lobes; a series of small spines often observed on the margins of the lobes.

Diameter 95 μ.; length 110 μ., of specimens from Florida; diameter 125-150 μ.; length 155-165 μ., of New Jersey specimens.

This species appears to be related to *M. radiosa*, var. *ornata*, Nord., but is smaller; the lobes are not so deeply, nor so often intersected, and the **polar lobe is more exserted and more dilated at the end.**

M. PAPILLIFERA, Breb.   Plate XXXVIII, figs. 8, 9.

**Orbicular,** with marginal gland-like teeth; semi-cells five lobed; lateral lobes dichotomously incised; incisions narrow **linear, the principal** sinuses bordered by a row of minute granules. The end lobe about as **wide** as the others, and emarginate, its angles dentate. Endochrome is usually yellowish or brownish green.

Diameter 95-112 μ.

Is found sparsely **in shallow pools, but in a wide range of** many States.

M. ROTATA, (Grev.), Ralfs.   Plate XXXVIII, figs. 1, 2, 3.

Orbicular, smooth; semi-cells five lobed; lobes dichotomously incised with ultimate subdivisions variously bidentate in different plants. End lobe somewhat exserted. **The** basal lobes have each four subdivisions, **and the intermediate lobes each eight.**

Diameter 200-250 μ.

M. DENTICULATA, (Breb.), Ralfs.   Plate XXXVIII, figs. 4-8.

**Near** the preceding, but separated by the usually obtuse **apices of the subdivision, often** more oval form of cells, and **equal number of** subdivisions in the basal and intermediate **lobes; polar lobe** not exserted. Size about the same, **but many smaller varieties.** Common.

M. VERRUCOSA, Roy.   Plate XLVII, fig. 10.

In outline this species agrees with smaller forms of *M. denticulata*, Ralfs, but differs from these and other described forms by the remarkable row of crenulated, circular or oval **basal** inflations, crossing **from** side to side, larger **towards the center,** gradually growing smaller towards the margins.

**The** original type was found in Scotland. The first from **this** country is from a pond near Minneapolis, Minnesota, in collections made by Miss E. Butler.

M. FIMBRIATA, Ralfs. Plate XL, figs. 1–8. Zygospores from Rochester, N. H.

Large circular; semi-cells five lobed; dichotomously incised; end lobe cuneate with a broad, shallow notch, or concave end, and two or three mucros, or spines, at each angle.

The ultimate subdivisions are rounded and slightly emarginate, each furnished with two spines usually divergently curved.

Diameter about 125–250 $\mu$. Frequent.

> Fruiting specimens, not heretofore observed, were received from Rochester, New Hampshire, collected by W. N. Hastings. The zygospores are orbicular, spinulose; spines rather slender, elongate, scattered, mostly furcate at the ends, and sometimes notched below the middle; punctate ends, with tips recurved.
>
> This species is found in various forms, as illustrated by the figures, and may be noted as

Forma,—GENUINA, (figs. 1, 2). The typical plant.

Forma,—NUDA, Wolle, (fig. 4). A form which occurs frequently with almost all the subdivisions nude, devoid of spines.

Forma,—ELEPHANTINA, Wolle, (fig. 3). Of gigantic size, diameter 400 $\mu$.

> Mount Everett, Mass.

Forma,—APICULATA, Menegh., (fig. 2). With series of minute spines bordering the sinuses.

Forma,—SIMPLEX, Wolle, (fig. 8). Small, oval, subdivisions with simply one small mucro.

> This may prove a distinct species; the two specimens I had from Florida were too imperfect from drying for satisfactory identification.

M. BRACHYPTERA, Lund. Plate XXXVI, figs. 6, 7.

About one-third longer than broad, elliptic, deeply constricted in the middle; sinus an acute angle somewhat ampliated; semi-cells five lobed; polar lobes longer than the intermediate lobes and separated from them by a wide sinus; neck moderately distending to the dilated apex; (neck tapering towards the apex, Lund.), depressed center forms a wide, shallow notch. Intermediate and basal lobes short and nearly equal in breadth; twice bisected; apices or lobules furnished each with two rather long, somewhat curved spines; angles and margins of the end lobe, and margins of the other lobes also, provided with a few scattered spines. The figures of two semi-cells show considerable variation in the arrangement of the spines and divisions of lateral lobes.

Diameter 140–150 $\mu$., without spines; length 200–210 $\mu$.

Collected near Minneapolis, Minn., by Miss E. Butler.

SECTION II.—Cells subelliptic; semi-cells three or five lobed; lobes radiate, the end lobe somewhat exserted, divided and arms divergent.

M. FURCATA, (Ag.), Ralfs.   Plate XXXIX, figs. 5, 6.

Cells five lobed; lobes bifid, their divisions linear, divergent, and forked at the apex. The end lobe exserted, its divisions divergent, producing a wide, shallow sinus.

Diameter 150–180 $\mu$.; Common.

Var. SIMPLEX, Wolle.   Plate XLVII, figs. 6, 7.

Cells equal in length and breadth, two lobed, terminal lobe exserted, its divisions spreading and producing a wide, shallow sinus; lateral lobes usually simple, but sometimes divided into two narrow, linear diverging sections, furcate at apices. Length and breadth 140–150 $\mu$.

A singularly variable species. Of the thirty-one fresh specimens examined during a stay at Winter Park, Florida, by Rev. H. D. Kitchel and myself, twenty were found of normal form as upper half of fig. 6, 7, no arms divided; five had all the lateral arms divided, like the lower half of figure; one had two arms divided and two single, like figure; two had only one arm divided, and three had each two arms divided. As two-thirds of the forms examined had all the arms single, this is considered the type; the others, one-third, variable, are varieties.

M. PSEUDOFURCATA, Wolle.   Plate XXXIX, fig. 4.

Five lobed, simple, not bifid; sometimes the lateral lobes appear more like one bifid lobe on each side; in either case only half as many lateral arms as characterize the preceding species, *M. furcata*.

Diameter 150–160 $\mu$.

Not as frequent as the true form, but it has a habitat in many localities in the Middle States.

Var. MINOR, Wolle.   Plate XLI, fig. 11.

Small, not one-half the diameter of the typical form, but so nearly like it in outline, I note it as a variety. Had but two or three specimens, from Minneapolis, Minn.

M. CRUX-MELITENSIS, Ehrb.   Plate XXXIX, fig. 3.

Semi-cells indistinctly five lobed; lobes bifid, subdivisions short, and furcate at the apices.

Plate XLV, figs. 4, 5, two semi-cells differing somewhat from the figures on Plate XXXIX, from Minnesota.

Diameter 100–125 $\mu$.

> Not so frequent as *M. furcata*, to which it often bears a close resemblance; it is similarly divided, but the incisions are not so deep, the subdivisions not so elongated, rather stouter and less divergent; end lobe less exserted.

M. DICHOTOMA, Wolle.   Plate LXIII, fig. 2.

Somewhat longer than broad, smooth or finely punctate; semi-cells three lobed; lateral lobes twice bifid; the ultimate lobules (four resulting from one) deeply furcate or clawed at the ends; the polar or end lobe exserted on a cylindrical neck with two diverging arms clawed at the ends.

Diameter with arms 175–200 $\mu$.; length the same to one-fourth greater. Length of body 115 $\mu$.; breadth of neck 15–17 $\mu$.

> Hitherto found this species in three localities only: ponds, Malaga, and Bamber, N. J., and Harvey Lake, Luzerne County, Pa.

M. RINGENS, Bailey.   Plate XXXIX, figs. 1, 2.

Oblong, semi-cells three lobed, with a series of granules inside of most of the margins; basal lobes divided by a deep notch into two spreading arms, obtuse or slightly dentate at the apices; terminal lobe exserted, emarginate, extremities obtuse.

Diameter 125–150 $\mu$.

> Obtained this species from Florida only, collected by J. D. Smith.

Var. SERULATA, Wolle.   Plate XLVII, fig. 15.

In size and form the same as the original type from Florida. Bailey describes it as "granular near the margins," but not so serrated. This new variety has the margins distinctly serrated, besides having the granules or mucros near the margins.

Diameter 115–130 $\mu$.; length 125–145 $\mu$.

> Found in large numbers in White Bear Lake, Minnesota, by Miss E. Butler.

SECTION III.—End lobe produced into four, more or less diverging, rigid, processes.

M. AMERICANA, (Ehrb.), Kg. Plate XXXVI, fig. 2 and Vars. 3–5.

Semi-cells three lobed; lateral lobes broad, cuneate, their margins concave, incised-serrate; end lobe broad cuneate and exserted, bipartite at the angles; the subdivisions straight, narrow, minutely dentate at the extremities, end concave.

Diameter 100–115 $\mu$.; length about one-third greater.

The wide distribution of this species entitles it to the name it bears.

There are several varieties, the one—

Var. RECTA, Wolle, (fig. 3).

Is distinct in the margin of the polar lobe, which is not concave and bisected, but straight with two small prominences.

Found it in a few localities in Pennsylvania and New Jersey.

Var. HERMANNIANA, Reinsch, (fig. 5.)

Distinct in the angular intersections and regularly serrate margins.

Collected in Florida. It is not an exact counterpart of the plant described by Reinsch, but very near it.

Var. SPINOSA, Turner. Plate XLIX, fig. 30.

A form not strictly from the United States, but near it, may be introduced. Mr. Turner describes it thus: A small compressed form. About one-eighth less in length and breadth than the type. Central portion of segments smooth; lobes ornamented with short stout spines; the end lobe bearing near its extremity a species of annular rugoso spinous coronet.

Diameter 112 $\mu$.; length 136 $\mu$.

Pictou, Nova Scotia.

M. MAHABULESHWARENSIS, Hobson. Plate XLI, fig. 10.

This form stands in close relation with the preceding species and varieties; it is separated by having the lateral lobes only once bisected, not twice. The margins are finely serrated.

Diameter 125 $\mu$., more or less.

Ponds, New Jersey, and eastern part of Pennsylvania.

M. APICULATA, Menegh. Plate XLV, fig. 3.

Large orbicular or oblong, with the surface more or less densely covered with mucros; semi-cells five lobed; lateral lobes equal in size, not close, bisected; lobulets bifid, each section emarginate, mucronate at each angle; polar lobe prominent, widely dilated, center notched, margins mucronate.

Diameter 175-200 $\mu$.

> Ponds, Pennsylvania, New Jersey and Minnesota; rather rare.

M. MAMILLATA, Turner. Plate XLVI, fig. 2.

Semi-cells papilionaceous, five lobed; end lobe broad; its ends and those of the other lobes divided into palmate shapes, with the points broadly rounded; surface adorned with mamilliform processes radiately arranged; provided with a process at isthmus, the purpose of which is apparently (?) to strengthen the segmental union. Only one specimen (semi-cell) seen. Seemingly related to *M. apiculata*.

Diameter 198 $\mu$.

> Inasmuch as this semi-cell was found in collections made in a swampy part of Harvey Lake, Pennsylvania, in which *M. apiculata* occurs freely, the author would emphasize the last remark.

M. ALATA, Wall. Plate XLVI, fig. 1.

In anticipation of the possible discovery of this interesting and unique form in Southern Florida, I quote it from G. von Lagerheim's *Bidrag till Amerikas Desmidie flora*. It is an Indian plant, but is now also found in Cuba. The figure is drawn direct from an India specimen in my herbarium.

M. NORDSTEDTIANA, Wolle. Plate LXIII, figs. 3-5.

Cells of equal length and breadth, smooth; semi-cells three lobed; the lateral lobes divided into two subcylindrical segments with a wide notch between; ends obtuse, furnished with three or four small spines. Polar lobe exserted on a long neck having a short conical prominence about the middle of each side; the ends diverge in two pair composed of one longer and one shorter, nearly horizontal, arms; the two are nearly parallel.

Diameter 150 $\mu$.

> Longwood Pond, Passaic County, N. J., and Harvey Lake, Luzerne County, Pa.
>
> This species has a number of distinct features; the four arms of the end lobe; the protuberances of the neck; the lateral lobes have something in common with *M. ringens*, but they are smooth or finely punctate, not granulate; there is something also to remind one of *M. pseudofurcata*, but the arms are not furcate at the ends.

SECTION IV.—Cells circular; semi-cells obscurely five lobed, the end lobe the broadest.

M. DECEMDENTATA, Naeg. Plate XXXVII, figs. 5, 6.

Suborbicular, granulate-punctate; semi-cells distinctly three lobed, or obscurely five lobed; lateral lobes divided by a small obtuse angled sinus into two lobelets, having straight, truncate margins, angles slightly produced and mucronate; polar lobe broadly truncate, separated from the adjoining lobe by a narrow linear sinus; apex broadly convex, sometimes sinuate, lateral angles slightly produced and mucronate.

Diameter 83–100 $\mu$.

Frequent in Florida; have not found it farther north. It differs from all forms described under this name, particularly in size. The author, *Naegeli*, gives the diameter 40 $\mu$. *Delponte* quotes subalpine forms at 50 $\mu$.; and *Lundell*, the Sweden plant also at 50 $\mu$., which is only half the size of our plant, but omitting the measure, the description proves them identical.

M. CRENATA, (Breb.), Ralfs. Plate XXXVII, figs. 7, 8.

Cells orbicular; semi-cells with five shallow lobes; end lobe very broad, cuneate, end convex, or slightly sinuate on the margin; lateral lobelets nearly entire.

Diameter 75–85 $\mu$.

This species is met with only occasionally, Pennsylvania, New Jersey, Florida.

M. TRUNCATA, (Corda), Ralfs. Plate XLIV, figs. 6–9.

Orbicular; semi-cells five lobed; lateral lobes shallow; end lobe very broad, truncate, angles bidentate; lateral ones incised-dentate.

Diameter 50–100 $\mu$.

One of the most common species of this genus. Variable in size and the structure of the margins; sometimes the lobelets are obscurely toothed; again very distinctly notched, and another form is frequent with the angles drawn out into long spine-like points, fig. 7. The truncate ends are usually more or less rounded; fig. 8 is a peculiar form with the ends perfectly flat, and not detached from one another after multiplication by division.

M. CONFERTA, Lund. (*M. granulata*, Wood). Plate LXIV, fig. 12.

Broad elliptic, central sinus deep, narrow linear; semi-cells five lobed, lobes and lobules always close; polar lobe subcuneate, more or less widened from the base to the end, sides concave and apex convex but roundly emarginate in the middle, angles furnished with two or three small papillae; lateral lobes nearly equal, bisected, and again divided, each lobule with apex furnished with two papilla-like points.

Var. HAMATA, Wolle. Plate XLIV, figs. 3, 4.

In this variety, the polar lobe is not *conferta*, compact, close against the adjoining lobes, as in the true form, but widely separated in the whole length; the open space is produced by the contraction of the lobe below the apex, thus giving it a hamate form.

Diameter 80-100 $\mu$., length slightly more.

> Ponds, Mount Everett, Mass.
>
> The only locality from which I received the typical form is Aiken, S. C., the same from which Wood had it. This species was first known in Sweden, and described by Cleve, as *M. crenata*. Lundell separated it from that species and named it *M. conferta;* it was so recorded with figure, in his *De Desmidiaceis, quæ in Suecia inventæ sunt*, published 1871, antedating Wood's contribution by at least one year; having a priority claim, Lundell's name is preferred. The membrane is distinctly and largely punctate, not granulate, except when in old condition.

M. TRIANGULARIS, Wolle. Plate XLIV, figs. 1, 2.

Cells large, orbicular or oblong; semi-cells five lobed. Polar lobe triangular, apex and sides nearly straight and nearly equal, the angles mucronate. The lateral lobes similar, twice bisected, apices of the lobelets emarginate or furcate.

Diameter 170-200 $\mu$.

> I found plants recognized as belonging to this new species in three distinct localities: ponds, Broad Mountain, Pa., Ocean Beach and Bamber, N. J., and Florida. They vary somewhat in outline and details of intersections, but all have the same broad more or less triangular terminal lobe with mucronate angles. Fig. 1 is the typical Pennsylvania form; fig. 2 the Florida type. The New Jersey plant had stouter terminal lobes, and the ultimate intersections of the lateral lobes were intermediate between the two.

SECTION V.—Cells oblong.

M. JENNERI, Ralfs. Plate XXXVII, figs. 1, 2.

Cells oblong, minutely granulated; semi-cells five parted, lobes closely approximate, cuneate lateral ones obscurely bipartite; the subdivisions emarginate.

Diameter 100-150 $\mu$.

This species differs from all others of this genus in the form of the cell, often twice as long as broad. Fig. 2 is very near a form which Reinsch denominated *M. angulosum*. It is proportionately shorter than the typical form of Ralfs, but otherwise so near, it scarcely admits of separation.

SECTION VI.—Lobes horizontal, attenuated, bidentate.

M. LATICEPS, Nord., 1869. (*M. disputata*, Wood, 1872.) Plate XLI, figs. 4, 5.

Quadrangular, about as long as broad, subpinnatisected, sinuses acute; terminal lobe nearly as long as the basal lobe; both the lobes strongly attenuated; the polar lobe into an acute point and the other into an acutely bidentate apex; ends rounded or emarginate.

Diameter 160–212 $\mu$.

This species made its first appearance from Brazil and was described by Nordstedt in 1869 in a scientific journal of Sweden. Wood gave the same plant a new name a few years later. The former has a claim of priority, hence should stand. The plant varies considerably in size, and in the form of the terminal lobes; some are more rounded than others.

It has been found in a large number of States.

M. OSCITANS, Ralfs. Plate XXXVII, figs. 3, 4.

Cells of nearly equal length and breadth; the end lobe separated from the adjoining lobe by a rounded or acute-angled sinus; lobe horizontal, conical, their extremities usually bidentate. One form has the ends of the terminal lobe acute. The end lobes are much shorter and narrower than the others. Transverse view fusiform; membrane punctate.

Diameter 150–160 $\mu$.

Bailey reports this species from Florida and Rhode Island, but makes the measures much less. I have specimens from Florida, Massachusetts and New Jersey. They were of the given measures.

M. PINNATIFIDA, Kg., Ralfs. Plate XLI, figs. 7, 8, 9.

Ends straight; semi-cells deeply constricted, lobes horizontal, more or less fusiform with apices bidentate.

Diameter varies from 83–110 $\mu$.

Somewhat like the preceding, but very much smaller, and lobes not so swollen.

Much more frequent than *M. oscitans*.

Some are found with the basal lobe wide (fig. 9); these I have named,

Var. INFLATA, fig. 9.

M. KITCHELII, Wolle.   Plate XLI, figs. 1, 2; Plate XLII, fig. 2.

Cells about as long as wide, sinus separating the semi-cells an acute angle, ampliated; basal lobes subconically produced, obliquely and broadly truncate with two angles drawn out into somewhat diverging processes, furcate at the ends; a rounded sinus between; polar lobe separated from the basal lobe by an ample, rounded, or oval sinus, sides produced and furcate as the others; apex slightly convex.

Diameter 125 $\mu$. in center; ends 75 $\mu$.; length 125 $\mu$.

First specimens were collected by H. S. Kitchel, in a pond, Mt. Everett, Mass. It has occurred since in many places in central and southern portions of New Jersey and Florida.

The general outline of this species has some resemblance to *M. adscendens*, Nord., found on the Sandwich Islands, but it is larger, the polar lobe is more exserted, and hence the sinuses between it and the basal lobes are much wider and deeper, broadly rounded, not "*amplo-acatangulo*," and the angles are not "*bidentate*," but are simply bifurcate.

It has a closer resemblance to *M. depauperata*, Nord., a form found in Brazil, but it is a decidedly larger plant.

M. ARCUATA, Bailey.   Plate XLIV, fig. 5.

Quadrangular; semi-cells three lobed; the basal lobes long and arcuate, subtended by the transverse projections from the ends of the slightly notched terminal lobes.

Diameter 90–110 $\mu$.

Collected in Florida and described by Bailey. I have found it repeatedly in New Jersey, Pennsylvania and Massachusetts.

M. EXPANSA, Bailey.   Plate XLI, fig. 12.

Semi-cells three lobed; basal lobes subconical, lower marginal line regularly convex; terminal lobe more slender, notched in center, spreading with an upward tendency to an acute, often mucronate point. Usually smaller than the preceding.

Diameter about 75 $\mu$.

This form is near *M. arcuata*, but somewhat smaller, stouter, with more regularly arched basal lobes; apices more acute, often mucronate.

Habitat the same as the preceding.

M. QUADRATA, Bailey.

Described by the author as "Large quadrangular, three lobed, basal lobes elongated, slightly curved, bidentate; terminal lobes with two slender transverse bidentate projections."

Diameter 110–120 $\mu$.

> Found good specimens in collections made in lakes, Winter Park, Florida. Besides the typical form also a variety which has the ends of the basal lobes deeply bisected, to nearly half the length.

M. BAILEYI, Ralfs. Plate XLI, fig. 6.

Cells small, granulate; semi-cells three lobed; basal lobes bipartite, apices obtuse, or finely dentate; terminal lobe much exserted, notched, spreading arms obtuse or bidentate at apices.

Diameter 75 $\mu$.

> New York, Rhode Island, South Carolina, Florida (Bailey). Ponds, New Jersey, Pennsylvania. Rather rare.

M. FOLIACEA, Bailey. Plate XLIV, figs. 10, 11.

Cells subquadrate, smooth; semi-cells three lobed; lateral lobes deeply bipartite, and again incised, their margins concave, incised-serrate; end lobe rhomboidal, exserted, angles entire, apex divided by a wide, rounded sinus, near the basal margin of which are two or more tooth-like spines.

Diameter of cell 80–95 $\mu$.

> Bailey reports this species from Worden's Pond, Rhode Island. I found it quite abundant in Gilder Pond, Mt. Everett, Mass. A singular feature was the union of many cells forming long filaments. In the process of multiplication by division (vide Introduction, p. 27), the terminal lobes lap one over the other and thus maintain a hold. The chains of cells collected were evidently mere fragments, or parts broken from longer filaments; they contained from 10 to 38 cells.
> The details of the terminal lobe vary somewhat from the form described by Bailey. This species has been found also in Florida and in Brazil, S. A.

M. MURICATA, Bailey. Plate XXXV, figs. 4–7.

"Semi-cells divided by deep indentations into three transverse portions; the basal with three sublinear processes on each side, the others with two on each side."

The divisions, in front view, do not diverge, but spread laterally, in such a manner that the one nearest the eye more or less conceals its companions.

Diameter 100–125 $\mu$.; length 150–200 $\mu$.

> Catskill Mountains, (Bailey); many localities in Pennsylvania, New Jersey, Massachusetts. Not abundant, but widely distributed.

M. RABENHORSTII, Kirch. Plate LXIII, fig. 6; Plate XLV, fig. 6.

Cells as long as broad, small, three lobed; terminal cell not much wider than the lateral lobes, widened from the base to the end, apex concave, angles terminating with two short teeth; lateral lobes divided by a wide, almost right-angled sinus, each half somewhat narrowed towards the end; apex indented, a small tooth at each angle. Membrane smooth.

Thus reads a free translation of Kirchner's diagnosis. The figure does not represent the type; merely a small form of it.

Diameter 62–85 $\mu$.

Collected in ponds in the vicinity of Minneapolis, Minn.

## Genus, STAURASTRUM, Meyen.

Cells in front view similar to *Cosmarium*, end view, three to six or more, angular; angles obtuse, acute, or drawn out into elongated horn-like processes. Chlorophyl more or less concentrated into a central mass, margins radiating towards the margins of the semi-cells. Zygospores provided with spines.

This genus contains a large number of species; as all are figured, a complete analysis does not appear important, but for a general guide they may be divided into four larger sections, in the order observed in the following list:

SECTION I.—Membrane of cells smooth, or rarely punctate or indistinctly granular.

SECTION II.—Membrane verrucose, or rough with pearly granules.

SECTION III.—Membrane hairy, spinulose or aculeated.

SECTION IV.—Membrane with angles extended into arms, or horn-like processes.

### SECTION I.

ST. MUTICUM, Breb. Plate L, figs. 11–15.

Cells in front view orbicular, smooth, deeply constricted, often involved in a mucous envelope; semi-cells elliptic; end view triangular, or rarely quadrangular; angles rounded, sides slightly concave.

Diameter 33–38 $\mu$. Frequent.

Var. MINUS (figs. 14, 15) does not differ from the typical form except in size; measures only about one-half.

Var. ELLIPTICUM. Fig. 13. This form is more elliptic in front view than the others. Plate XLIX, figs. 41, 42. A form differing from that of Plate L, and more strictly elliptical, semi-cells in front view slightly contracted near the ends.

Diameter 33–35 $\mu$.

Pond, St. Anthony Park, Minneapolis, Minnesota.

ST. ORBICULARE, (Ehrb.), Ralfs. Plate L, figs. 9, 10.

Orbicular, constriction narrow linear; semi-cells not elliptic, but semiorbicular; end view triangular, angles rounded, sides somewhat concave; smooth.

Diameter 30–45 $\mu$.

Plate XLIX, figs. 36-38 not so distinctly orbicular, sometimes approaching the form of a Turk's cap, sometimes the sides are more concave than figured and the sinuses between the semi-cells are not always so closely linear. It is a common species, and often involved in a mucous envelope.

ST. ANGULATUM, West., J. R. M. S., Nov., 1888. Plate XLIII, figs. 5, 6.

Semi-cells smooth, rhomboid, with a faint indication of an obscure mucro; end view triangular, with concave sides.

Length 76–78 $\mu$.; breadth 60 $\mu$.; sinus 17–18 $\mu$.

Pond near Amherst, Mass. Seen sparingly.

ST. VESICULATUM, Wolle. Plate XII, figs. 6, 7.

Small, smooth, about one-half longer than broad, constriction deep, sinuses acute angled, much ampliated; semi-cells subpyramidal, not as long as broad; base wide, inferior angles round, sides convex and inclining to a rounded apex; end view triangular, angles rather broadly rounded, sides slightly convex or straight.

Diameter 31 $\mu$.; length 45 $\mu$.

Differs from *St. cordatum*, F. Gay; in front view, sinuses are not narrow linear, but much ampliated, thereby giving the cell a more elevated appearance. Green's Lake, New Jersey.

ST. BACILLARE, Breb. Plate XLVIII, figs. 5, 6.

Cells small, deeply constricted, sinus a wide, acute angle; semi-cell narrow lanceolate, base convex, ends inflated, head-like, in vertical view 3–4–5 angled; angles radiately produced with ends enlarged and rounded.

Diameter 25–30 $\mu$.

Pond, Minnesota.

St. tumidum, Breb. Plate L, figs. 1, 2.

Large, somewhat longer than broad, deeply constricted, with a distinct colorless gelatinous covering; semi-cells elliptic or suborbicular; end view bluntly triangular, sides somewhat convex, slightly constricted near the angles, producing a nipple-like projection. Margins appear striated.

Diameter 112 $\mu$.

The only habitats hitherto discovered, are marsh pools, Bucks County, Pa., and Lee Pond, Mass.

St. grande, Bulnh. Plate L, figs. 3, 4.

Large, length and breadth the same, sinuses acute, much enlarged outwardly; semi-cells elliptic, angles obtuse; end view triangular, rarely quadrangular, sides slightly retuse, angles obtuse; membrane finely punctate.

Diameter 75–83 $\mu$.

Marsh pools, Minneapolis, Minn.

The specimens were some time in a weak solution of carbolic acid before being examined, and in consequence the arrangement of the chlorophyl was destroyed; omitting this consideration they agree well with measures and forms demanded by the diagnosis of the author.

St. magnum, Wolle. Plate L, figs. 7, 8.

Cells nearly one-third longer than broad; sinuses subrectangular; semi-cells broad elliptic with a short, stout, erect mucro at each end; end view triangular, sides straight or slightly concave, angles mucronate.

Diameter 82 $\mu$.; length 100 $\mu$.

This species, like *St. tumidum*, is usually surrounded by a wide, colorless, gelatinous sheath. I have this species from Florida, collected by J. D. Smith.

It is separated from the preceding by its intermediate size, proportionately greater length and the mucronate angles.

St. majusculum, Wolle. Plate L, figs. 5, 6.

Somewhat larger than *St. magnum*; in end view, sides not concave, but convex, mucronate; mucros not erect, but oblique; in front view they are curved inwardly.

Diameter 100–105 $\mu$.; length 108–112 $\mu$.

Two localities were productive of this form, Mt. Everett, Mass., and Longwood Pond, Passaic Co., N. J.

Found no gelatinous sheath around any of the many specimens examined.

St. DEJECTUM, Breb. Plate LI, figs. 7–11 and 17–21.

Semi-cells smooth elliptic, or extrorsely lunate with sides convex and ends nearly straight, concave, or convex; each angle furnished with a longer or shorter aculeus, or awn; these are sometimes horizontal, sometimes they converge, but more frequently they diverge, directed obliquely upward. End view triangular, or occasionally, four lobed.

Figs. 17–21 represent the more usual forms.

Var. MUCRONATUM, Ralfs. Fig. 8, front view and two end views.

Var. CONVERGENS, Wolle. Figs. 7, 9, 10, 11, are unusual forms collected near Minneapolis, Minn.; aculei are stout and often stand nearly at right angles with the sides; they are also of unusual size.

Diameter of the various forms 25–38 $\mu$. without the awns.

A common species.

St. MEGACANTHUM, Lund. Plate LXII, figs. 10, 11, 12.

Cells about as long as wide (without aculei) profoundly constricted; sinus acute-angled, or subrectangular; semi-cells triangular fusiform; sides somewhat convex, ends sub-truncate or lightly convex, angles each terminating in a strong and long aculeus; viewed from apex triangular, or rarely four lobed; sides retuse; angles produced into a long and firm aculeus; membrane finely punctate.

Diameter 50–57 $\mu$.; length about 50 $\mu$.; aculei 15–18 $\mu$.

Pennsylvania, New Jersey; rather rare.

St. BREVISPINA, Breb. Plate LI, figs. 1, 2; and Plate LXIV, figs. 2, 3.

Semi-cells smooth, turgid-elliptic, minutely mucronate; end view triangular with sides usually so sinuate as to produce a three lobed appearance; each lobe terminated by a short mucro.

Diameter 45–48 $\mu$. Smaller forms occur also.

The cells of this species vary in size and somewhat in form from elliptic to subreniform, turgid.
Neither very rare nor common.

Var. INERME, Wille. Plate LI, figs. 3, 4; Plate XLVI, figs. 9, 10.

Somewhat larger than the true form, but otherwise reminds one of it, notwithstanding the absence of the mucros. The author of the name adds, "semi-cells in vertical view triangular, sides lightly retuse, angles unarmed."

Diameter 60 $\mu$.

Northampton County, Pennsylvania; Florida.

ST. DICKIEI, Ralfs. Plate LI, figs. 5, 6, 20, 21.

Semi-cell smooth, subelliptic, turgid; spines short, curved towards those of the other semi-cell; end view triangular, sides sinuate, angles mucronate.

Diameter 36-44 $\mu$.

Cells are about as long as broad; semi-cells elliptic, but having the outer margin more convex than the inner one; the mucros or spines, short, curved, and directed inwardly. It occurs not infrequently in Pennsylvania, New Jersey, Massachusetts, and probably in every State.

ST. ARISTIFERUM, Ralfs. Plate LI, figs. 15, 16.

Semi-cells smooth, triangular, constricted near the angles, producing a mammillate appearance. Each angle furnished with a long awn; end view with three, or rarely four awned lobes.

Diameter 15-20 $\mu$. without the awns or spines, and with them fully twice the size.

Rather rare, but it has been found in many States, from Rhode Island, New Jersey, to Georgia.

ST. LEWISII, Wood. Plate LI, figs. 26, 27.

Smooth, with very ample sinus, obtuse-angled, which is armed with a small spine; semi-cells from the front broadly triangular; from the vertex, triangular, with the angles somewhat tumid and rounded; angles furnished with a very large, acute, robust spine.

Diameter with the spines, 62 $\mu$.

This species was first found by Lewis, in Saco Lake, N. H., and since only in one locality, the past Summer, 1883, by Miss Eloise Butler, of Minneapolis, Minn.

ST. CUSPIDATUM, Breb. Plate LI, figs. 23-25.

Semi-cells smooth, fusiform, connected by a long narrow band; aculei parallel or converging; end view triangular, or rarely quadrangular, with inflated aculeated lobes.

Diameter 25 $\mu$.; length 30 $\mu$.

Quiet waters, Pennsylvania and New Jersey, but not frequent.

ST. TRIHEDRALE, Wolle.  Plate LI, figs. 12, 13, 14.

Small punctate-granulate; semi-cells, in front view and in end view triangular, angles rounded, sides concave, sinus narrow linear.

Diameter 30 $\mu$.

Ponds, Mount Everett, Mass.

This species, in front view, has the appearance of a *Cosmarium* near *retusum*, Perty, and *angustatum*, Nord., but the side and end views are distinct. The semi-cells are three sided, pyramidal forms unlike those of a *Cosmarium*.

ST. TRIFIDUM, Nord.  Plate LI, figs. 28, 29.

Cells about as broad as long, deeply constricted; semi-cells short cuneate, with ends dilated, and lightly retuse; superior angles obtuse, trisected; viewed from vertex triangular, angles truncate, trifid; sides somewhat concave; membrane finely punctate.

Diameter 30-50 $\mu$.  Variable in size.

Not frequent, but met with in localities widely separated, Pennsylvania, New Jersey, and other States.

ST. AVICULA, Breb.  Plate LI, figs. 30, 31, 32.

Semi-cells twice as broad as long, with a forked spine on each side; each angle in end view terminated by a simple or forked spine; cytioderm smooth.

Diameter 25-30 $\mu$., without the spines.

Rather common species; appears to be found frequently in every State in which explorations are made.

ST. COMMUTATUM, Kg.  Plate LI, figs. 33, 34.

Smooth or punctate-granulate; semi-cells diverging, obverse semilunar; base broadly rounded, ends straight or somewhat concave; apices bifid; end view triangular, angles produced and apices bicuspidate; sides moderately retuse.

Diameter 35-38 $\mu$., omitting the spines.

Ponds, Lehigh Valley, Pennsylvania.

This form may not be strictly the plant described by the author, Kützing; it is near it, and appears to stand between it and *A. Bulnheimianum*, Rab. Have seen very few of them, hence record the name merely provisionally.

ST. BRACHIATUM, Ralfs.  Plate LI, figs. 37, 38, 39; and Plate LXIII, figs. 29, 30, 31.

Cells smooth; semi-cells with three diverging processes, or according to other authors, 2-4-5 radiate, which are deeply bifid or trifid at the apex; end view with three or four rays.

Diameter 33–55 $\mu$. Not frequent.

>The figures on Plate LXIII, represent a form noted as variety *Notarisii*, Rab. Collected in ponds Bamber and Brown's Mills, N. J.

St. paniculosum, Wolle. Plate LII, figs. 39, 40.

Cells hexangular, as long as broad, membrane punctate; punctules in radiating lines; semi-cells truncated triangles, angles rounded; inferior angles furnished with two short, straight aculei; end view triangular with one small aculeus visible on each rounded angle; sides moderately convex.

Diameter 40–50 $\mu$.

>Marsh pools, near Bethlehem, Pa.

St. bieneanum, Rab. Var. *ellipticum*, Wille. Plate LIII, figs. 1, 2.

Semi-cells elliptic; end view triangular with angles rounded, sides more or less deeply concave; membrane finely punctate, distinctly observable when the cell is empty; punctules regularly arranged in transverse lines.

Diameter 33–38 $\mu$.

>Not numerous, but hitherto found specimens in Minnesota, Massachusetts, New Jersey, Pennsylvania and Florida.

St. inconspicuum, Nord. Plate LXIV, figs. 4, 5.

Small, about equal in length and breadth; very indistinctly or not at all constricted in the middle; semi-cells subquadrangular, ends usually slightly retuse; superior angles produced obliquely into a geniculate arm with a truncate end; end view four radiate, sides concave. Membrane smooth or finely punctate.

Diameter 14–16 $\mu$.

>Occasional in ponds, New Jersey.

St. pseudopachyrhynchum, Wolle. Plate LXII, figs. 32–35.

Small, smooth or imperfectly punctate, slightly longer than broad, deeply constricted; sinus wide, base rounded; semi-cells subcuneate; from a narrow base somewhat undulately widened to the broad, subtruncate end; angles rather broadly rounded, with a slight constriction near the apex. End view tri- or quadrangular; sides sinuate. Isthmus about one-fourth the diameter of cell.

Diameter 20–24 $\mu$.; length 22–25 $\mu$.

Pond, Spring Lake, N. J.

I found this new species only in one pond, but numerous; it bears the appearance of a relation to a Brazil plant described by Nordstedt as *St. Clepsydra*, and also to a Spitzbergen species by the same author, *St. pachyrhynchum*. The name applies well to the new form, although only two-thirds the size and proportionately longer; the sides also of end view, are not "slightly concave," but deeply sinuate.

## SECTION II.
### CYTIODERM GRANULAR OR VERRUCOSE.

ST. MARGARITACEUM, Ehrb.  Plate LII, figs. 31-35.

Semi-cells in front view subelliptic, rough with pearly granules; outer margin convex, produced at each side into a more or less attenuate, short process, having the granules in transverse lines; blunt and entire at the apex. End view circular, bordered by from 4-6, rarely 7, short, narrow, obtuse, granulate marginal rays.

Diameter 30-35 $\mu$.

Found in all States explored, from Rhode Island to Florida.

ST. STRIOLATUM, Naeg.  Plate LXII, figs. 27, 28.

Small, as broad as long, sinus acute angled; semi-cells obverse reniform; angles rounded, end concave, transverse striate, five or six striae distinct on each lobe; end view triangular, angles rounded and sides concave; each lobe transversely striate. The striae are series of smaller or larger granules.

Diameter 22-35 $\mu$.

Not frequent, but found occasionally in distantly separated localities, New Jersey, Pennsylvania, South Carolina, and other States.

ST. TRICORNE, Breb.  Plate LII, figs. 36, 37, 38.

Cells rough, with puncta-like granules; semi-cells tapering on each side into a short, blunt, mostly entire, process; end view with three or four blunt angles.

Diameter 22-28 $\mu$.

Not in so many localities, but often numerously clustered together; Pennsylvania, New Jersey.

ST. CRENATUM, Bailey.  Plate LII, figs. 5, 6.

Semi-cells cuneate; outer margins crenate; end view with three truncate and crenate angles; sides concave.

This species was reported by Bailey to Ralfs as found in Rhode Island. Probably not seen since in this country.

St. pseudocrenatum, Lund. (St. maamense, Arch.)  Plate XLVIII, figs. 9, 10.

Cells nearly one-fourth part longer than broad, suboval ends somewhat truncate, deeply constricted, sinus narrow linear; semi-cells subsemicircular, base straight, sides subcrenate, crenae roughly truncate-emarginate; ends obsoletely erose-dentate, inferior angles subtruncate; in vertical view triangular, sides retuse, angles broadly subtruncate, dentate with three granules.

Diameter 30–35 $\mu$.; length 38–42 $\mu$.

Found this species frequent in ponds, Minnesota and California. This form is nearest to *St. crenatum*, Bailey, (In Ralfs' Br. Des., p. 215,) but differs in having a much narrower sinus between the semi-cells, and the semi-cells are not cuneate flabelliform.

St. erasum, Breb., var. espinulosa, Lund.  Plate XLVIII, figs. 16, 17.

Of medium size, as long as broad, coarsely granulate, sinus acute-angled, outwardly ampliated; semi-cells somewhat elliptic, back nearly straight, angles rounded, more or less dentate, with large granules; in vertical view triangular, angles broadly rounded, sides concave.

Diameter 34–38 $\mu$.

Green's Lake, New Jersey.

St. luteolum, Lagh.  Plate XLIX, figs. 22, 23.

Cells rather small, nearly circular, deeply constricted, sinus narrow linear; base of semi-cell straight, back arched, inferior angles obtusely rounded granulate-crenate. Membrane thick, punctate, yellowish.

Diameter 32 $\mu$.; length 33 $\mu$.; thickness 32 $\mu$.

Tewksbury, Massachusetts.

St. cosmarioides, Reinsch.  Plate XLVI. figs. 7, 8.

Cells large, composed in front view of two orbicular semi-cells attached, forming an isthmus of one-third the diameter of the cell; margins of sides finely dentate; in vertical view triangular, angles rounded, sides slightly convex.

Prof. Reinsch describes this form as found in Pennsylvania. To my knowledge it has not occurred since.

St. polymorphum, Breb.  Plate LIII, figs. 9, 10, 24, 25.

Semi-cells in front view broadly elliptic, with sides tapering into short, stout processes, ends tipped with three or four small spines; membrane rough with minute, sometimes acute granules; end view triangular, angles truncate, or drawn out into short, stout processes, ends tipped with small spines. Zygospores orbicular, armed with elongated spines forked at the ends.

Diameter 25–30 $\mu$.

Frequent in ponds and small pools.

ST. CRENULATUM, Naeg., (Delp.).   Plate LIII, figs. 26–29.

In front view hardly separable from the preceding; end view with four, five or six angles, each produced into a short, stout, somewhat tapering ray; ends tipped with short spines, which are sometimes merely rudimentary.

Diameter 30–38 $\mu$.

Frequent in ponds, ditches and the like.

Some authors unite these forms with the preceding species; others hold them as distinct for the reason that the rays often have transverse series of large granules, which give a crenulate appearance to the margins. Our artist failed to bring out this feature as distinctly as it should be.

ST. MURICATUM, Breb.   Plate LIII, figs. 3–6.

Suborbicular, deeply constricted, sinus narrow linear, or slightly enlarged outwardly; rough with somewhat conical granules; semi-cells subsemiorbicular, angles obtusely rounded, or truncate; end view triangular, sides convex, angles rounded or truncate spinous.

Diameter 40–45 $\mu$.

Pools and ditches in many distantly separated localities, but not very numerous.

ST. ASPERUM, Breb.   Plate LIII, figs. 7, 8.

In comparison with the preceding (*St. muricatum*), granules are emarginate, or divided; semi-cells broadly elliptic; sinus much wider, and sides in end view straight; otherwise very near it.

Habitat and size the same.

ST. RUGULOSUM, Breb.   Plate LII, figs. 41, 42.

Semi-cells elliptic, denticulate at their sides; end view triangular, with angles broadly rounded and sides slightly concave or straight.

Diameter about 38 $\mu$.

Very nearly related to the preceding, I quote the diagnosis of the author. Bailey reports it from New York and Rhode Island; I add it from Pennsylvania and New Jersey   Not a rare form.

St. punctulatum, Breb.  Plate LII, figs. 43-45.
 Cytioderm punctate-granulate, semi-cells elliptic, straight, ends broadly rounded; end view triangular, angles not produced, broadly rounded, sides lightly retuse.
  Diameter 30-35 µ.
   Frequent in marsh pools, ditches, on dripping rocks and the like.

St. pygmæum, Breb.  Plate LIII, figs. 14-21.
 Small, sinus wide, subrectangular; semi-cells cuneiform or broadly elliptic, often alternately attached, angles more or less obtuse, and sometimes spinous; membrane granularly rough.
  Diameter 16-25 µ.
   Variable in size and form. They may be separated into three divisions.

Forma,—genuina, Breb., figs. 14, 15.

Forma,—truncata, Wolle, figs. 16-19.

Forma,—rhomboides, Wolle, figs. 20, 21.
   Found in nearly all standing or quiet waters, sometimes in large numbers.

St. megalonotum, Nord., var. obtusum. Hast.  Plate XLII. figs. 6, 7.
 Small, about one-fourth longer than broad; cytioderm granulate; isthmus about one-half width of cell; sinuses acute angled, opening outwardly; semi-cells truncately conical, base convex, sides concave, the truncate end with six conical processes, only four of which are usually visible in side view, basal angles obtuse (differing in this respect from Arctic varieties); transverse view triangular, the angles rounded, the sides slightly concave.
  Diameter 45 µ.
   Ponds and brooks, Rochester, New Hampshire.

St. minneapoliense, Wolle.  Plate XLVIII, figs. 11-13.
 Small verrucose; semi-cells in front view subcuneate with the two opposite superior angles drawn out into a short arm with margins serrate, and apices finely toothed; arms diverging from the arms of the connected semi-cell; in vertical view arms straight, body much elevated on each side; in lateral view arms straight, short; body puffed out high on each side, crenate on the apices.

Diameter in front view, including arms, 50–58 $\mu$.; thickness of body 20–25 $\mu$.

The front presentation, not unlike other forms, but the vertical and lateral views are quite distinct in the usual inflation of the body.

The name indicates the habitat.

ST. ALTERNANS. Breb. Plate LII, figs. 26–28.

Semi-cells granulate, elliptic or oblong, two or three times as long as wide, and from their twisted position, unequal in front view; end view with three obtuse and rounded angles, forming short rays, alternating with those of the other semi-cell.

Diameter 20–28 $\mu$. Frequent.

ST. DILATATUM, Ehrb. Plate LXIII, figs. 32, 33.

Small, granulate; semi-cells fusiform, equal; end view with three, four or five short, broad, truncate rays, granules arranged in transverse lines.

Diameter 40 $\mu$. Frequent.

Distinguished from the preceding, mainly, by the semi-cells not being twisted.

ST. SILATATUM, Nord. Plate LIII, figs. 22, 23.

Cells in front view fully twice as wide as long, deeply constricted; sinus with rounded base, outwardly enlarged; semi-cells sublanceolate, ends straight, lightly undulate; end view five lobed, margins smooth.

Diameter 30 $\mu$.; length 13-16 $\mu$.

Ponds, Florida.

ST. CYRTOCERUM, Breb. Plate LIII, figs. 30, 31.

Cells rough with minute granules; semi-cells, front view, subcuneate, top broadly convex, superior angles produced into short, stout, curved processes; end view triangular; each angle produced into a curved horn-like process with end toothed or divided; granules arranged in transverse lines. Semi-cells often so twisted as to make one-half appear longer than the other half.

Diameter 35–40 $\mu$.

Var. MAJOR, Wolle. Plate LIV, figs. 1, 2.

Not unlike the typical form except in size; often attains to a diameter 120 $\mu$.

Var. PENTACLADUM. Wolle.  Plate LIII, figs. 32–35.

Separated from the other forms by the number of arms; they vary greatly in size, always symmetrically arranged with five curved arms.

Diameter 44–85 $\mu$.

Have one or the other form from every State hitherto explored.

ST. PARADOXUM, Meyen.  Plate LIII, figs. 36, 37.

Cells rough with minute granules; front view with elongated diverging processes which are bifid or trifid at the apices; end view triangular or quadrangular.

Diameter 40–60 $\mu$.

Ponds, New York, Pennsylvania, New Jersey, Massachusetts.

The figures represent an extraordinary form; usually the apices of the processes are more minutely trifid.

Var. OSCEOLENSE, Wolle.  Plate XLVII, figs. 8, 9.

This variety differs from the typical form in its larger size, quadrangular body and in the large trifid, hooked, apices of the arms.

Diameter of spread of arms 60–70 $\mu$.

Lake Osceola, Winter Park, Florida.

ST. ARACHNE, Ralfs.  Plate LIII, figs. 38–42.

Semi-cells minutely granular, suborbicular, with elongated, slender, often incurved processes; end view with three to five linear rays; apices obtuse.

Diameter 40–50 $\mu$.

Habitat same as that of the preceding.  Distinguished from it by its more slender arms and obtuse apices.

ST. COMPTUM, Wolle.  Plate LIII, figs. 43–46.

Small, granulate; semi-cells subfusiform, ends convex; arms more or less converging, separated by an elongated, cylindrical, somewhat swollen isthmus, ribbed in the center; vertical view six radiate; rays straight, tricuspidate at the ends.

Diameter 30–40 $\mu$.; length 40–50 $\mu$.

Not rare in ponds, New Jersey.

ST. ELONGATUM, Barker.  (*St. terebrans*, Nord.)  Plate LVII, figs. 11, 12.

Elongate; semi-cells subtriangular; base globosely inflated, produced into a cylindrical column inflated at the end, and drawn out into three arms somewhat reflexed at the ends; margins denticulate-undulate above, and **spinous below**; apices with three or four small spines. Inflated **base with three** transverse series of small papillae; end view triangular, **sides** concave, denticulate.

Diameter 43–45 µ.; length 60–75 µ.

Ponds, Pennsylvania.

Var. TETRAGONUM, Wolle. Plate LXII, fig. 31.

Separated from the typical form in having **in end view** four rays instead of three; in having the rays horizontal, **not** reflexed, and terminating with three or four strong **teeth; the ends of the cells are** rough with spine-like granules; the base of the semi-cells inflated, corrugated and **denticulate.**

Diameter 38 µ.; length 58 µ.

Pond, Brown's Mill, N. J.

ST. SCABRUM. Breb. Plate LII, figs. 29, 30.

Semi-cells elliptic, scabrous; **end view** triangular, fringed with minute emarginate spines; sides straight, angles obtuse.

Diameter 25–28 µ.

Occasional in ponds, trenches and ditches, Pennsylvania and New Jersey.

ST. FASCICULOIDES, Wolle. Plate LIII, figs. 54, 55.

Small, somewhat **longer than** broad, granular, sheaf-form, slightly constricted and notched in the middle, furnished with a **small protuberance** on **each side the notch** (front view), **apex 2-4 cuspidate.** Ends convex, angles drawn out, each into a horizontal, **short, stout,** tapering **process, apex dentate.** End **view triangular, sides** slightly convex, **angles dentate with two or** three acute, conical teeth.

Diameter 27–30 µ.; length 38 µ.

Wet rocks, Lehigh Valley, Pennsylvania.

ST. PUSILLUM, Wolle. Plate LIII, figs. 47–50.

Very small, **oblong, rectilinear, constriction** indistinct; angles produced into diverging **horn-like processes;** end view quadrangular, angles **drawn out into four diverging processes, ends obtuse; membrane granular.**

Diameter 8 µ.; length 14 µ., without the processes; about **twice** the measure with them. Larger form has with processes a diameter of 25 µ.

Not rare in ponds, Pennsylvania, **New Jersey.**

St. Franconium, Reinsch.  (*St. divaricatum*, Wolle.)  Plate LVII, fig. 22.

This species is separated from the preceding (*St. pusillum*) by its somewhat larger size and by having in end view, five processes with bifid apices, not obtuse. The typical plant is described by the author, "membrana glabra, (aut cornua verruculosa)." Our forms are always granular.

Diameter about 30 $\mu$. with processes.

> This, and the preceding, not common, but they appear in many widely separated localities in New Jersey and Pennsylvania.

St. Haaboeliense, Wille.  Plate LIII, figs. 51-53.

Small, about one-third more in breadth than length; constriction in the middle forms a wide sinus; semi-cells in front view subelliptic, ends bicuspidate, margins dentate; in vertical view triangular or rarely quadrangular, sides sinuate. Membrane granulate.

Diameter 24 $\mu$.; length 18 $\mu$.

> Found this form several times in ponds, New Jersey; it differs slightly from *St. tricorne* except in the apices, which are not obtuse but bicuspidate.

St. Botrophilum, Wolle.  Plate LIII, figs. 11-13.

Somewhat longer than broad, distinctly granular; granules arranged in concentric series; semi-cells, front view, subtriangular, with ends broadly truncate, sides moderately convex or nearly straight, converging, basal angles rounded; end view triangular, angles rounded, sides slightly convex or straight; lateral view, subelliptic.

Diameter 36-38 $\mu$.

> Collected in marsh ditches near Bethlehem, Pa. In front view it has the appearance of a *Cosmarium*, like some form of *Botrytis*, but in side and end views it is a *Staurastrum*.

St. Pringlei, Wolle.  Plate LXI, figs. 25.

Cytioderm granular; of equal length and breadth; constriction not deep, sinus wide; semi-cells subtriangular, sides rounded, end concave with a central inflation, angles acute. End view triangular, sides concave, angles acute. Membrane rough with fine granules. Surrounded by a thick gelatinous sheath.

Diameter 28-33 $\mu$.

> Found by C. G. Pringle, Nebraska Notch, Vt.

St. Donnellii, Wolle. Plate LXIII, fig. 20.

Small, twice as long as wide, oblong-quadrate; **cytioderm punctate** and sulcate; semi-cells quadrangular with **basal angles rounded, sides crenulate;** superior angles (four) produced into short, obtuse, diverging processes; end view **quadrangular.**

Diameter 15 $\mu$.

Collected by **J.** Donnell Smith in Florida.

This species is nearest *St. pusillum*, but unlike it in the proportionately longer cell, the almost smooth and sulcate membrane, and the crenulate sides.

St. incisum, Wolle. Plate LII, figs. 12-14.

Cytioderm granulate, margins serrately toothed; semi-cells in front view cuneate, base broad, sides diverging to a convex top; the upper portion on each side produced into short, obtuse, tapering **processes; end view, five or six radiate; rays with** broad **base,** somewhat tapering **to the obtuse apices;** sides serrately toothed; the rays **separated at their broad** base by an acute-angled, or linear incision.

Diameter 36-40 $\mu$.

Principally from Splitrock and other **ponds** of **New Jersey.** *St. pulchrum* and *St. distentum* have a **leading** feature **of this** species—the incision, or notch **between the bases** of the rays, **but they** are separated by the smooth **membrane and** differently formed notch.

St. Meriani, Reinsch. Plate LVII, figs. 17-19.

Cells in front view subrectangular, roughly granulate, slightly **constricted in the middle;** semi-cells somewhat enlarged in the upper **portion; sometimes** slightly constricted near the **end; apex rounded;** end view usually pentagonal, but varies, more rarely, **from four to six** angular.

Diameter 16-24 $\mu$.; **length** about one-half more.

Have found this species in various ponds **of New Jersey** and Pennsylvania.

St. Heleneanum, Wolle. Plate **LV, figs. 6, 7.**

Small, finely granular; **granules arranged in** transverse rows; semi-cells, front view, narrow, elliptic, ends slightly emarginate; angles somewhat produced, and apices furcate; vertical **view** triradiate, with large **central** inflation, rays **short, stout, tumid** at **base** and furcate **at** apices; basal inflation **furnished on each side with a** small bicuspidate **prominence.**

Diameter 30-36 $\mu$.

Frequent in Splitrock Pond, New Jersey.

There is a trace of similarity between this desmid and *St. vestitum*, Ralfs, but, while the latter has two or more slender forked spines in the middle of each side, mine has stouter forked prominences on the inflated base of each ray; the sides, moreover, are not concave, but undulate convex; size of plant much smaller.

ST. CERASTES, Lund.  Plate LIV, figs. 6, 7.

Rather broader than long; semi-cells in front view, ends lunate, drawn out in the middle of the concave side into a subconical column; the lateral horns are robust, short, incurved, apices obtuse; the exterior margin coarsely granulate and often very rough with large emarginate, bifid, verrucae; the interior margin nude; end view quadrangular, angles produced into stout, straight horns, apices tridentate; margins and areas variously roughened, with larger and smaller granules and often dentate with large conical, or emarginate-bifid verrucae.

Diameter 60–70 $\mu$.

> Not abundant, nevertheless a cosmopolite.
> The figures represent a smoother specimen.

ST. GRACILE, Ralfs.  Plate LIV, figs. 16, 17.

Semi-cells rough, elongated on each side into a slender process which is terminated by minute spines; end view triradiate.

Diameter 40–50 $\mu$.; length about one-third this measure.

> Ponds, pools, ditches from Vermont to Florida, and westward as far as explorations have been made.

ST. OPHIURA, Lund.  Plate LIV, figs. 10, 11.

Large, slightly constricted in the middle; semi-cells somewhat obovate, end convex and ornate with bifid papillae; superior angles produced laterally with elongated, thin, almost colorless, straight, or lightly incurved rays, with margins more or less denticulate, and apices dentate. Viewed from the vertex seven (rarely six or eight) rayed; rays attenuated, long, apices tridentate, margins serrate-dentate; center ornate with a crown composed of seven (rarely six or eight) four-parted papillae.

Diameter 140–150 $\mu$.; length 65–80 $\mu$.

> More abundant in the waters of New Jersey than of Pennsylvania; found specimens also in ponds, Massachusetts.

Var. TETRACERUM, Wolle. Plate LV, figs. 1, 2.
Var. PENTACERUM, Wolle. Plate LV, fig. 3.

The one four-armed, and the other five-armed; the crown papillae correspond in number with the arms; in other details they are not unlike the typical form; the serrate-dentate margins vary greatly in different specimens.

These varieties I collected only in Denmark Pond, Passaic County, N. J., where they occurred frequently.

ST. MACROCERUM, Wolle. Plate LIV, figs. 3, 4, 5.

Very large, granularly rough; semi-cells, front view, sub-cuneate, truncate base and rounded top; upper angles laterally produced into long, slightly tapering, straight or lightly incurved arms, margins serrate, ends bifid; end view six radiate. Separated from the preceding partly by the less number of arms, the less, central elevation (front view) and the absence of the crown of papillae.

Diameter 150–180 $\mu$.

Not rare in New Jersey waters.

ST. ODONTATUM, Wolle. Plate LIV, figs. 8, 9.

Of equal length and breadth; semi-cells in front view sub-quadrangular, end convex, upper angles drawn out laterally into straight or lightly incurved arms, as long as the breadth of the body of the cell; margins serrate, apices furcate; the lightly rounded inferior angles, each armed with a strong, short, aculeus. End view quadrangular, four rayed.

Diameter 62–75 $\mu$.; length 45 $\mu$.

Splitrock Pond, Passaic County, N. J.

ST. ROTULA, Nord. Plate LV, figs. 13, 14.

Large, punctate, profoundly constricted; semi-cells sub-hexagonal, top truncate and furnished with a few teeth; angles produced laterally into long, straight rays, margins with three (or four?) tooth-like prominences; end view circular with seven to nine straight rays, margins tri-dentate-crenate, apices trifid; at the base of each ray a large granule, area between, punctate.

Diameter 88–125 $\mu$. Florida specimens 50–62 $\mu$.

Denmark, Splitrock, and other ponds, Passaic County, N. J.; Florida. Very rare in Pennsylvania.

ST. CORONULATUM, Wolle. Plate LV, figs. 11, 12.

Twice as wide as long; semi-cells obovate; sides produced into somewhat tapering, incurved arms, margins dentate;

ends convex, bearing six oblong teeth arranged in crown-form; viewed from the vertex, six radiate, margins delicately serrate-dentate, apices tridentate.

Diameter 75–85 $\mu$.

 Denmark Pond, Passaic County, and pond near Malaga, New Jersey.

 This species has the crown teeth of *St. Rotula*, but not the size, number of arms, nor the serration.

Var. FLORIDENSE, Wolle. Plate LIV, figs. 12, 13, 14.

This form has points in common with the present species, with *St. Ophiura*, with *St. pentacladum*; but the form recognized under the latter name is very slender and usually smaller; *St. Ophiura* has seven arms, long, and coarsely dentate-serrate. Size, relative length of arms and breadth of body, and the marginal serration and crown papillae or teeth, make it appear most nearly allied to the present species.

Diameter 75–85 $\mu$.; exceptions 50 $\mu$.

 Frequent in pond water, Florida.

ST. PENTACLADUM, Wolle. Plate LIV, fig. 15; Plate LV, figs. 15, 16.

Of the same general type as the preceding. It has five rays, end view, but these are more slender, the body is smaller and the apices are more spreading.

Diameter 40–70 $\mu$.

 Gilder Pond, Mt. Everett, Mass., and in waters scattered throughout New Jersey and Pennsylvania.

ST. LEPTOCLADUM, Nord. Plate LV, figs. 4, 5.

Semi-cells subtriangular, end broadly rounded, furnished with small rudimentary teeth; within the margin a small tumor; margins serrate-crenate; base truncate, superior angles produced laterally, each into a long, thin, incurved, granularly rough arm with a bi-tri-furcate apex; in vertical view, fusiform with an obtuse angled inflation in the middle.

Diameter 80–100 $\mu$.; length about 25 $\mu$.

 The original, typical plant from Brazil, is described by the author, and figured by him with the arms strongly incurved and body longer than our form. The plants identified as of this species, have the arms nearly horizontal, and often strongly recurved.

 They occur frequently in ponds of New Jersey, Massachusetts, Minnesota, Pennsylvania, Florida and doubtless in many other States.

St. grallatorium, Nord.  Plate LV, fig. 19.

Semi-cells subquadrangular, top somewhat produced with one, or two, small aculei at each angle; inferior angles rounded; sides produced, each into a long, thin, colorless ray, margins crenate-dentate, apex bi-tri-furcate; vertical view oval, produced on opposite sides into a long thin arm.

Diameter 100–125 $\mu$.

Var. ungulatum, Wolle.  Plate LV, figs. 17, 18.

Besides having the apices of the rays tipped with a single claw-like spine, they are usually shorter and stouter, varying as the figures.

> This variety is from Florida; the typical forms from Denmark Pond, Passaic Co., New Jersey.

St. fusiforme, Wolle.  Plate LV, figs. 20, 21.

Semi-cells in front view, narrow fusiform, lateral angles drawn out into long, colorless arms, margins crenate-dentate, apices bifurcate; back or end broadly rounded or straight, crenate; end view fusiform.

Diameter 125–138 $\mu$.; length 38 $\mu$.

> This species appears to be related to the preceding two, but varies from both in form of cell; from *St. leptocladum*, in the longer, stouter, and straighter arms, and from *St. grallatorium*, in the absence of the produced back and the aculei.
>
> Denmark Pond, New Jersey.

St. iotanum, Wolle.  Plate LXII, figs. 5–7.

Very minute; semi-cells quadrangular, angles drawn out into thin, diverging, granular rays, each about as long as the diameter of the body; apices obtuse; end view triradiate.

Diameter, including the rays, 15–20 $\mu$.

> The rays are so minute, they appear like a single series of fine granules.
>
> Found this very small species quite numerous at Ocean Beach and at Malaga, N. J.

St. ankyroides, Wolle.  Plate LXII, fig. 4 and variety fig. 3.

About as long as wide, granularly rough; semi-cells cylindrical with enlargement towards the convex end; sides produced laterally into narrow, elongate, slightly tapering, incurved arms, margins granulate-crenate, apices bifurcate; end view quadrangular, four-rayed.

Diameter 82 $\mu$.; length 75 $\mu$.

> The only water which hitherto furnished this new species is a pond near Malaga, New Jersey.

Var. HEXACERUM, **Wolle.** Plate LXII, fig. 3.
Somewhat stouter than the typical form and furnished with six arms.

Ponds, northern counties of New Jersey.

In the possession of six arms it bears some resemblance to *St. coronulatum*, but with nearly twice the length, and in the absence of the circle of large granules on the convex end, which suggested the name, it appears more nearly related to *St. ankyroides*.

ST. NANUM, **Wolle.** **Plate LV, figs. 8, 9, 10.**
**Very** small, smooth, or granulate-punctate; semi-cells sub-cuneate, **sides somewhat** rounded, **ends broadly** convex; superior angles produced laterally **into straight** slightly diverging arms, nearly as long as the diameter of the cell, ends forked; viewed from the end tri-radiate, sometimes twisted so that the arms of the lower half cell alternate with those of the upper half.

Diameter 20–25 $\mu$.

Frequent in ponds, Mt. Everett, Mass.

This minute species is nearest *St. gracile*, Ralfs, but differs in its smaller size, more forked apices, and smoother membrane.

ST. VESTITUM, Ralfs. Plate LVI, figs. 28, 29, 30.
Cells rough with minute granules; **with this investment** there are also minute emarginate spines; semi-cells fusiform in front view; seen from the vertex, triradiate, **each side** having **two** slender, **forked spines in the** middle, **and often** accompanied by **other smaller ones.**

Diameter 62–90 $\mu$.

Has a home in many parts of the civilized world, so here also it is found widely scattered.

ST. SEBALDI, (*Sancti Sebaldi*), Reinsch. Plate LVII, figs. 1–6; 10.
One-fourth to one-half wider than long, coarsely granulate; margins in part granulate-crenate, and in **part** spinous. Semi-cells broad cuneate, base truncate, top convex, **with** sides more or less conically produced; apices bifid or trifid; near the top margin a series of emarginate **or** tricuspidate spines, which come to view at one or **the** other end of **the** cell as it is more or less inclined from a horizontal position. End **view triangular,** angles slightly produced, apices **tridentate; sides** nearly straight, or slightly convex.

Diameter 75–95 $\mu$.

A conspicuous species, large, stout and spinous; variable in the length of the lateral arms; in some cases short, stumpy; in others more elongated; the spines are also variously prominent; in exact horizontal position they are often not noticeable; when somewhat turned they become prominent on one end and indistinct on the other; the result of their being arranged not on the margin but within it.

The finest, largest and best developed forms, I found in small pools and ditches, Pennsylvania and New Jersey.

Var. SPINOSUM, Wolle. Plate LVII, fig. 7.

The spine (process) protruding near each lateral margin of the semi-cell, is the peculiarity of this variety.

Collected near Minneapolis, Minn.

ST. PSEUDOSEBALDI, Wille. Plate LVII, figs. 8, 9.

Cells one-fifth part more in width than length, profoundly constricted; spines of the end of the semi-cells bifurcate; rays nearly straight, granular, apices tricuspidate; vertical view, triangular, sides concave, furnished in the middle with short bifurcate spines.

Diameter about 75 $\mu$.

Ponds, Pennsylvania and New Jersey.

ST. ANATINUM, Cooke and Wills. Plate LXII, figs. 1, 2.

Large, granularly rough, or spinous; semi-cells in front view oval with ends drawn out into diverging arms, apices trifid. End view triangular, sides slightly concave, with angles produced into straight arms; margins in both views ornate with large, emarginate-bifid, or papilliform verrucae.

Diameter 60–80 $\mu$.; length about one-half the diameter.

Ponds, Mt. Everett, Mass.

This species differs from *St. Sebaldi*, in being more slender, not so turgid, arms more protracted, and more evenly clothed with large verrucae.

ST. ARCUATUM, Nord. (Var.) Plate LVII, figs. 13, 14.

In length and breadth about the same; constriction deep; sinus acute angled, much ampliated; semi-cells elliptic, granularly rough, granules arranged in transverse series; base convex, top convex or straight, each end furnished with large diverging twinned aculei; end view triangular, center smooth; arms short with granules in transverse series; sides furnished with four or more bicuspidate spines; angles with two aculei, only one of which is clearly visible in exact horizontal position of cell.

Diameter 30–36 $\mu$., without the aculei.

Splitrock Pond, Passaic Co., N. J.

Our species differs somewhat from the typical Norwegian form, but I adopt the name for our variety.

ST. SUBARCUATUM, Wolle. Plate LVII, figs. 15, 16.

This species is allied to the preceding, *St. arcuatum;* I have separated it because it is smaller, the aculei at the terminal angles are not so long and the marginal granules are only rarely bifid. In end view, the papilla-like granules are arranged concentrically, often protruding on the margins.

Since naming this desmid, three years since, I came across varieties of *St. Avicula* coarsely granulate, which are very near to this form. A *variety of Avicula* would have been equally appropriate.

ST. CRESCENTUM, Hast. Plate XLII, figs. 8-11.

Semi-cells subelliptic, or somewhat hexagonal, base truncate convex, undulate; superior lateral margins each with three teeth or verrucae, the upper two truncate; apex truncate undulate; each lateral angle furnished with two, or rarely three, diverging aculei, rarely unarmed; end view triangular, sides sinuous concave, sometimes furnished with a subulate spine near the angles; angles suddenly attenuate, rounded and usually furnished with two, sometimes three aculei, rarely unarmed; center of triangle smooth, surrounded by three pairs of crescentric teeth in a wide circle, these are surrounded by others, so that each limb of the triangle bears five crescentric teeth, two, two and one, all within the margin, the last one sometimes indistinct or obsolete.

Diameter, without aculei, 45–50 $\mu$.

From a small pond, Dover, N. H.

This at first view recalls *St. arcuatum,* also *St. forficulatum,* but in end view the crescentric markings, the suddenly attenuate angles; the sinuous concave sides and the lateral subulate spines make a good specific character.

### SECTION III.
#### MEMBRANE PILOSE, SPINOUS OR ACULEATED.

ST. ACULEATUM, Ehrb. Plate LVI, figs. 1, 2, 3.

Cells spinulose; semi-cells with sides somewhat drawn out, margined with smaller aculei, and terminated by larger ones; end view usually with three, but sometimes also with four angles.

Diameter, without aculei, about 50 $\mu$.

Pond, near Minneapolis, Minn. **Found no good specimens** elsewhere.

Semi-cells are elliptic or **fusiform, thickly spinulose**, the spines usually simple, rarely divided at **the apex**; the semi-cells taper on each side into a short process **tipped with three** or four larger aculei.

This form agrees well with *St. Saxonicum*, Reinsch. **Bulnheim has a different form with the same name which I have adopted in this monograph.**

St. TELIFERUM, Ralfs. **Plate LVI, fig. 4.**

Semi-cells **more or less** reniform, aculeated; the aculei **larger and** most densely set at the angles; end view triangular, sides concave, **angles** broadly **rounded** and bristly.

Diameter 33–38 $\mu$.

Not rare in pond waters **of New Jersey,** Pennsylvania **and** Massachusetts.

St. BREBISSONII, Arch. Plate LVI, **figs. 5, 6.**

Cells very near *St. teliferum*, but much **larger; semi-cells more** elliptic and aculei proportionately **smaller.**

Diameter 62 $\mu$.

Florida, the only habitat hitherto found.

St. SETIGERUM, Cleve. Plate LVI, figs. **26, 27.**

Semi-cells broadly elliptic, bristly; **the** bristles, or more properly aculei, have a firm **base** and sting-like apex; they are arranged on the margins, with two longer, and stronger, diverging ones on each lateral angle.

Diameter **with** aculei 45 $\mu$.; without **aculei 25 $\mu$.**

Not north of Florida, as far as I could discover.

St. SAXONICUM, Bulnh. (Not Reinsch's form.) Plate LVI, figs. 33, 34.

Large, **spinous;** semi-cells **elliptic,** evenly aculeated over the whole membrane; end view triangular, sides straight or **slightly concave.**

Diameter 68–75 $\mu$.

Budd's **Lake, N. J.** Compare note, *St. aculeatum*.

Var. PENTAGONUM. Plate XLII, figs. **14, 15.**

St. ECHINATUM, Breb. Plate LVI, figs. 31, 32.

Small, as long as broad, finely aculeated; semi-cells elliptic; end view triangular, angles broadly rounded, sides straight or lightly convex; whole membrane except the center of the semi-cells, aculeated; 7-10 aculei to a side, end view.

Diameter 27-30 $\mu$.

Not infrequent in pools and ponds, New Jersey, Pennsylvania and other States.

ST. PECTEN, Perty. Plate LVI, figs. 35, 36.

This looks like and probably is a depauperated variety of the last, *St. echinatum.*

Diameter 20 $\mu$.

Denmark Pond, Passaic County, N. J.

ST. HIRSUTUM, (Ehrb.), Breb. Plate LVI, figs. 19-21.

About as long as broad, more or less densely covered with thin, short, even, hair-like spines; semi-cells elliptic or sub-semiorbicular; end view triangular, angles obtusely rounded, sides straight or moderately convex.

Diameter 40-60 $\mu$.

A common species.

ST. SOCIATUM, Wolle. Plate LVI, figs. 22, 23.

Separated from the last two, mainly by the arrangement of the spines which are sociated, or twinned.

Diameter without spines 28-30 $\mu$., with spines 40-45 $\mu$.

This species has some resemblance to *St. geminatum*, Nord., but the twinned spines are smaller, and the number twice as large.

ST. XIPHIDIOPHORUM, Wolle. Plate XLVIII, figs. 21, 22, and Plate XLIX, fig. 19.

Small, one and one-half to two times as long as broad, deeply constricted, sinus narrow, widening irregularly outwardly; semi-cells transversely oblong, with lateral margins notched; the end margins drawn out into a sort of one-sided, hastate, poignard-like spines or slender points, usually nine in number; membrane smooth; with several verrucae; end view triangular, angles broadly truncate and usually each showing three prominences, the bases or supports of three spines, sides concave.

Diameter 25-30 $\mu$.; length 40 $\mu$. and upward.

Ponds, near Minneapolis and Stillwater, Minnesota.

Var. SIMPLEX, Wolle, differing from the type-form in having less spines, usually six; (Plate XLIX, fig. 19,) in end view the truncate angles have only two prominences each.

Found this form frequent in material collected in small pools near Lake Tahoe, California, by Mrs. Hanson and Miss Haggin, of San Francisco.

St. Minnesotense, Wolle.   Plate XLVIII, figs. 7, 8.

Cells large, punctate, spinous, about as long as broad; semi-cells broadly elliptic, twice as wide as long; lateral angles each with two large straight or incurved spines or aculei, three more pairs of similar spines placed within the margin of the end, one of each pair on opposite sides of the semi cell; six more, often inconspicuous, arranged around the center; end view triangular, with two spines at each angle and two pairs (near the margin) between the angles, on each side of the triangle; around the center are nine more spines, often indistinct.

Diameter 65–75 $\mu$. without, and 90–100 $\mu$. with the spines.

Frequent in Minnesota ponds.

St. Tridentiferum, Wolle.   Plate LVI, figs. 9, 10.

Very small, smooth, sinus ample; semi-cells elliptic, ends more or less convex, angles furnished with three, firm, diverging aculei; end view triangular, sides retuse, angles with three large aculei.

Diameter 17–20 $\mu$., without spines; with them 25–28 $\mu$.

Sluggish waters, Pennsylvania.

St. Cruciatum, Wolle.   Plate LVI, figs. 11–13.

Small, smooth, front view cruciform, lobes short linear, ends rounded; sinuses wide, rectangular; end view three or four lobed, slightly tapering, ends rounded and furnished with a number of more or less diverging setae, which are as long as the lobes.

Diameter 25 $\mu$., without setae.

Ponds, Northampton Co., Pa.

St. Cerberus, Bailey.   Plate LVI, figs. 7, 8.

"Cells small, deeply constricted, semi-cells three lobed; lobes with four teeth, two of which project upwards and two downwards, at each truncate angle."

Diameter 25–30 $\mu$.

This species is reported by Bailey, from lakes in Florida.

St. Hystrix, Ralfs.   Plate LVI, figs. 14–16.

Semi-cells in front view subquadrate, extremities somewhat rounded, end margins nearly straight, furnished with a few scattered, subulate, acute spines, chiefly confined to the lateral extremities; end view with three or four broadly rounded angles, the spines scattered, chiefly confined to the lateral extremities, sides concave.

Diameter 22–25 $\mu$.

Rhode Island, (S. T. Olney) Thwaites.

St. Ravenelii, Wood. Plate LVI, figs. 17, 18. Plate LXIII. figs. 7, 8.

A little longer than broad; semi-cells from the front, elliptical or oval, not semiorbicular; from the vertex triangular, with the sides convex or slightly retuse, and the angles rounded; connecting isthmus obsolete, broad sinus acute-angled; cytioderm armed with numerous acute robust spines.

Diameter 25–30 $\mu$.; length 35–38 $\mu$.

Still water, Aiken, South Carolina, collected by H. W. Ravenel.

Although in frequent correspondence with Mr. Ravenel, and having examined hundreds of specimens gathered by him the past years, I was not so fortunate as to find this desmid until December, 1883. The specimens were dried, and more or less collapsed and shriveled in consequence, but I was delighted to be able to identify ten to fifteen good specimens. A peculiarity is the somewhat irregular arrangement of the conical granules. The drawing, front view, of the semi-cells (fig. 18) is singularly incorrect; the inferior angles should be rounded so as to form a wide, acute-angled sinus. See Plate LXIII, fig. 8.

St. controversum, Breb. Plate LVI, figs. 24, 25.

Cells spinulose; semi-cells with a short, irregular process on each side terminated by minute spines; end view with three or four distorted rays.

Diameter 38–65 $\mu$.; length 75 $\mu$., more or less.

Marsh pool, Minneapolis, Minn.

A variable species in size, in distortions, and in arrangement and size of spines. The lateral angles of the semi-cells are often much incurved and tipped with minute subulate spines. In both views, the semi-cells show numerous conspicuous spines which are either subulate or forked at the end.

St. aspinosum, Wolle. Plate LXII, figs. 22, 23.

Semi-cells smooth, in front view oval, with each end protracted into a colorless arm about three times as long as the breadth of the body, diverging, apices tricuspidate, margins rough with minute, firm, perpendicular, irregularly placed aculei; end view triradiate.

Spread of the **arm 58–63** $\mu$.

Pond, Brown's Mills, New Jersey.

The vertical spines, like the thorns of a rose, give this plant a distinctive character.

ST. QUATERNIUM, Wolle. Plate LXIII, figs. 17, 18, 19.

**Small, smooth,** quadrangular in **front view; deeply constricted; sinus** acute-angled, much ampliated; semi-cells **oblong, sides** rounded, ends truncate, each angle furnished **with four firm** aculei; **end view triangular,** sides concave, angles broadly rounded **and** furnished with four aculei, two **on** the margin, somewhat separated, and two within the margin, one on each side of the cell, and projecting between **the other two.** By turning the cells two **smaller aculei may be** detected near the margins of the sides.

Diameter of body 25 $\mu$.; including **aculei 40–50** $\mu$.

Ponds, near Malaga, N. J., and Wilkes-Barre, Pa.

ST. CORNUTUM, Wolle. Plate XLVIII, figs. 3, 4, duplicated on Plate XLVI, figs. 11, 12.

Cells medium size, about one-fourth longer than broad, smooth; semi-cell oval or broadly elliptic, with a prominent, somewhat inwardly curved aculeus at each angle; end view triangular, angles rounded, each with a firm aculeus, sides straight or slightly concave.

Diameter 55–60 $\mu$.; length about 70 $\mu$., aculei not included. In front view resembles a large form of *Arthrodesmus convergens,* but the triangular end views prove it distinct.

Ponds, Minnesota; not infrequent.

ST. CALYXOIDES, Wolle. Plate XLVIII, figs. 14, 15.

Nearly equal in length and breadth; smooth or finely punctate; deeply constricted; semi-cells saucer- or calyx-shaped, bearing on the undulate margin five equally distant divergent spines; end view pentagonal, each angle produced and bearing a strong aculeus.

Diameter about 33 $\mu$. without, and 75 $\mu$. with, the aculei.

Pond, near Manchester, Ocean County, and Green's Lake, Warren County, New Jersey.

ST. FORFICULATUM, Lund. Plate LXII, figs. **16–19.**

Cells rather broader than long; deeply constricted; sinus wide; semi-cells subtrapezoid, end truncately rounded; **base** convex, sides somewhat produced and divided into two large diverging mucros; margins ornate with large emarginate verrucae, or more or less conspicuous prominences; in vertical aspect three, or more rarely, four or five angled; angles produced and divided, and sides furnished with spines as in front view.

Diámeter, including aculei, 70-80 $\mu$.

Bamber Pond, New Jersey.

The form of the semi-cells is more elliptic than trapezoid, but in other points it is a good representative of Lundell's Swedish plant.

ST. MONTICULOSUM, Breb. Var. *bifarium*, Nord. Plate LXII, figs. 24–26.

Semi-cells with a forked spine at each lateral angle, and at the end, two twinned, stout, acute, or furcate prominences; vertical view usually triangular, angles acute or bifid as the cell is in a horizontal position, or somewhat turned; sides with four single or two bifid prominences.

Diameter 38 $\mu$.; length 33–35 $\mu$.

Spring Lake, New Jersey.

The form I found is not the typical plant, but answers the description of Nordstedt's Norway variety, *bifarium*.

ST. TRICORNUTUM, Wolle. Plate LVIII, figs. 1, 2.

Large, as long as wide, smooth, semi-cells broad-elliptic with angles terminated by three long, stout, colorless, diverging, subulate spines; vertical view triangular, sides somewhat concave, or sometimes slightly convex, angles terminated with three subulate spines.

Diameter of body 90–100 $\mu$.; with the spines 175–200 $\mu$.

Frequent in Hammonton and other ponds of southern New Jersey.

ST. NOVÆ CÆSARÆ, Wolle. Plate LVIII, figs. 3, 4.

Cells as long as broad, or somewhat longer, coarsely granulate; semi-cells in front view elliptic, margins crenulate, angles produced into two long subulate, divergent spines; vertical view quadrangular, at angles somewhat constricted, often producing a mammiform appearance, and drawn out into two, long, subulate spines.

Diameter without spines 36–40 $\mu$.; with spines 62–70 $\mu$.

This species, hitherto found only in a pond near Hammonton, N. J., proves to have a home in Florida also. The plant differs somewhat from the more northern form, in having the subulate spines at the angles not so long, and the cell itself not quite so large. Jas. L. Bennett reports this plant from Providence, R. I., with end view *triangular*.

ST. LONGISPINUM, Bailey.  Plate LII, fig. 7.

Large, smooth, triangular, with two long spines at each angle.

Diameter of body 75 $\mu$.; with spines 150 $\mu$.

Lakes in Florida (Bailey).

ST. QUADRANGULARE, Breb.  Plate LII, figs. 1-4.

Cells smooth, nearly square, divided by a deep, linear constriction into rectangular-oblong semi-cells with a few marginal spines or teeth; end view quadrilateral, sides more or less concave, angles truncate and emarginate or dentate.

Diameter 23-30 $\mu$.

Not infrequent in ponds of Pennsylvania, New Jersey and Florida.

ST. BRASILIENSE, Nord.  Plate LIX, figs. 1, 2, 3.

Semi-cells short cuneate, top truncate, or moderately rounded, angles terminating in three firm, diverging aculei; end view pentangular; each angle produced into three more or less elongated firm subulate diverging spines, sides concave; membrane punctate.

Diameter 87-130 $\mu$., including the spines.

Three localities only have been developed for this species; Florida furnishes the smaller form figured; the other is from pond, Passaic County, New Jersey, and from vicinity of Mobile, Alabama. The original form from Brazil, is described by the author as usually quadrangular, and angles often furnished with four spines.

Var. TRIQUETRUM, Wolle.  Plate XLIX, figs. 39, 40.

The form hitherto found here is pentangular in vertical view; the form first discovered and described by Nordstedt, is quadrangular, found in Brazil. The present variety from California is triangular in vertical view; it appears so nearly related in character of cell, arrangement and character of aculei, think it best described as a variety of the same species.

Diameter of cells, including aculei, 63-67 $\mu$.

Smaller than the pentangular form, but about the same size as the original quadrangular form.

Collected in small pools near Lake Tahoe, by Mrs. Hanson and Miss Haggin, San Francisco, California.

SECTION IV.—Cells furnished with numerous processes usually divided at the ends.

ST. FURCIGERUM. Breb.   Plate LIX, figs. 12-14; Plate LXIII, figs. 23, 24.

Cells constricted at the middle, angular, with six processes to each semi-cell; in end view, triangular, one process at each angle and one within the angle, about half way between it and the center of the triangle. Plate LIX, fig. 12. Plate LXIII, fig. 24; semi-cell in front view somewhat elliptic, Plate LIX, fig. 13; Plate LXIII, fig. 23; each end drawn out into a short process, margins serrate, ends furcate or toothed; three other processes are usually in view, two on the end margin, and one intermediate. Cytioderm granular; granules arranged in transverse lines.

Diameter 50-62 $\mu$.

> Occurs in many localities, Rhode Island and southward to South Carolina and Florida.
>
> Foreign authors report a form, quadrangular in end view; such would have eight processes to a semi-cell.
>
> I find considerable diversity in the specimens of this species, particularly in the arrangement of the processes on the tops or ends of the cells; typically they are attached away from the center, and are directed towards the angles; a variety (Plate LIX, fig. 14), has them coming from the center and directed transversely, or at right angles with the sides.

ST. EUSTEPHANUM, (Ehrb.), Ralfs.   Plate LIX, figs. 9-11.

Of nearly equal length and breadth, granular, margins more or less serrate; semi-cells elliptic (fig. 9) with angles produced, furcate; end view triangular, furnished with nine processes, counting the three somewhat produced, and bifurcate angles; the other six are on the upper surface, attached, usually between the center and the margins, ends elevated above the surface; the processes extend to margins, or slightly over them; in front view, these present themselves on the outer margin in two pairs; the third pair is either under the cell, or stands towards the eye, and is invisible.

Diameter varies from 50-75 $\mu$.

Var. *a*. fig. 11 represents a form with more elongated processes.

Var. *b*. figs. 4-6 is another variety, very distinct; it is smaller in size and has spreading, swallowtail-like ends of processes.

The latter was collected in Minnesota; the others occur frequently in small ponds and ditches, New York, (Bailey; Ehrenberg); Pennsylvania, New Jersey, South Carolina, Massachusetts. Figs. 4-6 may represent a new species; it needs further verification.

ST. SENARIUM, (Ehrb.), Ralfs. Plate LXIII, fig. 1.

Smooth, each semi-cell furnished with fifteen processes; in end view triangular, each angle a process, two on each side, and six radiating, on the upper surface within the margins.

I have found no form to answer this description satisfactorily. Ehrenberg and Bailey report it from New York.

ST. PSEUDOFURCIGERUM, Reinsch. Plate LXIII, figs. 27, 28.

Cells smooth; semi-cells broadly elliptic, sides produced into a short, stout process, with margins smooth and apices bifurcate; end view triangular; one process at each angle, and two near the margin of each side, extending beyond it, making nine processes to each semi-cell.

Diameter 37–40 $\mu$.

Minnesota.

I am aware that this name is usually applied to a different plant, which has a granular cytioderm and margins undulate-serrate. Reinsch's figures indicate an absolutely smooth membrane, and in his description he writes *membrana glabra*. Satisfied I have Reinsch's prototype in size, and detail of construction, it is but just to retain the name given by him. The plants generally recorded for *pseudofurcigerum* would probably be better placed with *St. eustephanum*.

ST. CUNEATUM, Wolle. Plate LIX, figs. 7, 8.

As long as wide, divided by a deep constriction into two broadly cuneate semi-cells; base convex, broad; sides, each with three to six sharp teeth, converge from the base to a concave-truncate end; superior angles somewhat produced, making a short process, apex bifid or trifid; end view triangular, sides slightly convex, angles bisected; on the top six processes radiating from the center and extending to, or slightly over the margins.

Diameter 44–46 $\mu$.

Ponds, Pennsylvania.

In front view, this form bears much similarity to a plant found on the Island of Spitzbergen and named *St. megalonotum*, Nord., but in end view it is entirely distinct.

St. spongiosum, Breb.   Plate LVIII, figs. 5-8.

Thickly covered with short spines which are forked at the apex; semi-cells semiorbicular, spinulose; end view triangular, angles rounded; sides slightly convex and bordered with forked spines or short processes.

Diameter 45-50 $\mu$.

> This species appears to be sparsely but widely distributed. The specimens vary considerably in different localities; figs. 7, 8, represent the more frequent form; Naegeli supposed it to be a new species and named it *St. Griffitheanum*.

St. arctiscon, Ehrb.   Plate LVIII, figs. 9, 10.

Cells about one-fourth longer than broad, moderately constricted, sinuses obtuse angled; semi-cells subglobose, slightly depressed, furnished in the middle with (usually) nine straight divergent processes; above these another whorl consisting, usually, of six similar, but shorter processes, apices trifid. Membrane punctate.

Diameter 100-120 $\mu$.

> In addition to the forms represented on Plate LVIII, figs. 9, 10, I add another, apparently more highly developed, Plate XLVI, fig. 4, distinct in the large, wide-spreading points of the trifid apices of the arms.
>
> Green Lake and other waters of New Jersey.
>
> Wood describes *St. munitum* as a new species, but evidently it is the same as *St. arctiscon*. He had it from New Hampshire; I found it frequently in Massachusetts, Pennsylvania, New Jersey. No doubt it will turn up in all parts of the United States. Ehrenberg had his specimens from New York.

St. Wolleanum, Butler.   Plate XLVIII, figs. 1, 2.

Medium size, membrane punctate, about one-half longer than broad, moderately constricted, sinuses obtuse-angled; semi-cell broadly oval or subhexagonal; superior and lateral angles produced into subcylindrical, somewhat swollen processes or arms, slightly notched at the apices; four more similar processes within the margin; in vertical view regular hexagonal, each angle furnished with an arm in appearance as those in front view; within the margin, arranged in a circle around the center, are six, more or less conspicuous processes.

Diameter of body 40-50 $\mu$.; with processes 65-83 $\mu$.

> This species was discovered, identified as new and named by Miss E. Butler, Minneapolis, Minnesota, where it was found.

Var. KISSIMMENSE, Wolle. Plate XLVII, figs. 1, 2, 3.

Front, lateral and vertical views; a **large, smooth** and beautiful form fully one-half larger than the original type from Minnesota; the arms are similarly constructed and arranged, but in proportion with the body, are much longer, nearly equal in length to the diameter of the body; apices not notched but **tipped** with several small **spines**.

Diameter, including arms, 100–125 $\mu$.

Grassy shores of Lake at Kissimme, Florida, **March, 1885**.

ST. ELOISEANUM, Wolle. Plate LII, figs. 17, 18.

Small, equal in length and breadth, smooth or finely punctate; sinus an acute angle; semi-cells subhexagonal, basal and superior angles produced into short, bifurcate processes; sometimes two, but oftener only one discernible **at** each angle; **end** view circular, margin furnished with (usually) nine, short processes, ends notched.

Diameter 22–30 $\mu$.

This form has some resemblance to *St. spinosum*, Breb., but in front view the processes are less conspicuous, the **apices less** distended; in end **view**, circular, not triangular.

ST. TOHOPEKALIGENSE, **Wolle**. Plate XLVII, figs. **4, 5**.

Cells smooth, semi-cell **in front view** oval with **radiating** arms; in end view triangular, **each angle drawn out into a** smooth arm nearly as long as the diameter of the body; **two** similar arms **on each** side; all at nearly equal distances and bifurcate at the apices.

Diameter, including arms, 75 $\mu$.

This **species occurs** frequently **in small coves of** Lake Tohopekaliga, at Kissimme, Florida. It bears features in common with *St. furcatum*, Breb., but is about twice the size, has more arms, and has them differently arranged; the description "one spine at each angle, with two accessory spines at the base," or "three spines at each angle," does not apply.

ST. DUPLEX, **Wolle**. Plate LXIV, figs. 6, 7.

Small, subquadrangular, **constriction deep, sinus acute-angled**; semi-cell twice as broad as long, rectangular; angles truncate and **furnished with two short**, stout processes with ends truncate **granulate-spinous**; **end** view triangular, sides straight or **concave**, angles truncate, divided and drawn out into two short, somewhat diverging processes, apices finely toothed.

**Diameter 20–25** $\mu$.

Numerous in small pools, on the banks of river, Bethlehem, Pennsylvania.

The end view has a resemblance to Nordstedt's *St. gemelliparum*, but front view is quite distinct.

St. DISTENTUM, Wolle. Plate LII, figs. 15, 16.

Small, smooth; semi-cell obovate, end convex crenulate, sides in upper portion laterally produced into nearly straight elongated arms, margins smooth; apices divided into three parts and distended; end view five or six radiate; rays taper from a broad base to a distended trifid end. Between each two of the bases is a deep linear sinus.

Diameter 40 $\mu$., more or less.

Ponds, Denmark, Splitrock, Passaic County, N. J.

St. KITCHELII, Wolle. Plate LI, figs. 35, 36.

Cells smooth, about as long as wide; semi-cells subelliptic, bases more inflated than the ends, the angles produced into bifurcate processes; semi-cells furnished with three additional processes; end view triangular, angles produced, apices bisected; on the top surface three bifurcate processes, one extending over each of the three sides; membrane smooth or finely punctate.

Diameter 38-50 $\mu$.

Collected by Rev. H. D. Kitchel, in Gilder Pond, Mount Everett, Mass.

*St. spinosum*, Ralfs, bears some similarity, but is separated by having two or more spines on each side besides the one terminating each angle. *St. furcatum*, Ehrb., also appears related, but is possessed of more spines.

St. FURCATUM, (Ehrb.), Breb. Plate LI, figs. 40, 41; Plate LIX, figs. 15, 16; Plate LXIII, fig. 34.

Cells smooth, about as long as wide, sometimes shorter, furnished with numerous processes always more or less widely furcate at the apices; end view triangular, angles somewhat produced and furcate; sides each with two, or rarely three, furcate processes; normally a semi-cell has nine processes, one at each angle and two on each side between the angles; in front view, more or less broadly elliptic, angles drawn out and furcate; the end margin has usually four processes visible, projecting over the margin.

A variable form separated from *furcigerum*, *eustephanum* and others not only by the smooth, or punctate membrane which is very striking in contrast with the granular surface, and serrate margins of the others, but by the processes, particularly evident in end view, which do not spring from the upper surface more or less distant within the margin, but from the margin itself. This feature not evident in *St. pseudofurcigerum*, Reinsch, gives it a position for itself. The form, Plate LII, figs. 8, 9, from Minneapolis, Minn., is Ralfs' *St. spinosum*, now properly transferred to this "old name," has besides the marginal processes some smaller accessory ones within the margin, Plate LXIII, fig. 34. Plate LXIII, figs. 25, 26, is another variety from the same locality of unusual size and very marked in the wide-spreading forks of the processes; Ralfs admits of "sometimes three marginal spines, as seen in end view."

St. ENORME, Ralfs. Plate LII, figs. 19-25.

Cells irregular or quadrate, spinous; end view three or four lobed; lobes broad, more or less emarginate or bifid, and terminated by spines which are either simple or branched.

Ralfs, the author of this species, says of it, it "is by far the least symmetrical plant in this family, especially in front view, and it is very difficult to trace any division into the cells."

Some of the forms, as figs. 24, 25, may properly belong to this genus, but the others would be better placed under *Polyedrium*.

These forms occur frequently in ponds of New Jersey, Pennsylvania, Massachusetts.

St. LEPTACANTHUM, Nord. Var. TETROCTOCERUM, Wolle. Plate LXII. figs. 29, 30.

Cells about as long as broad; deeply constricted; semi-cells suborbicular, furnished with eight long thin rays, deeply forked, or clawed at the ends; this whorl is rather below the middle, and another above it with four similar rays; end view octangular, each angle produced into a long, thin ray, deeply clawed at the end; between the margin and the center four more similar rays go out; membrane smooth.

Diameter of body 25 $\mu$.; including the processes 75-80 $\mu$.

Pond near Malaga, N. J.

The only essential distinction between this form, and the typical, Brazil plant, is that it has *six* rays in the larger whorl, and ours has *eight*.

St. POTTSII, Wolle. Plate LXII, figs. 8, 9.

Small, smooth, sinus gaping; semi-cells in front view broadly elliptic, furnished on each side with three divergent processes, whose apices are rounded, bearing two small diverging aculei; end view triangular, sides concave, angles broadly truncate and produced into two processes with a wide, rounded sinus between, a third process from a position somewhat back of the sinus, rising at an angle of about 40 degrees, projects between the other two, thus constituting three divergent processes at each of the angles of the triangle.

Diameter, including the aculei, 30-38 $\mu$.

>Collected by Ed. Potts in Harvey Lake, near Wilkes-Barre, Pa., where it appeared in numbers.

>The three diverging, aculei-tipped processes at each angle make this form a distinct species.

## Family, PROTOCOCCACEÆ.

Cells chlorophyllous, strictly unicellular, **without** terminal growth, either single, segregate or associated **in** families.

Propagation by means of gonidia, which are of **two kinds**, *macrogonidia* the larger kind, and *microgonidia* the smaller **forms**; they are **ovate**; the smaller, anterior end, somewhat protruding and colorless, **is** provided with two ciliae; the posterior end is broadly rounded and green.

This family is subdivided into **a number of subfamilies, and these again into** *genera*. **There remains** for us to treat merely **of the subfamily** *Pediastreae*, **and genus** *Pediastrum*. The features **of the subfamily and of the genus being, in this case, the same, therefore**

### Genus, PEDIASTRUM, Meyen.

**Cells united** into definite families, known as *coenobiums;* **they are plane,** discoid or **stellate,** swimming free. **A *coenobium* is formed of cells** in a **single or rarely, in part, double stratum, which is continuous or perforated. Cells are polygonal, with four or more** sides; those of the center entire or **often emarginate,** and those of the periphery often **bilobed; the lobes cuneate, either** simple or bidentate, often produced into **short hair-like ends.** Cell contents green, **primarily homogeneous, then granular.**

In the propagation **of the species the granular chlorophyllous** contents of the cells break **up into small** subspherical bodies; these constitute the macrogonidia, **which break through the membrane. After** a short period **of motile life, they come to rest, then divide** and redivide, **and become invested with a gelatinous** covering; **the cells unite in a single** layer, then gradually **develop into the form of the matured, or mother plant.**

P. SIMPLEX, Meyen.   Plate LXIV, figs. 17-20.

Coenobium variously **composed of from one to three circles** of subquadrilateral cells, those of the **periphery with apex more or** less conically produced, **cuspidate.**

Var. *a*. **Composed of six simple cells radiately connected,** fig. 17.

Var. *b*. (*P. Sturmii*, Reinsch.)   Composed of six cells, with an open space in the center, fig. 18.

Var. *c.* (*P. duodenarius,* Bailey), fig. 20; composed of twelve cells in the periphery, and a circle of four cells in the middle, with open spaces between the two, and open center.

Var. *d.* A new form, with three circles of cells, of fourteen, seven, and four; the four constitute the center. The openings, or lacunae, first circle seven, second four.

> The only good locality found for this species and varieties is the Croton water supply of the City of New York. Bailey's specimens, collected more than thirty years ago, were from the same source.

P. MUTICUM, Kg. Plate LXIV, fig. 36.

Coenobium circular or oval, composed of two to five circles of cells, entire, smooth, regular; peripheric cells emarginate or with two slight protuberances.

Pond waters, Pennsylvania, New Jersey.

P. ANGULOSUM, (Ehrb.), Menegh. Plate LXIV, figs. 28, 37.

Minute, consisting of one or more circles of cells. Not perforated; marginal cells with angular lobes which are not extended into rays. A small form (fig. 37) has the center open.

Frequent in ponds, New Jersey.

P. FORCIPATUM, (Corda.), A. Br. Plate LXIV, figs. 21, 30, 31.

Coenobium orbicular, entire, marginal cells bilobed; lobules with apices acute, converging, leaving an oval sinus between; usually smooth or punctate, but sometimes coarsely granular, probably when in older condition.

Ponds, Pennsylvania, New Jersey.

P. BORYANUM, (Turpin), Menegh. Plate LXIV, figs. 22, 29, 32.

Coenobium orbicular, oblong or elliptic, bright green, variable in size, composed of 8–16–128 cells. Marginal cells two lobed, each drawn out into a colorless horn-like process, short or long, rather obtuse, sometimes a little thickened at the ends. Cells closely united, four to six angled. Membrane punctate.

Sometimes the cells and the horns are distinctly granulate. These constitute the variety *granulatum,* Kg.

Frequent, Massachusetts to Florida.

P. PERTUSUM, Kg. Plate LXIV, figs. 33, 34.

Coenobium, more or less orbicular, pierced with many lacunae; variable in size; composed of 16–32–64 cells. All the cells more or less loosely connected; attached at the angles only, leaving an opening between the sides, and between the connecting end of one, and the base of the adjoining cells. Cells of the periphery deeply bilobed; lobes conical or horn-like, sometimes acute, sometimes obtuse or truncate.

Frequent in pools everywhere.

Var. BRACHYLOBUM, A. Br. Plate LXIV, fig. 35.

Differs from the typical form in having the cells of the periphery emarginate, notched, or shortly two lobed, or lobes almost obsolete; cells of the disc perforated with smaller openings.

Var. CLATHRATUM, A. Br. Discs pierced with larger openings; the lacunae being often as large as the cells.

P. EHRENBERGII, (Corda.), A. Br. Plate LXIV, figs. 25–27.

Marginal cells closely united, bilobed, medianly deeply incised; each lobule with ends truncate and notched or incised. Coenobium not perforated, composed of 4–8–16–32 cells.

Var. CUSPIDATUM, A. Br. Plate LXIV, fig. 25.

A small form, with lobes of cells finely, and often indistinctly bidentate.

Not so frequent as the preceding forms, but widely distributed.

P. TETRAS, Ehrb. Plate LXIV, fig. 24.

Coenobium very small, four-celled, separated by colorless interstices which form a cross.

A. Braun. has a variety of *P. Ehrenbergii*, var. *truncatum*, very near this form, but differs in having the ends of the lobes notched—our form, as far as observed, is perfectly square, hence I retain the old name.

Occurs frequently from Rhode Island to Florida.

P. SELENÆA, Kg.

Coenobium orbicular; cells crescent-shaped, arranged in one or more circles round one or two central cells.

A form reported by Bailey from Rhode Island.

P. CONSTRICTUM, Hass.

Coenobium nearly orbicular, continuous, composed of 16–32 cells; cells of the periphery two lobed, or suddenly contracted into two short cylindrical, obtuse processes.

Bailey reports this species from South Carolina, Georgia and Rhode Island. It is very nearly allied to *Boryanum* and is probably a variety of that species.

# ADDENDA.

In addition to note on page 16 the following may be quoted from the "Journal of the Royal Microscopical Society of London," Feb., 1884. It relates to the *motion of granules in the vacuoles of Closterium*.

The occurrence of crystals of calcium sulphate, endowed with a peculiar *dancing* motion, has long been known in the terminal vesicles of *Closterium* and in other desmids; the phenomenon has now been carefully investigated by A. Fisher. Their chemical constitution was clearly established by different tests. They are always quite isolated from one another, and occur in all parts of the cells, though in the greatest quantity in the terminal vesicles; they are either carried along passively by the currents of protoplasm, or they *swarm* in the space filled with cell-sap, between the cell wall and the radiating chlorophyl bodies; these vesicles are not true vacuoles, but portions of cell-sap space. The crytals are not formed, nor do they grow, in the vesicle, but reach it in a mature condition from some other part of the cell, being formed apparently in the furrows between the bands of the chlorophyl bodies; from here they are carried to the terminal chambers of the protoplasmic currents.

Fisher found these crystals in all species of *Closterium* which he examined, also in various species of *Cosmarium* (though individuals are often entirely destitute of them) their form being the same as in *Closterium*. They occur in *Micrasterias*, *Euastrum*, in which genera also they are not invariably present, and always in *Pleurotaenium*, *Penium* and *Tetmemorus*, but were absent from all the specimens examined of *Staurastrum*, *Desmidium* and *Hyalotheca*. They appear to be entirely confined to the Desmidieae, other fresh water Algae containing calcium oxalate, especially species of *Spirogyra*, but not calcium sulphate.

DESMIDIUM DIAGONUM (*Aptogonum diagonum*).

    Filaments compressed, perforated, twisted, not vaginate; cells in end view oblong elliptic.

    Diameter 32 $\mu$.; thickness 14 $\mu$.; length of cell about half the diameter.

Found in Lake Jessup, five miles from Sanford, Florida.

This species described by Delponte in his DESMIDIACEARUM SUBALPINARUM is, in front view, scarcely separable from *D. aptogonum*, but in lateral view it is distinct. The cells oblong elliptic, in end view not triangular. The filaments are twisted, and being more than twice as wide as thick, present an irregular outline, parts showing the broad front and parts the narrow sides of the filaments. The margins of cells are notched, and the ends excavated as in *D. aptogonum*.

SPHAEROZOSMA PULCHRUM, var. CONSTRICTUM, Wolle. Plate XLVII, fig. 12.

Cells half as long as wide, with a decided constriction in each lobe between the axis and the apex.

Diameter 70–75 $\mu$.

Lake near Kissimme, Florida.

GONATOZYGON SEXSPINIFERUM, Turner. Plate XLIII, fig. 15.

Joints variable in length, ten to thirty times the breadth; base swollen, apex either rotundo-truncate or quite rounded; spines, or rather setae, very short and arranged longitudinally in six linear series. Forming long filaments.

Length of joints 88–180 $\mu$; diameter 6–8 $\mu$.

Minnesota.

CLOSTERIUM BREBISSONII, Delp. Plate VI, fig. 17.

Cells sublinear, ends attenuated, moderately curved, apices rounded; about thirty times longer than broad; cytioderm smooth.

Diameter 18 $\mu$.

Observed occasionally, Minnesota and Pennsylvania.

# ERRATA.

Page 37, 16th line from below, strike out Plate XXXVII.
" 40, insert C. Brebissonii, Plate VI, fig. 17.
" 41, third line, change Plate V to VI.
" 42, fourteenth line, insert Plate VI, fig. 12.
" 43, fourteenth line, change VII to VI.
" 45, twelfth line, change LIV to XLIII.
" 46, twenty-fifth line, change LIV to XLIII.
" 90, eighteenth line, change Laoense to Lagoense.

# INDEX.

| | PAGE. |
|---|---|
| ADDENDA, | 171 |
| ALGÆ—Characteristics of, | xi |
| Color of, | xii |
| Fresh-Water—How to find, collect and preserve, | xiii |
| Signification of term, | xi |
| Uses of, | xii |
| Varieties of, | xii |
| ARTHRODESMUS, Ehrb., | 103 |
| " convergens (Ehrb.), Ralfs, | 103 |
| " fragilis, Wolle, | 103 |
| " incus (Ehrb.). Hass., | 104 |
| " incrassatus, Lagh., | 105 |
| Var. cycladatus, Lagh., | 105 |
| " notochondrus, Lagh., | 105 |
| " orbicularis, Wolle, | 104 |
| " octocornis, Ehrb., | 104 |
| " ovalis, Wolle, | 103 |
| " pachycerous, Lagh., | 105 |
| " quadridens, Wood, | 104 |
| " Ranii, Wolle, | 103 |
| " subulatus, Kg., | 104 |
| " triangularis, Lagh., | 105 |
| AUTHORS AND BOOKS—Names of, | viii |
| BAMBUSINA, Kg.—Characteristics of, | 24 |
| " Brebissonii, Kg., | 24 |
| Var. gracilescens, Nord., | 25 |
| " gracilescens, Nord., | 25 |
| " delicatissima, Wolle, | 25 |
| CALOCYLINDRUS, D. By.—Description of, | 58 |
| " Clevei, Wolle, | 60 |
| " connatus, (Breb.), Kirch., | 59 |
| Var. minor, Nord, | 60 |
| " Cordanum, | 59 |

| | PAGE. |
|---|---|
| CALOCYLINDRUS, costatus, Wolle, | 61 |
| " Cucurbita (Breb.), Kirch., | 59 |
| " curtus (Breb.), Kirch., | 59 |
| " De Baryi, | 58 |
| " diplospora, Lund., | 60 |
| " minutus (Ralfs), Kirch., | 59 |
| " pseudoconnatus, Nord., | 60 |
| " Ralfsii (Kg.), Kirch., | 58 |
| " Thwaitesii, Ralfs, | 60 |
| CLOSTERIUM, Nitsch.—Observations concerning, | 38 |
| " acerosum (Schrank), Ehrb., | 42 |
| " acuminatum, Kg., | 47 |
| " acutum, Breb., | 46 |
| " amblyonema, Ehrb., | 46 |
| " angustatum, Kg., | 41 |
| " areolatum, Wood, | 46 |
| " attenuatum, Ehrb., | 44 |
| " Braunii, | 45 |
| " Brebissonii, | 72A |
| " costatum, Corda, | 45 |
| " Cucumis, Ehrb, | 42 |
| " decorum, Breb., | 45 |
| " decussatum, Kg., | 41 |
| " Delpontei, | 45 |
| " Dianæ, Ehrb., | 47 |
| " didymotocum, Corda, | 40 |
| " Ehrenbergii, Menegh., | 48 |
| Var. immane, Wolle, | 48 |
| " ensis, | 40 |
| " gracile, Breb., | 40 |
| " Jenneri, Ralfs, | 47 |
| " juncidum, Ralfs, | 39 |
| forma gracillima laevissima, Breb., | 39 |
| " Kuetzingii, Breb., | 50 |
| " lanceolatum, Kg., | 40 |

# INDEX.

CLOSTERIUM, Leibleinii, **Kg.**, . 49
  "  Var. curtum, . . 49
  "  lineatum, Ehrb., . 45
    Var. costatum, . 45
  "  Lunula, Ehrb., . . 42
    Var. striatum, Wolle, . 42
  "  macilentum, Breb., . 40
  "  moniliferum, Ehrb., . 48
  "  nasutum, Nord., . 43
  "  obtusum, Breb., . 39
  "  parvulum, Naeg., . 47
  "  prolongum, **Delp.**, . 43
  "  pronum, Breb., . . 50
  "  Ralfsii, Breb., . 49
  "  robustum, Hast., . 48
  "  rostratum, Ehrb., . 49
    Var. brevirostratum, West., . . . 49
  "  setaceum, Ehrb., . 50
  "  strigosum, Ehrb., . 44
  "  striolatum, Ehrb., . 44
  "  subcostatum, Nord., 43
  "  subdirectum, West, 46
  "  subtile, Breb., . 42
  "  turgidum, Ehrb., . 43
  "  Venus, Kg., . . 47

CONJUGATÆ—Family of, . 21

COSMARIUM, Corda—Divisions of, 62
  "  aculeatum, Wolle, . 71
  "  amœnum, Breb., . 85
    Var. tumidum, Wolle, 86
  "  Americanum, Lagh., 64
  "  anceps, Lund., . . 63
  "  anisochondrum **Nord.**, 78
  "  ansatum Kg., . . 74
  "  Baileyii, Wolle, . . 69
  "  bireme, Nord., . 89
  "  bioculatum, Breb., . 66
  "  biretum, Breb., . . 93
    Var. Floridense, **Wolle**, 93
  "  Blyttii, Wille, . 95
  "  Botrytis, Menegh., . 81
    Var. tumidum, Wolle, 82
  "  Braunii, Reinsch., . 72A
  "  Brebissonii, Menegh., . 82
  "  Broomei, Thwaites, . 93
  "  caelatum, Ralfs, . 93
  "  circulare, Reinsch, . 68

COSMARIUM conspersum, **Ralfs**, 82
    Var. retusum, . 82
  "  constrictum, Delp., . 63
  "  commisurale, Breb., . 91
  "  Cordanum, Breb., . 59
  "  contractum, Kirch., . 68
  "  crenatum, Ralfs, . . 73
    Var. crenulatum, Wolle, 73
  "  cruciatum, Breb., . . 89
  "  Cucumis, Corda, . 62
  "  DeBaryii, **Arch.**, . 62
  "  dentatum, Wolle, . 83
  "  depressum (Naeg.), Lund., 69
  "  Donnellii, Wolle, . 77
  "  elegantissimum, Lund., . 86
  "  Eloiseanum, Wolle, . 92
  "  Everettense, Wolle, . 92
  "  excavatum, Nord., . 85
    Var. trigonum, . . 85
    Var. duplo major, . 85
  "  exiguum, Arch., . . 72
  "  galeritum, **Nord.**, . 75
  "  globosum, Bulnh., . 65
  "  granatum, Breb., . 64
  "  Hammeri, Reinsch, . 86
  "  Holmiense, Lund., . 74
    Var. integrum, Lund., . 74
  "  homalodermum, Nord., 88
  "  inflatum, Wolle, . 67
  "  intermedium, Delp., . 83
  "  Kitchelii, Wolle, . 79
  "  Kjellmanii, **Wille,** . 94
  "  laeve, Rab., . . 72A
    Var. septentrionale, 72A
  "  lagoense, Nord., . 90
  "  latum, Breb., . . 84
  "  lobatulum, Wolle, . 66
  "  lunatum, **Wolle**, . 71
  "  margaritiferum, Menegh., 81
  "  margaritum, Wolle, . 88
  "  Meneghinii, Breb., . 70
    Var. simplicissimum, 71
  "  microsphinctum, . 81
    Var. parvula, Nord., 81
  "  moniliforme, Ralfs, . 65
  "  Naegelianum, Breb., . 73
  "  nasutum, Nord., . 96
  "  nitidulum, Be Not., . 62
  "  Nordstedtii, Delp., . 80
  "  notabile, Breb., . 72, 86

# INDEX.

| | | PAGE | | | PAGE |
|---|---|---|---|---|---|
| Cosmarium | Nymannianum, Grun., | 87 | Cosmarium | sendtnerianum, | 72A |
| " | obsoletum, Reinsch, | 70 | " | sexangulare, Lund., | 69 |
| " | ochthodes, Nord, | 84 | " | sinuosum, Lund., | 70 |
| " | octogonum, Delp., | 71 | " | Smolandicum, Lund., | 72 |
| " | oculiferum, Lagh, | 76 | " | speciosum, Lund., | 95 |
| " | ornatum, Ralfs, | 89 | " | sphalerostichum, Nord., | 76 |
| | Var. protractum, Wolle, | 90 | " | Sportella, Breb., | 90 |
| " | orbiculatum, Ralfs, | 85 | " | stenonotum, Nord., | 74 |
| " | orthosticum, Lund., | 86 | " | subcrenatum, Hantzsch, | 91 |
| " | ovale, Ralfs, | 62 | " | suberuciforme, Lagh., | 94 |
| " | pachydermum, Lund., | 75 | " | sublobatum, Arch., | 87 |
| " | Pardalis, Cohn, | 83 | " | suborbiculare, Wood, | 85 |
| " | parvulum, Breb., | 64 | " | supraspeciosum, Wolle, | 95 |
| " | Pectinoides, Wolle, | 96 | " | taxichondrum, Lund., | 77 |
| " | perforatum, Lund., | 65 | | Var. bidentatum, Lagh., | 77 |
| " | Phaseolus, Breb., | 89 | " | tetrophthalmum (Kg.), | |
| " | polygonum, Naeg., | 71 | | Breb., | 82 |
| " | polymazum, Nord., | 76 | " | tinctum, Ralfs, | 67 |
| " | polymorphum, Nord., | 80 | " | tithophorum, Nord., | 88 |
| " | Portianum, Arch., | 84 | " | trachypleurum, Lund., | 79 |
| " | protractum (Naeg.), Arch., | 90 | " | triplicatum, Wolle, | 79 |
| " | protuberans, Lund., | 91 | " | tumidum, Lund., | 67 |
| | Var. granulatum, Wolle, | 91 | " | Turpinii, Breb., | 87 |
| " | Pseudobroomei, Wolle, | 93 | " | undulatum, Corda, | 72 |
| " | pseudonitidulum, Nord., | 72A | | Var. crenulatum, | 73 |
| " | Pseudopectinoides, Wolle, | 96 | " | variolatum, Lund., | 68 |
| " | pseudogranatum, Nord., | 64 | " | venustum, Rab., | 73 |
| " | pseudopyramidatum, Lund., | 75 | " | Wolleanum, Lagh., | 64 |
| " | pseudotaxichondrum, Nord., | 77 | | Var. granuliferum, Lagh. | 64 |
| " | pulcherrimum, Nord., | 97 | | | |
| " | punctulatum, Breb., | 80 | Crystals in Desmids, | | — |
| " | pyramidatum, Breb., | 74 | Desmidieae—How generated and | | |
| | Var. stenonotum, | 74 | multiplied, | | 17 |
| " | pycnochondrum, Nord., | 97 | Desmidium, Ag.—Description of, | | 25 |
| " | quadratum, Ralfs, | 63 | " | aptogonium, Breb., | 27 |
| " | quadrifarium, Lund., | 94 | " | Baileyii, Ralfs, | 27 |
| " | Quasillus, Nord, | 92 | " | cylindricum, Grev., | 25 |
| " | Quimbyii, Wood, | 66 | " | diagonum, Delp., | 171 |
| " | quinarium, Lund., | 78 | " | longatum, Wolle, | 26 |
| " | radiosum, Wolle, | 97 | " | quadrangulatum, Kg., | 27 |
| " | Ralfsii, Breb., | 75 | " | quadratum, Nord,. | 26 |
| " | Regnesi, Zeinsch, | 70 | " | Swartzii, Ag., | 26 |
| " | reniforme, Ralfs, | 84 | | | |
| " | Reinschii, Arch., | 73 | Desmids—Characteristics of, | | 16 |
| " | retusum, Perty, | 87 | | How multiplied, | 17 |
| " | rhombusoides, Wolle, | 66 | | Regeneration of, | 18 |
| " | scenedesmus, Delp., | 63 | | Of the United States, | 21 |
| " | Schliephackeanum, Grun., | 89 | | Voluntary movements of, | 16 |
| " | Seelyanum, Wolle, | 80 | | Where found, | 15 |
| " | sejunctum, Wolle, | 68 | Didymoprium, Kg., | | 23 |

# INDEX.

DOCIDIUM, Breb.—Why name is retained, . . . . 50
" Archerii, Delp., . . 51
" Baculum (Breb.), D.By., . 52
    Var. Floridense, Wolle, 52
" breve, Wood. . . . 54
" clavatum (Kg.), D.By., 51
" constrictum, Bail., . . 54
" coronatum, Rab., . 53
" coronulatum, Grun., . 53
" costatum, Wolle, . 57
" crenulatum (Ehrb.), Rab., 51
" dilatatum (Cleve), Lund., 55
" Ehrenbergii, Ralfs, . . 53
    Var. Floridense, Wolle, 53
" Flotowii, Rab., . 52
" **gracile, Breb.,** 58
" Georgicum, . . 55
" hirsutum, Bail., 56
" minutum, Ralfs, . 57
" nodosum, Bail., 54
" nodulosum, 51
" rectum, Delp., . 52
" repandum, Wolle, . 54
" sinuosum, Wolle, 55
    Var. breve, Wolle, . 55
" spinosum, Wolle, 56
" Trabecula (Ehrb.), Naeg, 51
" tridentulum, Wolle, 57
" truncatum, Breb., . 52
" undulatum, Bail., 55
" verrucosum (Bailey), Ralfs, 56
" verticillatum, Bail., . 57
    **Var. turgidum, Wolle,** 58
" Woodii, . . . 55

EUASTRUM, Ehrb., . . . 106
" abruptum, Nord., 118
" **affine, Ralfs,** . . 110
" ampullaceum, Ralfs, 110
" ansatum (Ehrb.), Ralfs, . 109
" attenuatum, Wolle, 113
" binale (Turpin), Ralfs, . 117
" circulare, (Hass.), Ralfs, 112
" compactum, Wolle, . 117
" crassicolle, Lund., 115
" crassum (Breb.), Kg., 106
    Var. scrobiculum, 106
" cuneatum, Jenner, . 108
" **cuspudatum, Wolle,** . 115

EUASTRUM didelta (Turpin), Ralfs, 109
" divaricatum, Lund., . 114
" Donnellii, Wolle, . 114
" **elegans, Kg.,** . . 116
" erosum, Lund., . . 115
" Everettense, Wolle, . 112
" formosum, Wolle, . 114
" gemmatum, Breb., 112
" Hastingsii, Wolle, . 113
" humerosum, Ralfs, 107
" inerme, Lund., . 115
" insigne, Hass., 113
" insulare, Wittr., . 115
" integrum, Wolle, 117
" intermedium, Cleve, . 108
    Var. cuspadatum, Wolle, 103
" magnificum, Wolle, . 108
    Var. crassioides, Hast., 108
" mammillosum, Wolle, . 113
" multilobatum, Wood, . 107
" Nordstedtianum, Wolle, . 116
" **oblongum (Grev.), Ralfs,** 106
" **obtusum, Wolle,** . . 117
" ornatum, Wood, . . 106
" pectinatum, Breb., . 109
" pingue, Elf., . . 116
" **pinnatum, Ralfs,** . 107
" Pokornyanum, Grun., . 114
" **purum, Wolle,** . . 110
" rostratum, Ralfs, 116
" simplex, Wolle, . 117
" **spinosum, Ralfs,** . 116
" urnaforme, Wolle, . . 111
" ventricosum, Lund., . 110
" verrucosum (Ehrb.), Ralfs, 111
    Var. alatum, Wolle, 111
    " Crux Africanum, Lagh., . . 111
    " reductum, Nord., 112
    " simplex, Joshua, . 111
" Wollei, Lagh , . . 108
    Var. quadrigibberum, Lagh., . 108
" cuspidatum, Wolle 109

GONATOZYGON, D.By.—Description, 22
" asperum (Ralfs), Rab., 22
" pilosum, Wolle, . 22
" Ralfsii, D. By., . 22
" sexspiniferum, Turner, . 172

# INDEX.

| | PAGE |
|---|---|
| **HYALOTHECA**, Ehrb.—Characteristics of, | 22 |
| How to find and collect, | xiii |
| " dissiliens (Smith), Breb., | 22 |
| Var. hians, Wolle, | 22 |
| " dubia, Kg., | 24 |
| " mucosa (Mert.), Ralfs, | 23 |
| " undulata, Nord., | 23 |
| **MESOTÆNIUM**, Naeg.—Generation of, | 31 |
| " **Braunii, D. By.,** | 31 |
| " **Clepsydra, Wood,** | 33 |
| " **Endlicherianum, Naeg.,** | 32 |
| " **micrococcum, Kg.,** | 32 |
| **MICRASTERIAS**, Ag., | 118 |
| " Americana (Ehrb.), **Kg.,** | 124 |
| Var. spinosa, Tur., | 124 |
| " Hermanniana, Rh. | 124 |
| " recta, Wolle, | 124 |
| " alata, Wall, | 125 |
| " apiculata, Menegh., | 124 |
| " arcuata, Bailey, | 129 |
| " Baileyi, Ralfs, | 130 |
| " brachyptera, Lund., | 121 |
| " conferta, Lund., | 126 |
| " crenata (Breb.), Ralfs, | 126 |
| " Crux-Melitensis, Ehrb., | 123 |
| " decemdentata, Naeg., | 126 |
| " denticulata (Breb.), **Ralfs,** | 120 |
| " dichotoma, Wolle, | 123 |
| " expansa, Bailey, | 129 |
| " fimbriata, Ralfs, | 121 |
| Forma, genuina, | 121 |
| " apiculata, Menegh., | 121 |
| " Elephanta, Wolle, | 121 |
| " nuda, **Wolle,** | 121 |
| " simplex, Wolle, | 121 |
| " foliacea, Bailey, | 130 |
| " furcata (Ag.), Ralfs, | 122 |
| Var. simplex, Wolle, | 122 |
| " hamata, Wolle, | 127 |
| " Jenneri, Ralfs, | 127 |
| " **Kitchelii, Wolle,** | 129 |
| " laticeps, Nord., | 128 |
| " **Mahabuelshwarensis, Hn.** | 124 |
| " mamillata, Tur., | 125 |
| " muricata, Bailey, | 130 |
| " Nordstedtiana, Wolle, | 125 |

| | PAGE |
|---|---|
| MICRASTERIAS, oscitans, Ralfs, | 128 |
| " papillifera, Breb., | 120 |
| " pinnatifida (Kg.), Ralfs, | 128 |
| " pseudofurcata, Wolle, | 122 |
| Var. minor, Wolle, | 122 |
| " Pseudotorreyi, Wolle, | 118 |
| " quadrata, Bailey, | **129** |
| " Rabenhorstii, Kirch., | **131** |
| " radiosa (Ag.), Ralfs, | 119 |
| Var. punctata, West, | 119 |
| " ringens, Bailey, | 123 |
| Var. serulata, Wolle, | 123 |
| " rotata (Grev.), Ralfs, | 120 |
| " speciosa, Wolle, | 119 |
| " Swainei, Hast., | **119** |
| " Torreyi (Bailey), Ralfs, | 118 |
| " triangularis, Wolle, | 127 |
| " truncata (Corda), Ralfs, | 126 |
| " verrucosa, Roy, | 120 |
| " Multiplication of, | 17 |
| " Names of Authors, | ix |
| **PEDIASTRUM**, Meyen.—Description of, | 168 |
| " angulosum, Menegh., | 168 |
| " Boryanum (Turpin), | 169 |
| " brachylobum, A. Br., | 170 |
| Var. clathratum, A.Br., | **170** |
| " constrictum, Hass., | 170 |
| " duodenarius, Bailey, | 169 |
| " Ehrenbergii, A. Br., | 170 |
| Var. cuspidatum, | 170 |
| " forcipatum (Corda) A. Br., | 169 |
| " muticum, Kg., | 169 |
| " pertusum, Kg., | 169 |
| " Selenæa, Kg., | 170 |
| " simplex, Meyen, | **168** |
| " Sturmii, Reinsch, | 168 |
| " tetras, Ehrb., | 170 |
| **PENIUM**, Breb.—Description of, | 33 |
| " Brebissonii (Mengh.), Ralfs, | 37 |
| " Clevei, Lund., | 38 |
| " closterioides, Ralfs, | 36 |
| " crassa, D. By., | 36 |
| " cruciferum, (D.By.) Wittr | 38 |
| " Digitus (Ehrb.), | 34 |
| " interruptum, Breb., | 36 |
| " Jenneri, Ralfs, | 37 |
| " lamellosum, Breb., | 34 |

# INDEX.

| | PAGE |
|---|---|
| PENIUM, margaritaceum, Breb., | 35 |
| " minutum, Cleve, | 36 |
| " Navicula, Breb., | 37 |
| " oblongum, D. By., | 35 |
| " polymorphum, Perty, | 37 |
| " rupestre, Kg., | 38 |
| " spirostriolatum, Barker, | 35 |
| " tumidum, F. Gay, | 38 |
| " truncatum, Ralfs, | 36 |
| PHYMATODICIS, Nord., | 28 |
| " Nordstedtianum, Wolle, | 28 |
| PLEUROTAENIUM, see DOCIDIUM. | |
| Regeneration, | 18 |
| SPHAEROZOSMA, Corda—Wherein it differs from Phymatodocis | 28 |
| " excavatum, Ralfs, | 30 |
| " filiforme, Rab., | 29 |
| " moniliforme, Lund., | 30 |
| " Nordstediana, Turner, | 31 |
| " pulchellum (Arch.), Rab., | 29 |
| " pulchrum, Bailey, | 29 |
| Var. constrictum, Wolle, | 172 |
| " inflatum, Wolle, | 29 |
| " planum, Wolle, | 29 |
| " rectangulare, Wolle, | 31 |
| " serratum, Bailey, | 30 |
| " spinulosum, Delp., | 31 |
| " vertebratum (Breb.), Ralfs, | 30 |
| " Wallachi? Jacobson, | 31 |
| SPIROTAENIA, Breb., | 33 |
| " bryophila (Breb.), Rab., | 34 |
| " condensata, Breb., | 33 |
| " obscura, Ralfs, | 33 |
| STAURASTRUM, Meyen, | 119 |
| " aculeatum, Ehrb., | 153 |
| " alternans, Breb., | 142 |
| " anatinum, Cooke—Wills, | 152 |
| " angulatum, West, | 132 |
| " ankyroides, Wolle, | 150 |
| Var. hexacerum, Wolle, | 151 |
| " Arachne, Ralfs, | 143 |
| " aretiscon, Ehrb., | 163 |
| " arcuatum, Nord., | 152 |
| " aristiferum, Ralfs, | 135 |
| " asperum, Breb., | 140 |
| " aspinosum, Wolle, | 157 |

| | PAGE |
|---|---|
| STAURASTRUM, Avicula, **Breb.**, | **136** |
| " bacillare, Breb., | 132 |
| " Bieneanum, Rab., | 137 |
| " botrophilum, Wolle, | 145 |
| " brachiatum, Ralfs, | 136 |
| " Brebissonii, Arch., | 154 |
| " brevispina, Breb., | 134 |
| Var. inerme, Wille, | 134 |
| " Brasiliense, Nord., | 160 |
| Var. triquetrum, Wolle, | 160 |
| " calyxoides, Wolle, | 158 |
| " Cerastes, Lund., | 147 |
| " cerberus, Bailey, | 156 |
| " commutatum, Kg., | 136 |
| " comptum, Wolle, | 143 |
| " controversum, Breb., | 155 |
| " **cornutum**, Wolle, | 158 |
| " coronulatum, Wolle, | 148 |
| Var. Floridense, Wolle, | 149 |
| " cosmarioides, Reinsch, | 139 |
| " crenatum, Bailey, | 138 |
| " crenulatum, (Delp.), Naeg. | 140 |
| " crescentum, Hast., | 153 |
| " cruciatum, Wolle, | 156 |
| " cuneatum, Wolle, | **162** |
| " cuspidatum, Breb., | 135 |
| " crytocerum, Breb., | **142** |
| Var. major, Wlole, | **142** |
| " pentacladum, Wolle | **143** |
| " dejectum, Breb., | 134 |
| Var mucronatum, Ralfs, | 134 |
| " convergens, Wolle, | 134 |
| " Dickiei, Ralfs, | 135 |
| " dilatatum, Ehrb., | 142 |
| " distentum, Wolle, | 165 |
| " Donnellii, Wolle, | 146 |
| " duplex, Wolle, | 164 |
| " echinatum, Breb., | 154 |
| " Eloisianum, Wolle, | 164 |
| " elongatum, Barker, | 143 |
| Var. tetragonum, Wolle | 143 |
| " enorme, Ralfs, | **166** |
| " erasum, Breb., | 139 |
| Var. espinulosa, Lund., | 139 |
| " eustephanum, Ralfs, | **161** |
| " fasciculoides, Wolle, | 144 |
| " forficulatum, Lund., | 158 |
| " Franconium, Reinsch, | 145 |
| " furcatum, (Ehrb.), Breb., | 165 |
| " furcigerum, Breb., | 161 |

| | | PAGE |
|---|---|---|
| STAURASTRUM, | fusiforme, Wolle, | 150 |
| " | gracile, Ralfs, | 147 |
| " | grande, Bulnh., | 133 |
| " | grallatorium, Nord., | 150 |
| | Var. ungulatum, Wolle, | 150 |
| " | Haaboeliense, Wille, | 147 |
| " | Heleneanum, Wolle, | 146 |
| " | hirsutum (Ehrb.), Breb., | 155 |
| " | Hystrix, Ralfs, | 156 |
| " | incisum, Wolle, | 146 |
| " | inconspicuum, Nord., | 137 |
| " | iotanum, Wolle, | 150 |
| " | Kitchelii, Wolle, | 165 |
| " | leptacanthum, Nord., | 166 |
| " | leptocladum, Nord., | 149 |
| " | Lewisii, Wood, | 135 |
| " | longispinum, Bailey, | 160 |
| " | luteolum, Lagh., | 139 |
| " | manmense, Arch., | 139 |
| " | macrocerum, Wolle, | 148 |
| " | magnum, Wolle, | 133 |
| " | majusculum, Wolle, | 133 |
| " | margaritaceum, Ehrb., | 138 |
| " | megacanthum, Lund., | 134 |
| " | megalonotum, Nord., | 141 |
| " | Meriani, Reinsch, | 146 |
| " | Minneapoliense, Wolle, | 141 |
| " | Minnesotense, Wolle, | 156 |
| " | monticulosum, Breb., | 159 |
| " | munitum, Wood, | 163 |
| " | muricatum, Breb., | 140 |
| " | muticum, Breb., | 131 |
| | Var. minus, | 131 |
| | " ellipticum, | 132 |
| " | nanum, Wolle, | 151 |
| " | Novæ Cæsareæ, Wolle, | 159 |
| " | odontatum, Wolle, | 148 |
| " | Ophiura, Lund., | 147 |
| | Var. pentacerum, Wolle, | 148 |
| | " tetracerum, Wolle, | 148 |
| " | orbiculare (Ehrb.), Ralfs, | 132 |
| " | paniculosum, Wolle, | 136 |
| " | paradoxum, Meyen, | 143 |
| | Var. Osceolense, Wolle, | 132 |
| " | Pecten, Perty, | 155 |
| " | pentacladum, Wolle, | 149 |
| " | polymorphum, Breb., | 139 |
| " | Pottsii, Wolle, | 166 |
| " | Pringlei, Wolle, | 145 |
| " | pseudocrenatum, Wolle, | 139 |

| | | PAGE |
|---|---|---|
| STAURASTRUM, | pseudofurcigerum, Reinsch, | 162 |
| " | pseudopachyrhynchum, Wolle, | 137 |
| " | Pseudosebaldi, Wolle, | 152 |
| " | pusillum, Wolle, | 144 |
| " | punctulatum, Breb., | 141 |
| " | pygmæum, Breb., | 141 |
| | Forma—genuina, Breb., | 141 |
| | " rhomboides, Wolle, | 141 |
| | " truncata, Wolle, | 141 |
| " | quadrangulare, Breb., | 160 |
| " | quaternium, Wolle, | 158 |
| " | Ravenelii, Wood, | 157 |
| " | rotula, Nord., | 148 |
| " | rugulosum, Breb., | 140 |
| " | scabrum, Breb., | 143 |
| " | Saxonicum, Bulnh., | 154 |
| | Var. pentagona, | 154 |
| " | Sebaldi, Reinsch, | 151 |
| | Var. spinosum, Wolle, | 152 |
| " | senarium, Ralfs, | 162 |
| " | setigerum, Cleve, | 152 |
| " | silatatum, Nord, | 142 |
| " | sociatum, Wolle, | 155 |
| " | spongiosum, Breb., | 163 |
| " | striolatum, Naeg., | 138 |
| " | subarcuatum, Wolle, | 153 |
| " | teliferum, Ralfs, | 154 |
| " | tetroctocerum, Wolle, | 166 |
| " | Tohopekaligense, Wolle, | 164 |
| " | tricorne, Breb., | 138 |
| " | tricornutum, Wolle, | 155 |
| " | tridentiferum, Wolle, | 155 |
| " | trifidum, Nord., | 136 |
| " | trihedrale, Wolle, | 136 |
| " | tumidum, Breb., | 133 |
| " | ungulatum, Wolle, | 150 |
| " | vesiculatum, Wolle, | 132 |
| " | vestitum, Ralfs, | 151 |
| " | Wolleanum, Butler, | 163 |
| | Var. Kissimmense, Wolle, | 164 |
| " | xiphidophorum, Wolle, | 155 |
| | Var. simplex, Wolle, | 155 |
| TETMEMORUS, Ralfs—Description of, | | 98 |
| " | Brebissonii (Menegh.), Ralfs, | 98 |
| " | giganteus, Wood, | 99 |

| | PAGE |
|---|---|
| TETEMEMORUS, granulatus, Ralfs, | 98 |
| " laevis (Kg.), Ralfs, | 98 |
| " minutus, D. By., | 99 |
| " turgidus, Ralfs, | 98 |
| XANTHIDIUM, Ehrb., | 99 |
| " aculeatum (Ehrb.), Breb., | 99 |
| " antilopaeum (Breb.), Kg, | 101 |
| Var. polymazum, Nord., | 101 |
| " triquetrum, Lund., | 101 |
| ' Canadense, Joshua, | 102 |
| " truncatum, Hast., | 101 |
| " asteptum, Nord., | 100 |

| | PAGE |
|---|---|
| XANTHIDIUM, armatum (Breb.), Ralfs, | 99 |
| " bisenarium, Ehrb., | 100 |
| " Columbianum, Wolle, | 100 |
| " cristatum (Breb.), Ralfs, | 100 |
| ' fasciculatum (Ehrb.) Ralfs | 101 |
| Var. hexagonum, Wolle, | 101 |
| " minus, Wolle, | 101 |
| " subalpinum, Wolle, | 101 |
| " Minneapoliense, Wolle, | 101 |
| " rectocornutum, Wolle, | 102 |
| " tetracentrotum, Wolle, | 102 |
| ZYGOSPOREÆ—Order of, | 21 |

# EXPLANATIONS AND REFERENCES.

## PLATE I.

Figures magnified 500 diameters.

|  |  |  |  | PAGE. |
|---|---|---|---|---|
| Fig. 1. | GONATOZYGON ASPERUM, (*Ralfsii*), filaments and developed zygospore, | | | 22 |
| " 2. | " PILOSUM, | | | 22 |
| Figs. 3–5. | HYALOTHECA DISSILIENS; three forms, normal condition, | | | 22 |
| " 6, 8. | " | " | end views of two cells, | 22 |
| Fig. 7. | " | " | a cell separated from the **filament**, | 22 |
| " 9. | " | " | first stage of conjugation, one cell in front view, the other in end view, | 22 |
| Figs. 10, 11. | " | " | advancing stages; chlorophyl of the two cells concentrating in the gelatinous connecting tube, | 22 |
| Fig. 12. | " | " | the developed zygospore, | 22 |
| " 13. | HYALOTHECA MUCOSA, | | | 23 |
| " 14. | HYALOTHECA DUBIA, | | | 24 |
| " 15. | BAMBUSINA BREBISSONII, | | | 24 |
| " 16. | " | " | a developed zygospore, | 24 |
| " 17. | " | " | first stage of development from a zygospore; undeveloped cells enclosed in a gelatinous envelope, | 24 |
| " 18 | " | " | a second condition, the gelatinous envelope largely dissipated, | 24 |
| " 19. | " | " | **early form of** a developing filament, | 24 |
| " 20. | " | " | more advanced **stage**; appearance of **notch at the middle of** the cells, | 24 |
| " 21. | " | " | central inflation begins to show, | 24 |
| " 22. | BAMBUSINA DELICATISSIMA, fully developed, | | | 25 |
| " 23. | " | " | earlier stage, | 25 |
| " 24. | " | " | **younger still**, | 25 |

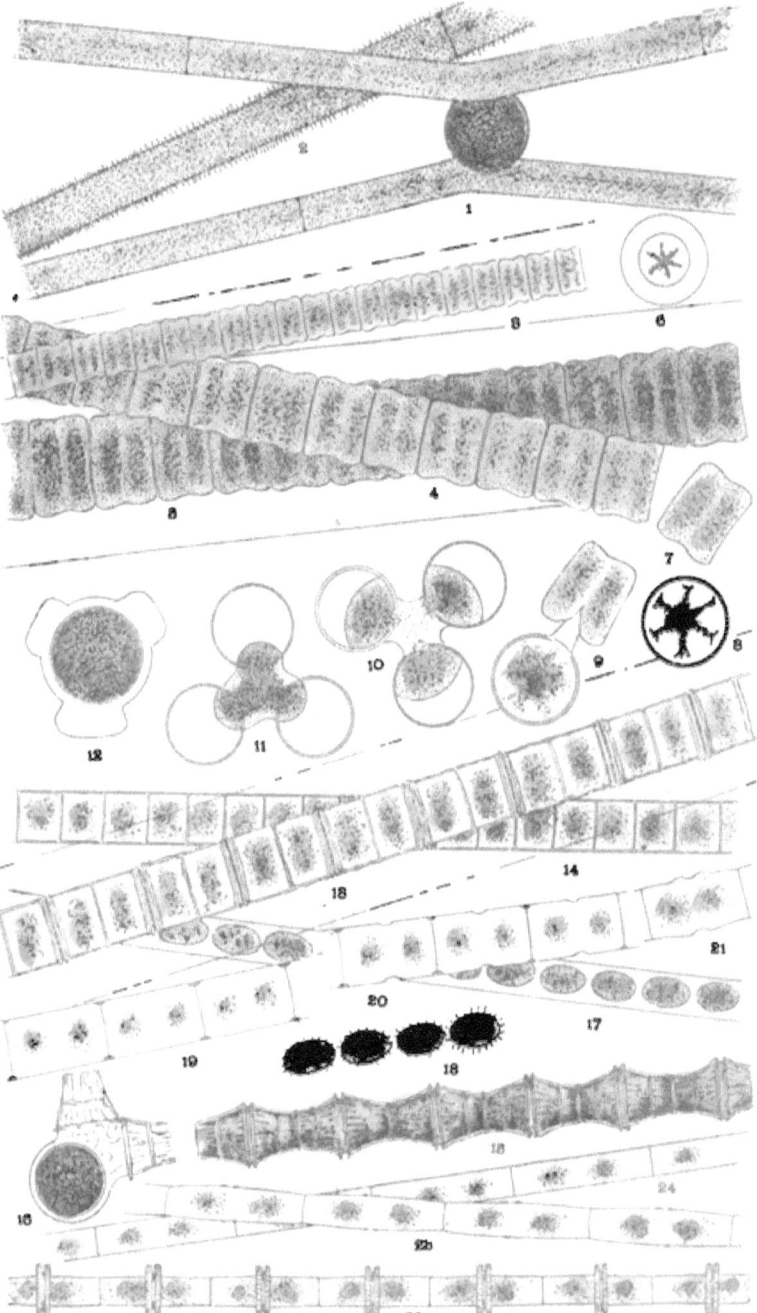

## PLATE II.

Figures magnified 500 diameters.

|  |  |  | PAGE. |
|---|---|---|---|
| Figs. 1, 2. | DESMIDIUM SWARTZII. | Two forms; filaments in vegetative condition, | 26 |
| Fig. 3. | " " | Filament in fruit; the spores, and empty cells forced apart by the growth of the spore, | 26 |
| Figs. 4, 5. | " " | End view of cells, showing the triangular form of the filaments, | 26 |
| Fig. 6. | DESMIDIUM APTOGONIUM, | a vegetative filament, | 27 |
| " 7. | " " | the triangular end view of the same, | 27 |
| Figs. 8, 9. | DESMIDIUM BAILEYI. | (*Aptogonum Baileyi.*) 8. the normal vegetative condition of the chlorophyl; 9. the same concentrating for the formation of the spores, (left hand figure is an end view), | 27 |
| Fig. 10. | " " | the fully developed spores, | 27 |
| " 11. | " " | spores matured and separating from the filaments, | 27 |
| " 12. | " " | end view of filament, | 27 |
| " 13. | DESMIDIUM QUADRANGULATUM; | part of a filament, | 27 |
| " 14. | " " | end view of filament, | 27 |

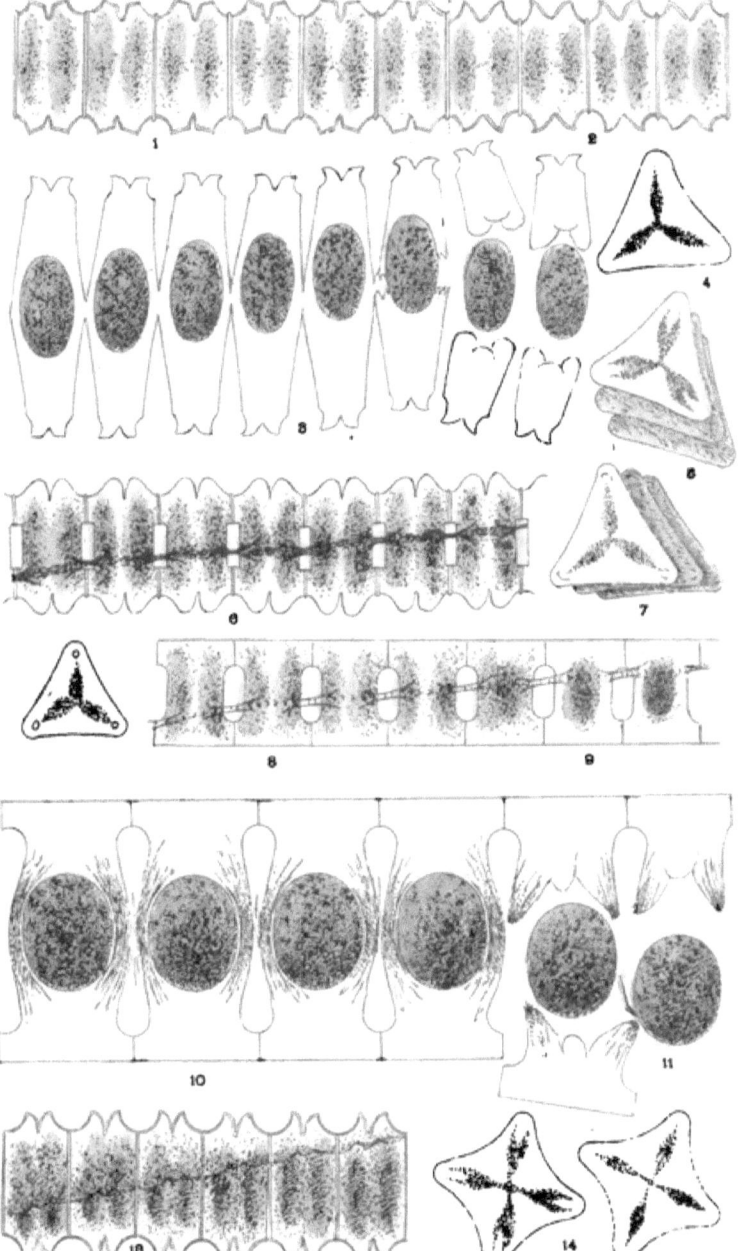

## PLATE III.

#### Figures magnified 500 diameters.

| | | | | PAGE. |
|---|---|---|---|---|
| Fig. 1. | DESMIDIUM CYLINDRICUM, (*Didymoprium Grevilli*), part of a vegetative filament, | | | 25 |
| " 2. | " " end view of a cell, | | | 25 |
| " 3. | " " two cells copulated; chlorophyllous contents passing through a gelatinous tube, from one cell to the other, | | | 25 |
| " 4. | " " Two developed zygospores; the two empty cells still connected, | | | 25 |
| " 5. | MESOTAENIUM BRAUNII, D. By. (*Palmoglœa macrococca*, Kg.), a group of three vegetative cells, | | | 32 |
| Figs. 6–9. | " " advancing stages of copulation and spore formation to the fully developed zygospore, | | | 32 |
| Fig 10. | MESOTAENIUM MICROCOCCUM, a group of seven cells, | | | 32 |
| " 11. | MESOTAENIUM ENDLICHERIANUM, a group of four cells, | | | 32 |
| " 12. | MESOTAENIUM CLEPSYDRA, three vegetative cells, | | | 32 |
| Figs. 13–15. | " " two cells copulating and two developed spores, husks remaining attached, | | | 33 |
| " 16–19. | SPIROTAENIA OBSCURA, | | | 33 |
| " 16, 17. | " " young stages of development in gelatinous envelopes, | | | 33 |
| " 18, 19. | " " more matured forms, | | | 33 |
| Fig. 20. | SPIROTAENIA BRYOPHILA, (*S. muscicola*), a group of four, | | | 34 |
| Figs. 21, 22. | SPIROTAENIA CONDENSATA, | | | 33 |

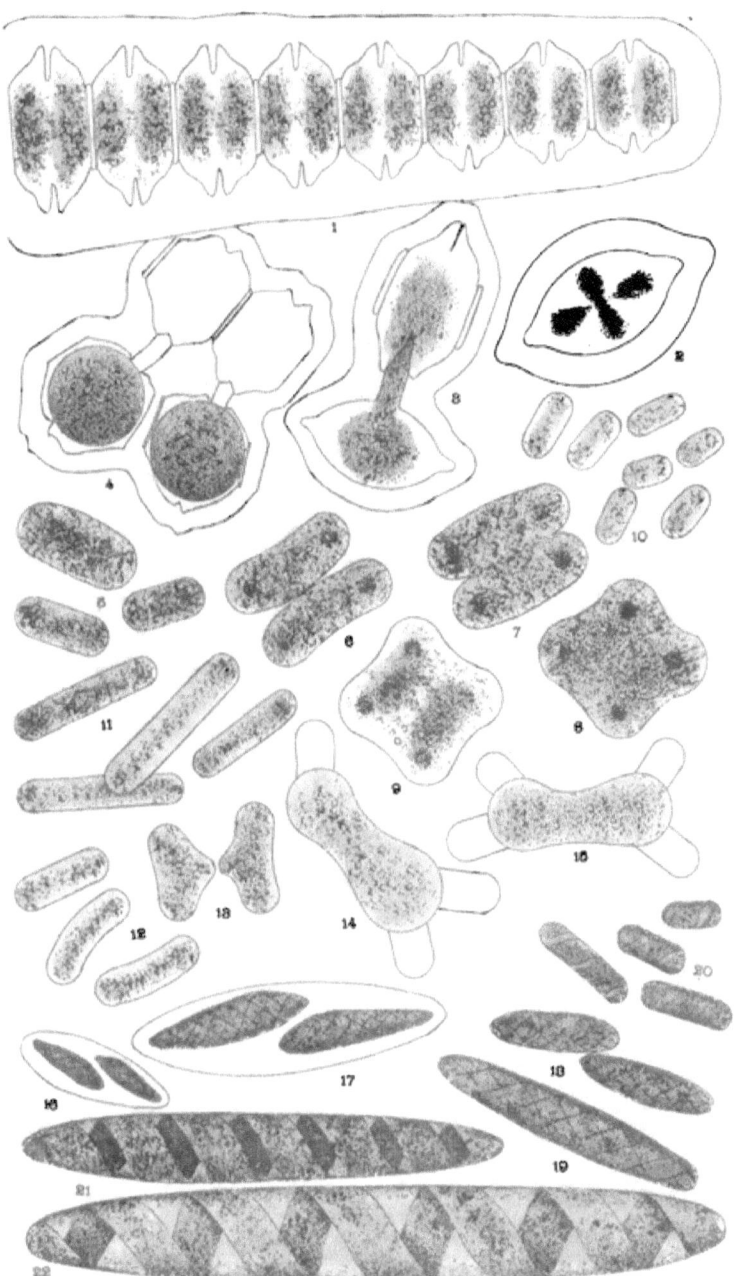

## PLATE IV.

### Figures magnified 50 diameters.

|  |  | PAGE |
|---|---|---|
| Figs. 1, 2. | SPHAEROZOSMA PULCHRUM, filament enveloped in a colorless gelatinous sheath; the irregular breadth is produced by the twist of the filament, | 29 |
| " 3, 4, | "         " Var. planum, | 29 |
| " 5, 6. | SPHAEROZOSMA FILIFORME, | 29 |
| Fig. 7. | SPHAEROZOSMA SERRATUM. See also Plate XLIII, | 30 |
| " 8. | SPHAEROZOSMA EXCAVATUM, with gelatinous sheath, | 30 |
| " 9. | "         " with sheath partially dispersed, | 29 |
| Figs. 10 12. | "         " developed spores with empty cells attached, | 29 |
| Fig. 13. | SPHAEROZOSMA VERTEBRATUM ? with a decided twist, | 30 |
| " 14. | SPHAEROZOSMA SPINULOSUM ? | 31 |
| " 15. | SPHAEROZOSMA WALLACHII ? | 31 |

For additional varieties see—

| | | | |
|---|---|---|---|
| Plate LX. | S. PULCHRUM, Var. inflatum, | | 29 |
| Plate XLVII. | S. var. CONSTRICTUM, | Addenda, | 172 |
| Plate LX. | S. RECTANGULARE, | | 31 |
| Plate XII. | S. PULCHELLUM, | | 29 |
| Plate XLVII. | S. MONILIFORME, | | 30 |
| Plate XLIII. | S. NORDSTEDTIANA, | | 31 |

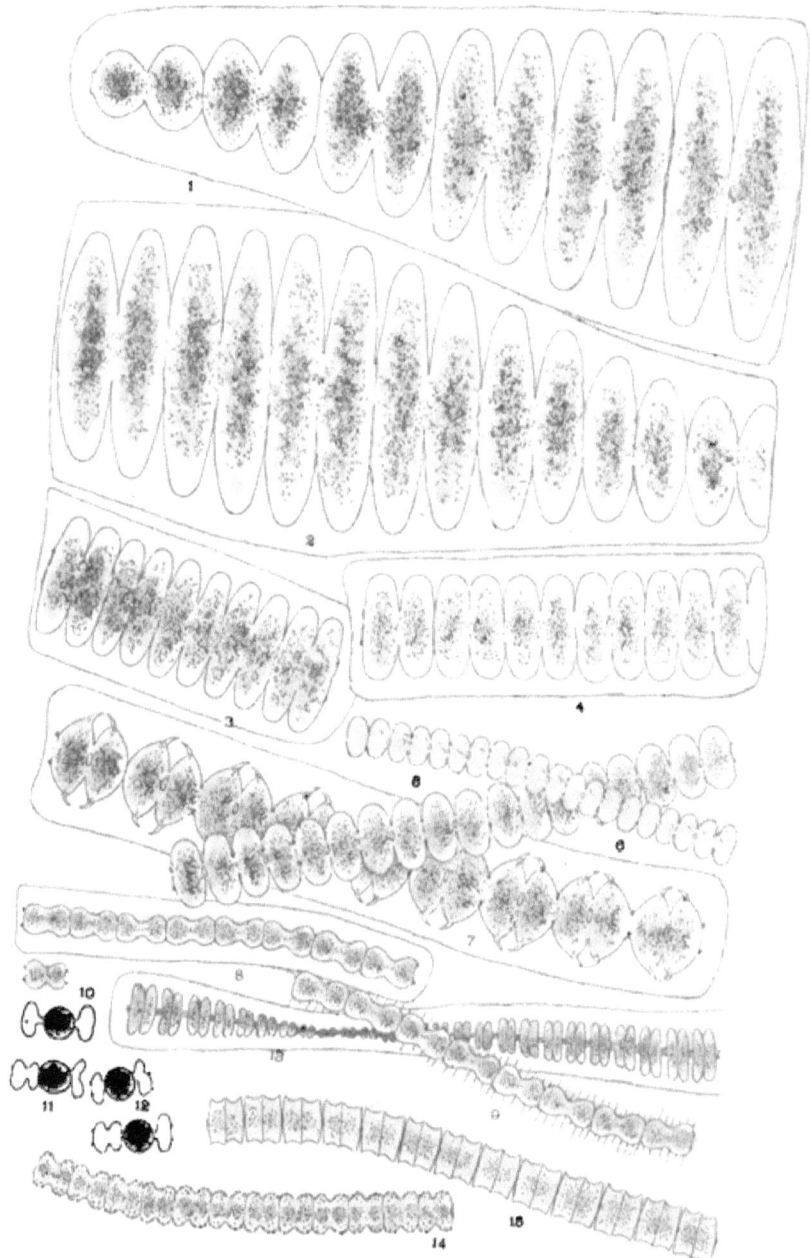

## PLATE V.

Figures magnified 500 diameters.

| | | PAGE. |
|---|---|---|
| Figs. 1, 2. | PENIUM DIGITUS; front view and transverse section. (See also Plate LXIV,) | 34 |
| Fig. 3. | PENIUM CRASSA, four specimens, | 37* |
| " 4. | PENIUM LAMELLOSUM, | 34 |
| " 5. | PENIUM MARGARITACEUM; empty cell, | 35 |
| " 6. | "          "         zygospore with empty cells attached, | 35 |
| " 7. | PENIUM BREBISSONII, zygospore and remains of cells, | 37 |
| " 8. | "          "         vegetative cell, | 37 |
| Figs. 9, 10. | PENIUM TRUNCATUM, and zygospore with husks of cells, | 36 |
| Fig. 11. | PENIUM MARGARITACEUM, vegetative cell, | 35 |
| " 12. | PENIUM POLYMORPHUM; group of four, | 37 |
| " 13. | PENIUM RUPESTRE; two cells, | 38 |
| " 14. | PENIUM INTERRUPTUM, (large form), | 36 |
| " 15. | "          "         (small form), | 36 |
| " 16. | PENIUM NAVICULA, two sizes of cells, | 37 |
| " 17. | PENIUM OBLONGUM, | 35 |
| " 18. | PENIUM CLOSTERIOIDES, | 36 |
| Figs. 19, 20. | PENIUM MINUTUM, (calocylindrus), | 36 |
| " 21, 22. | PENIUM TRUNCATUM, a variety of Fig. 10, | 36 |

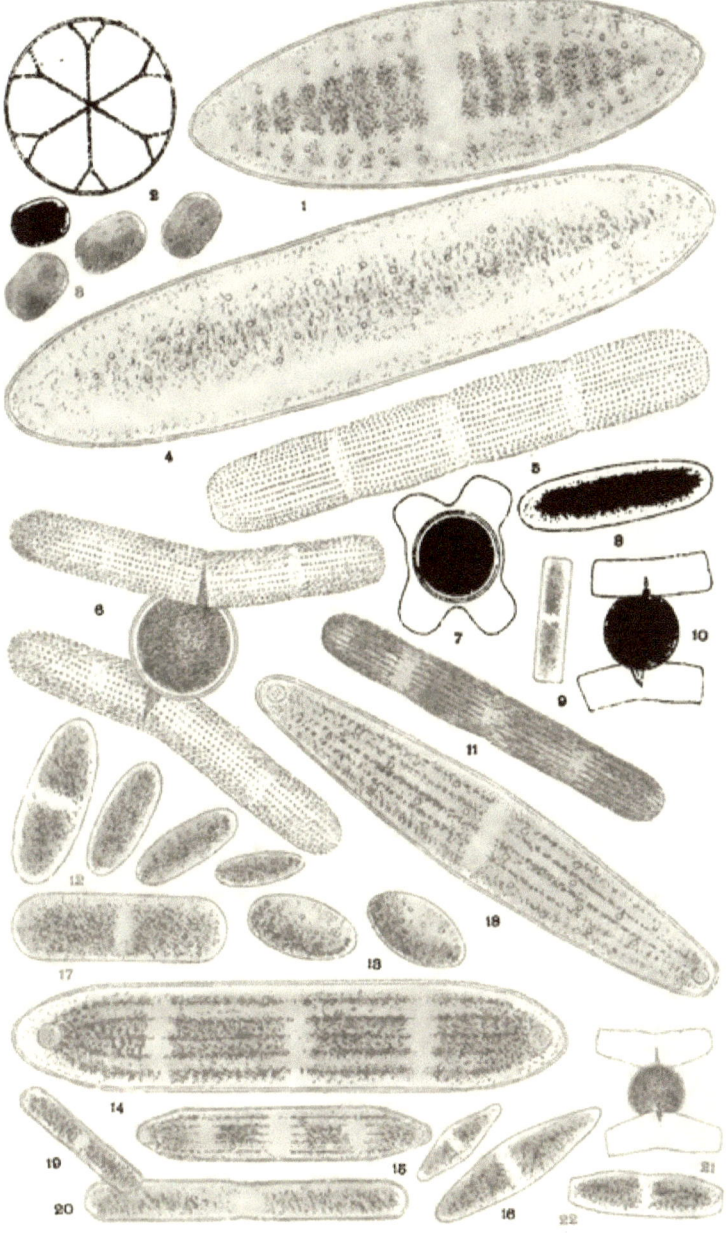

## PLATE VI.

Figures magnified 250 diameters.

|   |   |   | PAGE. |
|---|---|---|---|
| Figs. | 1, 2. | CLOSTERIUM DIANÆ, | 47 |
| " | 3, 4. | CLOSTERIUM TURGIDUM, | 43 |
| " | 5–8. | CLOSTERIUM STRIOLATUM, | 44 |
| Fig. | 9. | CLOSTERIUM DELPONTII, | 45 |
| " | 10. | CLOSTERIUM DIDYMOTICUM, | 41 |
| " | 11. | CLOSTERIUM SUBCOSTATUM, | 43 |
| " | 12. | CLOSTERIUM LUNULA. Var. striatum, | 42 |
| Figs. | 13, 14. | CLOSTERIUM ENSIS, | 40 |
| " | 15, 16. | CLOSTERIUM PRELONGUM, | 43 |
| Fig. | 17. | CLOSTERIUM BREBISSONII, (Addenda, p. 172), | 24 |
| Figs. | 18, 20. | CLOSTERIUM LANCEOLATUM, (also Plate IX, fig. 14), | 40 |
| Fig. | 21. | CLOSTERIUM JUNCIDUM, Var. gracillima-loevissima, | 39 |
| " | 22. | **CLOSTERIUM PRONUM,** | 50 |

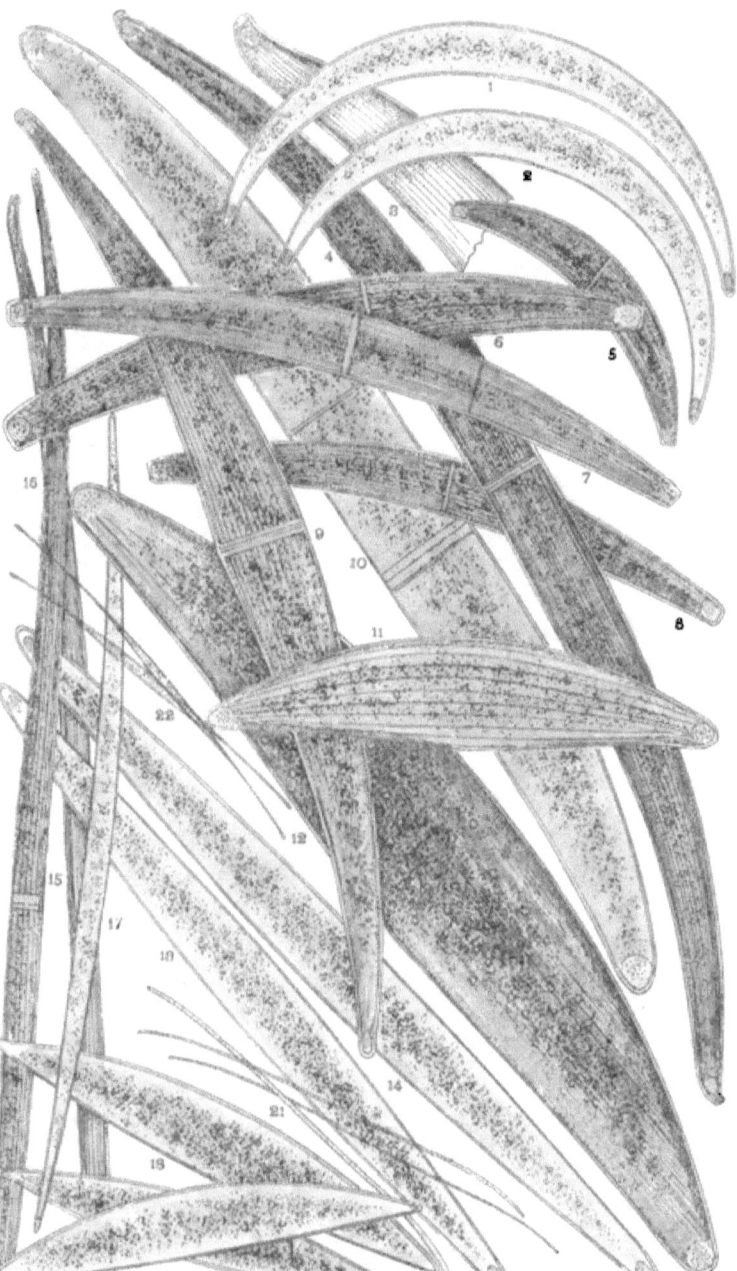

## PLATE VII.

### Figures magnified 250 diameters.

| | | PAGE |
|---|---|---|
| Fig. 1. | CLOSTERIUM OBTUSUM, | 39 |
| " 2. | CLOSTERIUM JUNCIDUM, | 39 |
| " 3. | "        "   two cells with developed zygospore, | 39 |
| Figs. 4, 5. | CLOSTERIUM GRACILE, | 40 |
| Fig. 6. | CLOSTERIUM MACILENTUM, | 40 |
| " 7. | CLOSTERIUM ACEROSUM, zygospore and empty cells, | 42 |
| " 8. | CLOSTERIUM STRIOLATUM, | 44 |
| Figs. 9, 10. | CLOSTERIUM DECUSSATUM, | 41 |
| Fig. 11. | CLOSTERIUM ACEROSUM, vegetative cell, | 42 |
| " 12. | CLOSTERIUM NASUTUM, | 43 |
| Figs. 13, 14. | CLOSTERIUM STRIGOSUM, | 44 |
| Fig. 15. | CLOSTERIUM TURGIDUM, | 43 |
| " 16. | CLOSTERIUM LINEATUM, two cells, (see Plate IX, fig. 15), | 45 |
| Figs. 17, 18. | CLOSTERIUM CUCUMIS, | 42 |
| Fig. 19. | CLOSTERIUM COSTATUM, | 45 |
| " 20. | CLOSTERIUM STRIOLATUM, (compare fig. 8, and Plate VI, figs. 5–8), | 44 |
| Figs. 21–23. | CLOSTERIUM ANGUSTATUM, and variety decussatum, | 41 |

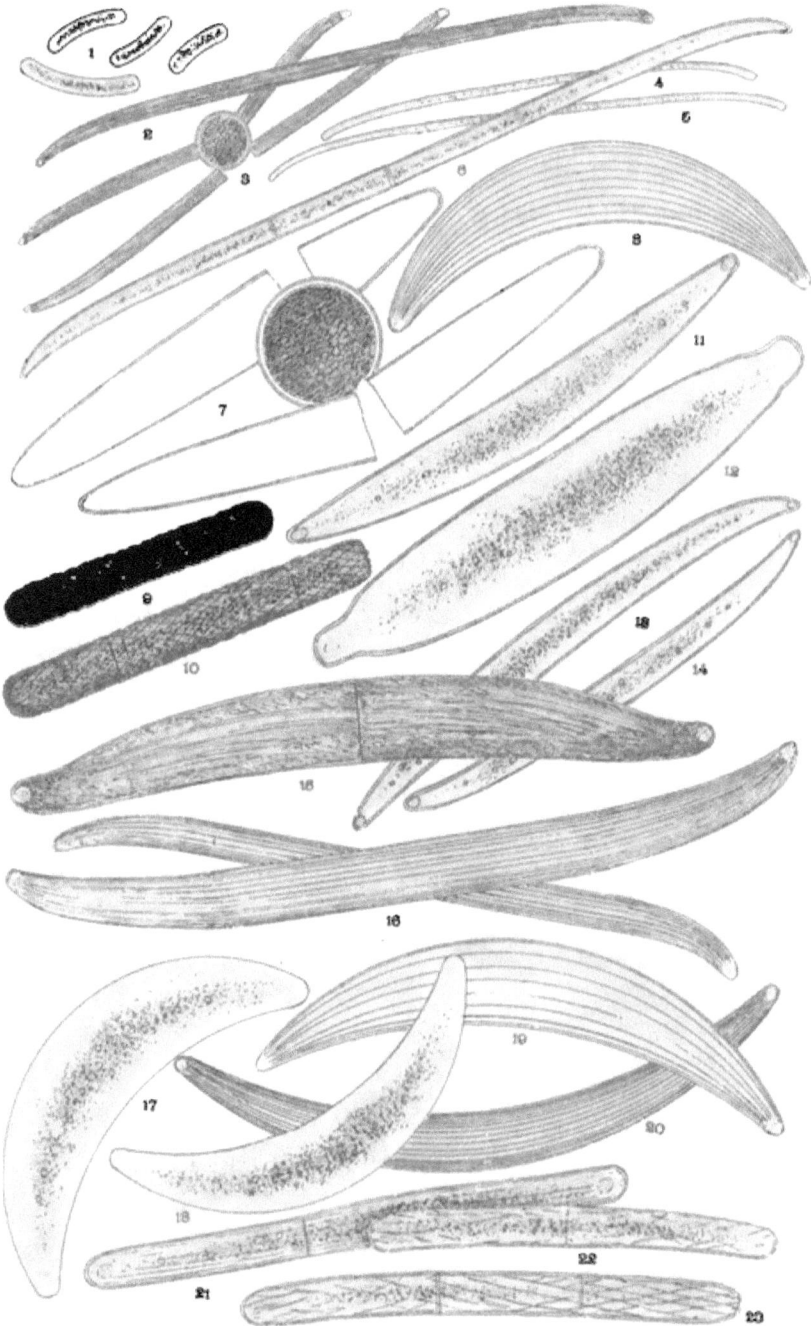

PLATE VII

# PLATE VIII.

Figures magnified 250 diameters.

|  |  |  | PAGE. |
|---|---|---|---|
| Fig. 1. | CLOSTERIUM DECORUM, | | 45 |
| " 2. | CLOSTERIUM SUBTILE, | | 42 |
| " 3. | CLOSTERIUM AREOLATUM, | | 46 |
| " 4. | " " end, more highly magnified, | | 46 |
| " 5. | CLOSTERIUM JENNERI, | | 47 |
| " 6. | CLOSTERIUM VENUS, (a group of three), | | 47 |
| " 7. | CLOSTERIUM PARVULUM, (a group of three), | | 47 |
| Figs. 8, 9. | CLOSTERIUM DIANAE, Var. arcuatum, and typical form, | | 47 |
| Fig. 10. | CLOSTERIUM RALFSII, one half-cell vegetative state, the other half lifeless, | | 49 |
| Figs. 11, 12. | CLOSTERIUM ACUTUM, and zygospore, | | 46 |
| " 13, 14. | CLOSTERIUM LEIBLEINII, | | 49 |
| Fig. 15. | CLOSTERIUM MONILIFERUM, | | 48 |
| " 16. | CLOSTERIUM EHRENBERGII, | | 48 |
| " 17. | " " Var. immane, | | 48 |
| " 18. | CLOSTERIUM ACUMINATUM, smaller form, | | 47 |
| " 19. | " " longer form, empty cells attached to zygospore, | | 47 |
| " 20. | CLOSTERIUM LEIBLEINII, zygospore, with empty membrane of the copulated cells, | | 49 |

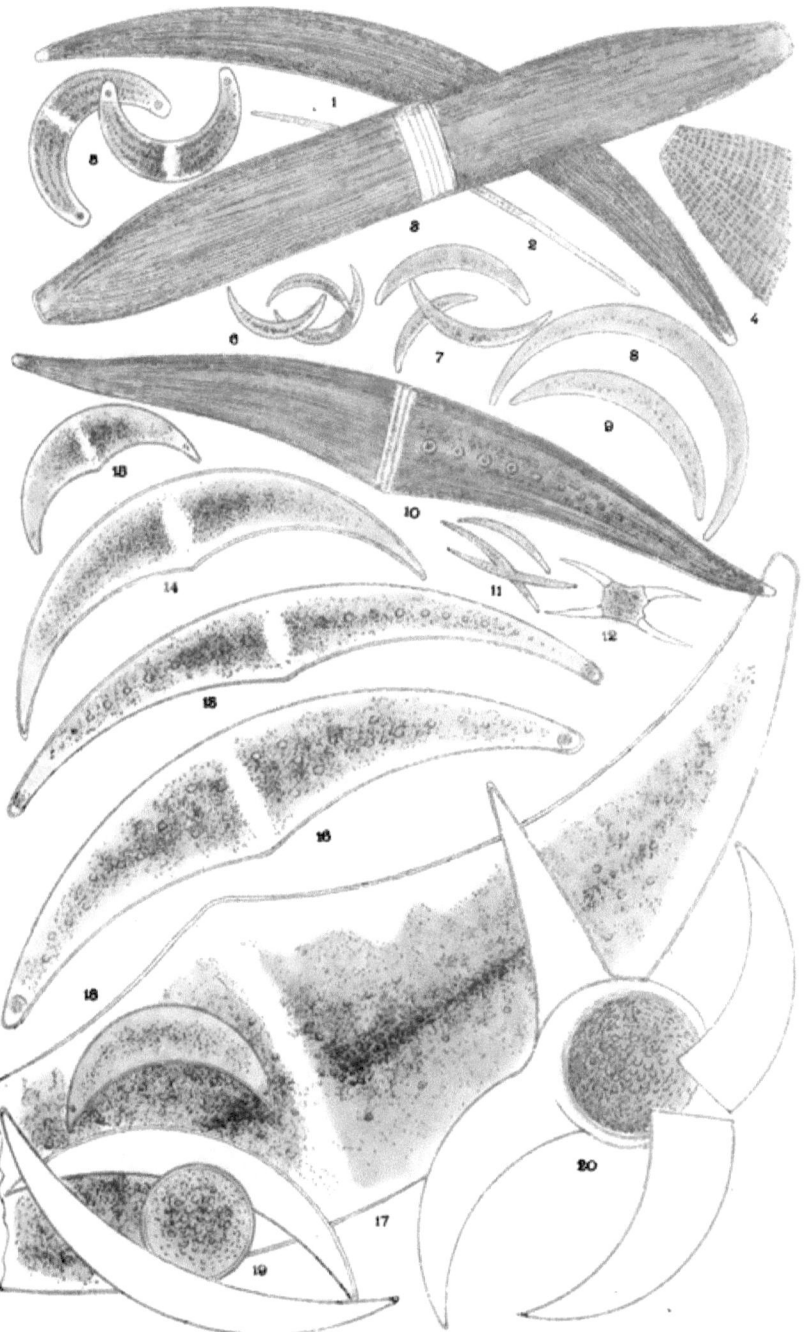

## PLATE IX.

#### Figures magnified 250 diameters.

|  |  |  | PAGE. |
|---|---|---|---|
| Fig. 1. | CLOSTERIUM ROSTRATUM, | | 49 |
| " 2. | " " first stage of the copulation of two cells, | | |
| " 3. | " " the developed zygospore and empty semi-cells, | | 49 |
| " 4. | CLOSTERIUM DIANÆ, zygospore and remains of empty cells, | | 47 |
| " 5. | CLOSTERIUM ATTENUATUM, | | 44 |
| Figs. 6, 7. | CLOSTERIUM SETACEUM. | | 50 |
| Fig. 8. | CLOSTERIUM KUETZINGII, | | 50 |
| Figs. 9–11. | CLOSTERIUM SETACEUM, three zygospores, before the emptied cells have been shed, | | 50 |
| " 12, 13. | CLOSTERIUM DIDYMOTICUM, two cells, | | 40 |
| Fig. 14. | CLOSTERIUM LANCEOLATUM, (see also Plate VI, figs. 18–20), | | 40 |
| " 15. | CLOSTERIUM LINEATUM; zygospore and emptied semi-cells, | | 45 |
| " 16. | CLOSTERIUM PARVULUM, zygospore, | | 47 |
| " 17. | CLOSTERIUM ACEROSUM, chlorophyl broken up and formed into small oval cells, | | 43 |

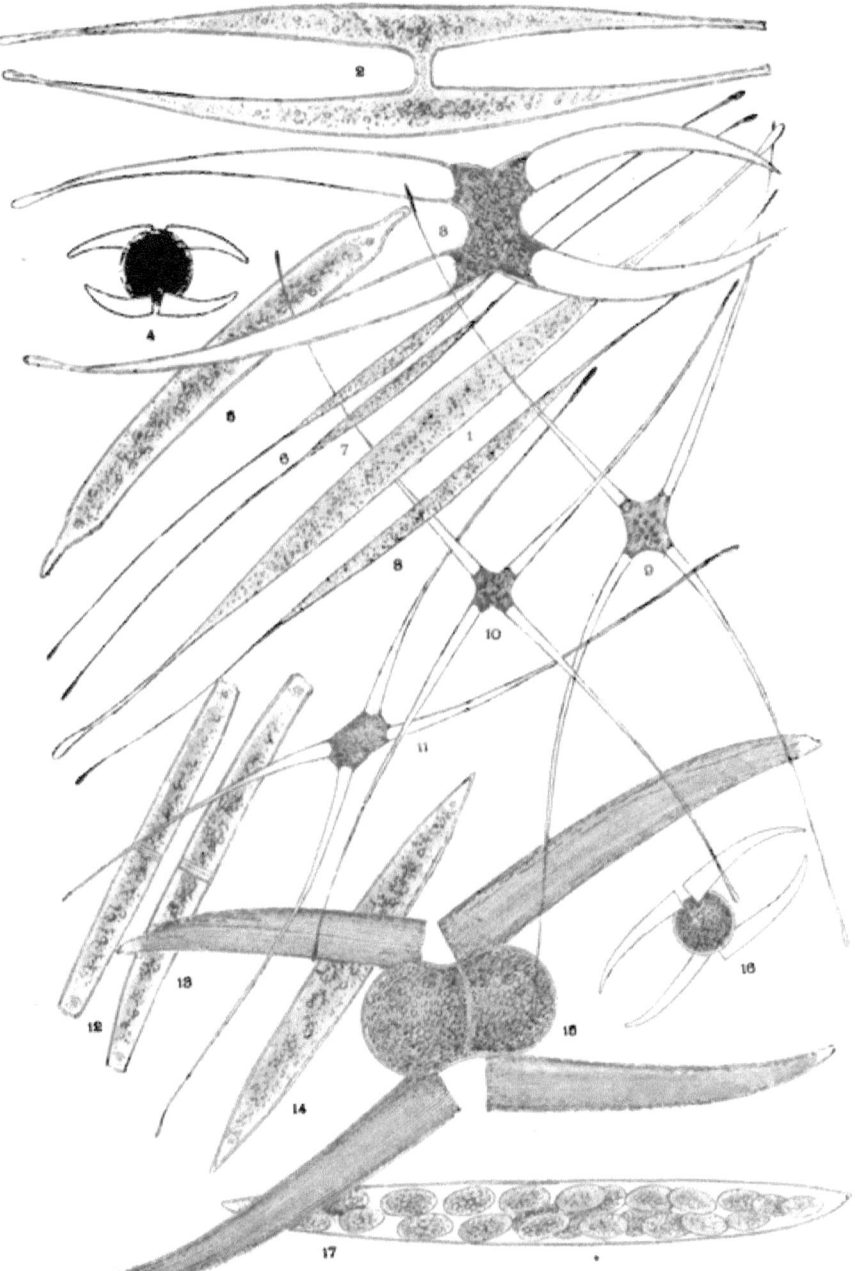

## PLATE X.

Figures magnified 500 diameters except Closterium, only 250 diameters.

| | | PAGE |
|---|---|---|
| Figs. 1, 2. | CLOSTERIUM ACEROSUM, forma striolatum with single and twin zygospores, | 42 |
| Fig. 3. | CLOSTERIUM LINEATUM, Var. costatum, with twin zygospores, | 45 |
| Figs. 4, 5. | ARTHRODESMUS NOTOCHONDRUS, in front and vertical views, | 105 |
| Fig. 6. | ARTHRODESMUS INCRASSATUS, Var. cycladatus, | 105 |
| Figs. 7, 8. | COSMARIUM OCULIFERUM, front and lateral views, | 76 |
| " 9–11. | PENIUM CRUCIFERUM, in different stages of division, | 38 |
| " 12, 13. | ARTHRODESMUS PACHYCERUS, front and lateral views, | 105 |
| " 14, 15. | ARTHRODESMUS TRIANGULARIS, front and vertical views, | 105 |
| Fig. 16. | DOCIDIUM GEORGICUM, | 55 |
| " 17. | PENIUM SPIROSTRIOLATUM, var., | 35 |
| " 19. | " " | 35 |
| " 18. | DOCIDIUM VERTICILLATUM, | 58 |
| Figs. 20, 21. | DOCIDIUM RECTUM, | 52 |

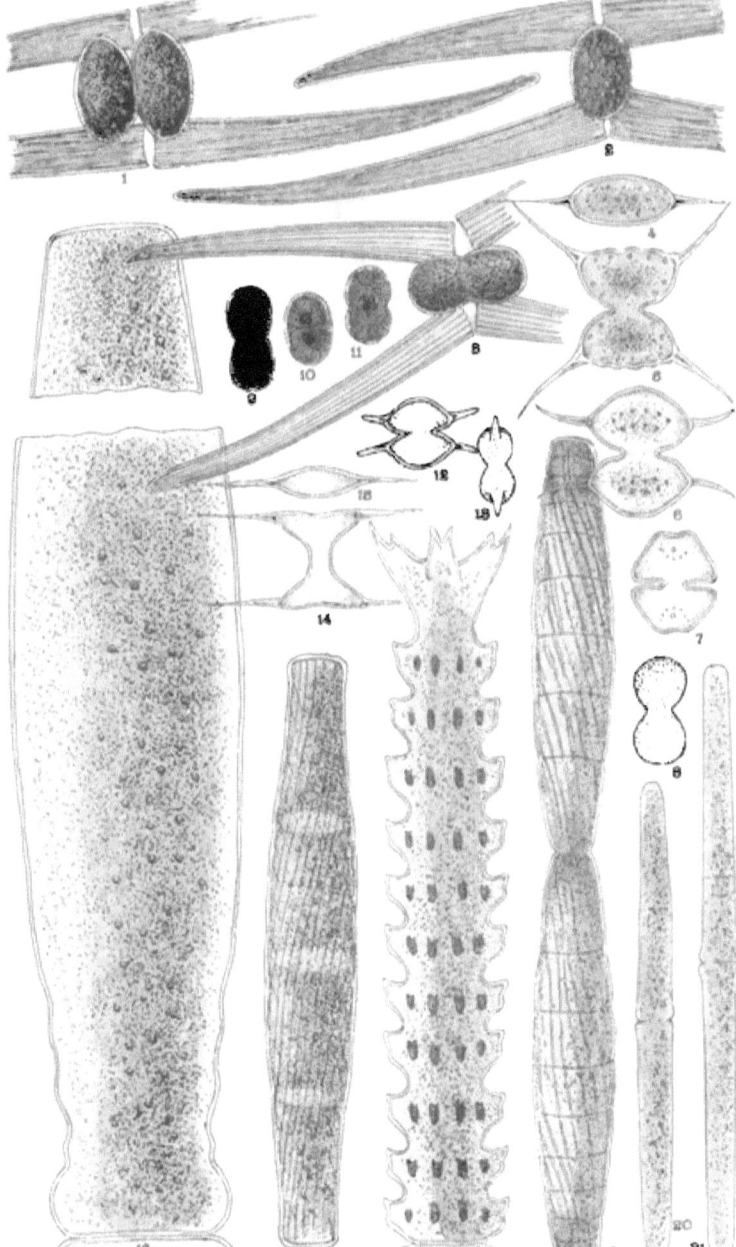

## PLATE XI.

Figures magnified **500 diameters**.

| | | PAGE. |
|---|---|---|
| **Fig.** 1. | Docidium crenulatum—(*C. nodulosum*), | 51 |
| **Figs.** 2, 3, 4. | Docidium Trabecula. Compare Plate XV, figs. 1–7, | 51 |
| **Fig.** 5. | Docidium Flotowii, Variety, | 52 |
| Figs. 6, 7. | Docidium truncatum, | 52 |
| **Fig.** 8. | **Docidium** clavatum, | 51 |

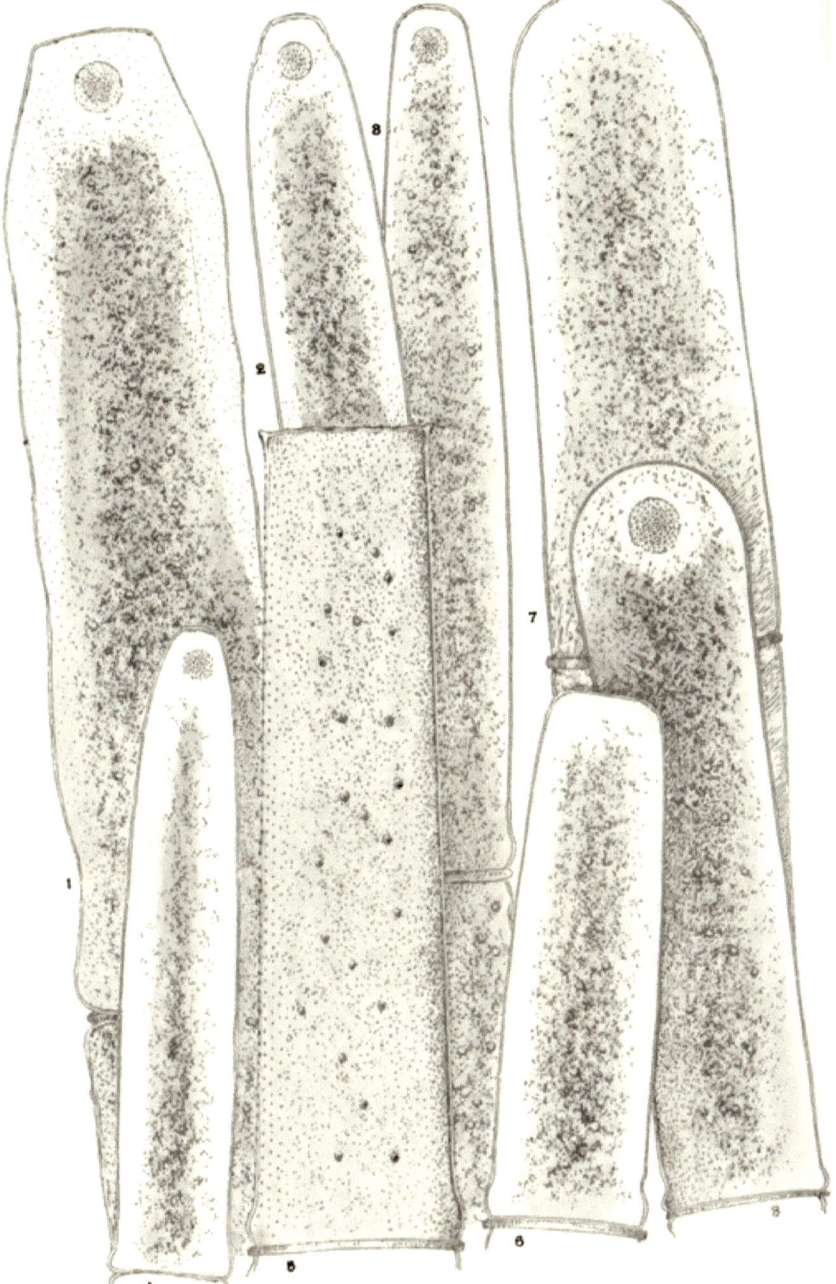

## PLATE XII.

Figures magnified 500 diameters.

| | | | PAGE. |
|---|---|---|---|
| Fig. | 1. | TETMEMORUS GIGANTEUS, | 99 |
| " | 2. | DOCIDIUM ARCHERII, | 51 |
| " | 3. | DOCIDIUM NODULOSUM, | 51 |
| " | 4. | DOCIDIUM WOODII, | 55 |
| " | 5. | DOCIDIUM BACULUM, Var. Floridense, | 53 |
| Figs. | 6, 7. | STAURASTRUM VESICULATUM, | 132 |
| " | 8, 9. | SPHAEROZOSMA PULCHELLUM, Var. bambusioides, | 29 |
| " | 10–13. | EUASTRUM PECTINATUM, front, lateral and transverse views, | 109 |
| " | 14–16. | HYALOTHECA DISSILIENS, Var. hians, | 22 |

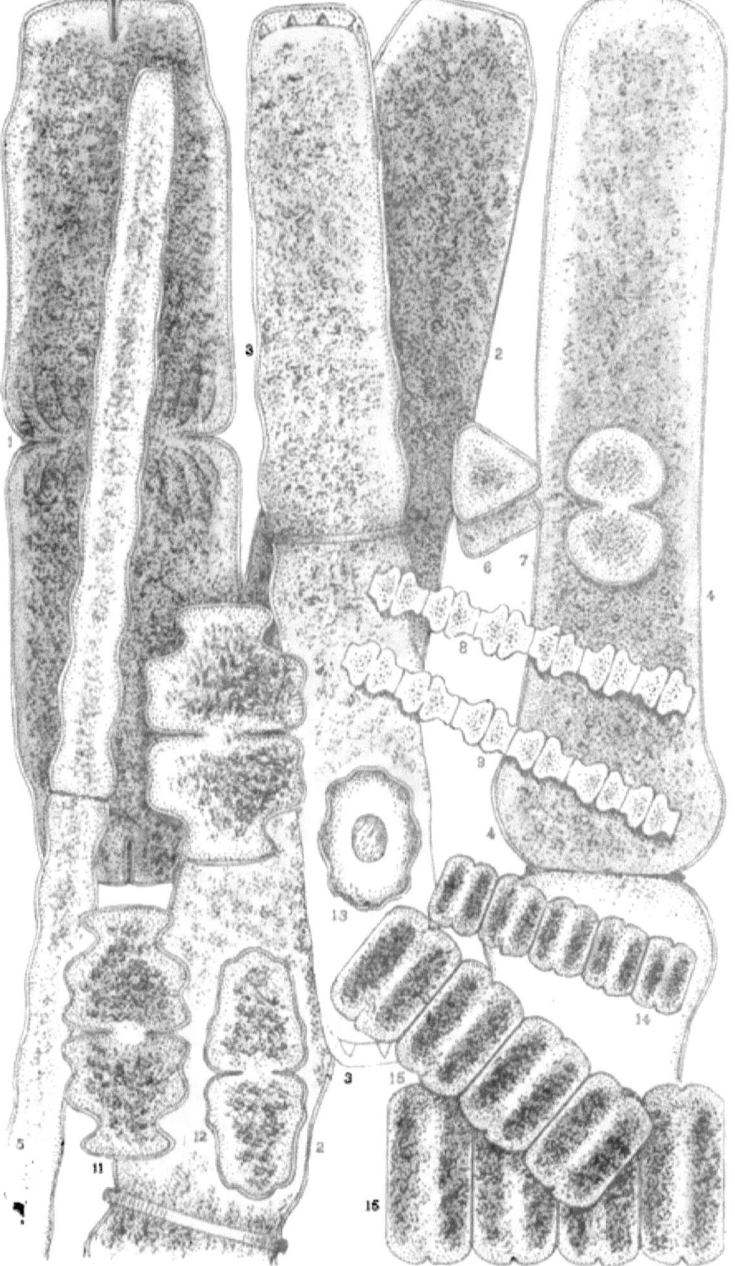

## PLATE XIII.

Figures magnified 500 diameters.

|  |  | PAGE. |
|---|---|---|
| Fig. 1. | DOCIDIUM VERTICILLATUM, | 57 |
| " 2. | DOCIDIUM COSTATUM, | 57 |
| " 3. | DOCIDIUM GRACILE, large form; whorls **evidently composed of two** rows of teeth, | 58 |
| " 4. | DOCIDIUM VERRUCOSUM, vegetative state, | 56 |
| " 5. | "            "      empty semi-cell, shows the arrangement of the verrucae, | 56 |
| " 6. | DOCIDIUM GRACILE, empty semi-cells, | 58 |
| " 7. | "            "      empty semi-cell, older condition before breaking into parts, | 58 |
| " 8. | "            "      small form, | 58 |
| " 9. | DOCIDIUM MINUTUM. Var. See Plate LXI, figs. 29–31. | 57 |
| " 10. | DOCIDIUM TRIDENTULUM, | 57 |
| " 11. | DOCIDIUM VERTICILLATUM, Var. turgidum, | 57 |
| " 12. | DOCIDIUM SPINOSUM, | 56 |
| " 13. | DOCIDIUM HIRSUTUM, | 56 |

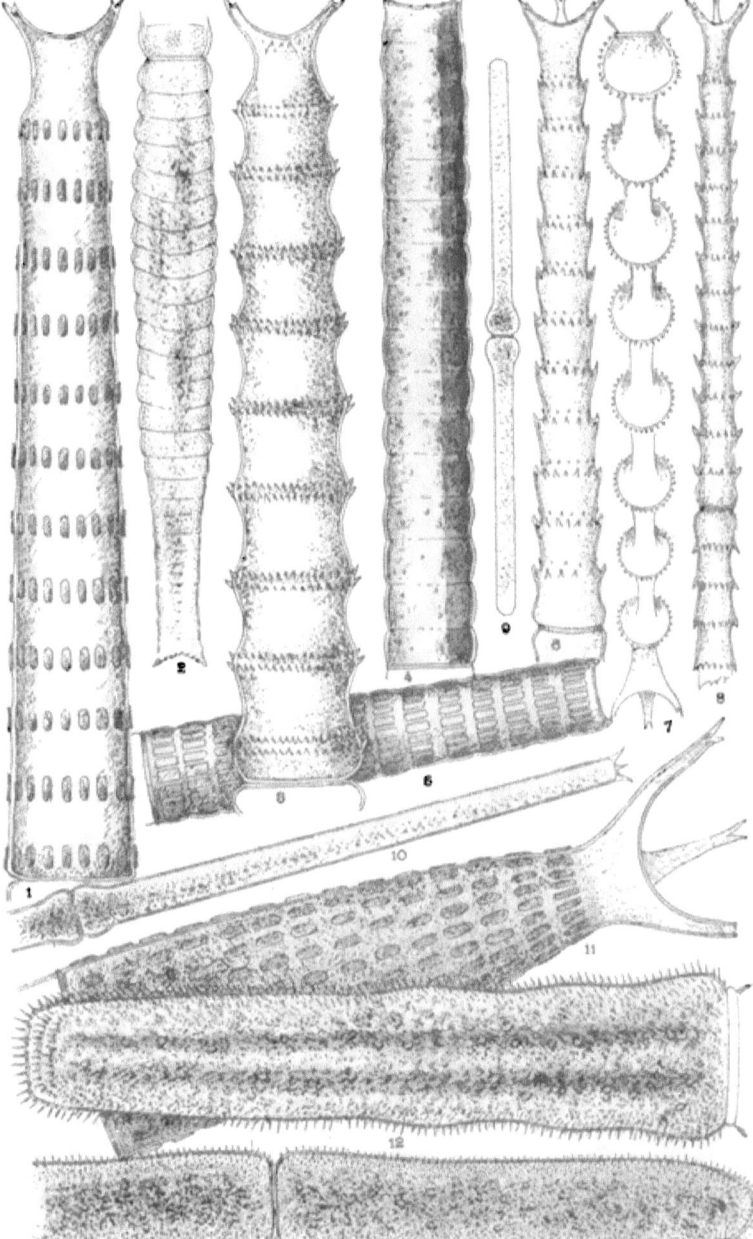

## PLATE XIV.

Figures magnified 500 diameters.

|  |  | PAGE |
|---|---|---|
| Fig. 1. | DOCIDIUM REPANDUM, | 54 |
| " 2. | DOCIDIUM CONSTRICTUM, | 54 |
| Figs. 3, 4. | DOCIDIUM BACULUM, two forms, | 52 |
| Fig. 5. | DOCIDIUM UNDULATUM, | 55 |
| Figs. 6–8. | DOCIDIUM SINUOSUM, | 55 |
| " 9, 10. | DOCIDIUM CORONATUM, two forms, | 53 |
| Fig. 11. | DOCIDIUM NODOSUM, falling to pieces through decay, | 54 |
| " 12. | " " a form of; See Plate XV, fig. 20, | 54 |

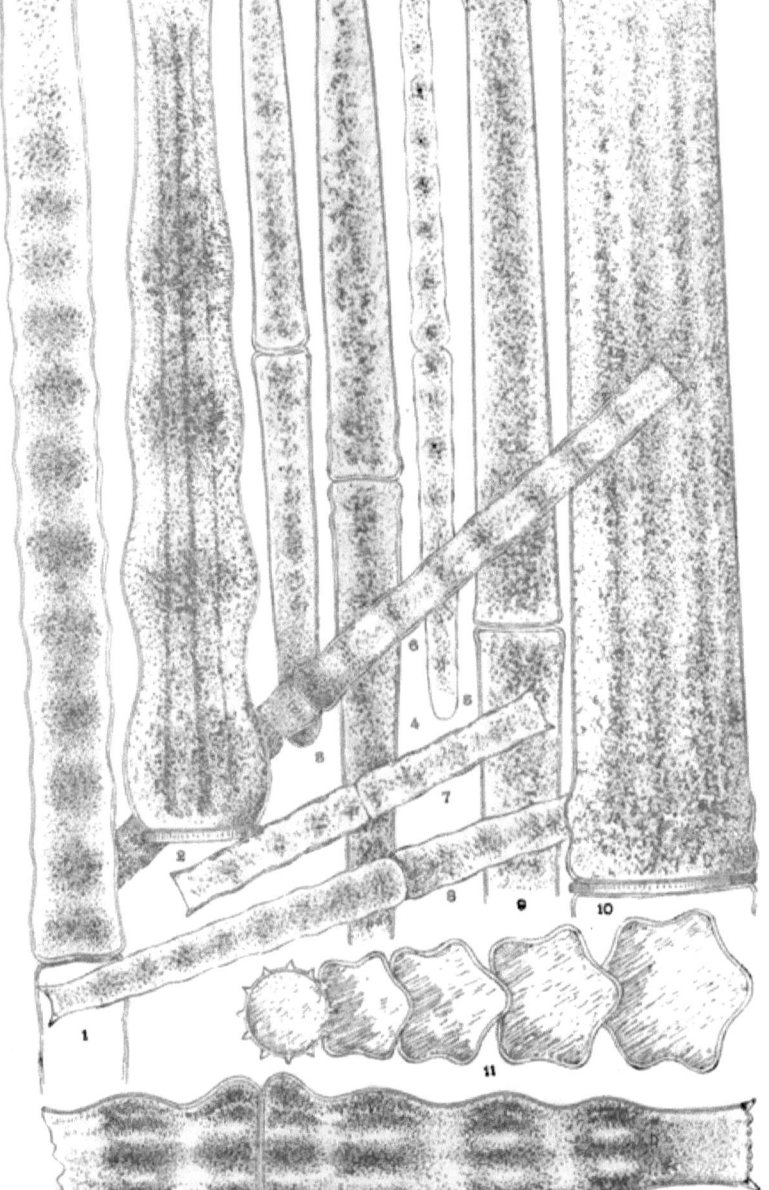

## PLATE XV.

#### Figures magnified 500 diameters.

PAGE.

Figs. 1–3. DOCIDIUM TRABECULA; two conjugated cells, pouring out the cytioplasm, or granular chlorophyllous contents and forming a zygospore, . 51
Fig. 4. " " a developed zygospore, 51
Figs. 5, 6. " " a cell dividing, . . . . 51
Fig. 7. " " early stage of outgrowth, or new semi-cells, . . . . . 51
" 8. CALOCYLINDRUS CONNATUS, very near Delps. *C. ellipticum*, 59
" 9. " " . . . . . 59
" 10. " " Var. minor, 60
" 11. CALOCYLINDRUS PSEUDOCONNATUS, . . 60
" 12. CALOCYLINDRUS MINUTUS, 59
" 13. CALOCYLINDRUS COSTATUS, . . 61
" 14. CALOCYLINDRUS CUCURBITA, 59
" 15. CALOCYLINDRUS CURTUS, larger form, 59
" 16. " " smaller form, . 59
" 17. CALOCYLINDRUS RALFSII—*C. cylindricum*, . . 58
" 18. CALOCYLINDRUS DIPLOSPORA, . . 61
" 19. CALOCYLINDRUS THWAITESII, . . . . 60
" 20. DOCIDIUM NODOSUM. (Compare Plate XIV, fig. 12), 54

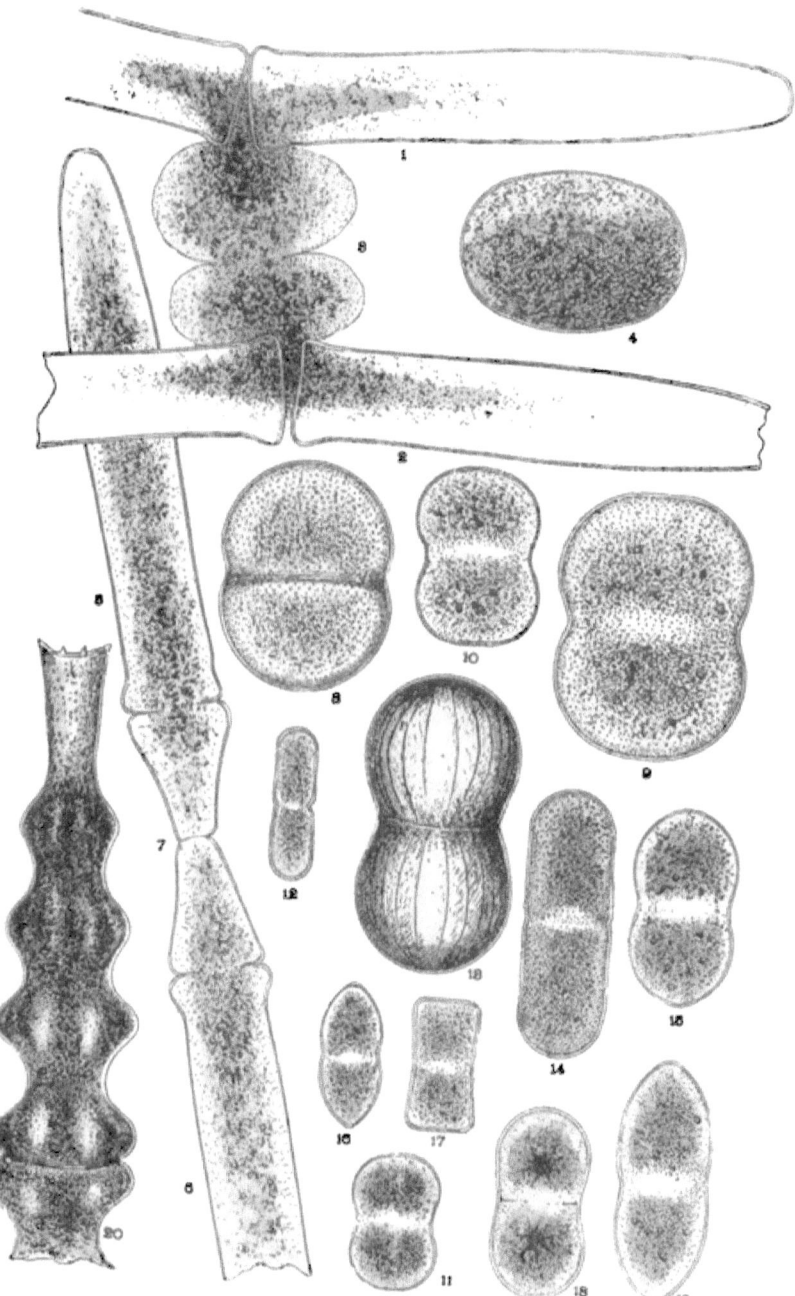

## PLATE XVI.

### Figures magnified 500 diameters.

|  |  | PAGE. |
|---|---|---|
| Figs. 1, 2. | COSMARIUM MARGARITIFERUM; normal, front view, and empty semi-cells, transverse view, | 81 |
| Fig. 3. | "          "          zygospore with the empty semi-cells, | 81 |
| " 4. | COSMARIUM PUNCTULATUM, | 81 |
| Figs. 5–7. | COSMARIUM BOTRYTIS, three forms. (Compare Plate XXVII, fig. 27), | 81 |
| " 8, 9. | COSMARIUM OVALE, smaller and larger form, | 62 |
| " 10, 11. | COSMARIUM BREBISSONII, two forms, | 82 |
| Fig. 12. | COSMARIUM INTERMIDIUM, | 83 |
| " 13. | COSMARIUM TETROPTHALMUM, | 82 |
| " 14. | COSMARIUM LATUM, ends too convex for typical form, | 84 |
| " 15. | COSMARIUM DENTATUM, | 83 |

PLATE XVI

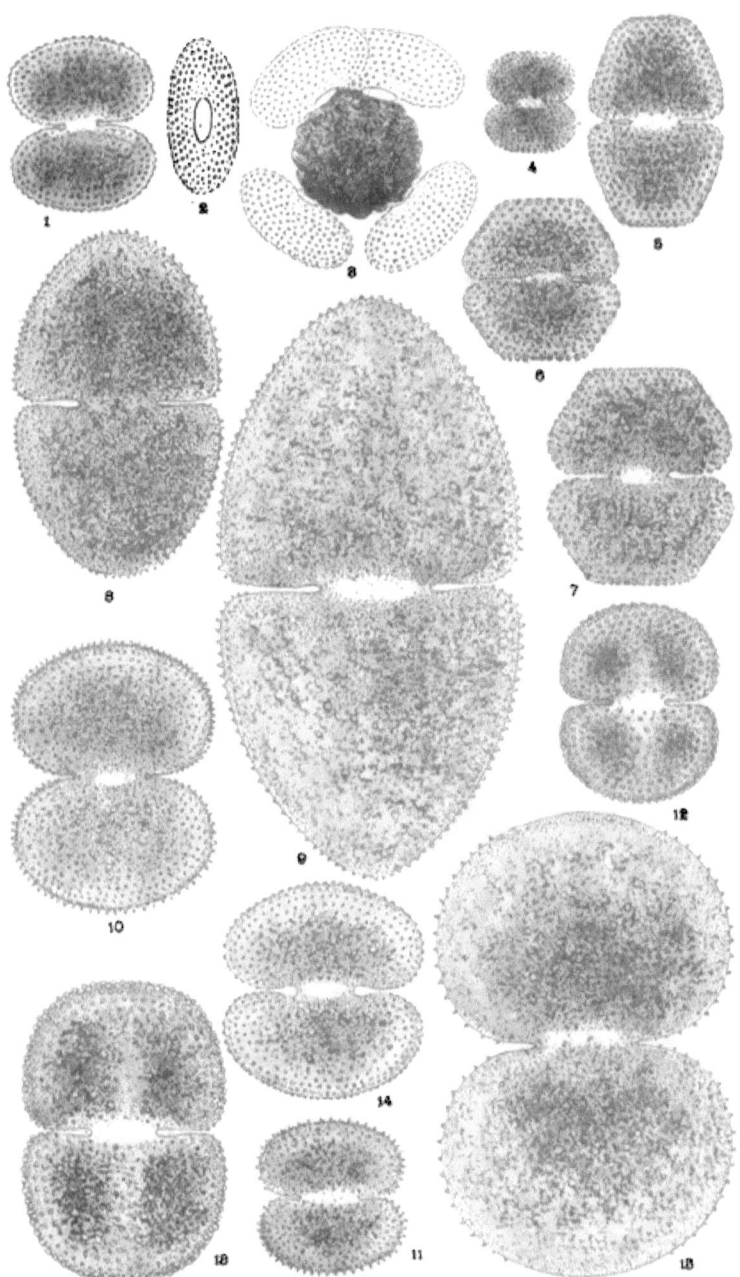

## PLATE XVII.

### Figures magnified 500 diameters.

| | | PAGE |
|---|---|---|
| Figs. 1, 2. | COSMARIUM CONSPERSUM; two forms, | 82 |
| Fig. 3. | COSMARIUM OCHTHODES, | 84 |
| "   4. | "         "         empty cell of smaller form, | 84 |
| Figs. 5, 6. | COSMARIUM AMŒNUM, | 85 |
| Fig. 7. | "         "         Var. tumidum, | 85 |
| Figs. 8, 9 | COSMARIUM ELEGANTISSIMUM, | 86 |
| Fig. 10. | COSMARIUM RENIFORME, | 84 |
| "   11. | "         "         smaller form, empty cell, | 84 |
| "   12. | COSMARIUM PORTIANUM, | 84 |
| "   13. | "         "         cell dividing, | 84 |
| "   14. | "         "         zygospore and emptied semi-cells, | 84 |
| "   15. | COSMARIUM BROOMEI, Var. (Compare Plate XX, figs. 6-9), | 93 |
| Figs 16, 17. | COSMARIUM PYRAMIDATUM, two forms, one cell empty, | 74 |
| "   18, 19. | "         "         Var. stenonotum, | 74 |
| "   20, 21. | COSMARIUM ORBICULATUM, | 85 |

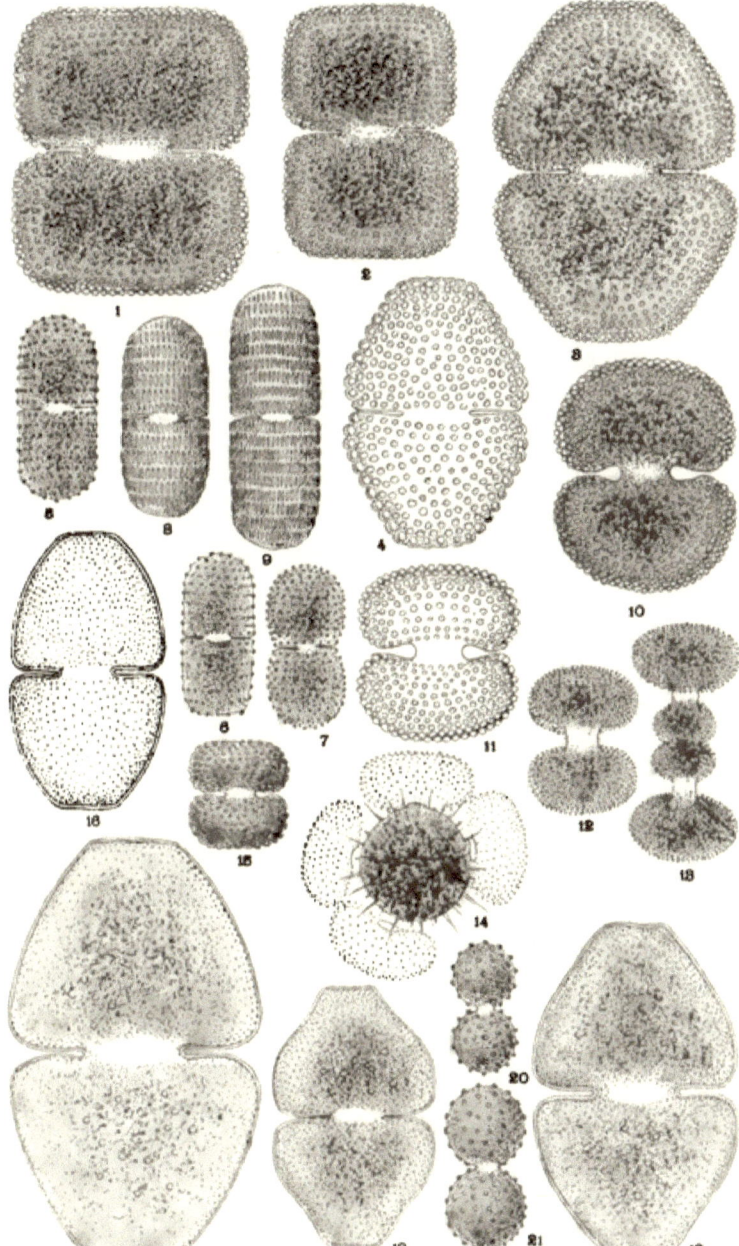

## PLATE XVIII.

#### Figures magnified 500 diameters.

|  |  | PAGE |
|---|---|---|
| Fig. 1. | COSMARIUM RALFSII, | 75 |
| Figs. 2–4. | COSMARIUM PACHYDERMUM; three forms, | 75 |
| Fig. 5. | COSMARIUM DE BARYI. (Compare Plate XLV, fig. 12), | 62 |
| Figs. 6–9. | COSMARIUM CUCUMIS, four sizes, | 62 |
| Fig. 10. | COSMARIUM LAEVE, a variety. (Compare Plate XLIII, fig. 14), | 70a |
| Figs. 11, 12. | COSMARIUM PSEUDOPYRAMIDATUM. (Compare Plate XIX, figs. 5, 6), | 75 |
| Fig. 13. | " " zygospore, and husks of cells, | 75 |
| Figs. 14, 15. | COSMARIUM GRANATUM, Var. elongatum, for typical form See Plate LXI, fig. 13, | 64 |
| " 16, 17. | COSMARIUM MONILIFORME, two forms, | 64 |
| Fig. 18. | " " after division, new semi-cells enlarged, | 64 |
| " 19. | " " zygospore, | 64 |
| " 20. | COSMARIUM GLOBOSUM; a variety; See typical form, Plate LX, figs. 14–17, | 65 |
| " 21. | COSMARIUM BIOCULATUM, | 66 |
| " 22. | " " zygospore, | 66 |
| " 23. | COSMARIUM TUMIDUM, | 67 |

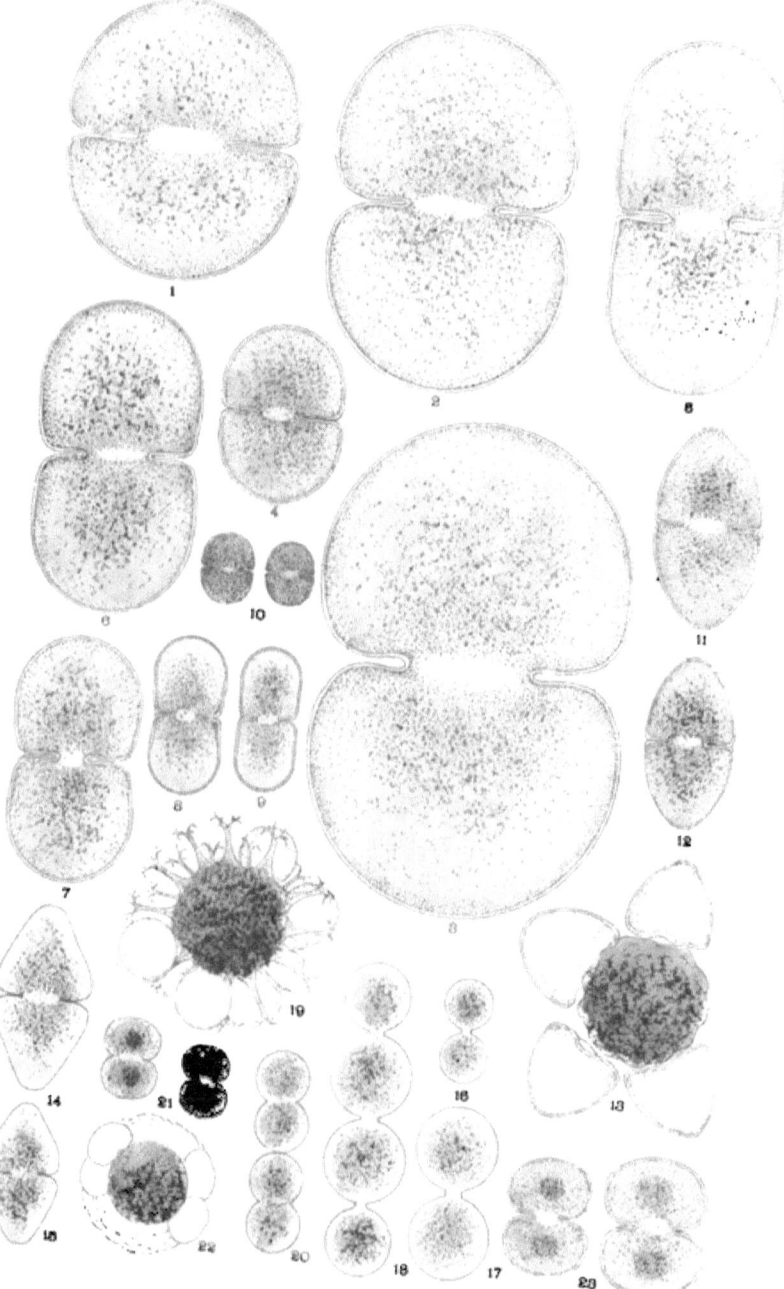

## PLATE XIX.

Figures magnified 500 diameters.

|  |  | PAGE |
|---|---|---|
| Fig. 1. | COSMARIUM CONTRACTUM, | 68 |
| " 2. | COSMARIUM SINUOSUM, | 70 |
| Figs. 3, 4. | COSMARIUM VARIOLATUM, | 68 |
| " 5–6. | COSMARIUM PSEUDOPYRAMIDATUM, small variety. (Compare Plate XVIII). | 75 |
| Fig. 7. | COSMARIUM MENEGHINII, four forms, | 76 |
| Figs. 8, 9. | COSMARIUM SEXANGULARE. (Compare Plate LX, fig. 13), | 69 |
| Fig. 10. | COSMARIUM UNDULATUM, Var. crenulatum, | 73 |
| " 11. | COSMARIUM NOTABILE, | 72, 86 |
| " 12. | COSMARIUM REINSCHII, | 73 |
| Figs. 13, 14. | COSMARIUM EXIGUUM, | 72 |
| Fig. 15. | COSMARIUM ACULEATUM, | 71 |
| " 16. | COSMARIUM LUNATUM, | 71 |
| Figs. 17, 18. | COSMARIUM BAILEYI; (C. depressum, Bail.), | 69 |
| " 19, 20. | COSMARIUM UNDULATUM; and Var. crenulatum, | 72 |
| Fig. 21. | " " a zygospore, | 72 |
| " 22. | COSMARIUM ANSATUM, | 74 |
| Figs. 23–25. | COSMARIUM HOLMIENSE, varieties, | 74 |
| " 26, 27. | COSMARIUM TRACHYPLEURUM, normal state and cell dividing, | 79 |
| " 28, 29. | " " transverse and side views, | 79 |
| Fig. 30. | COSMARIUM POLYGONUM, | 71 |
| " 31. | COSMARIUM TINCTUM, | 67 |
| Figs. 32–34. | COSMARIUM TAXICHONDRUM; two forms and lateral view of empty cell, | 77 |
| " 35, 36. | COSMARIUM SMOLANDICUM, | 72 |
| Fig. 37. | COSMARIUM VENUSTUM, | 73 |
| Figs. 38–40. | COSMARIUM POLYMAZUM, front, end and lateral views, | 76 |
| " 41, 42. | COSMARIUM DONNELLII, | 77 |
| " 43–45. | COSMARIUM ANISOCHONDRUM, front, end and side views, | 78 |
| " 46–48. | COSMARIUM GALERITUM, three varieties, | 75 |

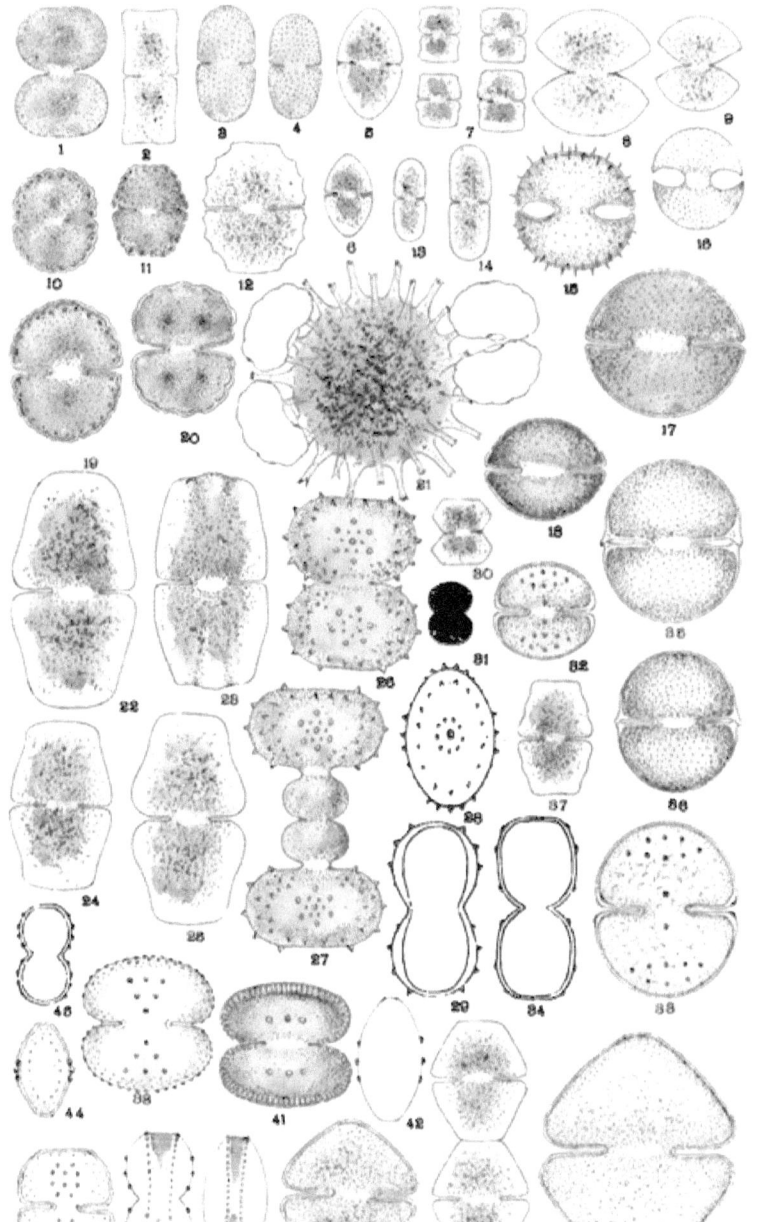

## PLATE XX.

Figures magnified 500 diameters.

| | | PAGE. |
|---|---|---|
| Figs. 1, 2. | COSMARIUM BIRETUM, front and end view, | 93 |
| " 3, 5. | COSMARIUM BOTRYTIS, Var. tumidum, Wolle, front and side views, | 82 |
| Fig. 4. | " " zygospore, husks attached, | 82 |
| Figs. 6, 7. | COSMARIUM BROOMEI, front and end views, | 93 |
| " 8, 9. | " " smaller variety and zygospore, | 93 |
| " 10–12. | COSMARIUM EVERETTENSE; front, end and lateral views, | 92 |
| " 13–15. | COSMARIUM QUASILLUS; front, lateral and end views, | 92 |
| " 16–18. | COSMARIUM QUADRIFARIUM; front, lateral and end views, | 94 |
| " 19, 20. | COSMARIUM HOMALODERMUM; front and end views, | 88 |
| " 21–33. | COSMARIUM WOLLEANUM (*C. pseudogranatum*), front, transverse and lateral views, | 64 |
| " 24–26. | COSMARIUM TURPINII; front, end and lateral views, | 87 |
| " 27, 28. | COSMARIUM PROTRACTUM; front and end views, | 90 |
| Fig. 29. | COSMARIUM ORNATUM, Var. minor, (*Protractum?*) | 90 |

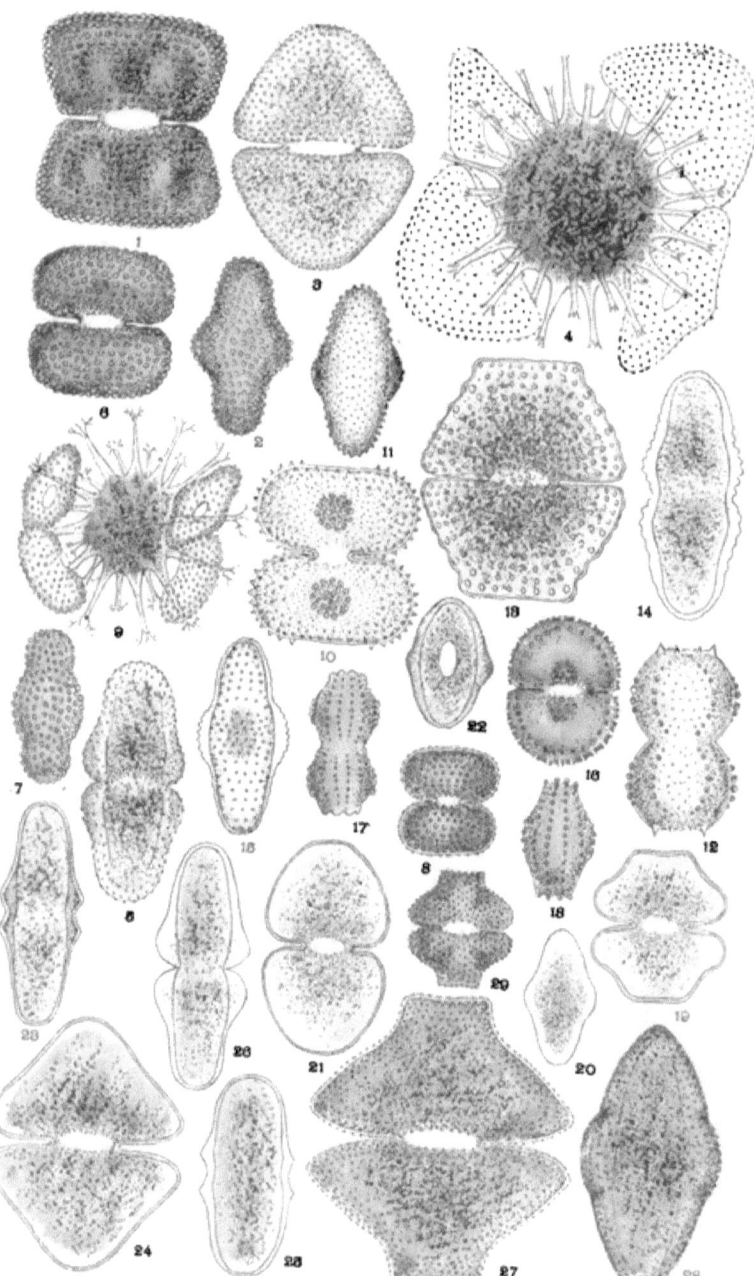

## PLATE XXI.

Figures magnified 500 diameters.

|  |  | PAGE. |
|---|---|---|
| Figs. 1-3. | COSMARIUM KITCHELII, front, end and lateral views, | 79 |
| " 4, 5. | COSMARIUM ORTHOSTICUM, front and lateral views, | 86 |
| " 6, 7. | COSMARIUM SUBCRENATUM, front and lateral views, | 91 |
| " 8, 9. | COSMARIUM QUADRATUM, front and end views, | 63 |
| Fig. 10. | "         "         larger form. | 63 |
| " 11. | COSMARIUM ANCEPS, | 63 |
| Figs 12, 13. | COSMARIUM PARVULUM, front and side views, | 64 |
| " 14, 15. | COSMARIUM SCHLEIPACHEANUM, front and end views, | 89 |
| " 16-18. | COSMARIUM NITIDULUM; a form; ends not usually so convex, | 72A |
| Fig. 19. | COSMARIUM PSEUDONITIDULUM, | 72A |
| " 20. | COSMARIUM TUMIDUM, a coarsely granulate variety, | 82 |
| Figs. 21, 22. | COSMARIUM SUBLOBATUM, | 87 |
| " 23, 24. | COSMARIUM CRUCIATUM, front and end aspect, | 89 |
| " 25, 26 | COSMARIUM RETUSUM, front and end aspect, | 88 |
| Fig 27. | COSMARIUM HAMMERI, Var. intermedium, | 86 |
| Figs. 28-30. | COSMARIUM PHASEOLUS, three views, | 89 |
| " 31, 32, | "         "         smaller variety; zygospore with husks of cells attached, | 89 |
| " 33-35. | COSMARIUM SEELYANUM, front, end and side views, | 80 |
| " 36, 37. | COSMARIUM HAMMERI, Var. inflated sides, | 86 |
| Fig. 38. | "         "         zygospores with remains of cells, | 86 |
| Figs. 39-42. | COSMARIUM ORNATUM, two sizes, four views, | 89 |
| " 43-45. | "         "         a variety, front, side and end views, | 89 |
| " 46-48. | COSMARIUM CAELATUM, front and side views; transverse view of an empty semi-cell, | 93 |
| " 49, 50. | COSMARIUM COMMISURALE, front and transverse views, | 91 |
| Fig. 51. | "         "         zygospore, husks of cells not detached, | 91 |

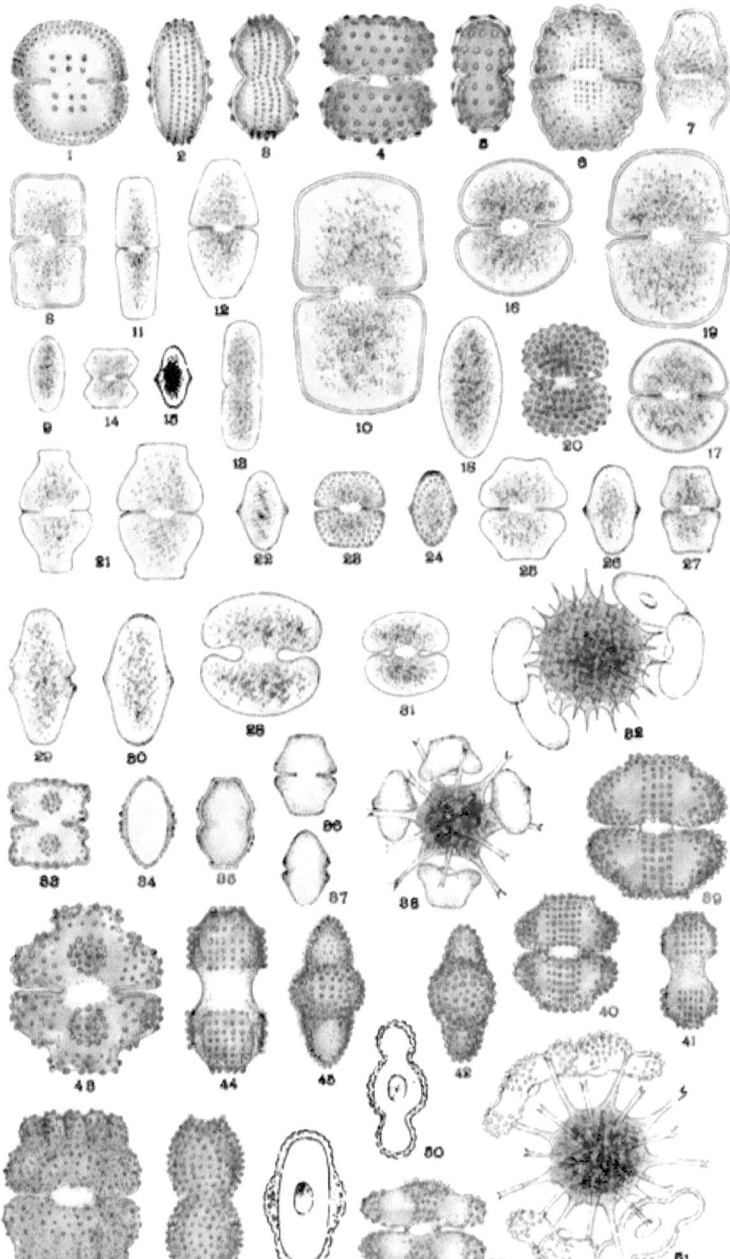

## PLATE XXII.

Figures magnified 500 diameters.

|  |  | PAGE |
|---|---|---|
| Figs. 1, 2. | COSMARIUM ELOISEANUM, front and end views, | 92 |
| " 3–6. | COSMARIUM TRIPLICATUM, front, lateral and end views, and zygospore, | 79 |
| " 7, 8. | COSMARIUM SPECIOSUM, | 95 |
| Fig 9. | " " smaller form, | 95 |
| Figs. 10, 11. | COSMARIUM PYCNOCHONDRUM, front and lateral views, | 97 |
| " 12, 13. | COSMARIUM PECTINOIDES, front and side views, | 96 |
| " 14, 15. | COSMARIUM SPECIOSUM, small variety, | 95 |
| " 16–18. | COSMARIUM PSEUDOPECTINOIDES; two in front view, one in side view, | 96 |
| Fig. 19. | COSMARIUM NASUTUM, | 96 |
| " 20. | COSMARIUM SUBCRENATUM. (Compare Plate XXI, figs. 6, 7), | 91 |
| Figs. 21–22. | COSMARIUM RADIOSUM, | 97 |
| " 23, 24. | COSMARIUM BIREME, in three views, front, side and end, | 89 |
| " 25, 26. | COSMARIUM MARGARITUM, in three views, | 88 |
| Fig. 27. | " " zygospore, with the remains of the semi-cells attached, | 88 |
| Figs. 28–30. | COSMARIUM TITHOPHORUM, from three points of view, | 88 |
| " 31–33. | COSMARIUM BLYTTII, front, side and end views, | 95 |

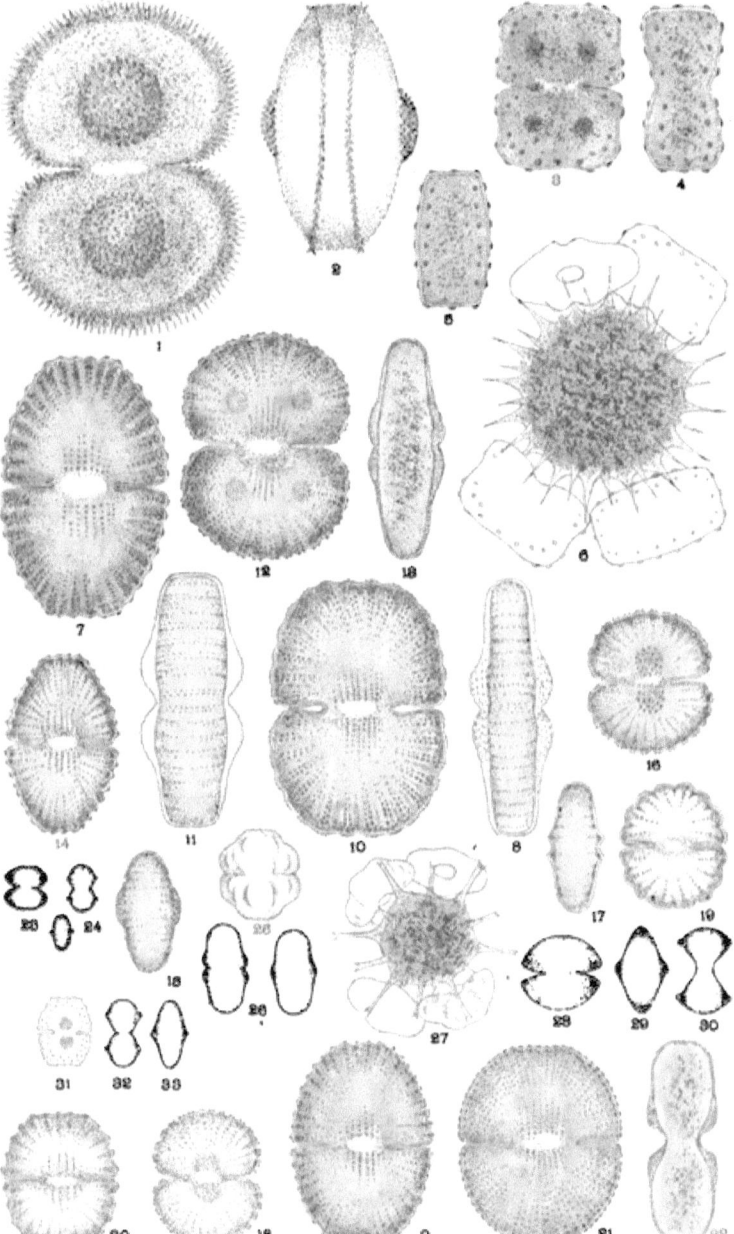

## PLATE XXIII.

Figures magnified 500 diameters.

|  |  | PAGE. |
|---|---|---|
| Fig. 1. | TETMEMORUS BREBISSONII, long form, | 98 |
| " 2. | "          "    shorter and more usual form, | 98 |
| " 3. | TETMEMORUS LAEVIS, | 98 |
| Figs. 4, 5. | TETMEMORUS BREBISSONII, Var. turgidus, two forms, front view, | 98 |
| Fig. 6. | TETMEMORUS GIGANTEUS, (See also Plate XII), | 99 |
| Figs. 7, 8. | TETMEMORUS MINUTUS, conjugating and more advanced condition of spore, | 99 |
| Fig. 9. | "          "    zygospore fully developed, | 99 |

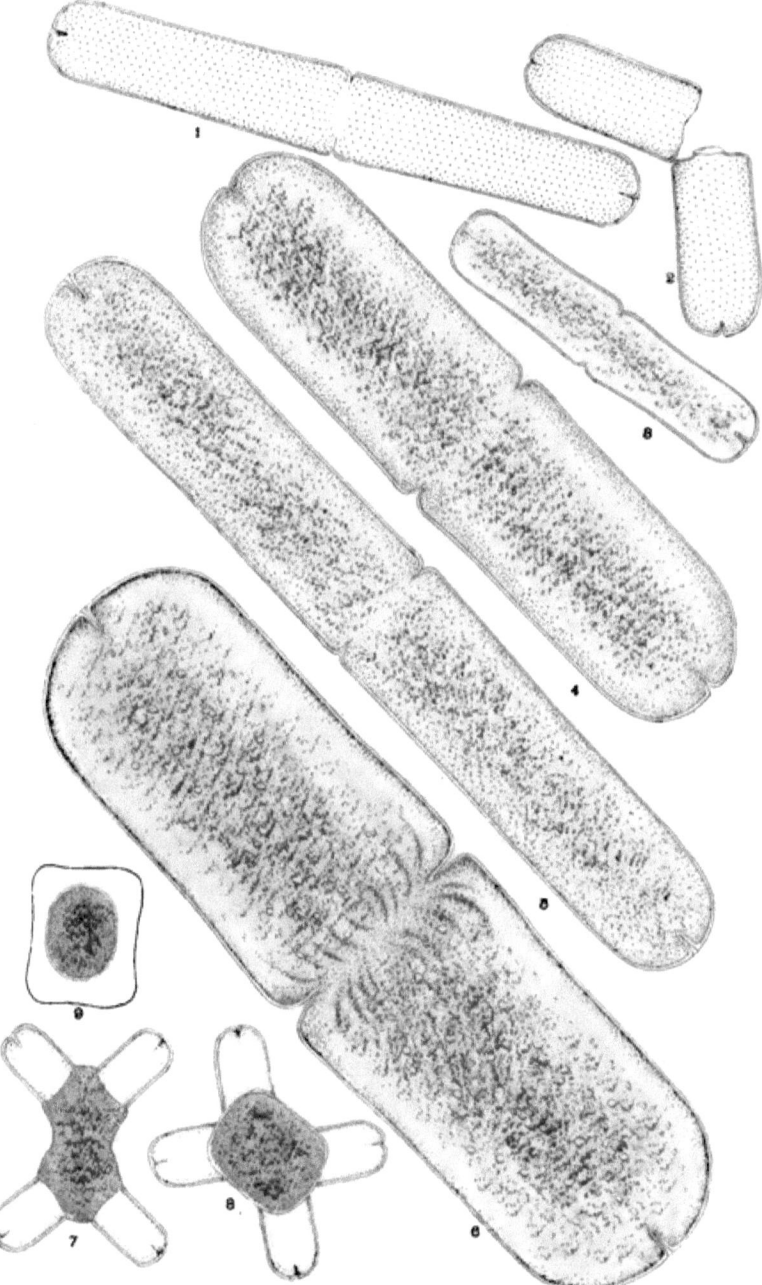

## PLATE XXIV.

### Figures magnified 500 diameters.

|  |  | PAGE. |
|---|---|---|
| Fig. 1. | XANTHIDIUM ARMATUM, from Mount Everett, Mass., | 99 |
| Figs. 2, 3. | "         " more common forms and sizes, | 99 |
| Fig. 4. | "         " transverse view of a semi-cell, | 99 |
| Figs. 5–7. | XANTHIDIUM CRISTATUM, three forms, | 100 |
| Fig. 8. | "         " end view, | 100 |
| Figs. 9, 10. | XANTHIDIUM ASEPTUM, two forms, | 100 |
| Fig. 11. | "         " lateral view, | 100 |

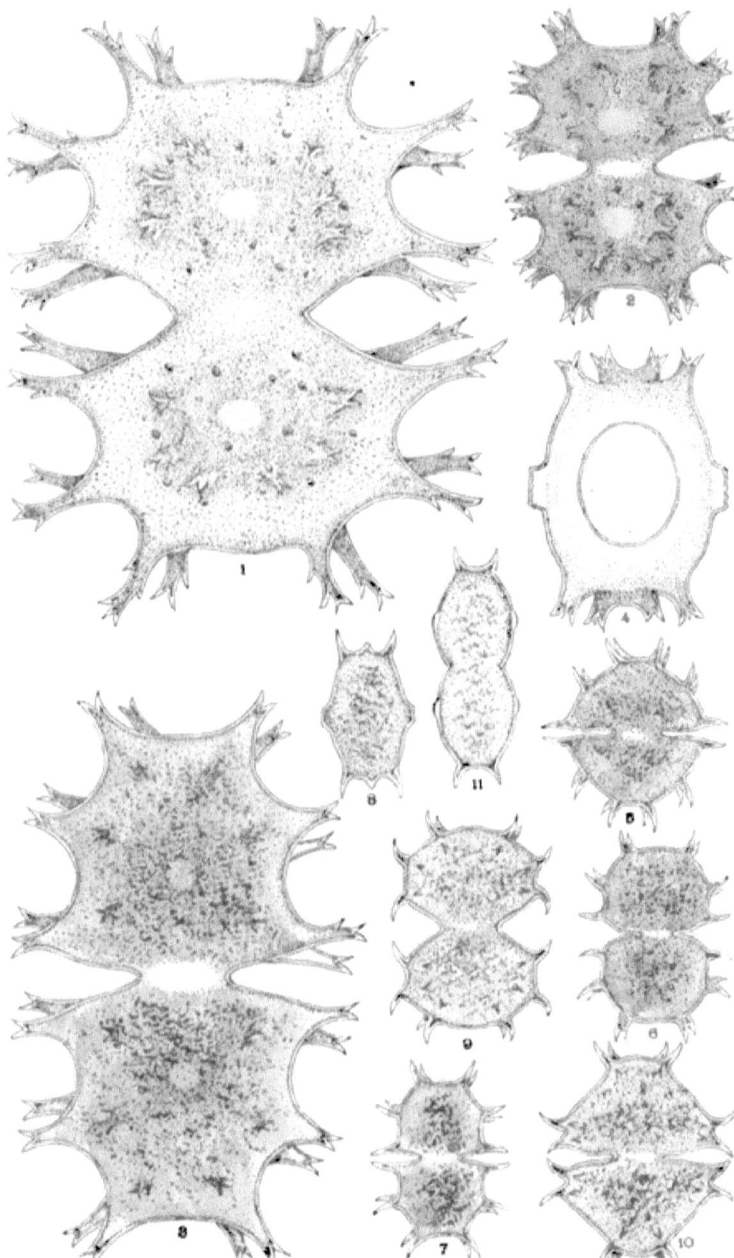

## PLATE XXV.

Figures magnified 500 diameters.

|  |  |  |  | PAGE. |
|---|---|---|---|---|
| Fig. 1. | XANTHIDIUM ANTILOPAEUM, | Var. triquetrum, front view, | | 101 |
| " 2. | " | " | triangular end view, | 101 |
| " 3. | " | " | zygospore with the empty semi-cells attached, | 101 |
| " 4. | XANTHIDIUM FASCICULATUM, | . | | 101 |
| " 5. | " | " | in process of dividing, | 101 |
| Figs. 6, 7. | " | " | a semi-cell in two views, develping a sort of spore without conjugation; an abnormal process, | 102 |
| Figs. 8, 9. | XANTHIDIUM TETRACENTROTUM, front and end views | | | 102 |
| " 10, 11. | " | RECTOCORNUTUM, front and end views, | . | 102 |

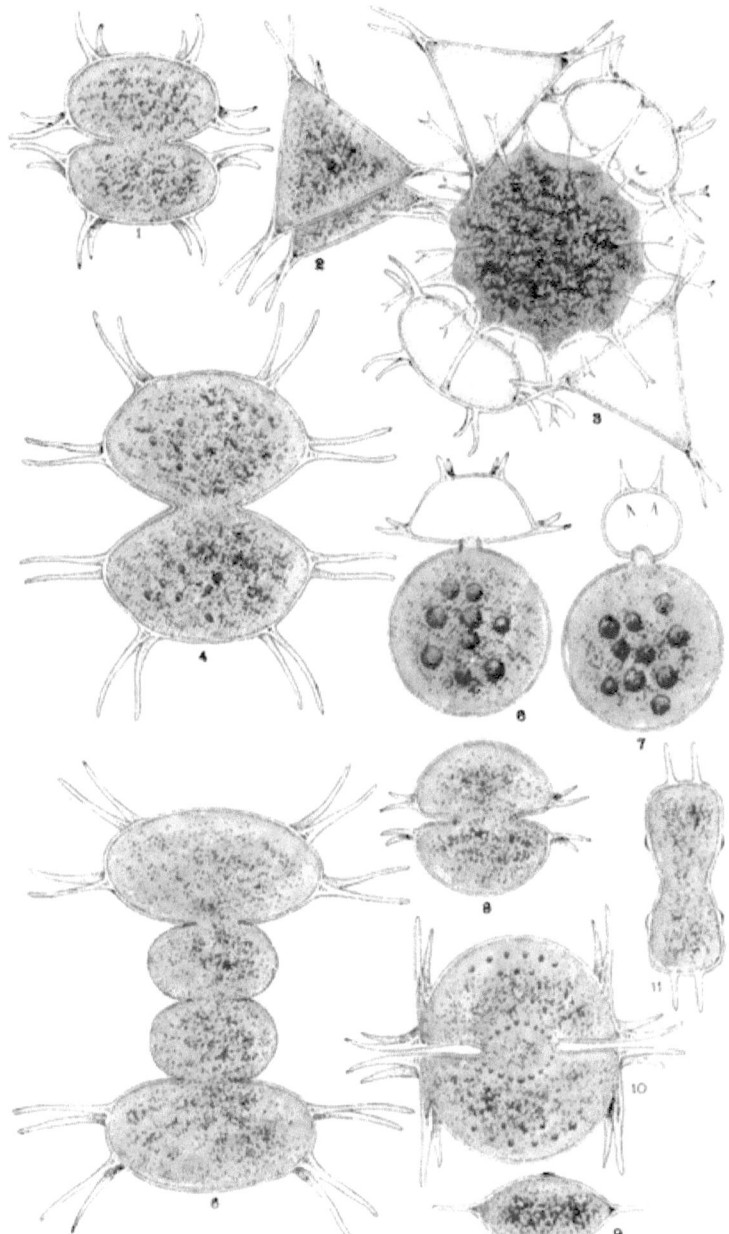

## PLATE XXVI.

Figures magnified 500 diameters.

|  |  | PAGE. |
|---|---|---|
| Fig. 1. | XANTHIDIUM ANTILOPAEUM, typical form, front view, | 101 |
| " 2. | "          "     transverse view of semi-cell, | 101 |
| " 3. | "          "     Var. polymazum, front view, | 101 |
| " 4. | "          "     lateral view, | 101 |
| " 5. | XANTHIDIUM FASCICULATUM, Var. hexagonum, | 101 |
| " 6. | "          "     lateral view, | 101 |
| Figs. 7–9. | XANTHIDIUM BISENARIUM, front, side and end views, | 100 |
| " 10–12. | XANTHIDIUM ACULEATUM, front, side and end views, | 99 |
| " 13–15. | ARTHRODESMUS RAUII, front, end and side views, | 103 |
| " 16–18. | ARTHRODESMUS FRAGILIS, two front and one end view, | 103 |
| " 19–21. | ARTHRODESMUS CONVERGENS, two front and one end view, | 103 |
| " 22, 23. | "          "     variety with short aculei, | 103 |

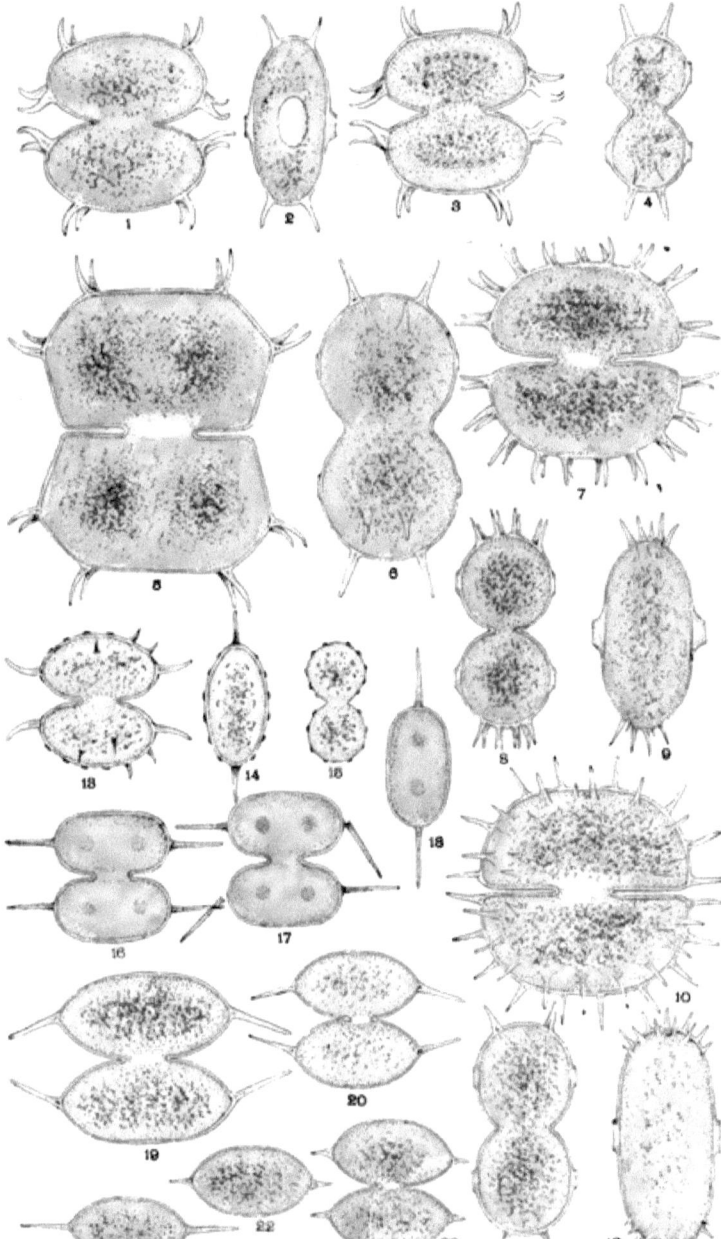

## PLATE XXVII.

Figures magnified 500 diameters.

|  |  |  |  | PAGE |
|---|---|---|---|---|
| Fig. 1. | ARTHRODESMUS INCUS, | **large form,** | | 104 |
| " 2. | " | " | smaller form, | 104 |
| " 3. | " | " | long spined variety, | 104 |
| " 4. | " | " | depressed variety, | 104 |
| " 5. | " | " | quadrate variety, | 104 |
| " 6. | " | " | quadrate variety, smaller, | 104 |
| " 7. | " | " | crenate-cuneate, . | 104 |
| " 8. | " | " | two cells conjugating, | 104 |
| " 9. | " | " | zygospores developed, | 104 |
| " 10. | " | " | end view of **cell,** | 104 |

Figs. 11, 12. ARTHRODESMUS SUBULATUS, front and end view, . 104
" 13, 14. ARTHRODESMUS OVALIS, front and end view, 103
" 15, 16. ARTHRODESMUS ORBICULARIS, front end view, . 104
" 17, 18. ARTHRODESMUS QUADRIDENS, **front and end view,** . 104
" 19, 20. ARTHRODESMUS OCTOCORNIS, Var. twin spined, . 104
" 21-23. " " larger and smaller typical form, 104

Fig. 24. COSMARIUM SUBORCULARE, . . 85
" 25. DESMIDUM CYLINDRICUM, (Compare Plate III, fig. 1,) to illustrate the division of a cell **in the** process of growth, . 26
" 26. HYALOTHECA DISSILIENS, (Compare Plate I, figs. 4, 5, etc.), the middle cell is normal, the other two enlarging preparatory to division in the process of growth, 22
" 27. COSMARIUM **BOTRYTIS,** two cells, opening on one side, putting forth cytioplasm, uniting, thus performing the first act of conjugation, 81
" 28. The whole contents, cytioplasm, of the cells, poured out commingled and formed into the zygospore, 19
" 29. The tubercles on the membrane formed around the mass of cytioplasm (fig. 28,) developed into spines. In the process of further development the membrane breaks, lets out some of the cytioplasm; (fig. 29,) this assumes a spherical form, (fig. 30,) membrane increases in thickness and number of layers; **the** contents divide in one direction, **(fig. 31,)** then subdivided **in** a transverse direction, (fig. 32). Two or four daughter cells are thus formed in all respects like the mother cell, except in the granules of the membrane; these develop later, 19
" 33. A cyst containing a number of small Closteriums; supposed to be the development of a zygospore by another process, 19

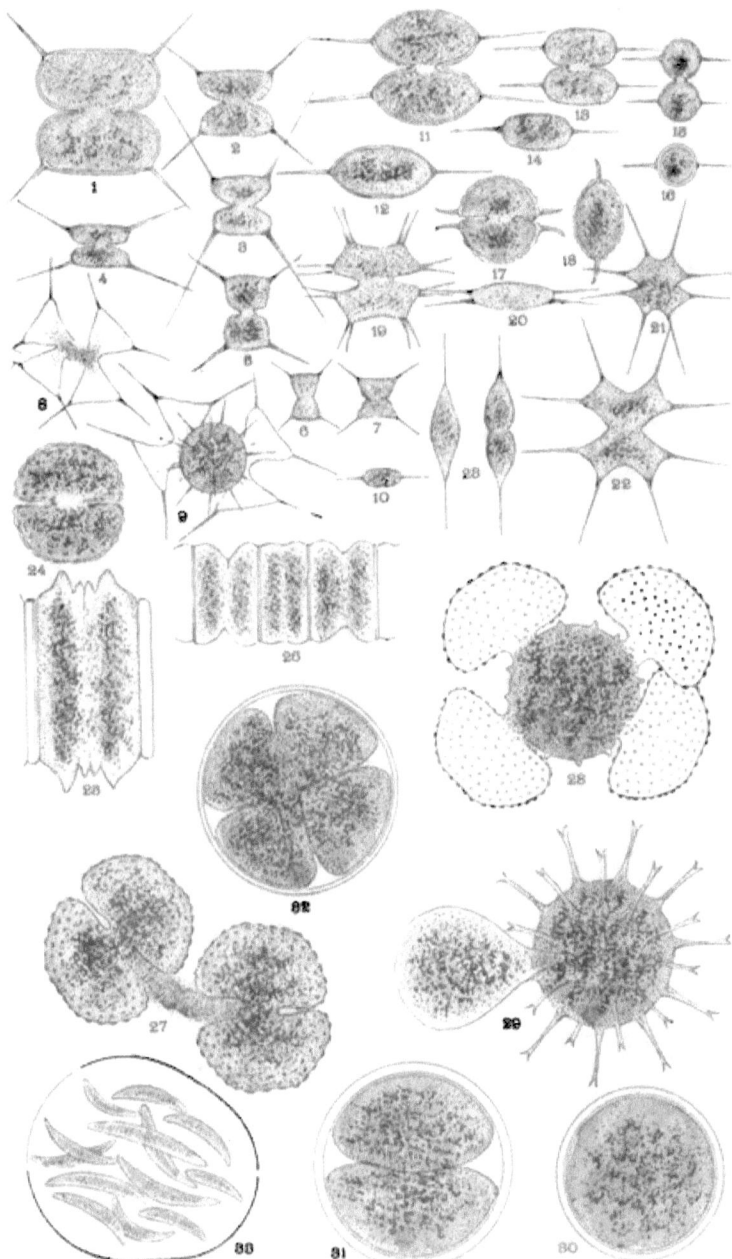

## PLATE XXVIII.

Figures 3, 7, 10, 12 magnified 350 diameters; others 500 diameters.

|  |  | PAGE |
|---|---|---|
| Fig. 1. | EUASTRUM CRASSUM, | 106 |
| " 2. | "        "   semi-cells of very large form, | 106 |
| " 3. | "        "   transverse view of semi-cell, | 106 |
| " 4. | EUASTRUM ORNATUM, a form of " E. crassum." | 106 |
| Figs. 5, 6. | EUASTRUM OBLONGUM, two forms, | 106 |
| Fig. 7. | "        "   transverse view of semi-cell, | 106 |
| Figs. 8, 9. | EUASTRUM ANSATUM, two forms, | 109 |
| Fig. 10. | "        "   transverse view of semi-cell, | 109 |
| Figs. 11, 12. | EUASTRUM AFFINE, front and transverse views, | 110 |

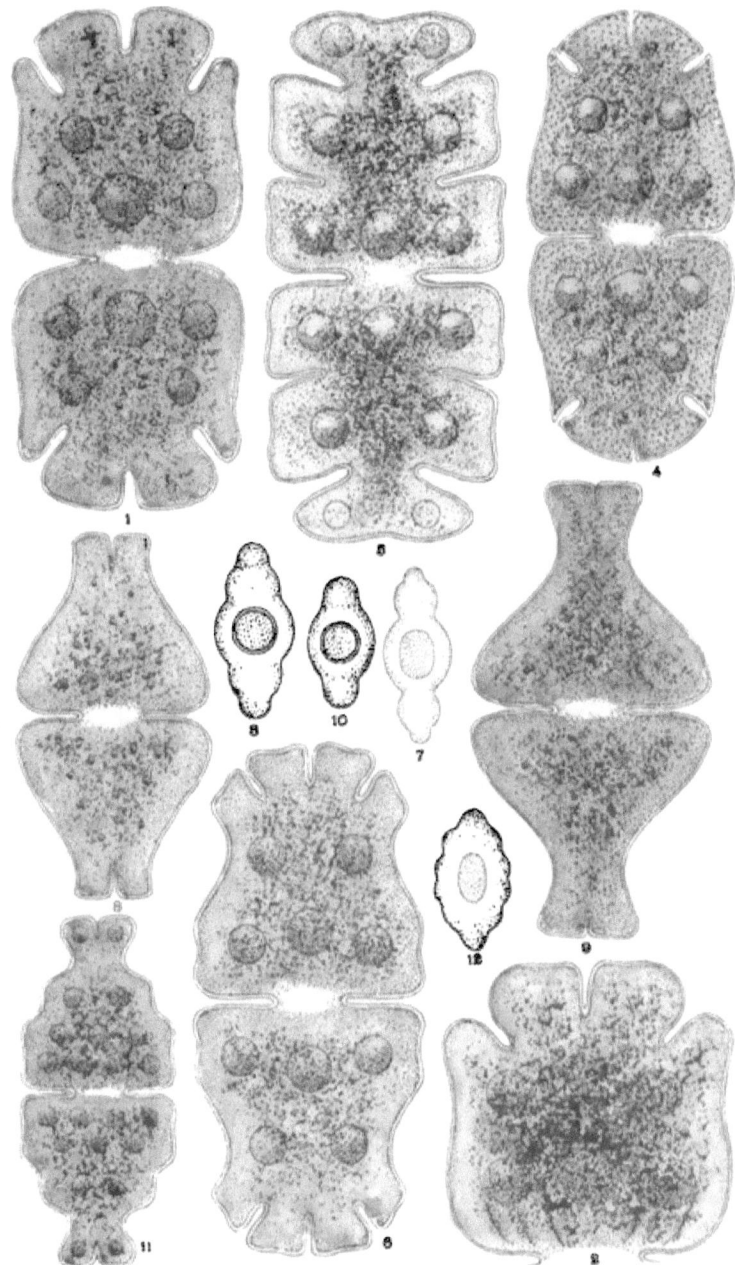

## PLATE XXIX.

Figures magnified 500 diameters.

|  |  | PAGE |
|---|---|---|
| Fig. 1-3. | EUASTRUM VENTRICOSUM, zygospore, lateral and end views of cell, | 110 |
| Figs. 4, 5. | EUASTRUM CRASSUM, Var. SCROBICULATUM, front and lateral views, | 106, 108 |
| " 6-8. | EUASTRUM MAGNIFICUM, front, lateral and end views, | 108 |
| " 9-11. | EUASTRUM PURUM, two front and one lateral view, | 110 |
| " 12, 13. | EUASTRUM CUNEATUM, front and lateral views, | 108 |

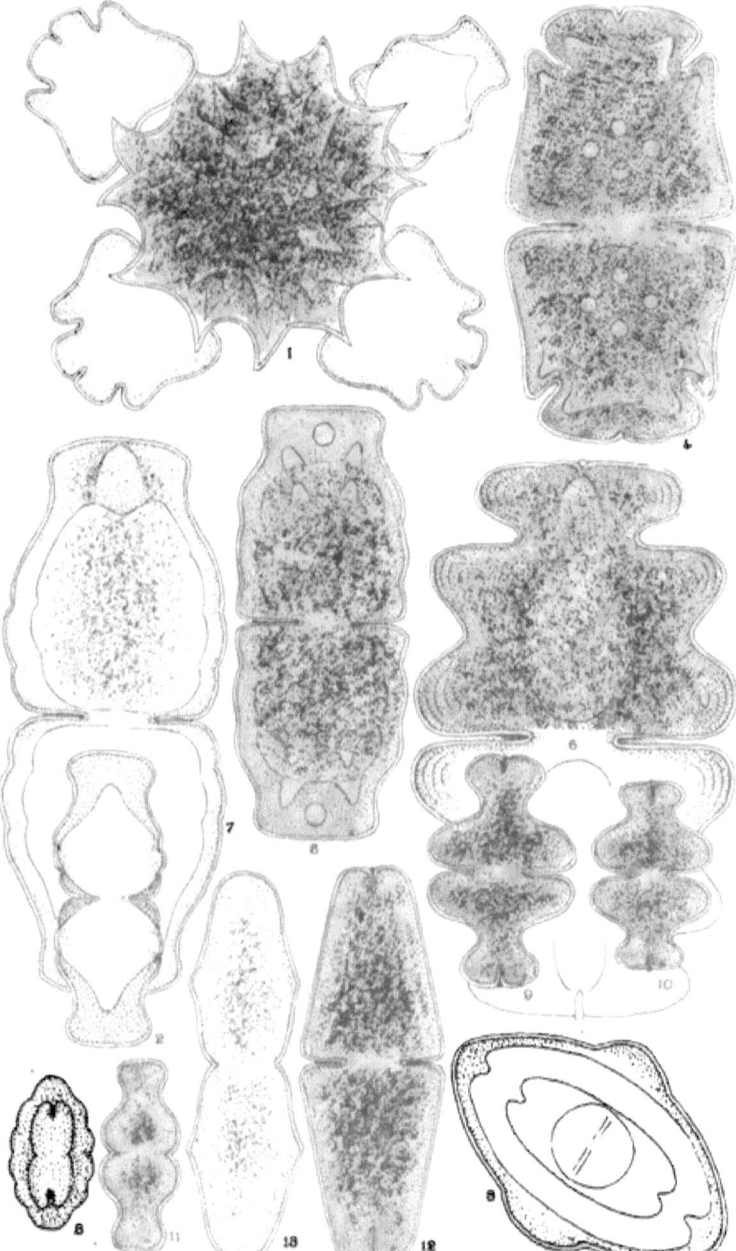

## PLATE XXX.

### Figures magnified 500 diameters.

| | | | | PAGE |
|---|---|---|---|---|
| Fig. 1. | EUASTRUM VERRUCOSUM, typical form, | | . | . 111 |
| " 2. | " | " | Var. Crux Africanum, . | 111 |
| " 3. | " | " | Var. reductum, | . 111 |
| " 4. | " | " | Var. alatum, | 111 |
| " 5. | " | " | transverse view, | . 111 |
| " 6. | EUASTRUM DONNELLII, | | . | 114 |
| " 7. | EUASTRUM NORDSTEDTIANUM, . | | . | . 116 |
| " 8. | " | " | Var. minor, | 116 |
| Figs. 9–12 | " | " | typical varieties, | . 116 |
| Fig. 13. | " | " | lateral view, | 116 |
| " 14, 15. | EUASTRUM MAMMILLOSUM, front and end views, | | | . 113 |
| " 16. | EUASTRUM FORMOSUM, | | . | 114 |
| " 17. | EUASTRUM ATTENUATUM, | | | 113 |
| Figs. 18, 19. | EUASTRUM DIVARICATUM, front and end views, | | | 114 |

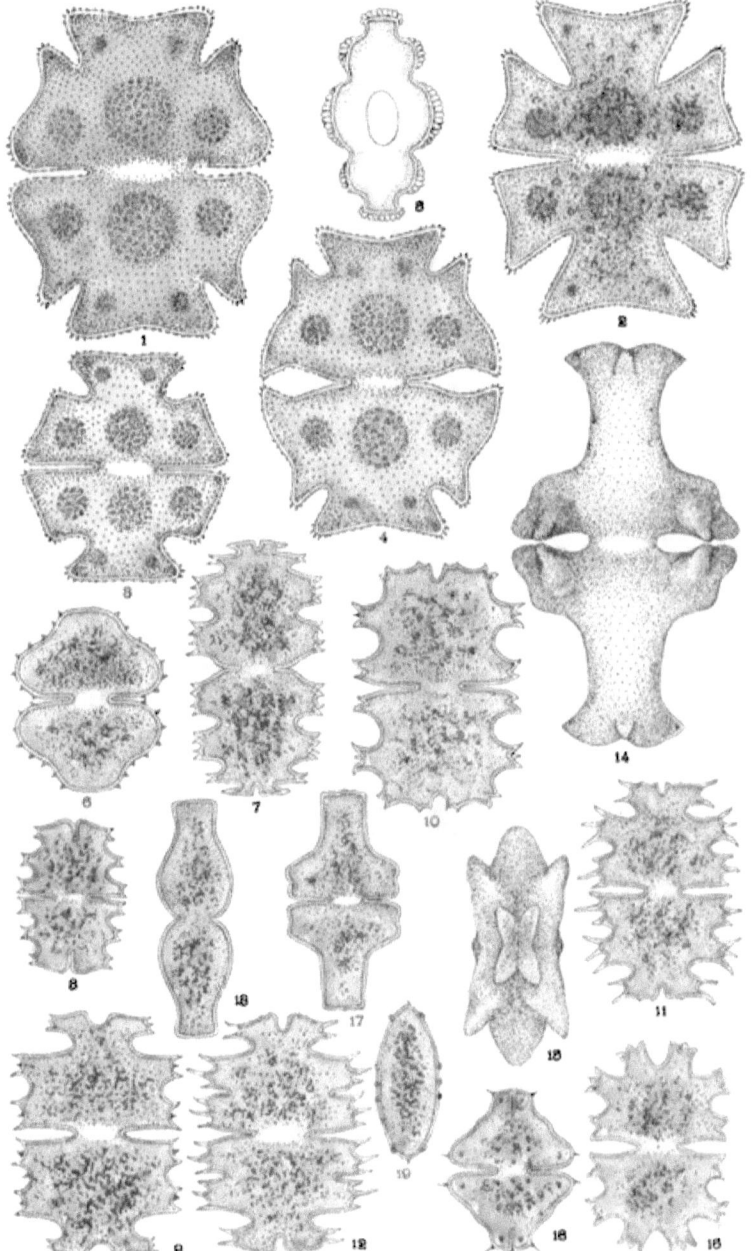

## PLATE XXXI.

### Figures magnified 500 diameters.

| | | PAGE |
|---|---|---|
| Figs. 1–3. | EUASTRUM PINGUE, front, side and end views, | 116 |
| " 4–6. | EUASTRUM SPINOSUM, three forms, | 116 |
| Fig. 7. | " " lateral view, | 116 |
| Figs. 8, 9. | EUASTRUM ROSTRATUM, | 116 |
| " 10–15. | EUASTRUM ELEGANS, | 116 |
| Fig. 16. | " " zygospore, | 116 |
| " 17. | EUASTRUM SPINOSUM, side view of cell. | 116 |
| Figs. 18–22. | EUASTRUM INTEGRUM, | 117 |
| " 23, 24. | EUASTRUM BINALE, | 117 |
| " 25, 26. | EUASTRUM ELEGANS, | 116 |
| Fig. 27. | EUASTRUM ROSTRATUM, a form of, | 116 |
| Figs. 28, 29. | EUASTRUM COMPACTUM, | 117 |
| " 30, 36. | EUASTRUM INERME, | 115 |
| Fig. 31. | EUASTRUM OBTUSUM, | 117 |
| " 32. | EUASTRUM CUSPIDATUM. | 115 |
| Figs. 33–35. | EUASTRUM POKORNYANUM, | 114 |
| Fig. 36. | EUASTRUM INERME, | 115 |
| Figs. 37, 38. | EUASTRUM CRASSICOLLE, | 115 |
| " 39–42. | EUASTRUM INSIGNE, | 113 |
| Fig. 43. | " " end view, showing the cruciform apex and the quadrate base of the semi-cell, | 113 |

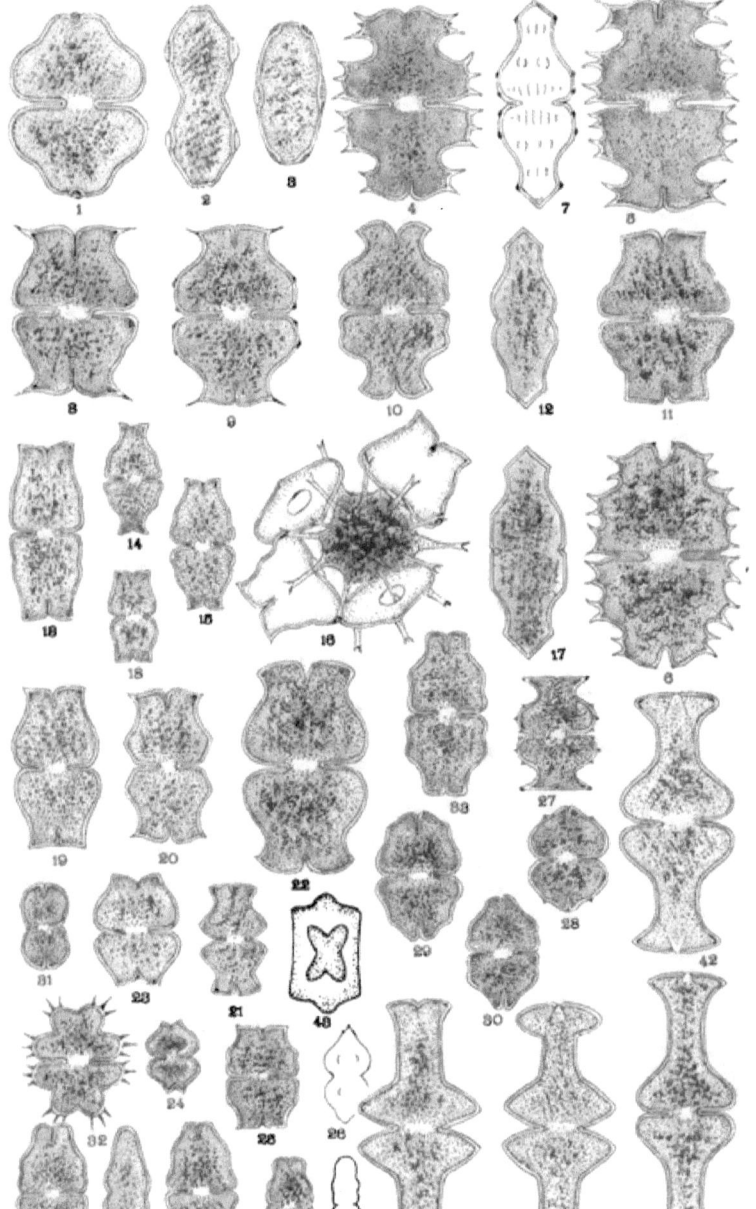

## PLATE XXXII.

Figures magnified 500 diameters.

|  |  | PAGE. |
|---|---|---|
| **Figs. 1, 2.** | EUASTRUM CIRCULARE, front and transverse views of semi-cell, | 112 |
| **Fig. 3.** | EUASTRUM GEMMATUM, . | 112 |
| " 4. | "       "    transverse view of semi-cell, | 112 |
| " 5. | EUASTRUM EVERETTENSE, . | 112 |
| Figs. 6, 7. | "       "    transverse and lateral aspect of semi-cell, | 112 |
| " **8–10.** | EUASTRUM AMPULLACEUM, three forms, . . . | 110 |
| Fig. 11. | "       "    **transverse view of semi-cell.** . | 110 |
| " **12.** | EUASTRUM HUMEROSUM, | 107 |
| " 13. | " ·     "    basal view of semi-cell, | 107 |
| Figs. 14, **15.** | EUASTRUM PINNATUM, . . . | 107 |
| **Fig. 16.** | "       "    **basal aspect of semi-cell,** | 107 |

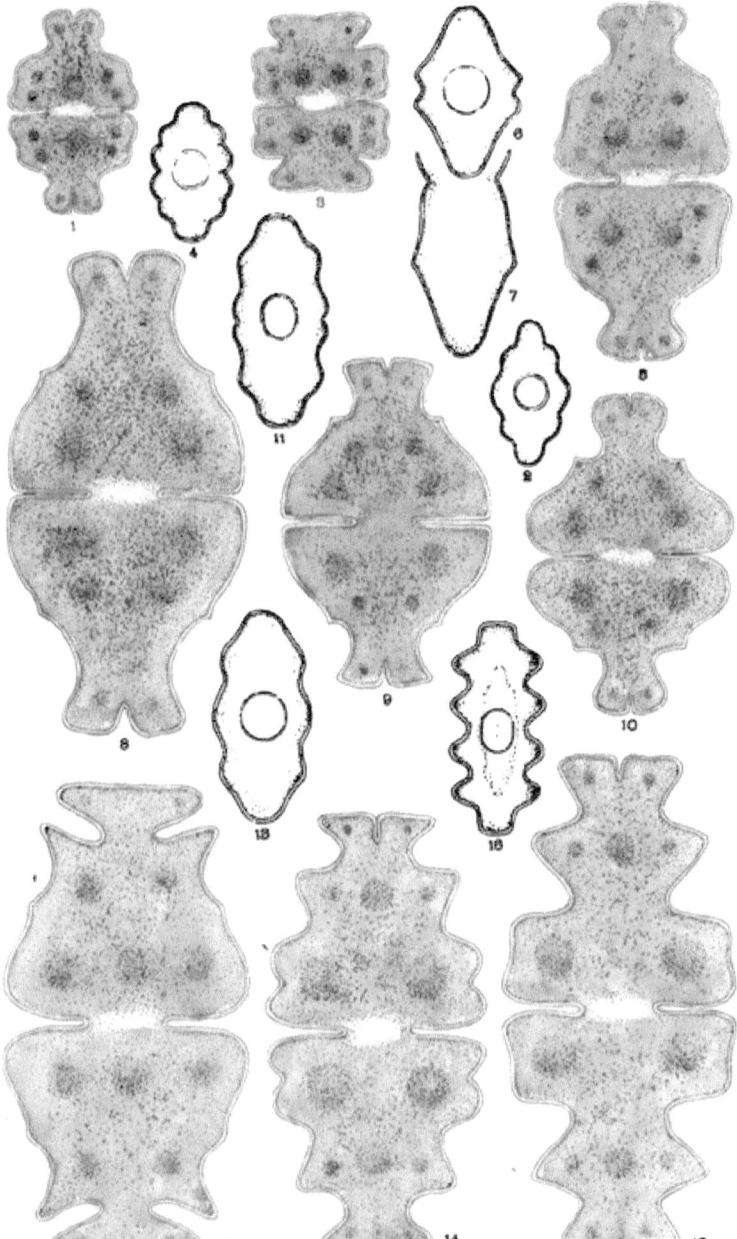

## PLATE XXXIII.

#### Figures magnified 500 diameters.

|  |  |  |  | PAGE. |
|---|---|---|---|---|
| Fig. 1. | EUASTRUM WOLLEI, | | | 108 |
| " 2. | " | " | transverse view of semi-cell. . | 108 |
| " 3. | " | " | Var. cuspidatum, . | 108 |
| Figs. 4, 5. | " | " | lateral and end views, | 108 |
| " 6–8. | EUASTRUM INERME, three forms, | | | 115 |
| " 9, 10. | EUASTRUM DIDELTA, two forms, | | | 109 |
| " 11, 12. | EUASTRUM ANSATUM—E. Ralfsii, | | | 109 |

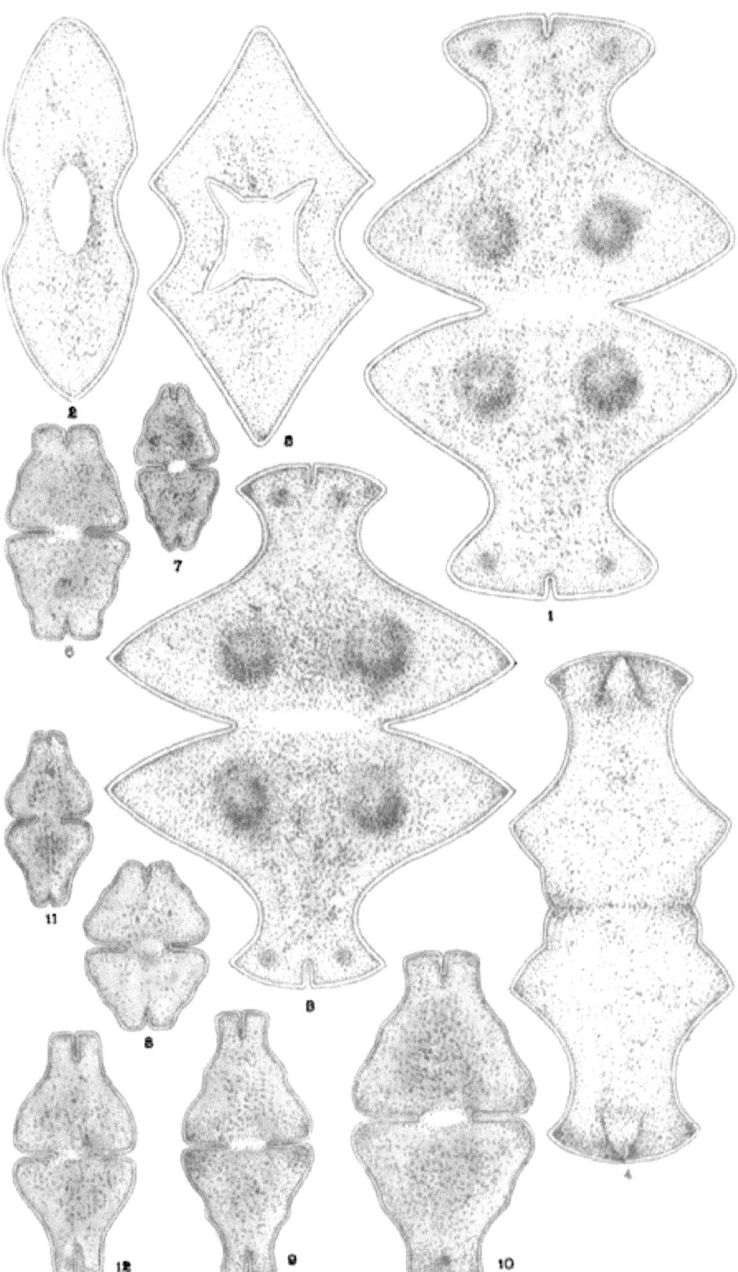

## PLATE XXXIV

Figures magnified 375 diameters.

|  | PAGE. |
|---|---|
| Figs. 1-8. MICRASTERIAS TORREYI, in eight varieties, each **represented by one-fourth of a cell. The varieties** effected by the process of multiplication by division; two semi-cells of entirely different outline being in **many cases united, as part** of the same plant, | 118 |

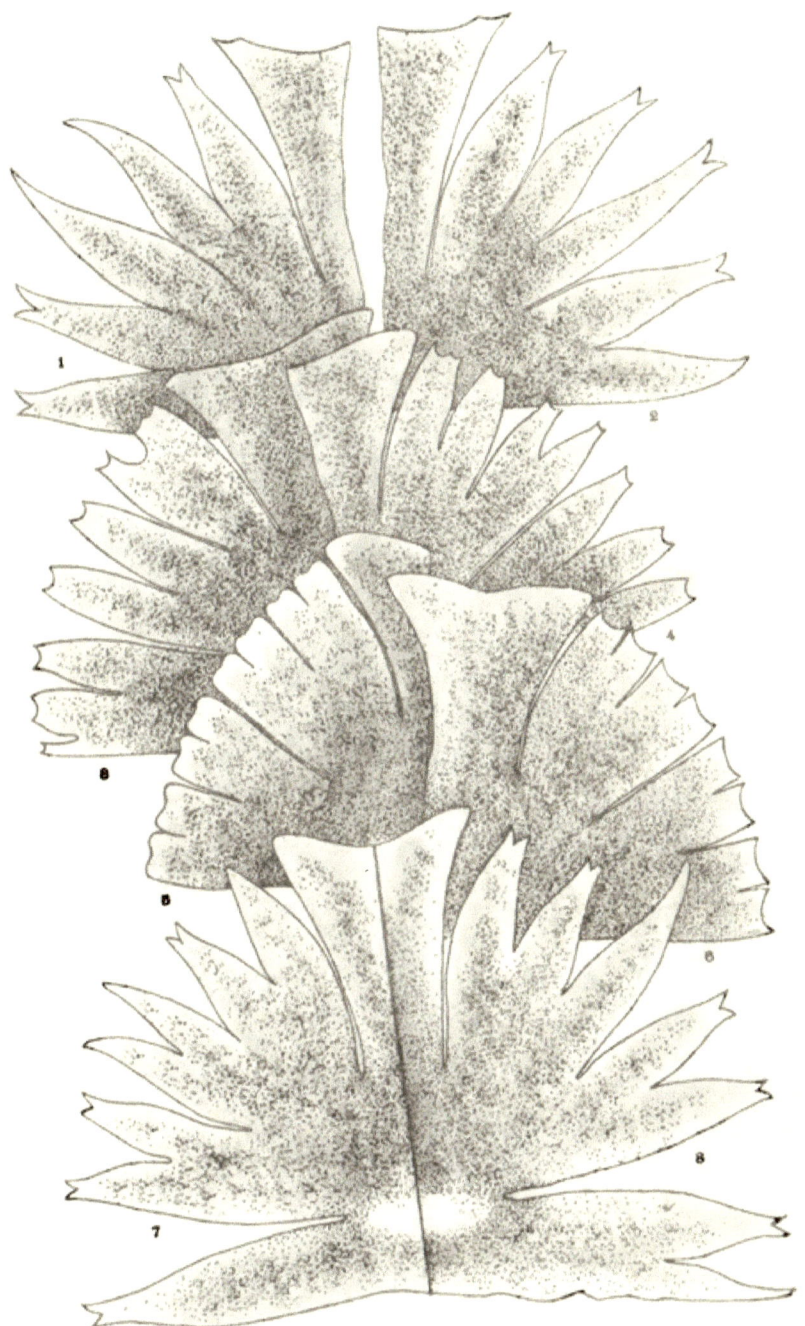

## PLATE XXXV.

Figures magnified 375 diameters.

|  |  |  |  |  | PAGE. |
|---|---|---|---|---|---|
| Fig. 1. | MICRASTERIAS RADIOSA, larger form containing about forty biparted lobelets, with apices furcate or bidentate, | | | | 119 |
| " 2. | " | " | smaller form of about twenty bipartite lobelets, | | 119 |
| " 3. | " | " | another form with about twenty-four similar lobelets, some of the apices indicating by the smaller indentations a further division, | | 119 |
| " 4. | MICRASTERIAS MURICATA, small variety, | | | | 130 |
| " 5. | " | " | larger form, | | 130 |
| " 6. | " | " | transverse view of semi-cell, | | 130 |
| " 7. | " | " | end view, | | 130 |

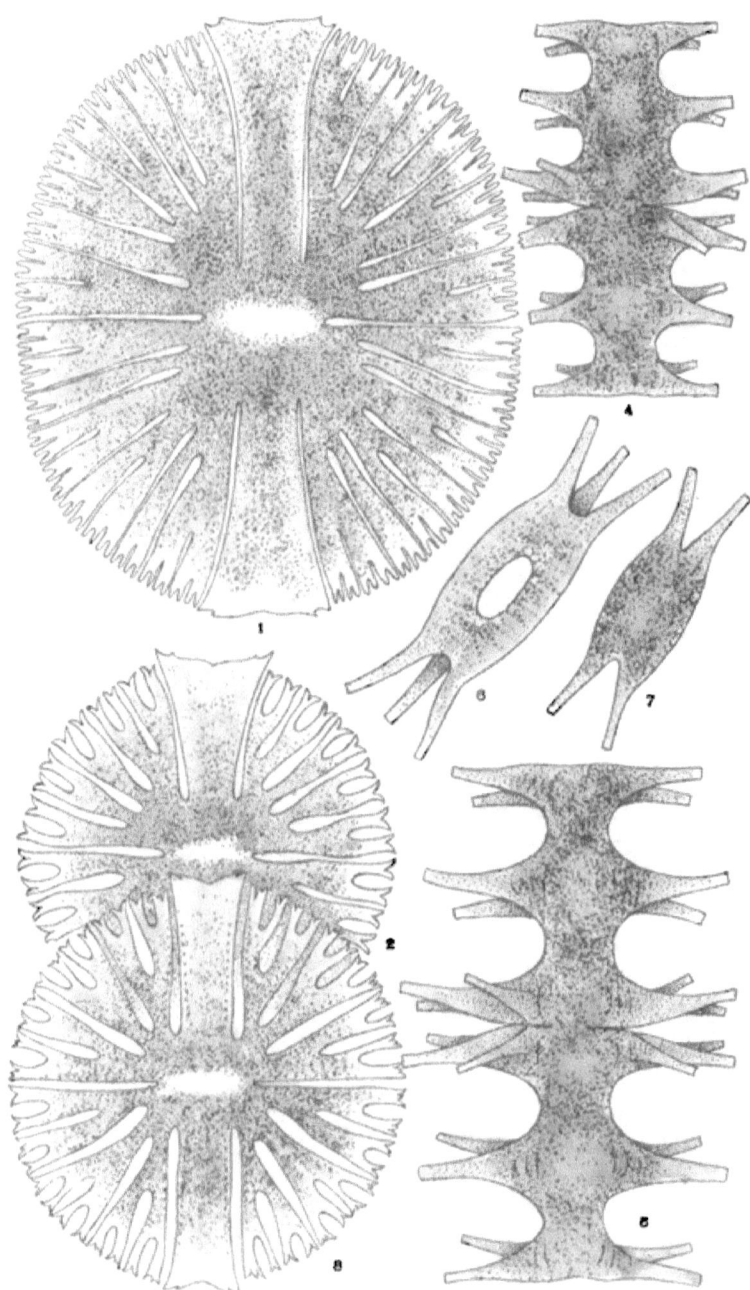

## PLATE XXXVI.

Figures magnified 375 diameters.

|   |   |   |   |   | PAGE. |
|---|---|---|---|---|---|
| Fig. 1. | MICRASTERIAS PSEUDOTORREYI, | | | | 118 |
| " 2. | MICRASTERIAS AMERICANA, | | | | 124 |
| " 3. | " | " | Var. recta, | | 124 |
| " 4. | " | " | transverse view, | | 124 |
| " 5. | " | " | Var. Hermanniana, | | 124 |
| Figs. 6, 7. | MICRASTERIAS BRACHYPTERA, two semi-cells varying somewhat in details, | | | | 121 |
| " 8, 9. | MICRASTERIAS PAPILLIFERA, two forms, | | | | 120 |

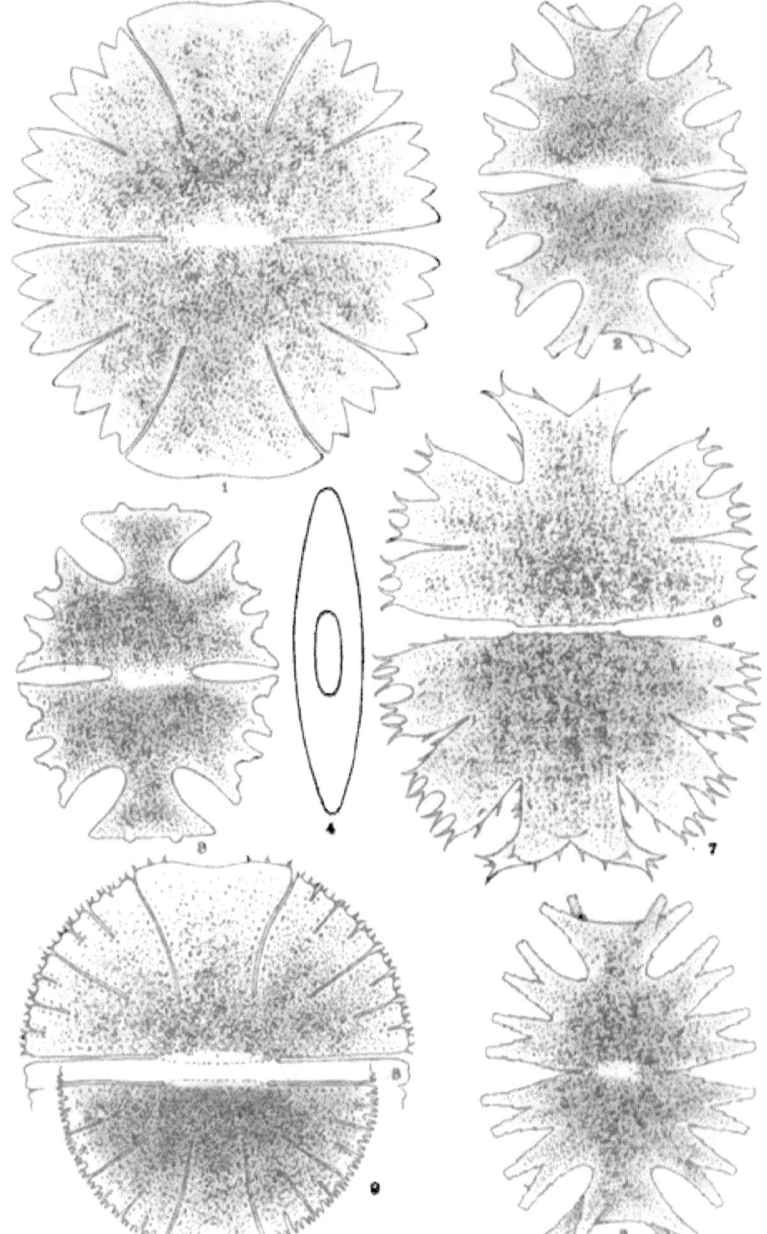

## PLATE XXXVII.

### Figures magnified 375 diameters.

|  |  | PAGE. |
|---|---|---|
| Fig. 1. | MICRASTERIAS JENNERI, . . . . | 127 |
| " 2. | "    "    Var. angulosa, | 127 |
| Figs. 3, 4. | MICRASTERIAS OSCITANS, two semi-cells, varying mainly in the apices of the polar lobes; in the one simple, in the other **divided**, . | 128 |
| " 5, 6. | MICRASTERIAS DECEMDENTATA, a large form, two sizes, | 126 |
| " 7, 8. | MICRASTERIAS CRENATA, two forms, | 126 |

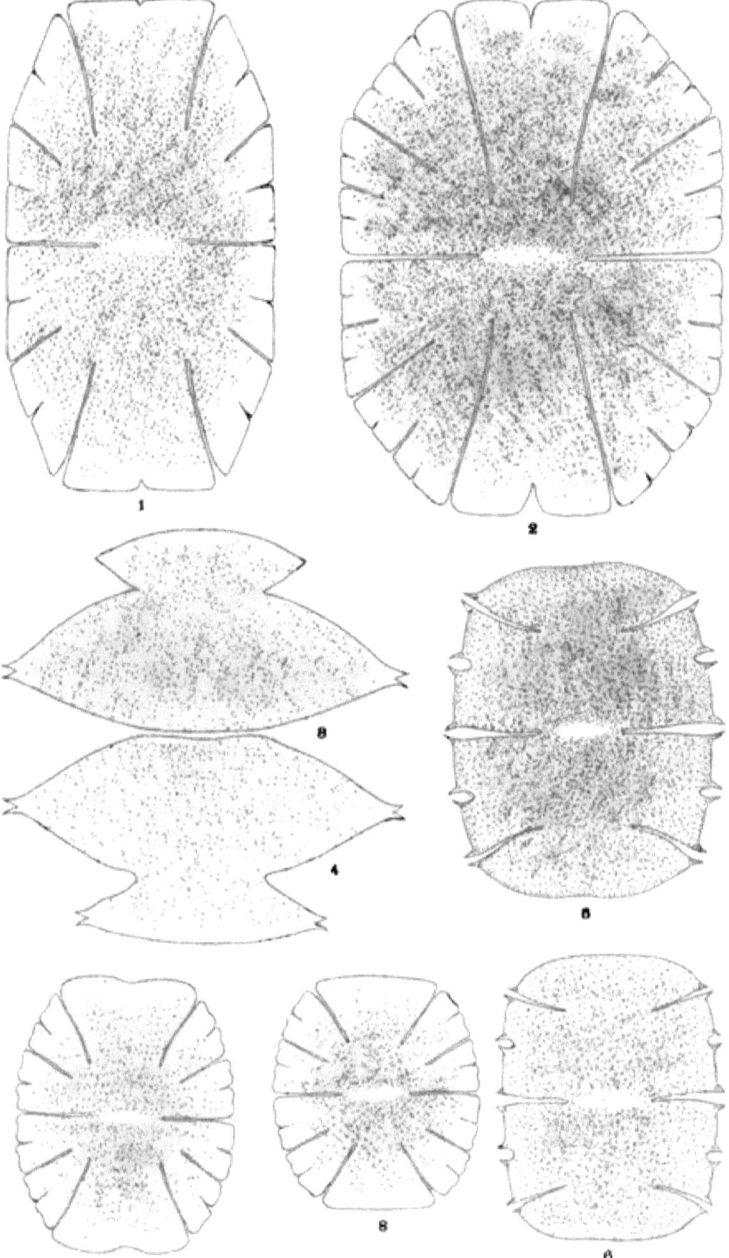

## PLATE XXXVIII.

Figures magnified 375 diameters.

|  |  | PAGE. |
|---|---|---|
| Figs. 1, 2. MICRASTERIAS ROTATA, two forms, | | 120 |
| Fig. 3. " " Var. simplex, | | 120 |
| " 4. MICRASTERIAS DENTICULATA, circular form, | | 120 |
| " 5. " " more oblong in outline, | | 120 |
| " 6. " " larger variety, near M. angulosa of Reinsch, | | 120 |
| Figs. 7, 8. " " semi-cells of two smaller forms, | | 120 |

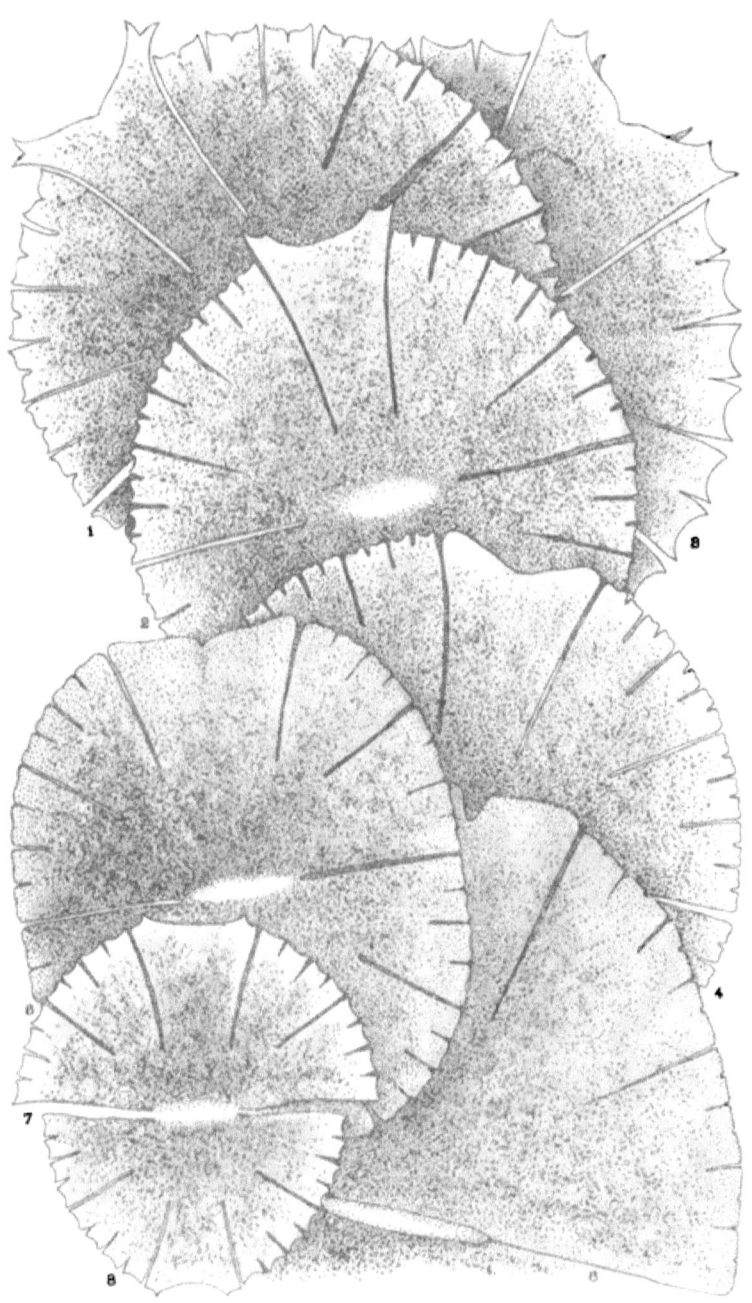

## PLATE XXXIX.

Figures magnified 375 diameters.

| | | PAGE. |
|---|---|---|
| Figs. 1, 2. | MICRASTERIAS RINGENS, two forms, | 123 |
| Fig. 3. | MICRASTERIAS CRUX **MELITENSIS**, | 123 |
| " 4. | MICRASTERIAS PSEUDOFURCATA, | **122** |
| Figs. 5, 6. | MICRASTERIAS FURCATA, two forms, . | 128 |

## PLATE XL.

Figures magnified 375 diameters.

|  |  | PAGE. |
|---|---|---|
| Fig. 1. | MICRASTERIAS FIMBRIATA, semi-cell, typical form, | 121 |
| " 2. | " " other semi-cell, Var. apiculata, | 121 |
| " 3. | " " one-fourth cell, Var. Elephantina, | 121 |
| " 4. | " " Var. nuda, | 121 |
| Figs. 5, 6. | " " two varieties of polar lobes, | 121 |
| Fig. 7. | MICRASTERIAS SUBFIMBRIATA, has the form of lobelets, but not the specific number, | 121 |
| " 8. | MICRASTERIAS SIMPLEX, unlike all other forms in the simple, acute, ultimate division of the lobules, | 121 |

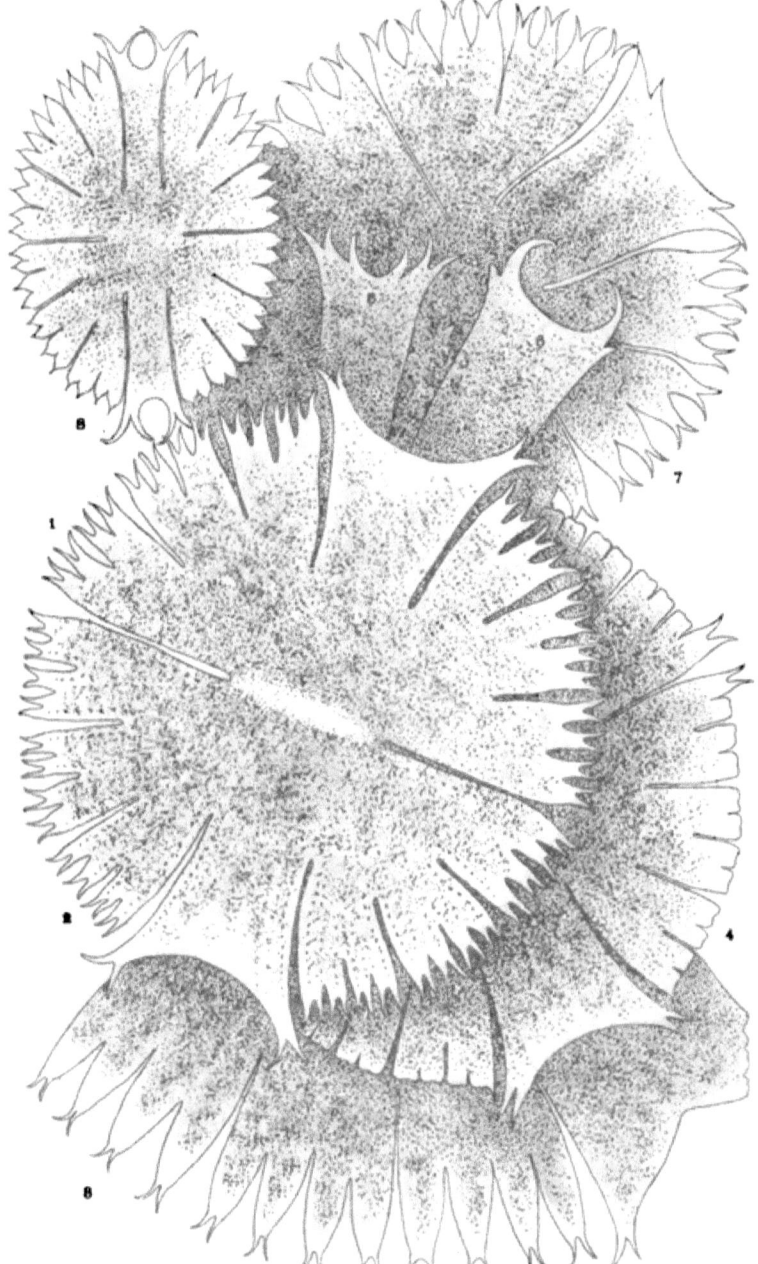

## PLATE XLI.

**Figures magnified 375 diameters.**

|  |  | PAGE |
|---|---|---|
| Figs. 1, 2. MICRASTERIAS KITCHELII, two forms, | | 129 |
| Fig. 3. " " lateral view, | | 129 |
| Figs. 4, 5. MICRASTERIAS LATICEPS,—*M. disputa*, Wood, | | 128 |
| Fig. 6. MICRASTERIAS BAILEYI, | | 130 |
| Figs. 7, 8. MICRASTERIAS PINNATIFIDA, two forms, | | 129 |
| Fig 9. " " Var. inflata, | | 129 |
| " 10. MICRASTERIAS MAHABULESHWARENSIS, | | 124 |
| " 11. MICRASTERIAS PSEUDOFURCATA, Var. minor, | | 122 |
| " 12. MICRASTERIAS EXPANSA, | | 129 |

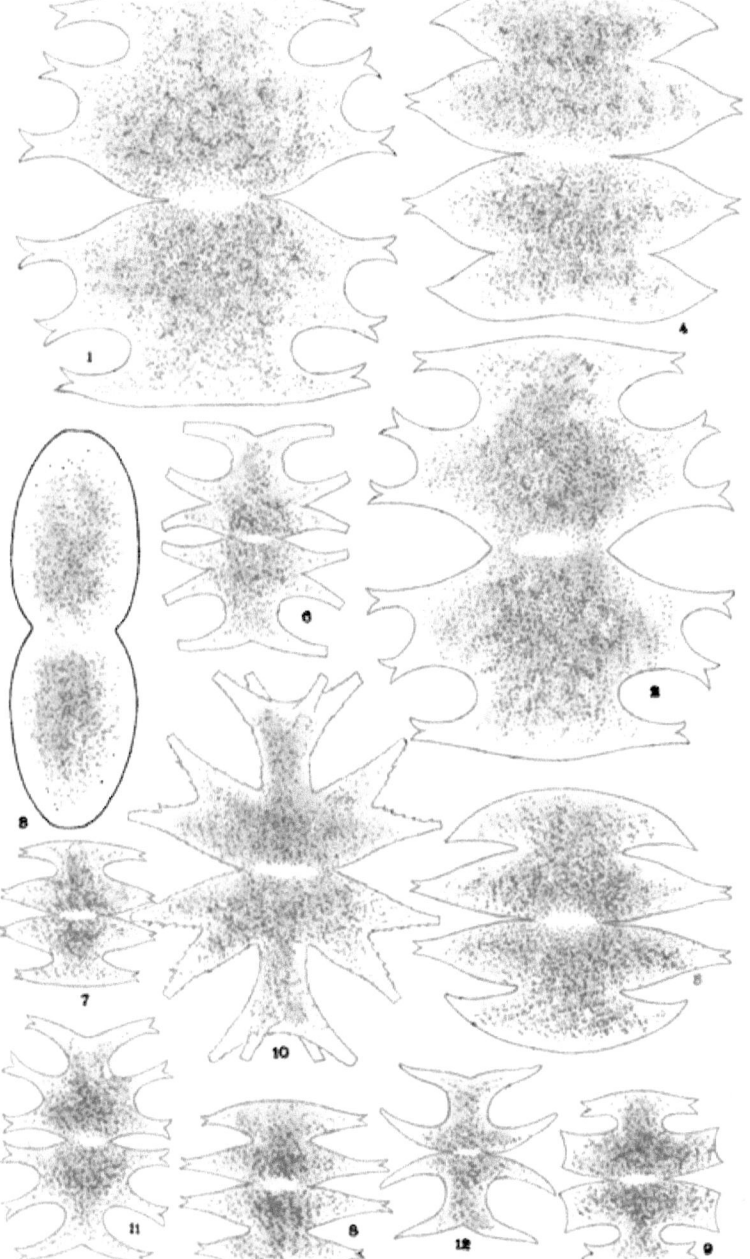

## PLATE XLII.

Figures magnified 500 diameters, excepting the Micrasterias only about one-half as much.

|  |  |  | PAGE. |
|---|---|---|---|
| Fig. 1. | MICRASTERIAS SWAINEI, Hastings, | . . . . | 119 |
| " 2. | MICRASTERIAS KITCHELII, Wolle, variety. Pond, Malaga, New Jersey, | . . | 129 |
| Figs. 3–5. | XANTHIDIUM ANTELOPAEUM, Kg., . | . . . | 101 |
|  | Var. truncatum, Hastings, front, lateral and end views, | . | 101 |
| " 6, 7. | STAURASTRUM MEGALONOTUM, Nord., . | . | 141 |
|  | Var. obtusum, Hastings, | . | 141 |
|  | Nord.'s Spitz., Des. Arcto. and Des. Groen. |  |  |
| " 8–11. | STAURASTRUM CRESCENTUM, Hast., front and end views, | . | 153 |
| " 12, 13. | EUASTRUM VERRUCOSUM, Ehrb., . | . | 111 |
|  | Var. simplex, Joshua, | . | 111 |
| " 14, 15. | STAURASTRUM SAXONICUM, Bulnh., | . . . | 154 |
|  | Var. pentagonum, Wolle, front and end views, | . . | 154 |
| " 16, 17. | EUASTRUM HASTINGSII, Wolle, | . . . | 113 |

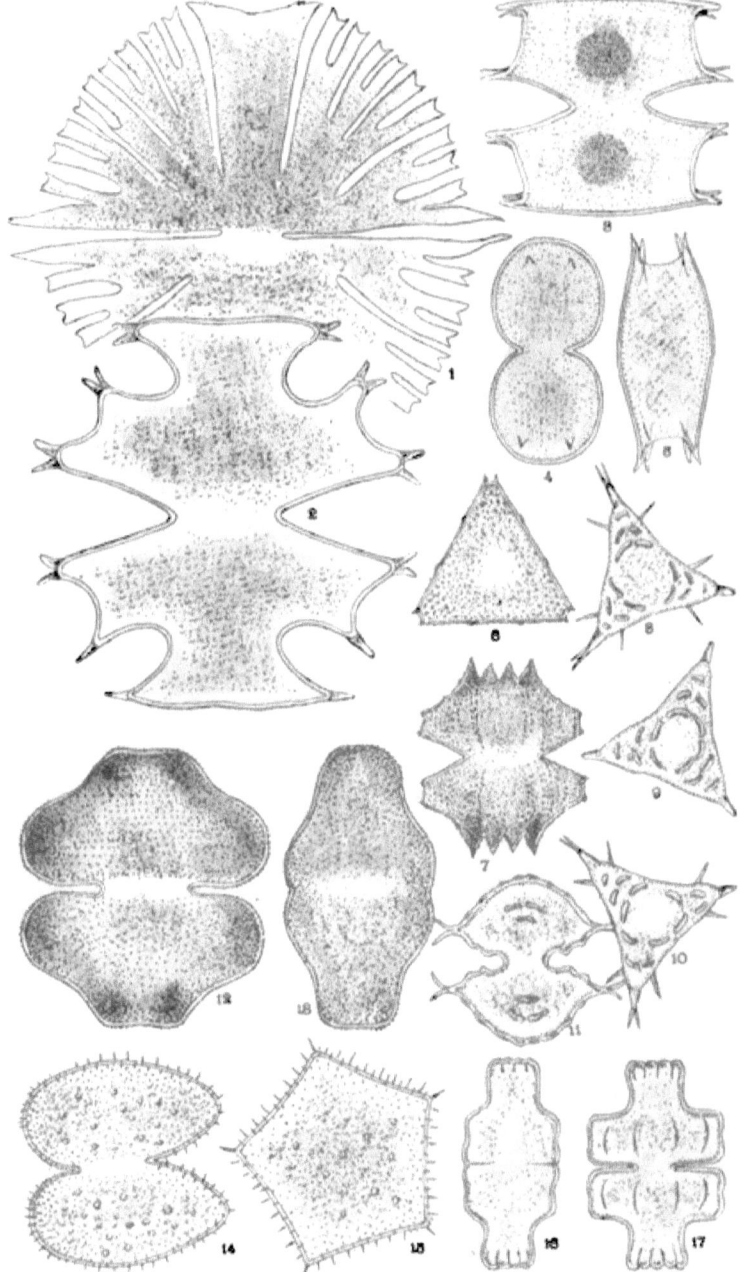

## PLATE XLIII.

Figures magnified 500 diameters, except the *Micrasterias* and *Closteriums* only about one-half.

| | | PAGE. |
|---|---|---|
| Fig. 1. | MICRASTERIAS RADIOSA, Ralfs, Var. PUNCTATA, West, | 119 |
| Figs. 2, 3. | XANTHIDIUM ANTILOPAEUM, Kg., | 101 |
| | Var. CANADENSE, Joshua, front and end views, | 102 |
| Fig. 4. | COSMARIUM REGNESI, Reinsch, | 70 |
| Figs. 5, 6. | STAURASTRUM ANGULATUM, West, | 132 |
| " 7, 8. | SPHAEROZOSMA SERRATUM, Bailey; two varieties from Florida, | 30 |
| " 9, 10. | SPHAEROZOSMA (Onychonema), NORDSTEDTIANA, Turner, | 31 |
| " 11–13. | COSMARIUM MENEGHINII, Breb., forma octangularis, Wille, | |
| | Var. simplicissimum, Wille, | 70 |
| Fig. 14. | COSMARIUM LAEVE, Rab., Var Septemtrionale, Wille, | 72A |
| " 15. | GONATOZYGON SEX-SPINIFERUM, Turner, | 172 |
| " 16. | CALOCYLINDRUS CUCURBITA (Breb.), Kirch., | 59 |
| Figs. 17, 18. | COSMARIUM (Calocylindrus) CORDANUM, Breb., | 59 |
| Fig. 19. | CLOSTERIUM BRAUNII, Reinsch, | 45 |
| " 20. | CLOSTERIUM SUBDIRECTUM, West, | 46 |
| " 21. | CLOSTERIUM ROSTRATUM, Ehrb., | 49 |
| | Var. brevirostratum, West, | 49 |
| " 22. | CLOSTERIUM LEIBLEINII, Kg., | 49 |
| | Var. curtum West, | 49 |

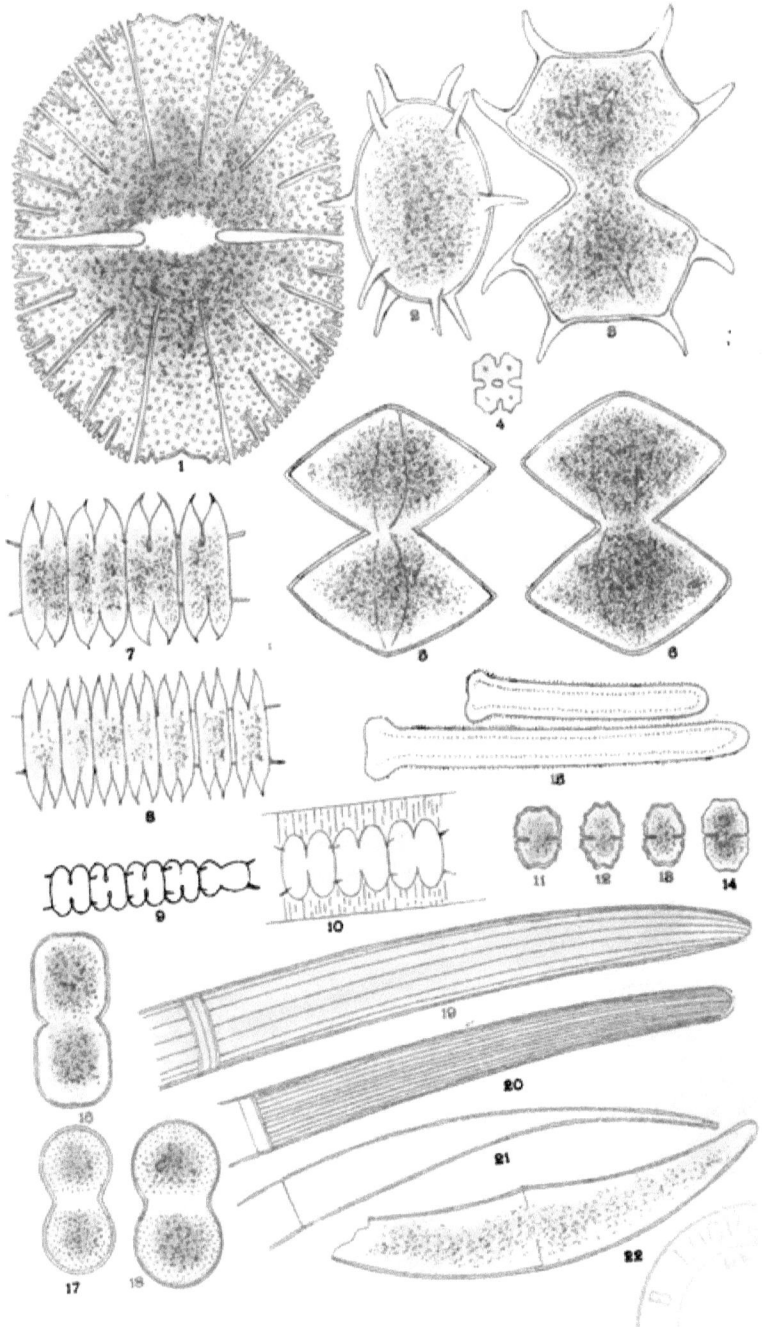

## PLATE XLIV.

### Figures magnified 375 diameters.

|  |  | PAGE |
|---|---|---|
| Fig. 1. | MICRASTERIAS TRIANGULARIS, Pennsylvania and New Jersey form, | 127 |
| " 2. | "          "          Florida variety, | 127 |
| Figs. 3, 4. | MICRASTERIAS CONFERTA, Var. hamata, | 127 |
| Fig. 5. | **MICRASTERIAS ARCUATA,** . | 129 |
| 6. | MICRASTERIAS TRUNCATA, . . . | 126 |
| " 7. | "          "    Var. semiradiata, Naeg., | 126 |
| " 8. | "          "    Var. concatenata, Wolle, | 126 |
| " 9. | "          "    Var. minor, Wolle, | 126 |
| " 10. | MICRASTERIAS FOLIACEA, a single cell, | 130 |
| " 11. | "          "    part of a series of more than forty cells, | 130 |

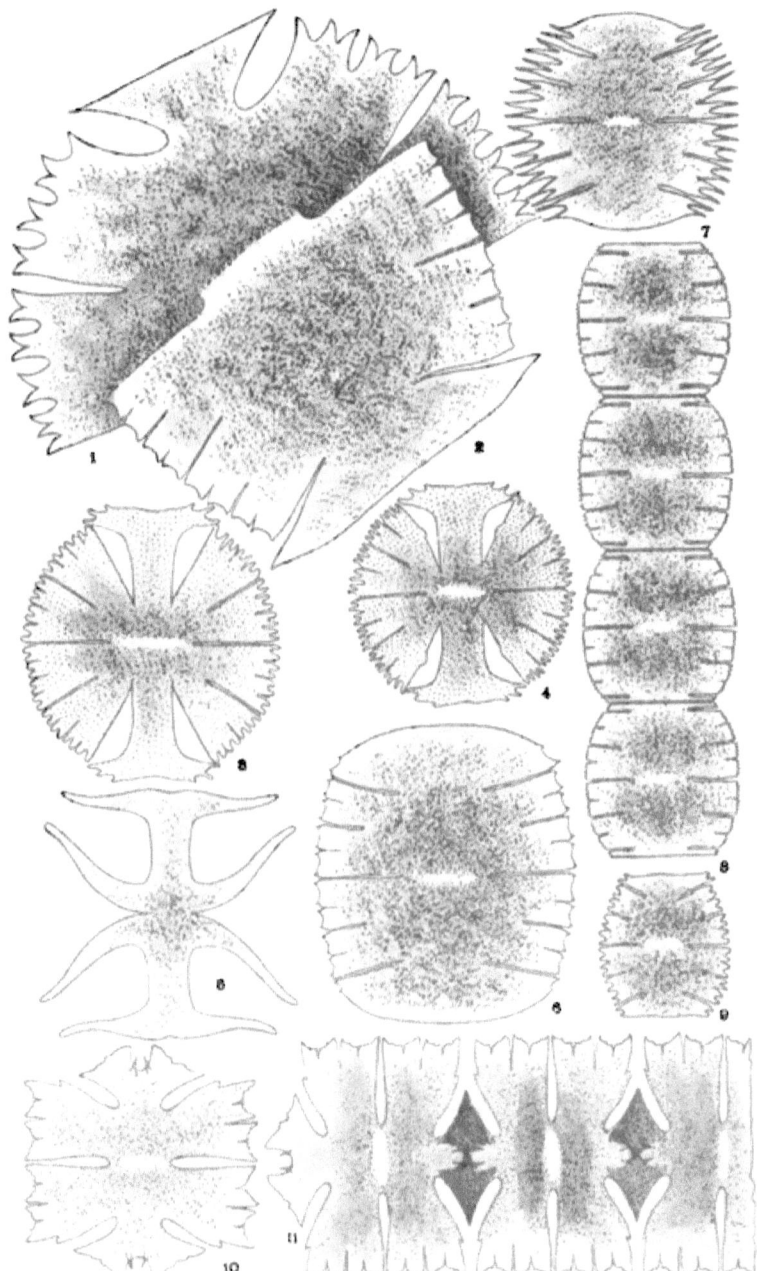

## PLATE XLV.

Figures magnified 375-500 diameters.

| | | PAGE. |
|---|---|---|
| Figs. 1, 2. | MICRASTERIAS SPECIOSA, | 119 |
| Fig. 3. | MICRASTERIAS APICULATA, | 124 |
| Figs. 4, 5. | MICRASTERIAS CRUX MELITENSIS, | 123 |
| Fig. 6. | MICRASTERIAS RABENHORSTII, Var., | 131 |
| Figs. 7, 8. | CYLINDROCYSTIS TUMIDUM, | 38 |
| Fig. 9. | XANTHIDIUM FASCICULATUM, Var. Subalpinum, | 101 |
| Figs. 10, 11. | XANTHIDIUM COLUMBIANUM, | 100 |
| Fig. 12. | CYLINDROCYSTIS DE BARYI, | 58 |
| Figs. 13, 14. | XANTHIDIUM TORREYI. (See Fresh-Water Algæ. p. 35), | — |

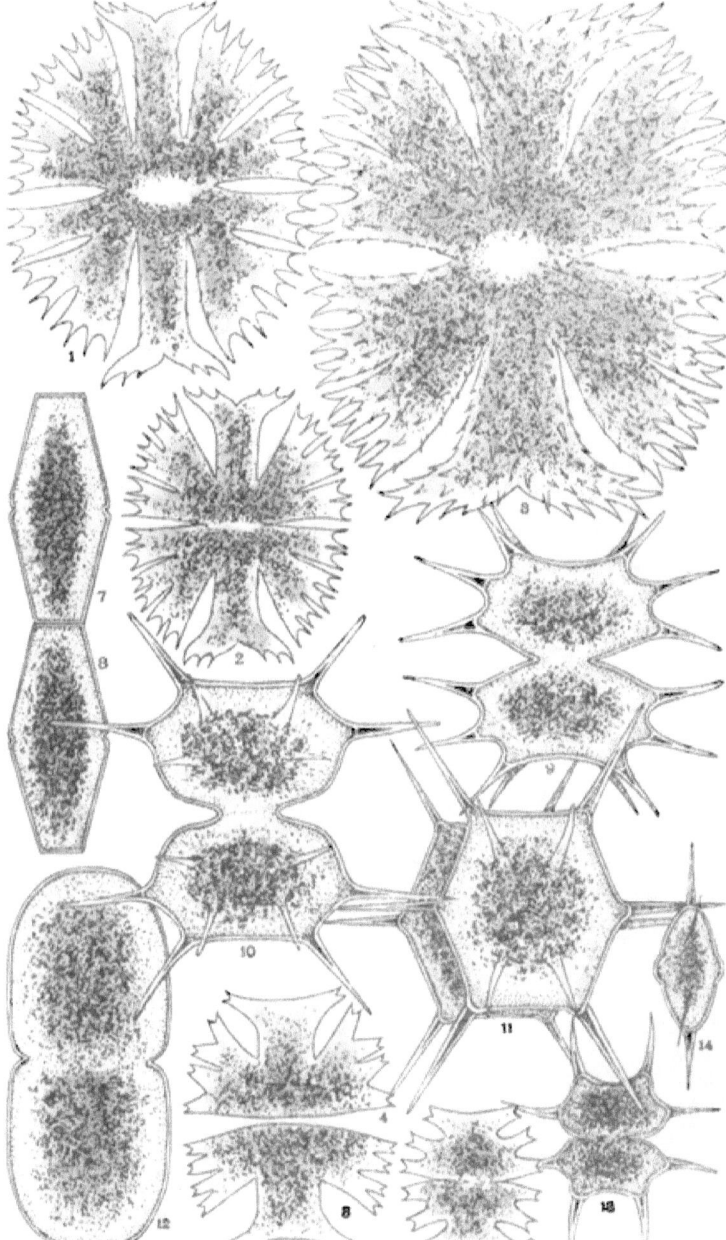

## PLATE XLVI.

Figures magnified 500 diameters; the Micrasterias 375 diameters.

|  |  | PAGE |
|---|---|---|
| Fig. 1. | MICRASTERIAS ALATA, . | 125 |
| " 2. | MICRASTERIAS MAMILLATA, | 125 |
| " 3. | MICRASTERIAS DENTICULATA, zygospore, | 120 |
| " 4. | STAURASTRUM ARCTISCON, Var., | 163 |
| " 5. | COSMARIUM CONSPERSUM, Var. retusum, front view, . | 82 |
| " 6. | COSMARIUM BIRETUM, Var. Floridense, front view, | 93 |
| Figs. 7, 8. | STAURASTRUM COSMARIOIDES, front and vertical views, | 139 |
| " 9, 10. | STAURASTRUM BREVISPINA, Var. inerme, . | 134 |
| " 11, 12. | STAURASTRUM CORNUTUM, front and vertical views, . | 158 |

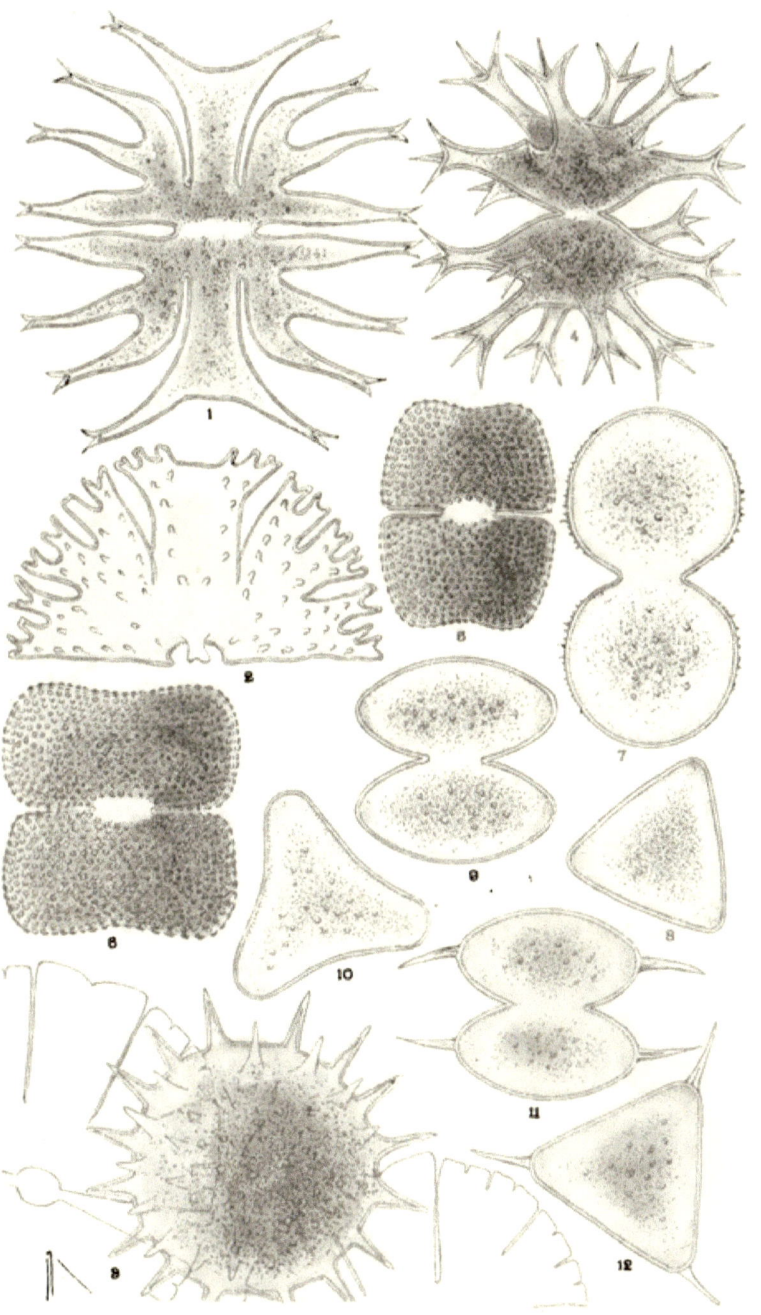

## PLATE XLVII.

Figures magnified 500 diameters.

|  |  | PAGE |
|---|---|---|
| Fig. 1–3. | STAURASTRUM **WOLLEANUM**, Var. **KISSIMENSE**, | 163 |
| Figs. 4, 5. | STAURASTRUM TOHOPEKALIGENSE, front, lateral and end views, | 164 |
| " 6, 7. | MICRASTERIAS FURCATA, Var. SIMPLEX, | 122 |
| " 8, 9. | STAURASTRUM **PARODOXUM**, Var. OSCEOLENSE, | 143 |
| Fig. 10. | MICRASTERIAS VERRUCOSA, | 120 |
| " 11. | SPHAEROZOSMA MONILIFORME, | 30 |
| " 12. | SPHAEROZOSMA PULCHRUM, Var. CONSTRICTUM, | 172 |
| Figs. 13, 14. | BAMBUSINA GRACILESCENS, with zygospores, | 25 |
| Fig. 15. | MICRASTERIAS RINGENS, Var. SERRULATA, | 123 |

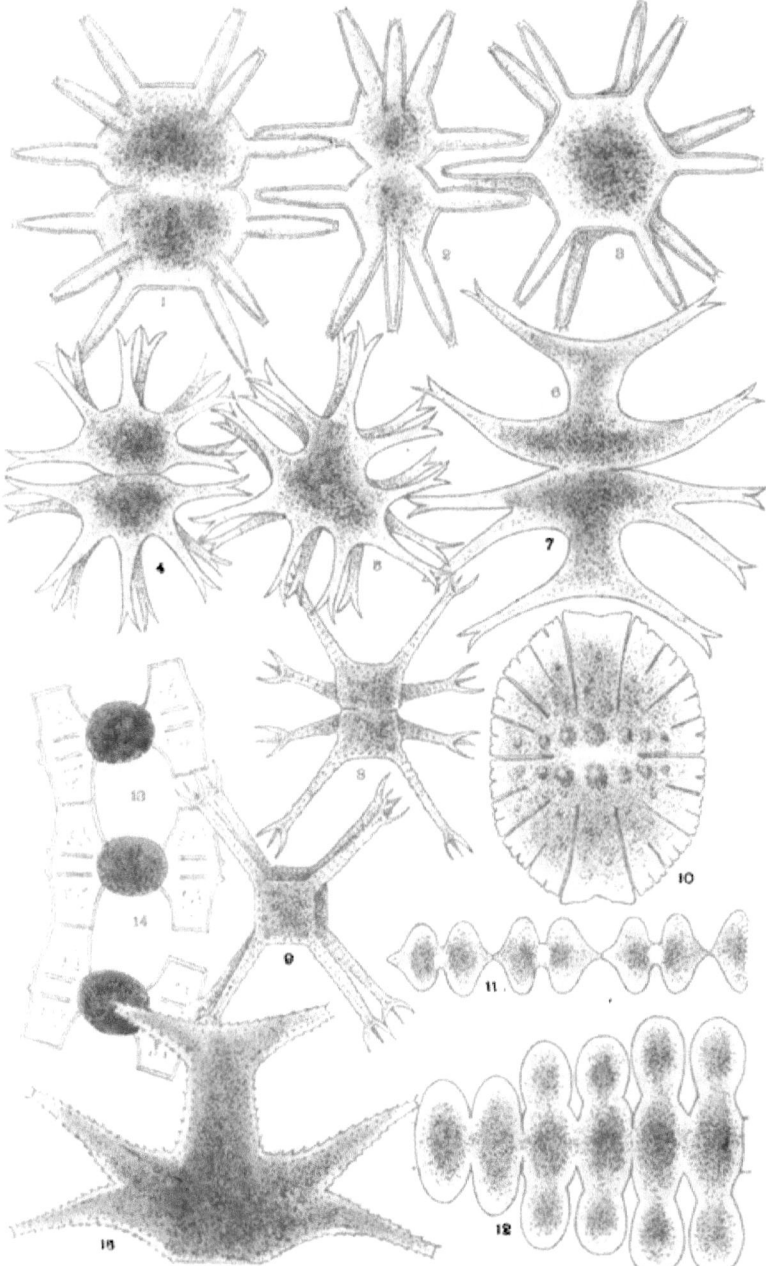

## PLATE XLVIII.

Figures magnified 500 diameters.

|  |  | PAGE. |
|---|---|---|
| Figs. 1, 2. | STAURASTRUM WOLLEANUM, | 163 |
| " 3, 4. | STAURASTRUM CORNUTUM, . | 158 |
| " 5, 6. | STAURASTRUM BACILLARE, | 132 |
| " 7, 8. | STAURASTRUM MINNESOTENSE, | 156 |
| " 9, 10. | STAURASTRUM PSEUDOCRENATUM, | 139 |
| " 11–13. | STAURASTRUM MINNEAPOLIENSE, . | 141 |
| " 14, 15. | STAURASTRUM CALYXOIDES, | 158 |
| " 16, 17. | STAURASTRUM ERASUM, | 139 |
| " 18–20. | COSMARIUM INFLATUM, . | 67 |
| " 21, 22. | STAURASTRUM XIPHIDIOPHORUM, | 155 |
| " 23–25. | COSMARIUM NORDSTEDTII, | 80 |
| " 26, 27. | COSMARIUM SPHALEROSTICHUM, | 76 |
| " 28, 29. | COSMARIUM BRAUNII, forma MAJOR, | 72A |
| " 30, 31. | COSMARIUM SENDTNERIANUM, | 72A |
| Fig. 32. | COSMARIUM PERFORATUM, | 65 |
| Figs. 33, 34. | COSMARIUM LOBATULUM, | 66 |
| " 35, 36. | COSMARIUM LOEVE, | 72A |
| Fig. 37. | COSMARIUM CIRCULARE, | 68 |

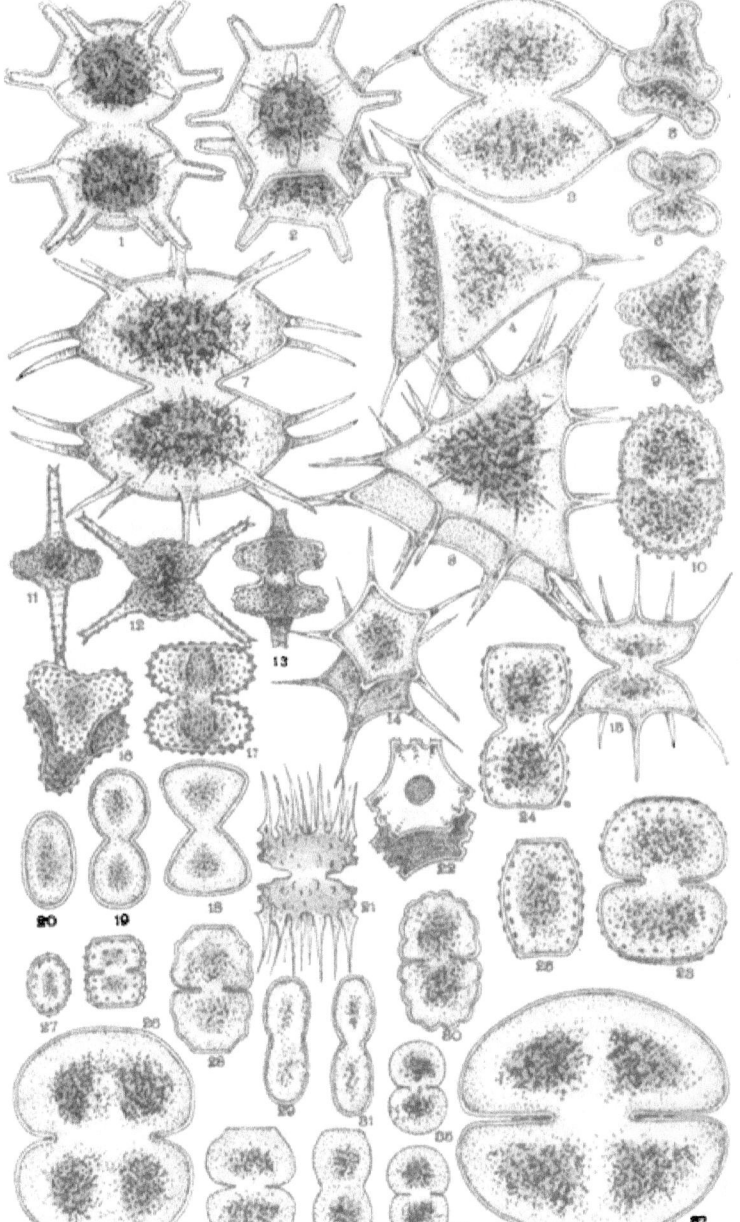

## PLATE XLIX.

Figures magnified 500 diameters.

|  |  | PAGE |
|---|---|---|
| Figs. 1, 2. | Cosmarium Wolleanum, Var. graniliferum, front and lateral views, | 64 |
| " 3-5. | Cosmarium Pardalis, front, lateral and transverse views, | 83 |
| " 6, 7. | Cosmarium rhombusoides, front and transverse views, | 66 |
| " 8, 9. | Staurastrum Novæ Cæsareæ, front and vertical views, | 159 |
| " 10, 11. | Cosmarium quinarium, front and vertical views, | 78 |
| " 12-14. | Cosmarium subcruciforme, front, lateral and vertical views, | 94 |
| " 15, 16. | Cosmarium Americanum, front and vertical views, | 64 |
| " 17, 18. | Cosmarium taxichondrum, Var. bidentulum, front and vertical views, | 77 |
| Fig. 19. | Staurastrum xiphidiophorum, Var. simplex, front view, | 155 |
| Figs. 20, 21. | Cosmarium microsphinctum, front and vertical views, | 81 |
| " 22, 23. | Staurastrum luteolum, front and vertical views, | 139 |
| " 24, 25. | Cosmarium excavatum, Var. trigonum, front and vertical views, | 85 |
| " 26, 27. | Cosmarium lagoense, front and vertical views, | 90 |
| Fig. 28. | Cosmarium cordanum, front view, | 59 |
| " 29. | Euastrum Wollei, Var. quadrigibberum, vertical views, | 108 |
| " 30. | Micrasterias Americana, Var spinosa, front view of semi-cell, | 124 |
| Figs. 31-33. | Cosmarium polymorphum, front, lateral and vertical view, | 81 |
| " 34, 35. | Cosmarium octogonum, front and vertical views, | 71 |
| " 36-38. | Staurastrum orbiculare, Var. oblique and front views, | 132 |
| " 39, 40. | Staurastrum Brasiliense, Var. triquetum, front and vertical views, | 160 |
| " 41, 42. | Staurastrum muticum, Var. ellipticum, front and vertical views, | 132 |

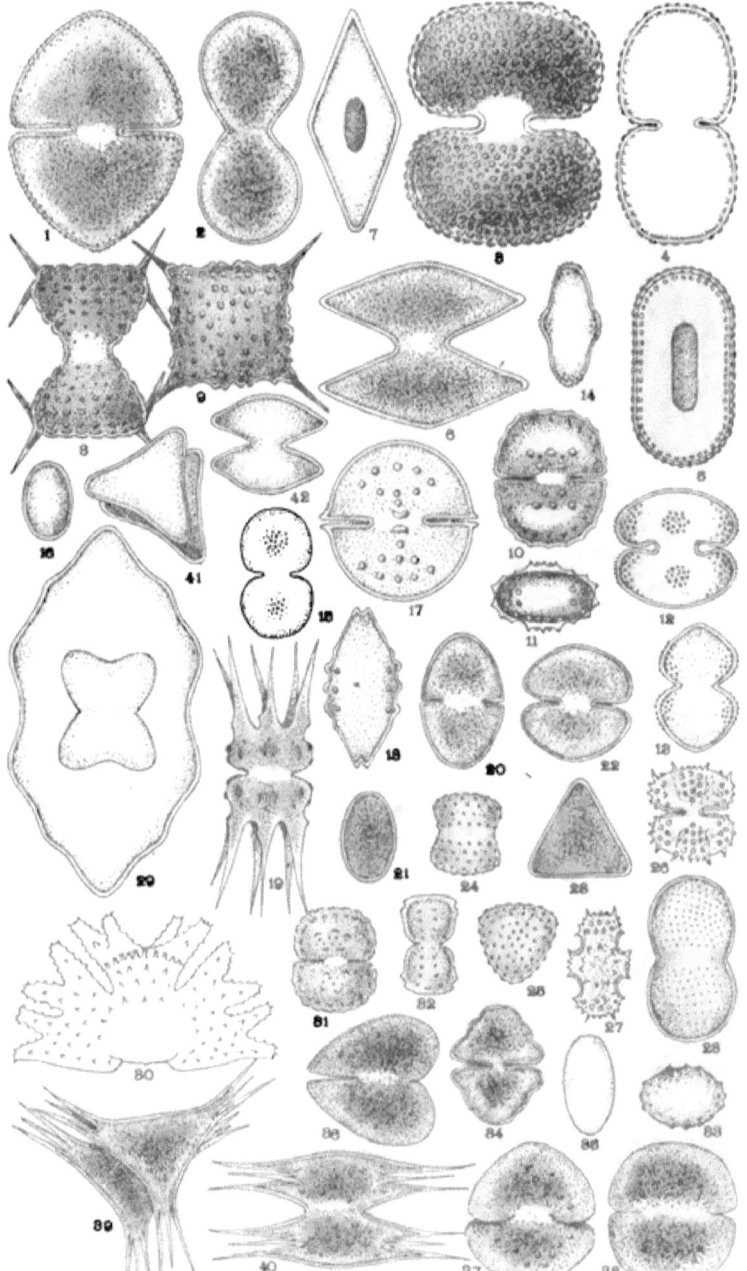

## PLATE L.

Figures magnified 500 diameters.

|  |  | PAGE. |
|---|---|---|
| Figs. 1, 2. | STAURASTRUM TUMIDUM, front and end views, | 133 |
| "  3, 4. | STAURASTRUM GRANDE, front and end views, | 133 |
| "  5, 6. | STAURASTRUM MAJUSCULUM, front and end views, | 133 |
| "  7, 8. | STAURASTRUM MAGNUM, front and end views, | 133 |
| "  9, 10. | STAURASTRUM ORBICULARE, front and end views, | 132 |
| "  11, 12. | STAURASTRUM MUTICUM, front and end views, | 131 |
| Fig. 13 | "          "     Var. ellipticum, | 132 |
| Figs. 14, 15. | "          "     Var. minus, | 131 |

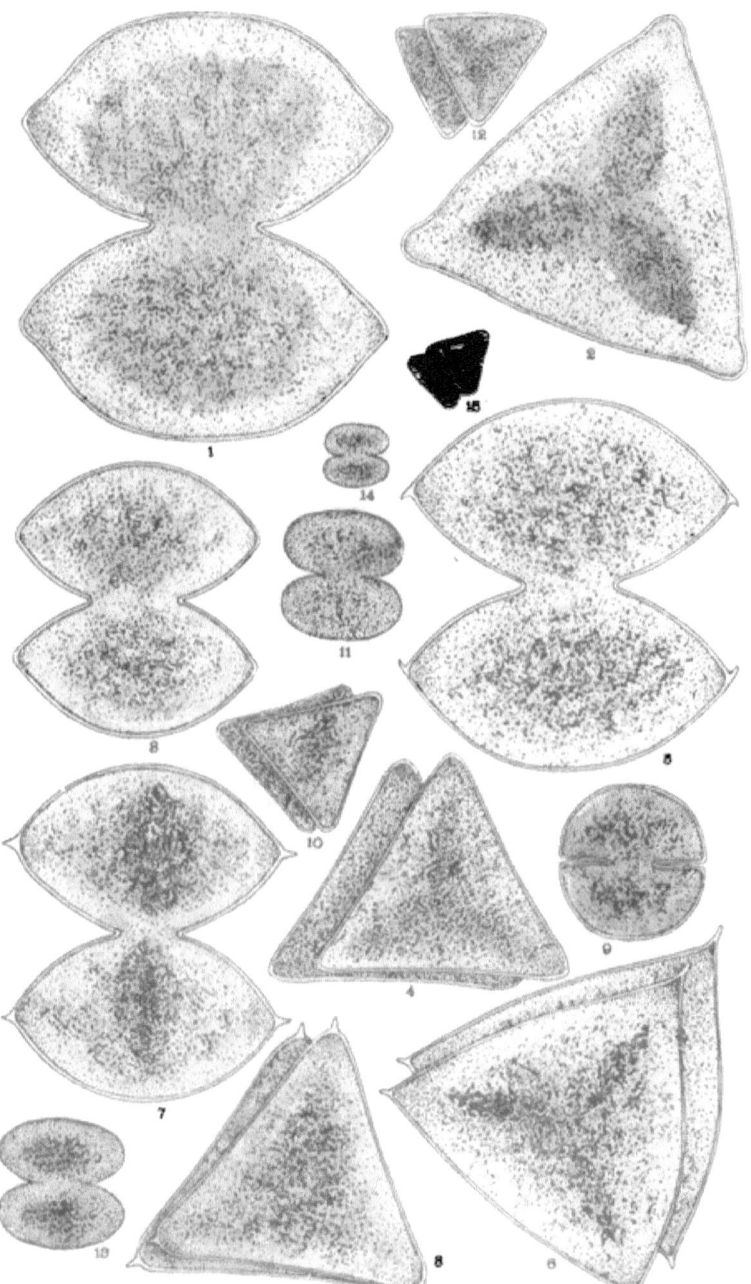

## PLATE LI.

Figures magnified 500 diameters.

|  |  | PAGE |
|---|---|---|
| Figs. 1, 2. | STAURASTRUM BREVISPINA, Var., front and end views, | 134 |
| " 3, 4. | "          "      Var. inerme, | 134 |
| " 5, 6. | STAURASTRUM DICKIEI, two aspects, | 135 |
| " 7, 9, 10, 11. | STAURASTRUM DEJECTUM, Var. convergens, | 134 |
| Fig. 8. | "          "      Var. mucronatum, | 134 |
| Figs. 12-14. | STAURASTRUM TRIHEDRALE, in three aspects, | 136 |
| " 15, 16. | STAURASTRUM ARISTIFERUM, | 135 |
| " 17-22. | STAURASTRUM DEJECTUM, four forms and a zygospore, | 134 |
| " 23, 25. | STAURASTRUM CUSPIDATUM, | 135 |
| " 26, 27. | STAURASTRUM LEWISII, front and end views, | 135 |
| " 28, 29. | STAURASTRUM TRIFIDUM, front and end views, | 136 |
| " 30, 32. | STAURASTRUM AVICULUM, | 136 |
| " 33, 34. | STAURASTRUM COMMUTATUM, | 136 |
| " 35, 36. | STAURASTRUM KITCHELII, two views, | 165 |
| " 37-39. | STAURASTRUM BRACHIATUM, | 136 |
| " 40, 41. | STAURASTRUM FURCATUM, a form of a variable species, | 165 |

PLATE LI

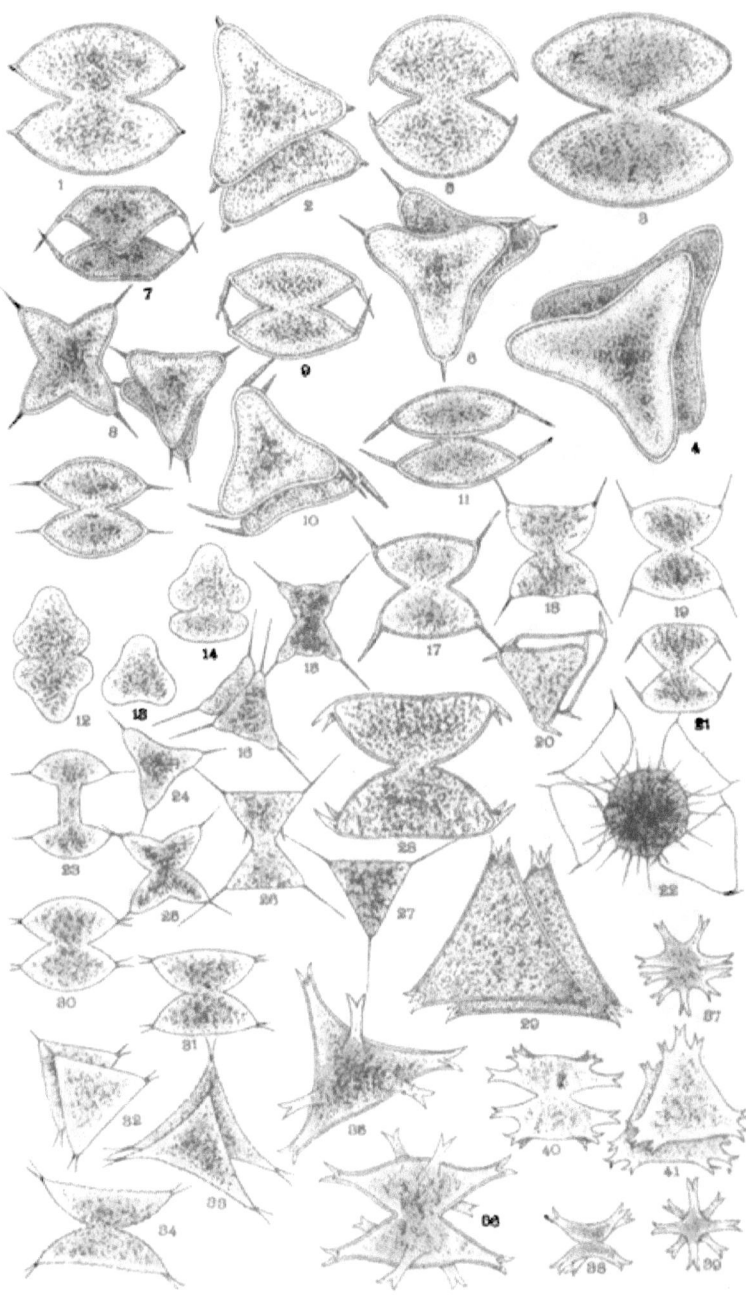

## PLATE LII.

Figures magnified 500 diameters.

| | | | PAGE |
|---|---|---|---|
| Fig. 1. | STAURASTRUM QUADRANGULARE, a Minnesota variety, | | 160 |
| " 2. | " " a Pennsylvania and New Jersey variety, | | 160 |
| Figs. 3, 4. | " " end view of Florida forms, | | 160 |
| " 5, 6. | STAURASTRUM CRENATUM, | | 138 |
| Fig. 7. | STAURASTRUM LONGISPINUM, | | 160 |
| Figs 8, 9. | STAURASTRUM SPINOSUM. *See St. furcatum* and *Kitchelii*, | | 152 |
| " 10, 11. | STAURASTRUM PULCHRUM,* | | 147 |
| " 12, 13. | STAURASTRUM INCISUM, | | 146 |
| Fig. 14. | " " six rayed form, | | 146 |
| Figs 15, 16. | STAURASTRUM DISTENTUM, | | 165 |
| " 17, 18. | STAURASTRUM ELOISEANUM, | | 164 |
| " 19-25. | STAURASTRUM ENORME, | | 166 |
| " 26-28. | STAURASTRUM ALTERNANS, | | 142 |
| " 29, 30 | STAURASTRUM SCABRUM, | | 144 |
| " 31-35. | STAURASTRUM MARGARITACEUM, | | 138 |
| " 36-38. | STAURASTRUM TRICORNE, | | 138 |
| " 39, 40. | STAURASTRUM PANICULOSUM, | | 137 |
| " 41, 42. | STAURASTRUM RUGULOSUM, | | 140 |
| " 43-45. | STAURASTRUM PUNCTULATUM, | | 141 |

* Compare note under *St. incisum*, p. 146. This species from ponds, New Jersey, was described in the "Bull. Tor. Bot. Club, New York, 1880." Membrane smooth; end view five-rayed; apices of rays obtusely **rounded**, bases **wide, separated by a** rounded sinus.

PLATE LII

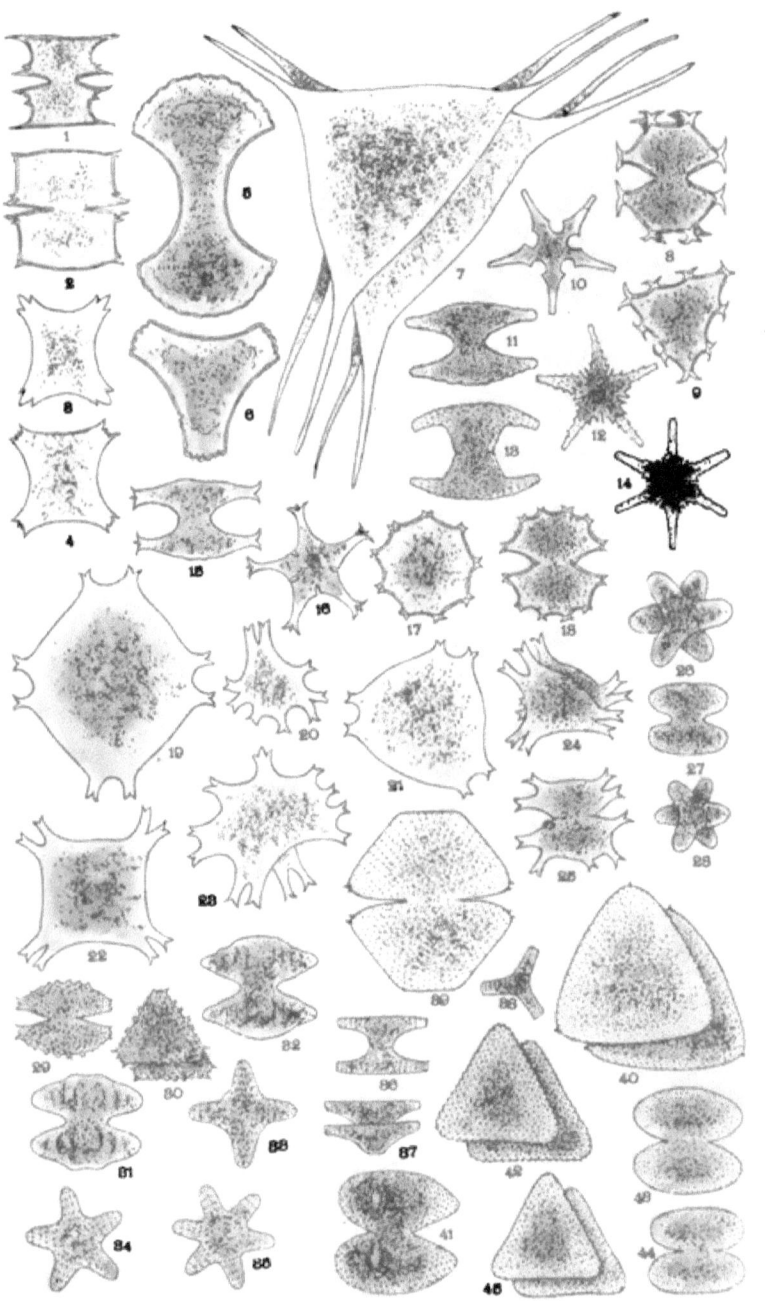

## PLATE LIII.

Figures magnified 500 diameters.

|  |  | PAGE |
|---|---|---|
| Figs. 1, 2. | Staurastrum Bieneanum, Var. ellipticum, | 137 |
| " 3, 4. | Staurastrum muricatum, | 140 |
| " 5, 6. | " " Var., | 140 |
| " 7, 8. | Staurastrum asperum, | 140 |
| " 9, 10. | Staurastrum polymorphum, | 139 |
| " 11–13. | Staurastrum botrophilum, | 145 |
| " 14, 15. | Staurastrum pygmaeum, | 141 |
| " 16–19. | " " Var. truncatum, | 141 |
| " 20, 21. | " " Var. rhomboides, | 141 |
| " 22, 23. | Staurastrum dilatatum, | 142 |
| " 24, 25. | Staurastrum polymorphum, | 139 |
| " 26–29. | Staurastrum crenulatum, | 140 |
| " 30, 31. | Staurastrum cyrtocerum, | 142 |
| " 32, 33. | " " Var. pentacladum minor, | 143 |
| " 34, 35. | " " pentacladum major, | 143 |
| " 36, 37. | **Staurastrum paradoxum**, | 143 |
| " 38–42. | **Staurastrum arachne**, | 143 |
| " 43, 44. | Staurastrum comptum, front and end views, | 143 |
| " 45, 46. | " " Var. major, front and end views, | 143 |
| " 47, 48. | Staurastrum pusillum, | 144 |
| " 49, 50. | " " smaller variety, two **views**, | 144 |
| " 51–53. | Staurastrum Haardeliense, front and two end views, | 147 |
| " 54, 55. | Staurastrum fasciculoides, front and end views, | 144 |

PLATE LIII

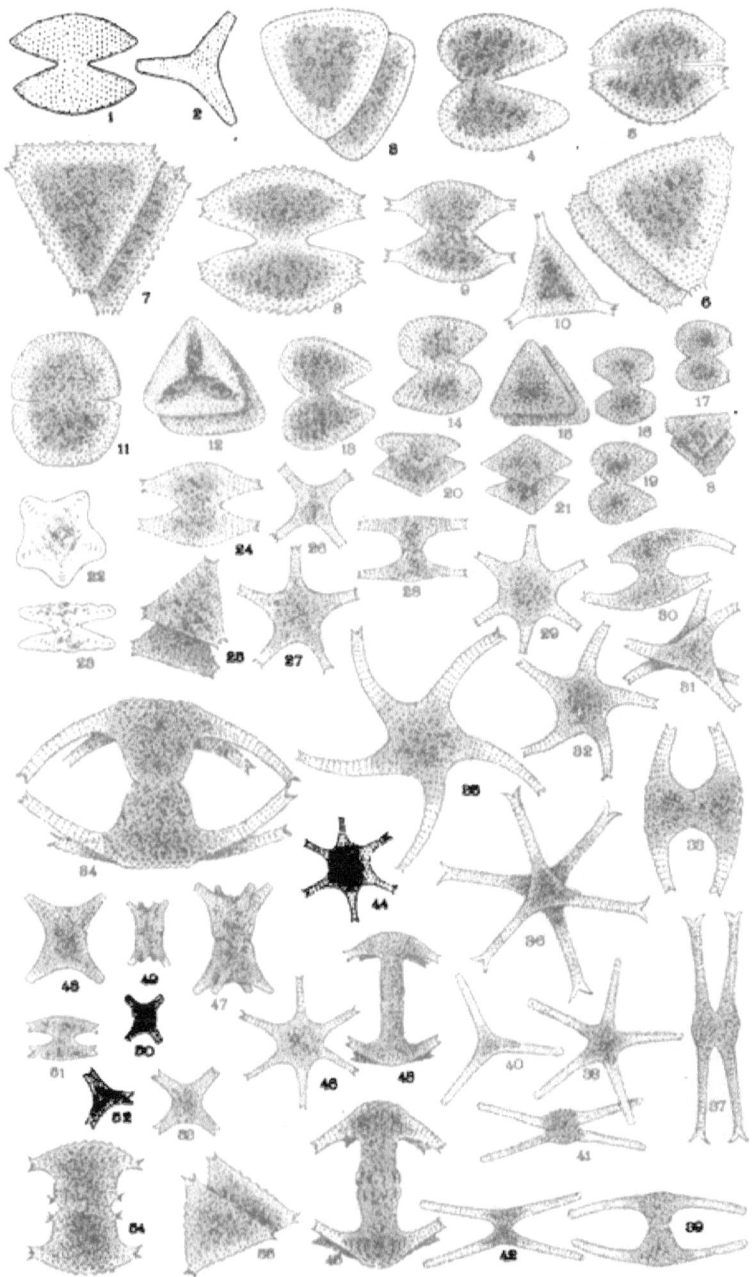

## PLATE LIV.

Figures magnified 500 diameters.

|  |  | PAGE |
|---|---|---|
| Fig. 1. | STAURASTRUM CYRTOCERUM, Var. major, end view, | 142 |
| " 2. | "         "         Var. major, front view, | 142 |
| Figs. 3–5. | STAURASTRUM MACROCERUM, three views, | 148 |
| " 6, 7. | STAURASTRUM CERASTES, front and end views, | 147 |
| " 8, 9. | STAURASTRUM ODONTODUM, front and end views, | 148 |
| " 10, 11. | STAURASTRUM OPHIURA, front and end views, | 147 |
| " 12, 13, 14. | STAURASTRUM CORONULATUM, Var. Floridense, | 149 |
| Fig. 15. | STAURASTRUM PENTACLADUM, front and end views, | 149 |
| Figs. 16, 17. | STAURASTRUM GRACILE, front and end views, | 147 |

PLATE LI

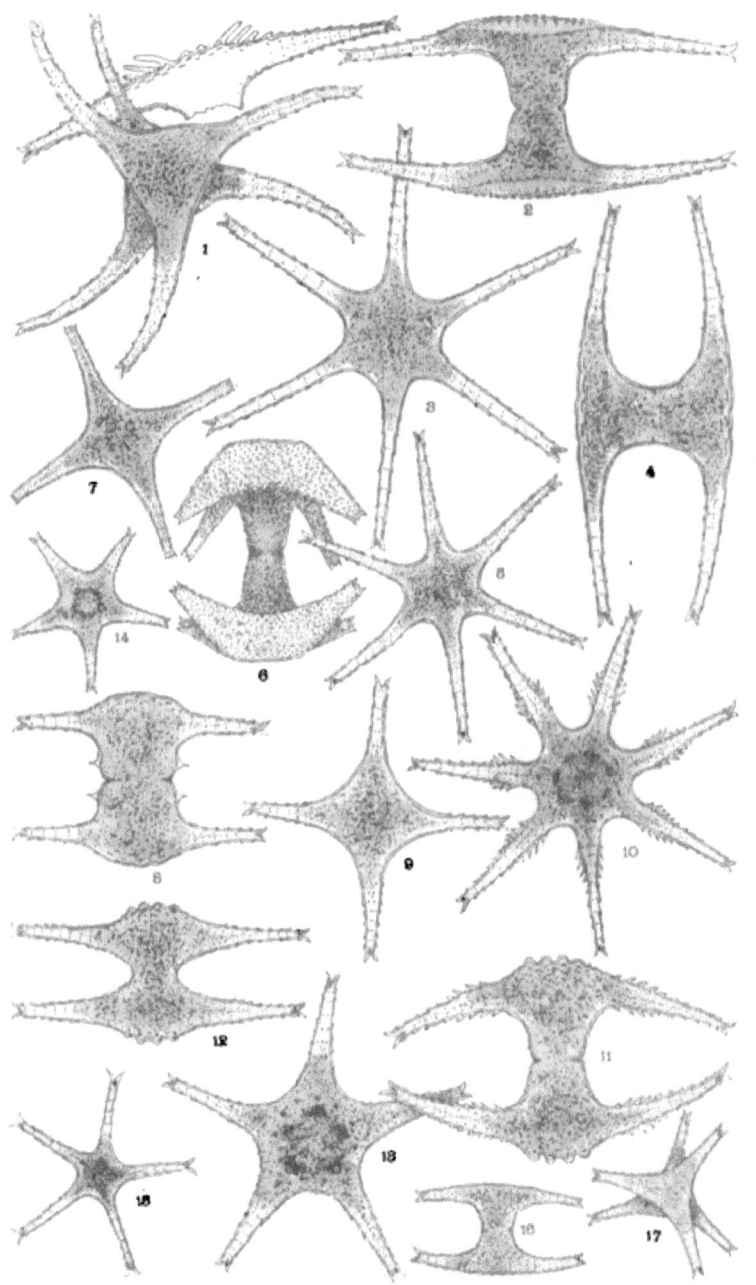

## PLATE LV.

#### Figures magnified 500 diameters.

| | | PAGE. |
|---|---|---|
| Figs. 1, 2 | STAURASTRUM OPHIURA, Var. tetracerum, | 148 |
| Fig. 3. | " " Var. pentacerum, lighter form than Plate LIV, fig. 13, | 148 |
| " 4 | STAURASTRUM LEPTOCLADUM, | 149 |
| " 5. | " " Var. divergens, | — |
| Figs. 6, 7. | STAURASTRUM HELENEANUM, front and end views, | 146 |
| " 8, 9, 10. | STAURASTRUM NANUM, three aspects, | 151 |
| " 11, 12. | STAURASTRUM CORONULATUM, | 148 |
| " 13, 14. | STAURASTRUM ROTULA, end and front views, | 148 |
| " 15, 16. | STAURASTRUM PENTACLADUM, end and **front views**. (Compare Plate LIV, fig. 15), | 149 |
| " 17, 18. | STAURASTRUM GRALLATORIUM, Var. ungulatum, | 150 |
| Fig. 19. | " " typical form, | 150 |
| Figs. 20, 21. | STAURASTRUM **FUSIFORME**, front and end views, | 150 |

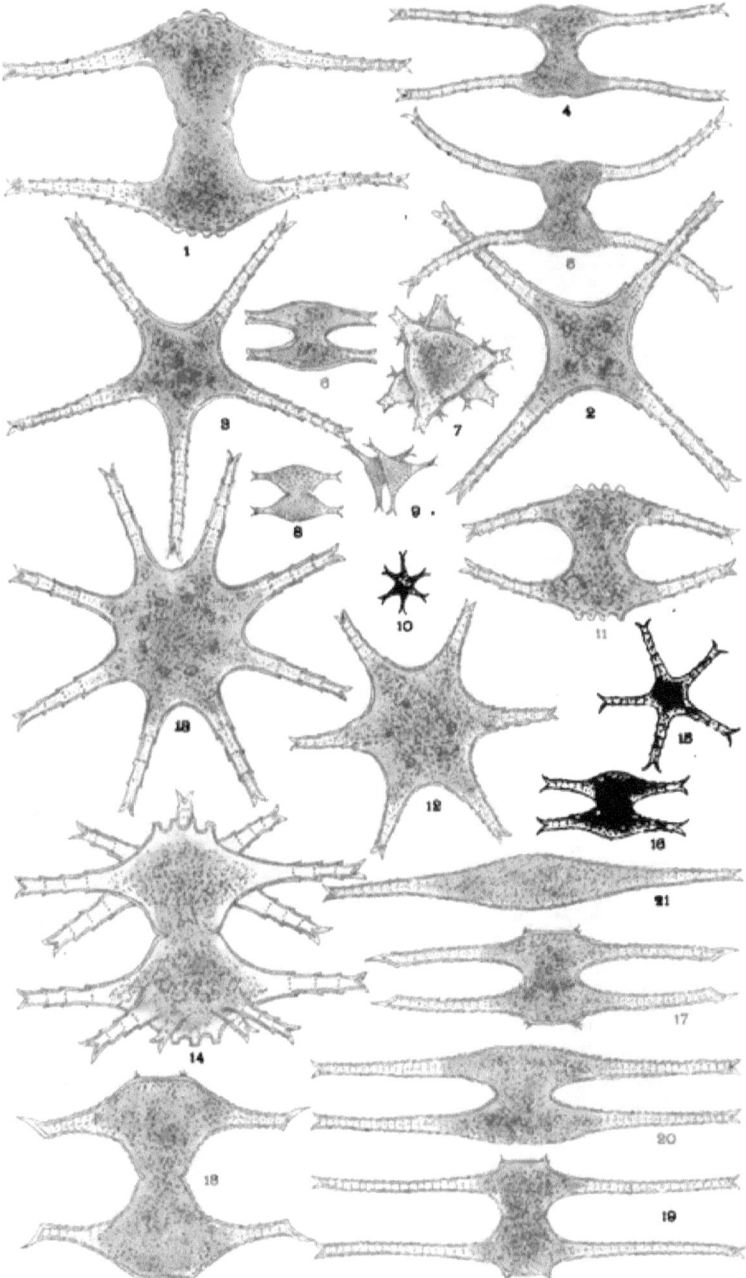

## PLATE LVI.

Figures magnified 500 diameters.

|  |  | PAGE |
|---|---|---|
| Figs. 1-3. | STAURASTRUM ACULEATUM, in **three aspects**, . | 153 |
| Fig. 4. | STAURASTRUM TELIFERUM, normal size, | 154 |
| " 5, 6. | STAURASTRUM BREBISSONII, | 154 |
| " 7, 8. | STAURASTRUM CERBERUS, . | 156 |
| " 9, 10. | STAURASTRUM TRIDENTIFERUM, | 156 |
| " 11-13. | STAURASTRUM CRUCIATUM, . | 156 |
| " 14-16. | STAURASTRUM HYSTRIX, . . . . . | 156 |
| " 17, 18. | STAURASTRUM RAVENELII. (Compare Plate LXIII, figs. 7, 8), | 157 |
| Fig. 19. | STAURASTRUM HIRSUTUM. | 155 |
| " 20. | " " dividing, . . . | 155 |
| " 21. | " " zygospore with empty cells attached, | 155 |
| Figs. 22, 23. | STAURASTRUM SOCIATUM, | 155 |
| " 24, 25. | STAURASTRUM CONTROVERSUM, . | 157 |
| " 26, 27 | STAURASTRUM SETIGERUM. | 154 |
| Fig. 28. | STAURASTRUM VESTITUM, zygospore with remains of cells, . | 151 |
| Figs. 29, 30. | " " large form, front and end views. | 151 |
| " 31, 32. | STAURASTRUM ECHINATUM, front and end views, | 154 |
| " 33, 34. | STAURASTRUM SAXONICUM, front and end **views**, . | 154 |
| " 35, 36. | **STAURASTRUM PECTEN, front and end views,** . | 155 |

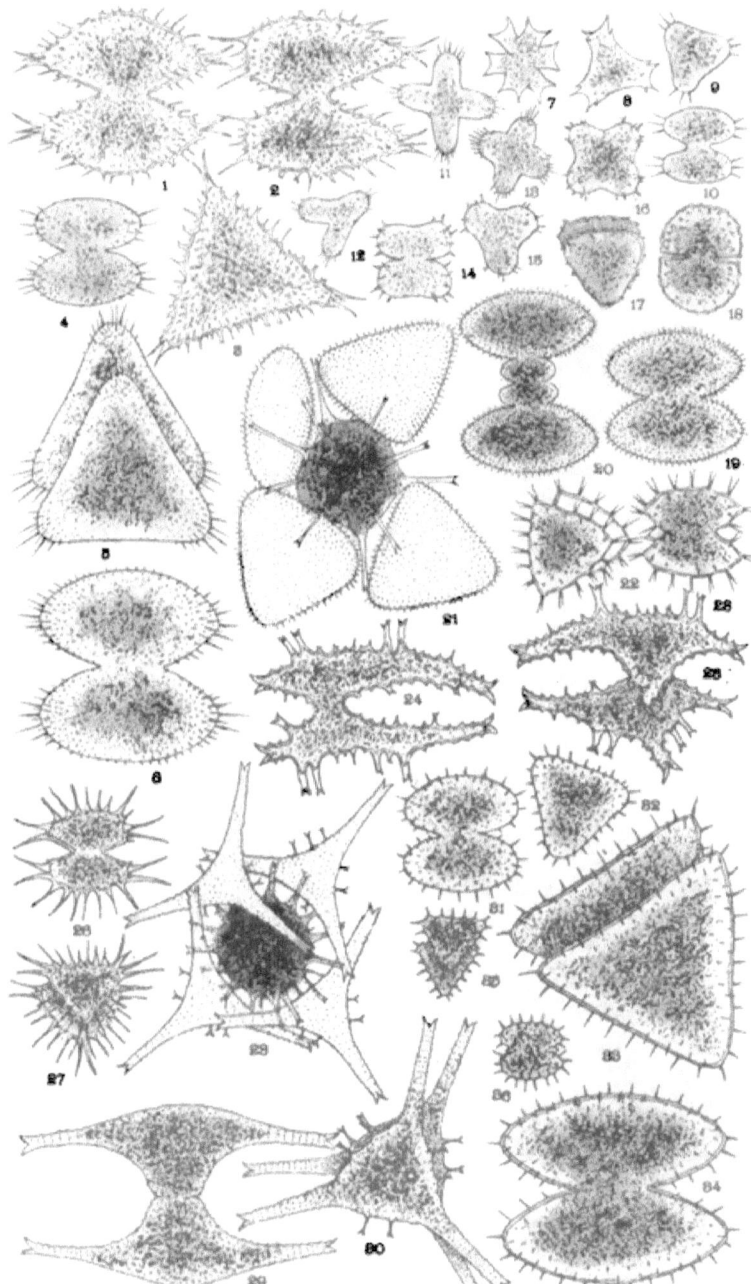

## PLATE LVIII.

### Figures magnified 500 diameters.

|  |  | PAGE |
|---|---|---|
| Figs. 1, 2. | STAURASTRUM TRICORNUTUM, front and end views, | 159 |
| " 3, 4. | STAURASTRUM NOVÆ CÆSAREÆ, front and end views, | 159 |
| " 5, 6. | STAURASTRUM SPONGIOSUM, front and end views, | 163 |
| " 7, 8. | "          "          other form, front and end views, | 163 |
| " 9, 10. | STAURASTRUM ARCTICON,—(M. munitum Wood), | 163 |

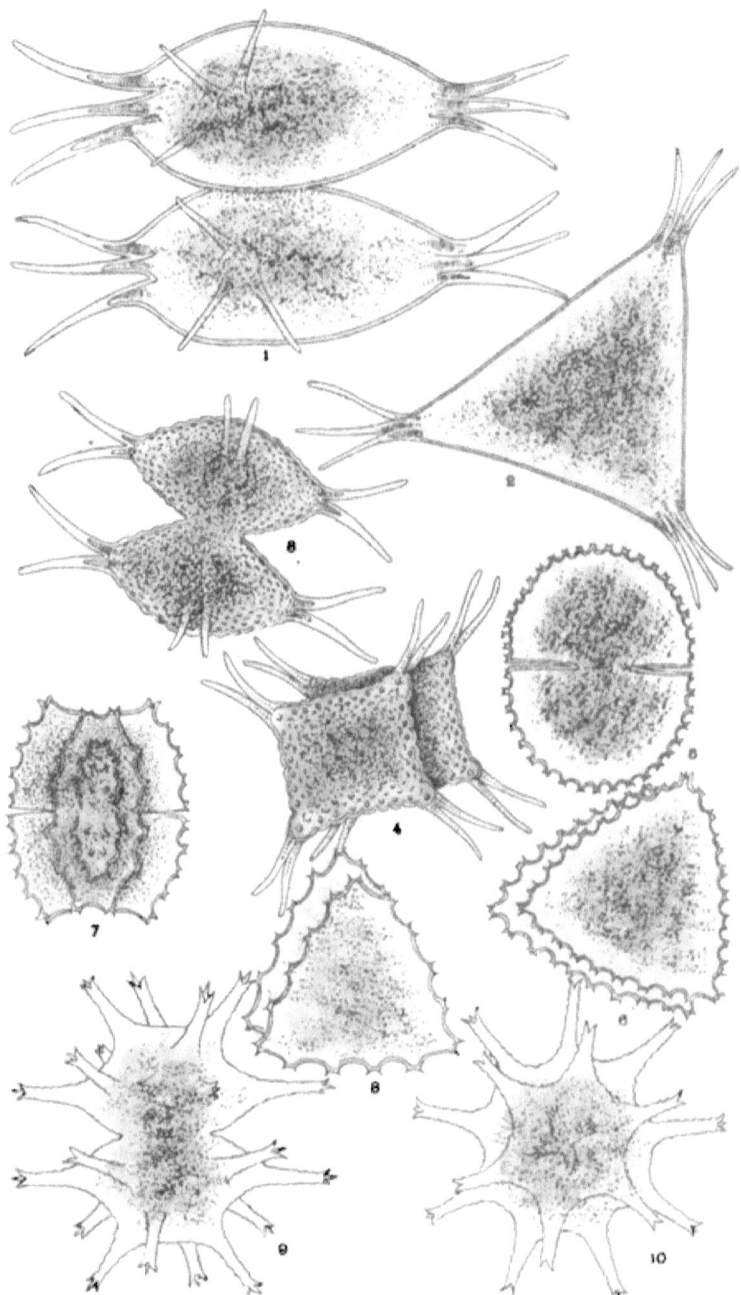

## PLATE LIX.

Figures magnified 500 diameters.

|  |  | PAGE. |
|---|---|---|
| Fig. 1. | STAURASTRUM BRASILIENSE, | 160 |
| Figs. 2, 3. | "  "  two end views, Florida and New Jersey forms, | 160 |
| "  4, 5, 6. | STUARASTRUM EUSTEPHANUM, **Minnesota form**, | 161 |
| "  7, 8. | STAURASTRUM CUNEATUM, front and end views, | 162 |
| "  9, 10. | STAURASTRUM EUSTEPHANUM, (typical form), | 161 |
| Fig. 11. | "  "  (elongated processes), | 161 |
| Figs. 12, 13. | STAURASTRUM FURCIGERUM, end and front views, | 161 |
| Fig. 14. | "  "  a variety, | 165 |
| Figs. 15, 16. | STAURATRUM FURCATUM, variety, | 165 |

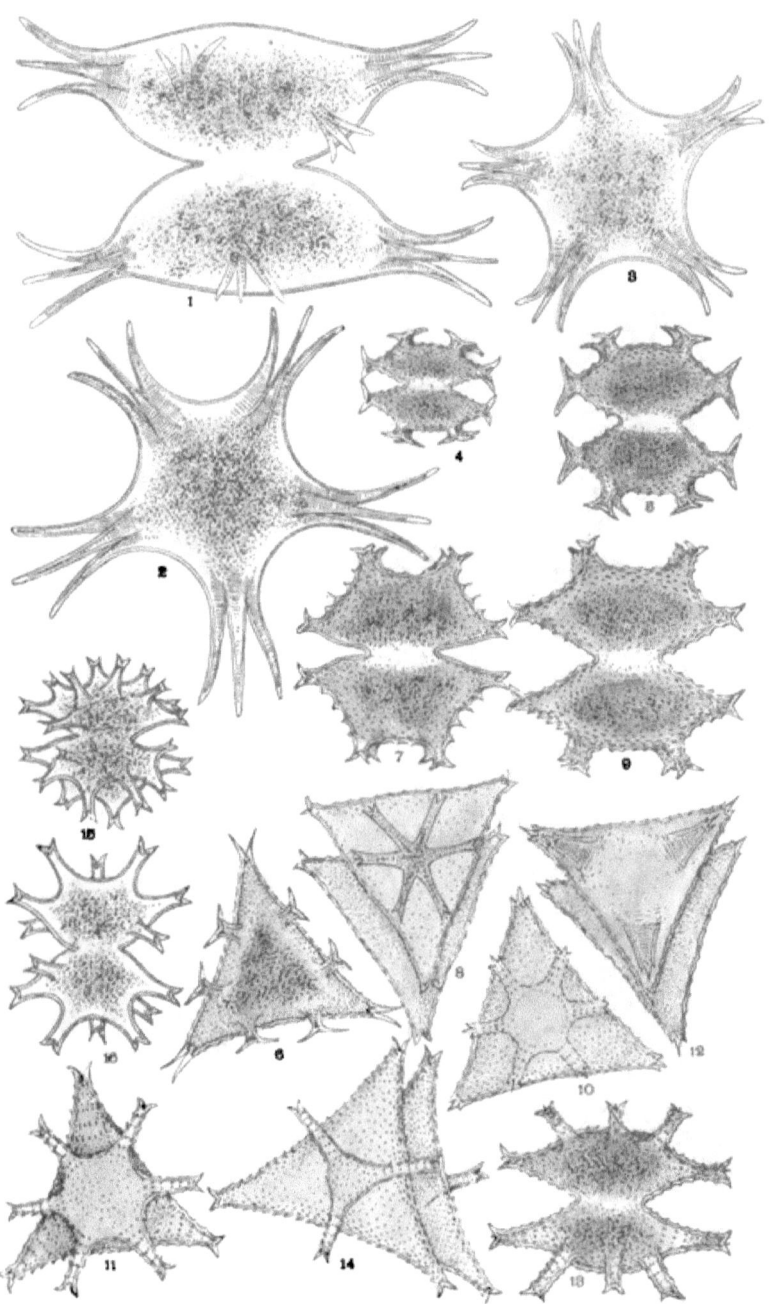

## PLATE LX.

Figures magnified 500 diameters.

| | | PAGE |
|---|---|---|
| Fig. 1. | PHYMATODOCIS NORDSTEDTIANUM, | 28 |
| " 2. | "        "        a cell dividing, | 28 |
| Figs. 3, 4. | "        "        transverse view, and front view of a cell, | 28 |
| Fig. 5. | DESMIDIUM (*Didymoprium*) QUADRATUM, front and side views made evident by the twist of the filament, | 26 |
| " 6. | DESMIDIUM (*Didymoprium*) LONGATUM, front and side views of cells, | 27 |
| " 7. | DESMIDIUM APTOGONIUM, partially advanced in process of division. (Compare normal condition, Plate II, fig. 6), | 27 |
| " 8. | SPHAEROZOSMA PULCHRUM, Var. inflatum, | 29 |
| " 9. | SPHAEROZOSMA RECTANGULARE, | 31 |
| " 10. | CALOCYLINDRUS PSEUDOCONNATUS, Var. (Compare Plate XV), | 60 |
| " 12. | COSMARIUM OBSOLETUM, Var. major, | 70 |
| " 13. | COSMARIUM SEXANGULARE, | 69 |
| Figs. 14-17. | COSMARIUM GLOBOSUM, | 65 |
| Fig. 18. | COLOCYLINDRUS CONNATUS, Var. minor, | 60 |
| " 19. | COSMARIUM KJELLMANII, | 94 |
| Figs. 20, 21. | "        "        end and side views, | 94 |
| Fig. 22. | COSMARIUM ORNATUM, Var. protractum, | 90 |
| Figs. 23, 24. | "        "        front and side views, | 90 |
| Fig. 25. | COSMARIUM PULCHERRIMUM, Var. minor, | 97 |
| Figs. 26, 27. | "        "        side and end views, | 97 |
| Fig. 28. | COSMARIUM SPORTELLA, | 90 |
| Figs. 29, 30. | "        "        lateral and vertical views, | 90 |
| " 31, 32. | COSMARIUM CRENATUM, | 73 |

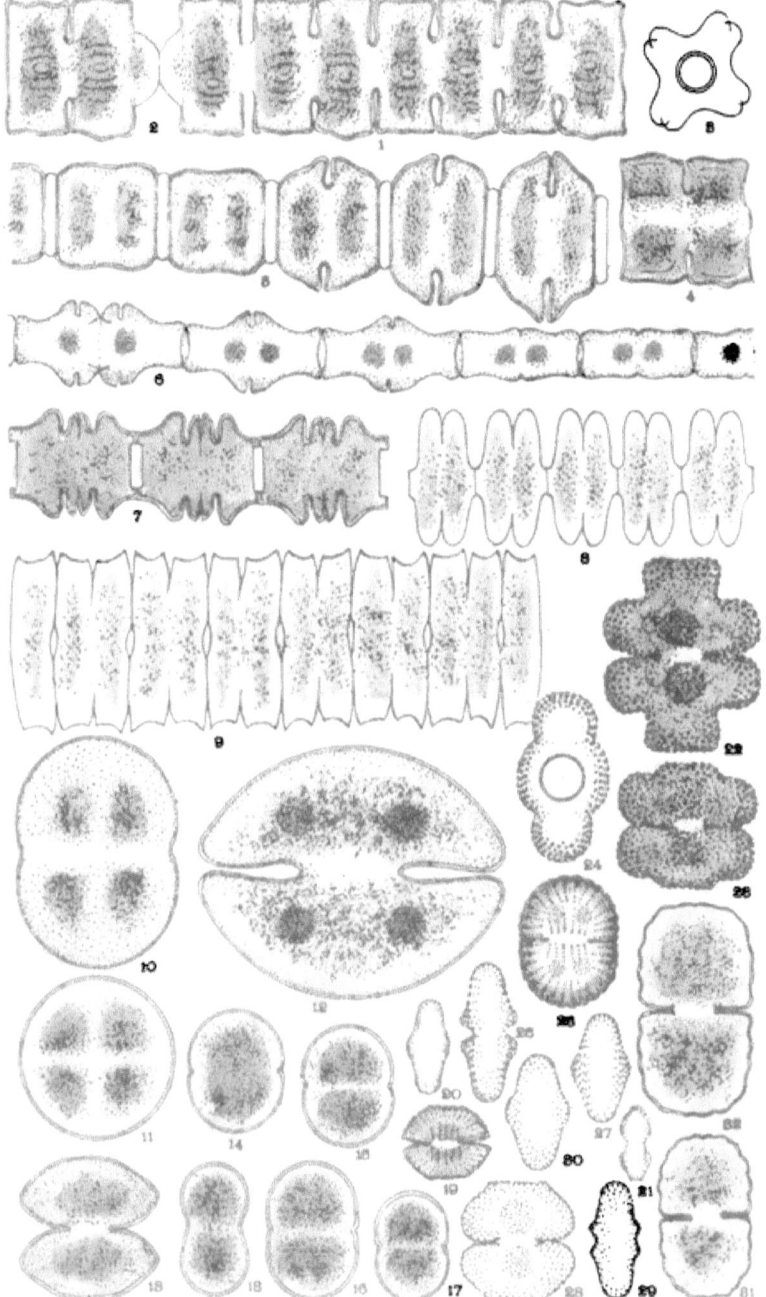

## PLATE LXI.

Figures magnified 500 diameters.

| | | PAGE. |
|---|---|---|
| Figs 1–4. | COSMARIUM CONSTRICTUM, | 63 |
| " 5, 6. | COSMARIUM SUPRASPECIOSUM, front and side views, | 95 |
| " 7, 8, 9. | COSMARIUM SCENEDESMUS, in three views, | 63 |
| " 10, 11, 12. | COSMARIUM DEPRESSUM, in three views, | 69 |
| Fig. 13. | COSMARIUM GRANATUM, | 64 |
| Figs. 14–17. | COSMARIUM BECKEI,* | — |
| " 18–20. | COSMARIUM SEJUNCTUM, front, end and side views, | 68 |
| Fig. 21. | COSMARIUM NAGELIANUM, | 73 |
| Figs. 22, 23. | COSMARIUM PSEUDOTAXICHONDRUM, | 77 |
| Fig. 24. | COSMARIUM CONTRACTUM, | 68 |
| " 25. | STAURASTRUM PRINGLEI, in three views, | 145 |
| " 26. | CLOSTERIUM LUNULA, | 42 |
| " 27. | CALOCYLINDRUS CLEVEI, | 60–38 |
| " 28. | CALOCYLINDRUS THWAITESII, | 60 |
| Figs. 29, 30, 31. | DOCIDIUM MINUTUM, | 57 |
| Fig. 32. | DOCIDIUM DILATATUM, | 55 |
| " 33, 34. | TETMEMORUS GRANULATUS, | 98 |
| " 35. | TETMEMORUS LAEVIS, | 98 |
| " 36. | TETMEMORUS BREBISSONII, | 95 |
| Figs. 37–39. | STAURASTRUM (*Polyedrium*) ENORME, | 166 |

* C. Beckel, Willie. (Omitted in proper place.) Cells slightly longer than broad; semi-cells nearly semicircular, apices truncate five crenate; sides incised crenate; two series of granules of about 15 and 9 near the margins; center inflated and sparsely granular; variable in size; larger form about 28 Mic. M. long; 25 Mic. M. wide.

Not quite, but nearly in accord with **Willie's diagnosis.**

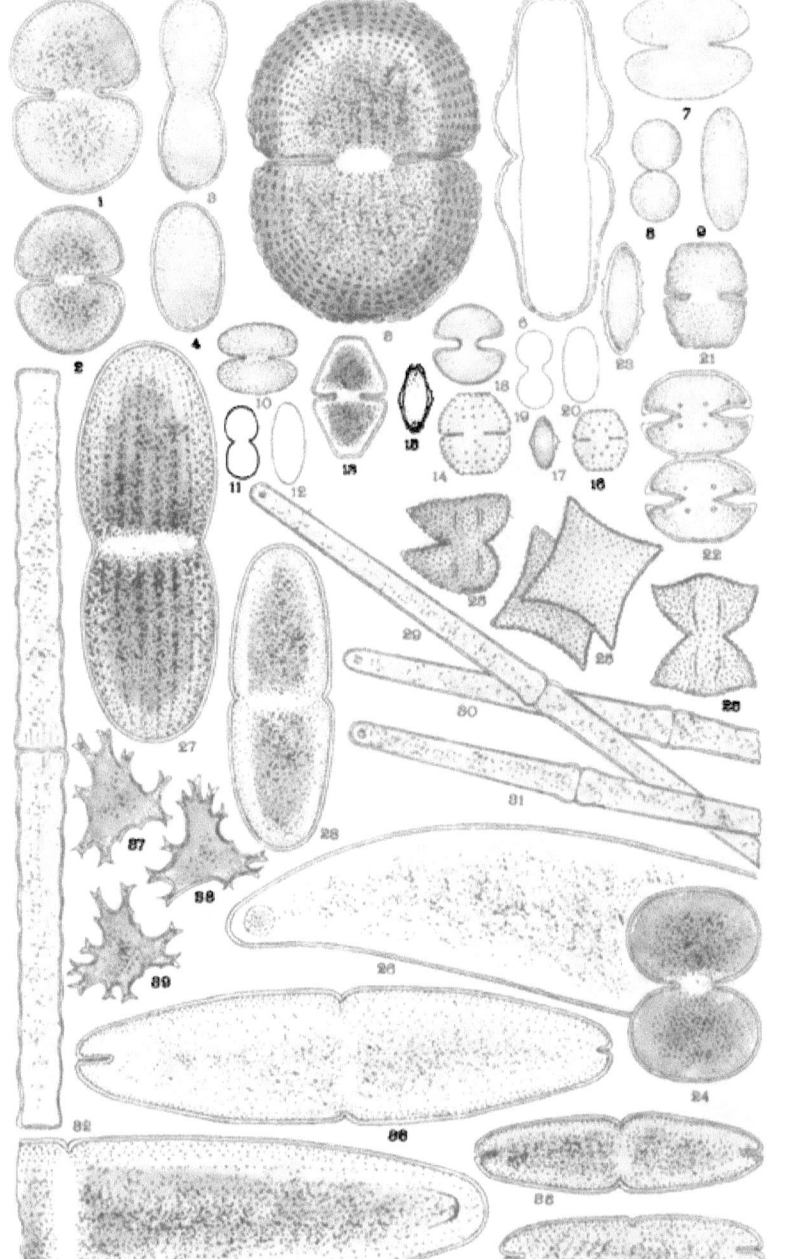

## PLATE LXII

Figures magnified 500 diameters.

| | | PAGE |
|---|---|---|
| Figs. 1, 2. | Staurastrum anatinum, | 152 |
| Fig. 3. | Staurastrum ankyroides, Var. hexacerum, | 151 |
| " 4. | Staurastrum ankyroides, typical form, | 150 |
| Figs. 5 7. | Staurastrum iotanum, | 150 |
| " 8–9. | Staurastrum Pottsii, | 166 |
| " 10–12. | Staurastrum megacanthum, | 134 |
| " 13–15. | **Cosmarium** protuberans, Var. granulatum, | 91 |
| " 16, 17. | **Staurastrum forficulatum**, forma tetragona, | 158 |
| " 18, 19. | "  forma trigona, | 158 |
| " 20, 21. | Staurastrum Dickiei, front and end views. (Compare Plate LI, figs 5, 6), | 135 |
| " **22, 23.** | Staurastrum aspinosum, | 157 |
| 24–26. | Staurastrum monticulosum, | 159 |
| " 27, 28. | Staurastrum striolatum, | 138 |
| " 29, 30. | Staurastrum leptacanthum, Var. iretroctocerum. | 166 |
| Fig. 31. | Staurastrum elongatum, Var. tetragonum, | 144 |
| Figs. 32–35. | Staurastrum pseudopachyrhynchum, two front and two end views, | 137 |
| " 36, 37. | **Cosmarium pseudobroomei**, front and end view, | 93 |

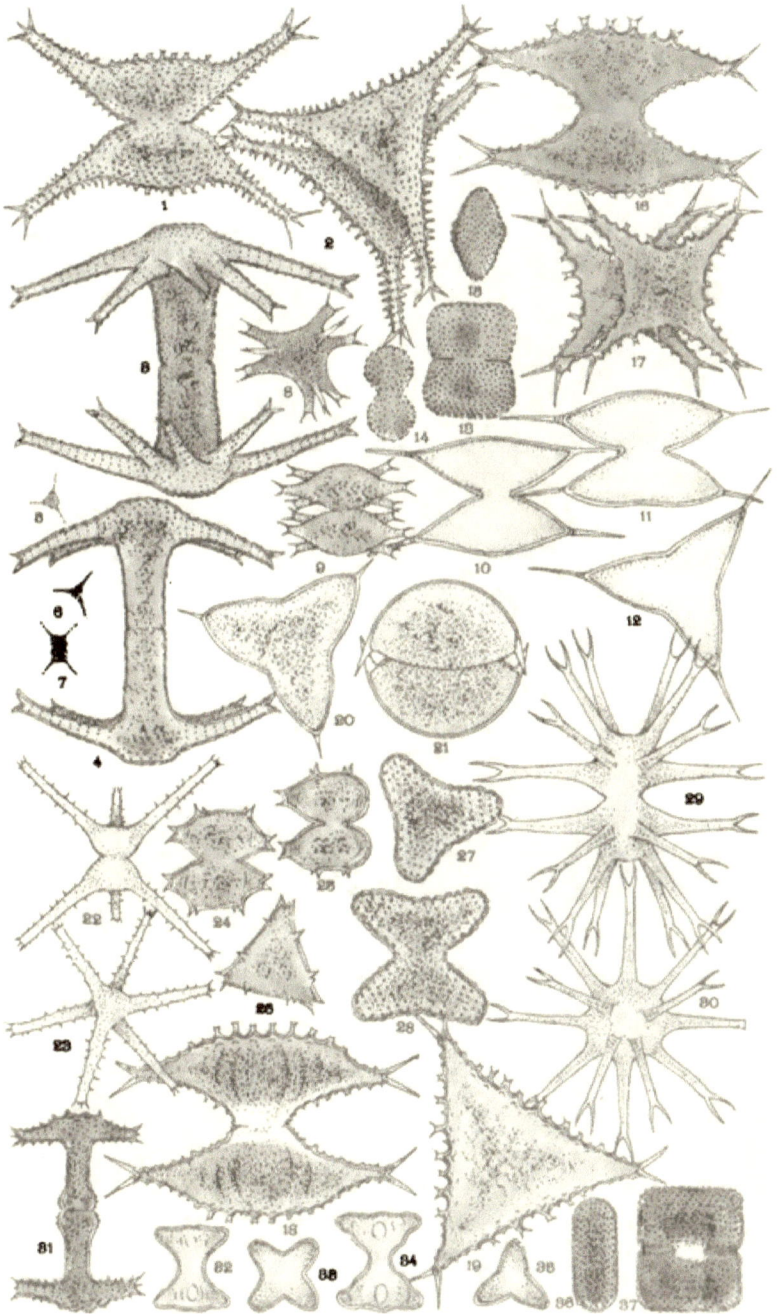

## PLATE LXIII.

Figures magnified 500 diameters, except the Micrasterias 375.

|  |  | PAGE |
|---|---|---|
| Fig 1. | STAURASTRUM SENARIUM, end view, | 162 |
| " 2. | MICRASTERIAS DICHOTOMA, | 123 |
| " 3. | MICRASTERIAS NORDSTEDTIANUM, | 125 |
| Figs 4, 5. | "           "           end and lateral views, | 125 |
| Fig. 6. | MICRASTERIAS RABENHORSTII, | 131 |
| Figs. 7, 8. | STAURASTRUM RAVENELII, | 157 |
| " 9, 10. | COSMARIUM NITIDULUM, | 72A |
| " 11, 12. | EUASTRUM URNAFORME, front and transverse views, | 111 |
| " 13-15. | EUASTRUM NORDSTEDTIANUM, side, transverse and end views, | 116 |
| Fig. 16. | XANTHIDIUM ANTILOPAEUM, Var. Minneapoliense, | 101 |
| Figs. 17-19. | STAURASTRUM QUATERNIUM, end and front views, | 158 |
| Fig. 20. | STAURASTRUM DONNELLII, | 146 |
| Figs. 21, 22. | EUASTRUM ABRUPTUM, variety, | 118 |
| " 23, 24. | STAURASTRUM FURCIGERUM, front and end views, | 161 |
| " 25, 26. | STAURASTRUM FURCATUM, (St. spinosum), | 165 |
| " 27, 28. | STAURASTRUM PSEUDOFURCIGERUM, front and end views, | 165 |
| " 29, 31. | STAURASTRUM BRACHIATUM, | 136 |
| " 32, 33. | STAURASTRUM DILATATUM, | 142 |
| Fig. 34. | STAURASTRUM FURCATUM, (St. spinosum), | 165 |

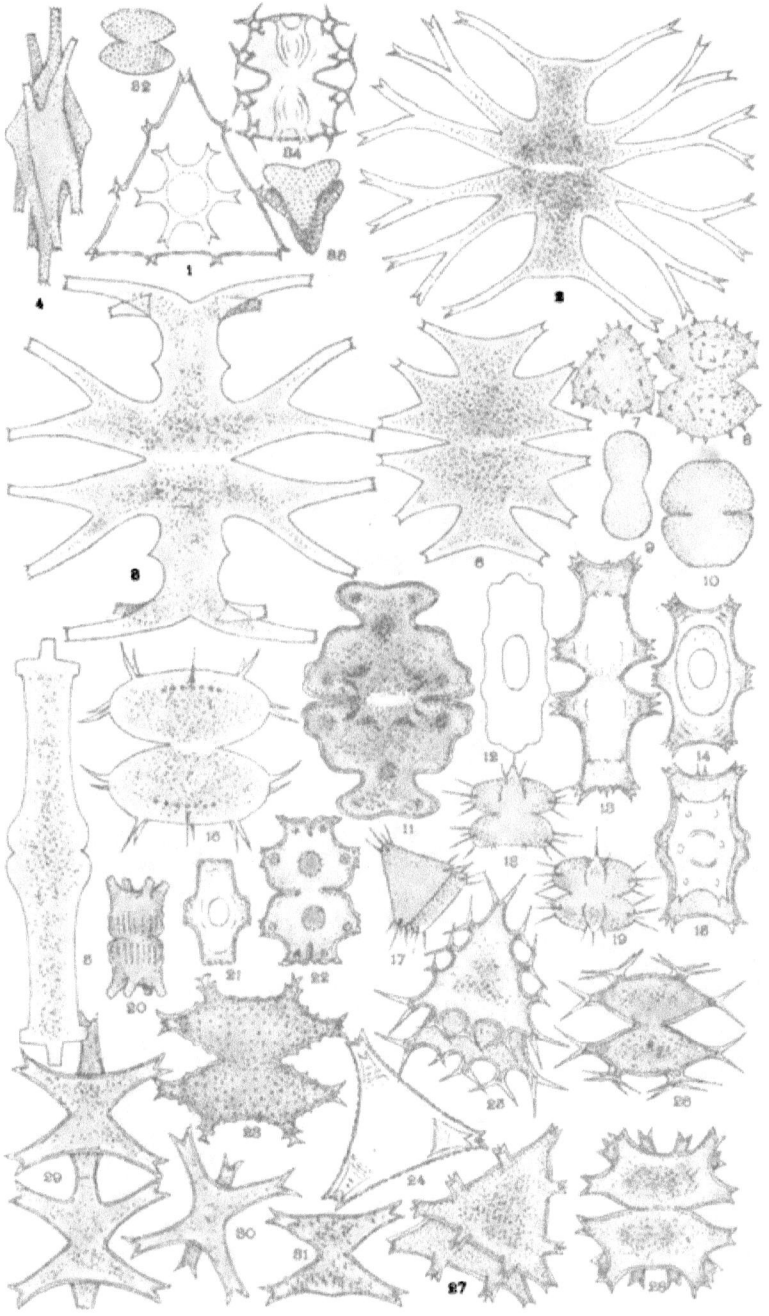

## PLATE LXIV.

### Figures magnified 500 diameters.

| | | PAGE. |
|---|---|---|
| Fig. 1. | PENIUM DIGITUS, | 34 |
| Figs. 2, 3. | STAURASTRUM BREVISPINA, front and end views, | 134 |
| " 4, 5. | STAURASTRUM INCONSPICUUM, | 137 |
| " 6, 7. | STAURASTRUM DUPLEX, | 164 |
| Fig. 8. | HYALOTHECA UNDULATA, | 23 |
| Figs. 9, 10. | CLOSTERIUM STRIGOSUM, two zygospores with empty cells attached, | 41 |
| Fig. 11. | EUASTRUM MULTILOBATUM, | 107 |
| Figs. 12, 13. | MICRASTERIAS CONFERTA, | 126 |
| " 14, 15. | COSMARIUM **EXCAVATUM**, | 85 |
| Fig. 16. | DOCIDIUM CORONULATUM, | 53 |
| " 17. | PEDIASTRUM **SIMPLEX**, | 168 |
| " 18. | PEDIASTRUM STURMII, | 168 |
| " 19. | PEDIASTRUM SIMPLEX, Var., | 168 |
| " 20. | PEDIASTRUM DUODENARIUS, | 168 |
| " 21. | PEDIASTRUM **FORCIPATUM**, | 169 |
| Figs. 22, 23. | PEDIASTRUM EHRENBERGII, | 170 |
| Fig. 24. | **PEDIASTRUM TETRAS**, | 170 |
| Figs. 25, 26. | PEDIASTRUM EHRENBERGII, | 170 |
| Fig. 27. | " " variety, | 170 |
| " 28. | PEDIASTRUM ANGULOSUM, | 162 |
| " 29. | PEDIASTRUM BORYANUM, | 169 |
| Figs. 30, 31. | PEDIASTRUM FORCIPATUM, | 169 |
| Fig. 32. | PEDIASTRUM BORYANUM, | 169 |
| Figs. 33, 34. | PEDIASTRUM PERTUSUM, | 169 |
| Fig. 35. | " " Var. brachylobum, | 170 |
| " 36. | PEDIASTRUM MUTICUM, | 169 |
| " 37. | PEDIASTRUM ANGULOSUM, **variety**, | 162 |

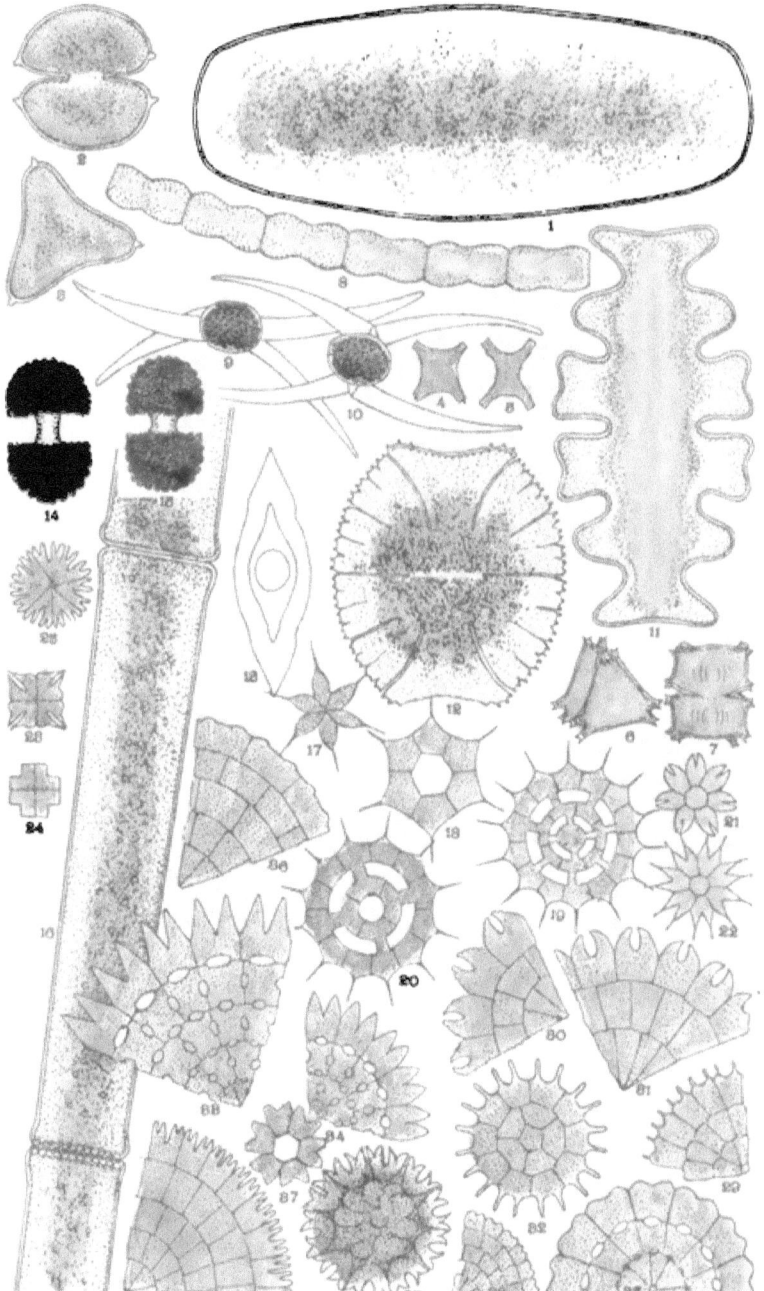

www.ingramcontent.com/pod-product-compliance
Lightning Source LLC
Chambersburg PA
CBHW020534300426
44111CB00008B/654